Theories of Truth

Theories of Truth
A Critical Introduction

Richard L. Kirkham

A Bradford Book
The MIT Press
Cambridge, Massachusetts
London, England

This book was set in Times Roman by Associated Publishing Services, England, and was printed and bound in the United States of America.

Library of Congress Cataloging-in-Publication Data

Kirkham, Richard L.
  Theories of truth : a critical introduction / Richard L. Kirkham.
      p.   cm.
  Includes bibliographical references and index.
  ISBN 0-262-11167-5
  1. Truth. I. Title.
BC171.K55   1992   91-42394
121—dc20   CIP

Contents

Preface

You are holding in your hand the only book-length introduction to theories of truth. This is a surprising state of affairs in view of the importance theories of truth have had for philosophy of language, formal model theory, and epistemology. It is also a debilitating state of affairs for philosophy. As I shall note repeatedly in this book, a failure to grasp the big picture about truth is the root cause of many philosophical mistakes. That failure is reflected in the fact that too many theorists of truth have been lax in explaining what question they suppose themselves to be answering and what relevance their answer to the question has for broader intellectual problems.

Among the many differences between an introductory book and an encyclopedia is that the latter takes things in alphabetical order and makes some claims to comprehensiveness, in breadth if not in depth. This book is not an encyclopedia. My purpose is to introduce, not to exhaust, the subject. Readers who already have some familiarity with the subject are hereby forewarned: your favorite theorist of truth may not be among those who receive extended discussion in this work. An exhaustive survey of every theory of truth ever offered would be unnecessary and, indeed, counterproductive. I do not want to intimidate my intended audience: I hope to convey something of the importance of theories of truth for broader philosophical, logical, and linguistic problems.

As to the intended audience, I have in mind, first, upper-level undergraduates, for whom this book may be the last as well as the first thing they ever read about theories of truth; second, graduate students studying epistemology, philosophy of language, logic, or semantics; and third, philosophers, linguists, and others planning to self-educate themselves about theories of truth and for whom this book will be only a first step.

There are two sections, 9.5 and 9.8, in which I presuppose greater knowledge than most undergraduates and even many professional scholars are likely to possess. The sections in question describe Saul Kripke's solution and also Jon Barwise and John Etchemendy's solution to the Liar Paradox and use advanced formal techniques. I found it impossible to summarize these views fairly without presupposing some knowledge of elementary set theory and its standard formalization, but these two views are too important to omit. Also, section 8.3 will be difficult for undergraduates on first reading.

Aside from these exceptions, I chose what to include and what not to include by keeping in mind my goals and intended audience. Accordingly, I discuss one, but usually only one, example of each major type of theory (coherence, correspondence, etc.). Moreover, in selecting examples, I have chosen the clearest of each type rather than the most sophisticated. For instance, as my example of the correspondence-as-congruence theory, I treat Bertrand Russell, not Ludwig Wittgenstein. (Of course, some theories, e.g., Alfred Tarski's, are too important not to include, however unclear they might be. In such cases I hope I have made them clear.) Further, I devote to each philosopher just the amount of discussion needed to make clear his theory and some of the problems that confront it. So the amount of space given over to a particular philosopher is inversely proportional to the clarity of his original presentation, and hence it is *not* always proportional to his historical importance.

Of course, the book is likely to be read also by many who are already thoroughly expert in the field. Writers of introductory texts often fear that such expert readers will think them shallow or unthorough, and many a purportedly introductory text has been ruined when its author gave in to these fears. So, if you are one such expert reader, I must ask you to remember your place: You are a city native who has hitched a ride on a tour bus. You are welcome along for the trip, but when the tour guide says, "And on our left is the Plaza of Martyrs," it is not polite to demand further details about the plaza that the tourists are not ready to grasp or do not yet need to know. I have, however, been much more indulgent of expert readers in the notes. A nonexpert should feel that he does not *need* to understand any note he does not understand.

No tool is more important to a writer than critical feedback on his work, and I am happy to say that my toolbox has been fuller than I deserve: Robert Audi, Irving Copi, and Paul Moser all took time to read a first draft of this book some years ago. Each of them will find that I've taken to heart a good eighty percent of his suggestions for improvement. A late draft was read by Lee Basham, Ray Elugardo, and Adam Morton. The advice of the earlier troika ensured that the later one was pained by fewer of my stupidities, and the later group has performed the same service for the reader. In between, a number of people commented on various parts of this work. They include Simon Blackburn, Roderick Chisholm, Michael Dummett, John Etchemendy, Richard Foley, Peter Markie, Scott Shalkowski, Cindy Stern, Chris Swoyer, and Crispin Wright. All of them, as well as the six named above, disagree strongly, albeit not quite violently, with much of what I say herein.

Since this is my first book, let me thank my undergraduate teachers Paul Gray and Bill Debbins, who get the credit, or blame, for encouraging my interest in philosophy. My thanks go also to C. J. F. Williams and James Sterba, who were the first to suggest to me that I might have some talent as an original philosopher. Al Neiman and Richard Foley encouraged me in that delusion at critical times in my career.

Finally, my greatest debts are to Dougie, his parents and siblings, and to Karen, Emory, Kendall, and Collin.

Theories of Truth

1 Projects of Theories of Truth

1.1 Four-Dimensional Confusion

Ideally, one begins any philosophical book by posing the question the book is supposed to answer or by describing the philosophical problem the book is supposed to solve. Even the briefest survey of writings about truth, however, reveals that there is little agreement about what the philosophical problem of truth is. Of course, this is not unusual in philosophy. But in most philosophical disputes, philosophers are conscious of the different opinions about exactly what the problem is and are therefore careful to avoid the fallacy of criticizing a theory for not accomplishing what it was not intended to accomplish in the first place.[1] Surprisingly, however, very few writers on *truth* show any awareness that the philosophers with whom they disagree may have had a different conception of the philosophical problem of truth. Even when a given writer does show such an awareness, he as often as not fails to make clear what his own conception of the problem is. Typically, books, chapters, or articles presenting a theory of truth begin with a statement of the problem so brief and ambiguous that it could be interchanged with the beginning of any other book, chapter, or article about truth and no one save the two authors would notice the difference. In other words, these descriptions of the problem of truth are too ambiguous to differentiate the various conceptions of the problem that have been held. By contrast, one of the ten chapters and many parts of other chapters of this book are devoted to the three related questions: What is (are) the philosophical problem(s) of truth? What questions should a theory of truth answer? What should a theory of truth do?

Let me begin by listing some of the purposes that philosophers have had for their own theory of truth or the purpose they thought someone else had for his or hers. By no means should you feel you must understand any of these examples. Read through them quickly. I am deliberately trying to overwhelm you, for I want to simulate in your mind the degree of confusion you would face if you approached the literature about truth without having first read this book.[2]

- To answer the question, What is truth?[3]
- To answer the question, What is it for something to be true? (Mackie 1973, 17)
- To answer the question, What do we mean by the terms 'truth' and 'falsehood'?[4]
- To find a "criterion of truth" (Haack 1978, 91) and (Mackie 1973, 30–32)
- To provide an account of the *use* of 'true' (Mackie 1973, 50)
- To find the "criteria of evidence" (Chisholm 1982, 182; 1977, 98)
- To show "how the truth conditions of any sentence depend on the structure of that sentence" (Harman 1973, 71)
- To answer the question, What are the necessary and sufficient conditions of a statement's truth? (Hamlyn 1970, 113–114)

There is also a dispute about what *kind* of things can be true or false. Are they beliefs, propositions, statements, or what? Fortunately, we need not complicate the story with this issue until sections 2.3 to 2.7. There are several dimensions of confusion in the story as it is. The first dimension is vagueness.[5] Many of the descriptions, particularly the project of answering "What is truth?" are vague enough that virtually any theorist could endorse it as a description of his project. The second problem is one of ambiguity: some of these descriptions can be taken in any number of ways (e.g., 'to find a criterion of truth'). Third, just as the same words could be used to describe two different projects, so too some of these apparently different descriptions are just two ways of describing the *same* project. This is obvious when an author gives two different descriptions of his own project. More important, two different authors may have the same project in mind, though they have different ways of describing it. Finally, some theorists have had more than one project in mind; that is, they offer a theory of truth that they believe will answer two distinctly different questions about truth or will fulfill two distinctly different projects. And this too will confuse one coming to the subject of truth for the first time. So we have a four-dimensional confusion.[6] And we must dissolve this confusion before we can evaluate any of the various theories of truth, for no theory, unless it is self-contradictory or incoherent in some way, can be judged good or bad until we know what its author intended to accomplish.

1.2 How to Resolve This Confusion

The method of dissolving confusion of this sort is similar to the process of solving one of those Magic Sphere puzzles in which several odd shaped pieces of wood must be fitted together to form a sphere: one must try various combinations until everything fits. So too we have a number of "pieces" or clues about the different conceptions of what the philosophical problem of truth is. Our job is to try to put them together so that everything fits. Fitting in this case would mean, first, a picture of the various conceptions of the problem or, to put the same thing another way, a list of the different questions about truth, each one precise and unambiguous, that the various theorists have been trying to answer. Second, making everything fit also means assigning each theorist to the particular question(s) he or she was trying to answer with his or her theory of truth.

Among the clues, or pieces of the puzzle, we must fit together are, first, the description each theorist provides for his or her project, or the question he or she poses. These, however, are not very good clues in and of themselves because, as we have seen, they tend to be vague or ambiguous. Better clues are the statements philosophers of truth make when comparing their own project with what they take to be the project of other theorists. Third, and better still, are the *criticisms* theorists make about each other's theories. Particularly significant is the type of complaint involved when philosopher *a* says either that philosopher *b*'s theory is not even the *kind* of thing that could serve as a theory of truth, or that it fails to provide any answer to the key question about truth. Complaints of this type are nearly certain signs that philosopher *a*, whether he knows it or not, has a different notion of what a theory of truth should do than philosopher *b* has. Finally, the relative similarity of two theories can be a clue. If we have already determined what sort of project philosopher *c* has in mind and we find that philosopher *d*'s theory is similar to *c*'s, then, in the absence of contrary clues, we can conclude that philosopher *d* had the same sort of project in mind for his theory. We shall return to these issues of exegesis in section 1.8.

1.3 Extensionality

It turns out that one cannot make all the pieces of the puzzle fit together unless one postulates three different projects: the speech-act project, the metaphysical project, and the justification project. And one must also postulate certain subdivisions and sub-subdivisions within the first two of these. I shall describe and distinguish these projects in later sections, but making the distinctions requires that we understand the concepts of extension and intension as they are used by philosophers and linguists. It is to this task that I now turn.

Since the seminal work of Gottlob Frege (1892), it has been a commonplace that the meaning of an expression has at least two components: the sense and the reference. The sense of an expression is often called the *connotation* or the *intension* of the expression, and the reference is often called the *denotation* or *extension* of the expression.[7] The extension of an expression is the object or set of objects referred to, pointed to, or indicated by, the expression. The extension of 'Gottlob Frege' is a certain turn-of-the-century German scholar. The extension of 'the morning star' is a certain planet, Venus. The extension of a *predicate* is the set of all objects to which the predicate truly applies. The extension of 'red' is the set of all red things. The extension of 'vertebrate with a liver' is the set of all vertebrates with livers. Abstract objects can also serve as the extensions of terms. Love, hate, and anger, are all members of the set that is the extension of 'is an emotion'. What is the extension of the predicate 'is true'? Trivially, it is the set of all true things, but this, being circular, is not a very informative answer. In some cases we can specify noncircularly the extension of a predicate by simply listing, one by one, each of the objects that are members of the extension. But when the extension of a term has an infinite number of members, or even a finite but very large number of members, this is a practical impossibility. In such cases we can only specify the set in question by describing it. And if our description is to be informative, it must be noncircular. The attempt to produce such a noncircular description of the set of all true things (the extension of the predicate 'is true') is what I shall call the extensional project. More about this below.

Note that two different expressions can have the same extension. The set consisting of only the morning star and the set consisting of only the evening star are in fact the same set. There is only one planet here and thus only one set. Hence the extensions of 'the morning star' and 'the evening star' are identical. These are just two names for the same planet. Similarly, it happens to be the case that all vertebrates with livers also have hearts and vice versa. Thus, the set of all vertebrates with livers is the same set as the set of all vertebrates with hearts. Accordingly, the extension of 'vertebrate with a heart' and 'vertebrate with a liver' are identical. When two terms have identical extensions, we say they are *extensionally equivalent*. The fact that two terms can have identical extensions is often of great help in explaining the meaning (or at least the extension) of a term. Imagine someone in the process of learning English. He has learned the meaning of, and hence the extension of, 'vertebrate with a liver', but he does not yet know the meaning of 'vertebrate with a heart'. By informing him that the extension of 'vertebrate with a heart' is identical to the extension of 'vertebrate with a liver', we have effectively specified for him the extension of the former. (We shall not, however, have completely explained the meaning of 'vertebrate with a heart' until we have accounted for the other component of its meaning, its *intension*.) One upshot of this is that 'the set of vertebrates with livers', is itself a description of the extension of 'vertebrate with a heart'. Thus an alternative way of conceiving of the extensional project is to think of it as the search for an expression that is extensionally equivalent to the predicate 'is true'. But notice that the extensional project is *not* about finding an expression that *means the same thing* as, or is synonymous with, 'is true'. Two expressions may be extensionally equivalent and still fail to *mean* the same thing. This happens whenever their *intensions*, the other component of their meaning, are not identical. As we shall see, the case of 'vertebrate with a heart' versus 'vertebrate with a liver' is one in which identity of intension, and thus synonymy, fails despite the identity of extension.

Four more points about extensional equivalence should be made before we turn our attention to intensionality. First, two extensionally equivalent expressions need not have the same degree of syntactic complexity. The simple predicate 'is an American citizen', for example, is extensionally equivalent to the disjunctive predicate 'was born on American territory and has not been naturalized by any other country *or* is the child of American citizens and has not been naturalized by any other country *or* has been naturalized as an American'. In principle, there is no limit to the complexity one could discover in one or the other (or both) of two extensionally equivalent expressions.

Second, being a vertebrate with a liver is a necessary and sufficient condition for being a vertebrate with a heart. It is a necessary condition because no vertebrate in the world, the actual world, has a heart unless it also has a liver. It is a sufficient condition because any vertebrate in the world with a liver also has a heart. Similarly, being born on American territory and not having been naturalized by any other country is a sufficient condition for being an American citizen, because anyone with the former characteristic also has the latter characteristic. But it is not a necessary condition for being an American citizen, because some American citizens were not born on American territory. On the other hand, no one is an American citizen unless she was born on American territory or is the child of American citizens or has been naturalized, so the disjunction of all three of these conditions is itself a necessary condition for American citizenship. There is a general principle here: when expressions x and y are extensionally equivalent, then y can be thought of as specifying the individually necessary and jointly sufficient condition(s) for something being an x.[8] Now we have still another way of characterizing the extensional project: it is the search for a set of necessary and sufficient conditions for something's being true. (Just what sort of something can be true or false is a disputed issue that I shall take up in sections 2.3 to 2.7. In the meantime, note that beliefs, sentences, propositions, and statements have all been proposed as the sort of something that can bear truth or falsity.)

Third, extensionally equivalent expressions do not just come in pairs. Any number of expressions can all be extensionally equivalent to each other. Before the invention of dialysis machines, 'vertebrate with a kidney' was extensionally equivalent to 'vertebrate with a heart', and thus also to 'vertebrate with a liver'. So being a vertebrate with a kidney was also a necessary and sufficient condition for being a vertebrate with a heart. This sounds contradictory at first glance. If, among vertebrates, having a liver was a sufficient condition for having a heart, how could having a kidney have been a *necessary* condition for having a heart? But we can see that there really is no contradiction when we notice that because 'vertebrate with a liver' was extensionally equivalent to 'vertebrate with a kidney', having a kidney was, among vertebrates, also a necessary condition to having a liver.

So in attempting to fix the extension of a given term, say 'is x', we may find that there is more than one way to do it, more than one extensionally equivalent expression, and thus more than one list of individually necessary and jointly sufficient conditions for something's being an x. What counts in such cases as the "correct" extensional analysis of a term will depend on what motivated us to seek an extensional analysis of the term in the first place. Although they have been accused of doing so, analytic philosophers do not really analyze terms just for the sake of it. Analysis is a tool one uses in the service of some broader philosophical program. A given extensional analysis of 'is x' may accurately and noncircularly specify the set of things that are x, and it may still fail to be informative with regard to the problem that motivated us to seek an extensional analysis of 'is x' in the first place. Consider again a man who is just learning English. If he has no better idea of the extension of 'vertebrate with a liver' than he has of 'vertebrate with a heart', he will not be helped a bit to be told that having a liver is, among vertebrates, a necessary and sufficient condition for having a heart. But if he does know the extension of 'vertebrate with a kidney' (and if dialysis machines had not been invented), then he will learn something (albeit not everything) about the meaning of 'vertebrate with a heart' by being told that having a kidney is, among vertebrates, a necessary and sufficient condition for having a heart. Clearly, in this situation, describing the extension of 'vertebrate with a heart' as the set of vertebrates with kidneys is preferable to describing it as the set of vertebrates with livers.

The fourth and final point to be made about extensional equivalence is that when two terms are extensionally equivalent, certain sentences in which those terms appear will bear an interesting logical relationship to one another: if 'John has a heart' is true, then 'John has a liver' is also true. We can express this logical relationship with the following statement:

John has a heart $\supset$ John has a liver

This means that 'John has a heart' *materially implies* 'John has a liver'. The statement can be translated as 'If John has a heart, then John has a liver'. Because the set of things with hearts is more than just a proper subset of the things with livers and is indeed the identical set, the following statement is also true:

John has a liver $\supset$ John has a heart

It is a principle of logic that when two statements materially imply each other they are materially equivalent. So this statement is also true:

John has a liver $\equiv$ John has a heart

Here, the '$\equiv$' says that the statements on either side of it are materially equivalent. The '$\equiv$' can be translated 'if and only if'. So the statement as a whole says that John has a liver if and only if John has a heart. We may say, then, that the extensional project is the project of correctly filling in the blank in

x is true $\equiv$ ____ .

I mean by this that the extensional project is looking for some statement about x that is materially equivalent to a statement that asserts that x is true. But not just any materially equivalent statement will do. On pain of making the analysis circular, what fills the blank cannot contain any form of the word 'true', nor can it contain any term that can be understood only parasitically on a prior understanding of 'true'; thus 'x is not false' will not do. Moreover, what fills the blank must be *informative* given the broader program that motivated the search for an extensional analysis of 'is true' in the first place. (There are other complexities that must be added to this description of the extensional project, but they can wait.)

1.4   Intensionality

Let us turn now to the other component of the meaning of a term: the sense or connotation or, as I shall most often call it, the *intension* of the term. Put in a very general way, the intension of an expression is the informational content of the expression, as distinct from the set of objects denoted by the expression. An example makes this clear. 'Vertebrate with a heart' and 'vertebrate with a liver' obviously do not mean the same thing. So since their extensions are identical, their intensions must be different. The intension of 'vertebrate with a heart', its informational content, is 'vertebrate possessing a blood-pumping organ'. The intension of 'vertebrate with a liver' is 'vertebrate possessing a blood-cleaning organ'. But, again, since pumping and cleaning are two different things, we have two different intensions here. The intension of 'the morning star' can be worded as 'the star visible around dawn', while the intension of 'the evening star' is 'the star visible around sunset'.[9] But being visible around dawn is not the same thing as being visible around sunset, so while 'the morning star' and 'the evening star' are extensionally equivalent, they are not intensionally equivalent. They convey different information. And since intension is one component of meaning, the two expressions do not *mean* the same thing, despite the fact that they both name the same planet.

Embedding the key terms in a sentence can make the differences very obvious. 'He awoke to the morning star' means something very different from 'He awoke to the evening star'. The first suggests that he is an early riser, the other implies that he sleeps late. Similarly, 'If you have a heart, you should practice jogging' is good advice, but 'If you have a liver, you should practice jogging' is at best puzzling advice.

The task of discovering the informational content, the intension, of the predicate 'is true' is what I shall call the assertion project. The latter is a subdivision of the speech-act project. More about this below.

Some terms *are* intensionally equivalent.[10] 'Has a heart' is intensionally equivalent to 'possesses a blood-pumping organ'. Another, classic example of intensional equivalence is 'bachelor' and 'unmarried man'. The reader may already have noticed that each of these cases of intensional equivalence is *also* a case of extensional equivalence. The set of things with hearts is the same set as the set of things with blood-pumping organs. (Keep in mind that an *artificial* blood-pumping device *is* a heart. It is just an artificial heart.) So too the set of unmarried men is identical to the set of bachelors. This is a universal rule: if two terms are intensionally equivalent, then they are also extensionally equivalent. The converse, as we have seen, is *not* the case. It is in this sense that intensional equivalence is a *stronger* relation than mere extensional equivalence. The former "includes," as it were, the latter. Since both meaning components are identical when x and y are intensionally equivalent, we may say in such cases that x *means that* y. One implication of the intensional equivalence of x and y is that we can substitute y for x in any English sentence in which the latter appears without changing the meaning or, hence, the truth value, of the sentence. This principle does not hold good in cases of mere extensional equivalence.[11]

So we have two additional ways of describing the assertion project. It is the attempt to find an expression intensionally equivalent to (that is, synonymous with) 'is true'. Alternatively, it is the attempt to figure out what 'is true' *means*. A puzzle arises here. The extensional project is the search for an expression extensionally equivalent to 'is true' and the assertion project is the search for an expression intensionally equivalent to 'is true'. But if an expression is intensionally equivalent to 'is true' it is also, per force, extensionally equivalent. So why are there two projects here? Is not a solution to the assertion project *eo ipso* a solution to the extensional project? I shall deal with this puzzle in section 1.6.

Some of the characteristics that mark relations of mere extensional equivalence also mark relations of intensional equivalence. First, x and y can be intensionally equivalent even if y is syntactically much more complex than x. Second, intensionally equivalent expressions do not just come in pairs. 'Has a pulmonary organ' is intensionally equivalent to both 'has a heart' and 'possesses a blood-pumping organ'. Third, certain sentences containing intensionally equivalent expressions have interesting logical relations to each other. Because intensional equivalence includes extensional equivalence, all of the following are true:

John has a heart $\supset$ John possesses a blood-pumping organ

John possesses a blood-pumping organ $\supset$ John has a heart

John has a heart $\equiv$ John possesses a blood-pumping organ

But the intensionally equivalent terms involved here allow us to assert another, tighter logical connection between the sentences in question that we would not be able to assert if the terms were merely extensionally equivalent. The tighter logical connection may be called *essential implication* and is expressed by placing the word 'necessarily' at the head of an assertion of mere material implication. Thus both of the following are true:

Necessarily (John has a heart $\supset$ John possesses a blood-pumping organ)

Necessarily (John possesses a blood-pumping organ $\supset$ John has a heart)

And these two entail:

Necessarily (John has a heart $\equiv$ John possesses a blood-pumping organ)

I shall call the relation asserted by the last example *essential equivalence*. But what exactly do assertions of essential implication and essential equivalence *say*, and how does it differ from what is said by an assertion of mere material implication or material equivalence?

The best way of explaining the meaning of the word 'necessarily' is with the help of the concept of a *possible world*. We all recognize that the universe might have been different from the way it actually is in many different ways. If your parents had never met, you would not have been born, and there is really nothing in the world that logically guaranteed that your parents would meet. The fact that they met was largely happenstance, what philosophers call a historical accident. There are also grander ways in which the universe might have been different. Had Hitler not been born, there would likely not have been a second world war. Had the earth not had a moon, 'Neil Armstrong' would not be a household name. There is *almost* no limit to the ways the world might have been different. China might have been French-speaking. China might not have even existed (had the history of continental drift been different than it was). The solar system might have had fifteen planets, or none. Or the Milky Way galaxy itself might not have existed. A *possible world* is a hypothetical entity postulated as an aid to talking about and studying the various ways the universe might have been different.[12] ('Possible universe' would be a more accurate term, but I shall stick to standard terminology.) A possible world is a complete universe that differs in some way or another (or in more than one way) from the actual universe. There is a possible world in which your parents did not meet. There is another in which Hitler was not born. There is still another in which your parents did not meet *and* Hitler was not born. Indeed, for every way or combination of ways in which the world might have been different, there is a possible world that *is* different from the actual world in just that way or combination of ways. Instead of saying 'Ford Motors could have gone bankrupt in 1955', we can say 'There is a possible world in which Ford Motors went bankrupt in 1955'. Instead of saying 'It is possible I shall fail', we can say 'There is a possible world in which I *do* fail'.

There are even possible worlds in which the laws of nature themselves are different from what they are in the actual world. There are possible worlds in which gravity does not effect copper the way it effects other objects. Copper in these worlds floats around weightlessly. There are possible worlds in which species do not evolve. There are some in which there is only one species. And there are some in which there are no living things at all. It may help to think in theistic terms: God, if there is one, could have created the world differently than he did. He might have made it with different laws of nature and/or with different creatures in it. A possible world is one of the worlds God could have made had he wanted to.

There is, however, a limit on what can count as a possible world. There is no possible world in which something logically impossible occurs. There is no world with a round square or with a married bachelor. This follows from the fact that there are limits on how the actual world might have been different from the way it is. We intuitively recognize that no matter how different the history of the world might have been, there could never have been a round square. A round square is just an impossible entity. (Of course, the *words* 'round' and 'square' might have had different meanings from what they do have, but this does not change the fact that we in the actual world can recognize that the sort of thing we call a square could never have the shape we call round.)

There would be no point to postulating possible worlds if all they did were to give us an alternative way of saying things like 'I might not have been born'. But possible-worlds talk also allows us to analyze the meaning of some very important philosophical terminology. We can define an *impossible* thing (or event) as a thing that does not exist (or take place) in either the actual world or in *any* possible world. For simplicity I shall follow common practice hereafter and count the actual world as one of the possible worlds. So an impossible event does not happen on any possible world. Correspondingly, a possible thing (or event) is one that exists (or happens) in a least one possible world. (So, of course, anything that actually happens or exists counts as a possible event or thing, since it happens in at least one possible world, namely this one.) A *necessary* event is one that happens in *every* possible world, and a necessary thing is one that exists in every possible world.

Now we are in a position to understand what the word 'necessarily' means in assertions of essential equivalence. Recall again that the set of vertebrates with hearts is identical to the set of vertebrates with livers. But there are possible worlds where this is not the case. Some possible worlds have vertebrates with livers but no hearts. Their blood needs to be cleaned, but it does not circulate by means of a pump. Perhaps it just sloshes around when they move about. And there are worlds where some of the vertebrates with hearts do not ever need to have their blood cleaned, so they do not have livers. So although

John has a heart ≡ John has a liver

is true in this, the actual, world, it is not true in certain other worlds. But notice that it is impossible for anything to have a heart and not possess a blood-pumping organ and vice versa, because a heart just is a blood-pumping organ. So there is no possible world containing a creature with a heart but not a blood-pumping organ, and there is no world with a creature possessing a blood-pumping organ but not having a heart. This in turn means that in any given possible world the set of things in that world with hearts is identical to the set of things in that world with a blood-pumping organs.[13] So

John has a heart ≡ John possesses a blood-pumping organ

is true in *every* possible world. It is precisely *this* point that is expressed by

Necessarily (John has a heart ≡ John possesses a blood-pumping organ).

So the word 'necessarily' can be translated as 'in all possible worlds', and the assertion as a whole is claiming that in all possible worlds, John has a heart if and only if John has a blood-pumping organ. So in any world where 'John has a heart' is true, so too is 'John has a blood-pumping organ', and in any world where 'John has a heart' is false, 'John has a blood-pumping organ' is false as well. Hence, two sentences are essentially equivalent when in every possible world, each has the same truth value as the other.

The preceding example of an assertion of essential equivalence is true, but one can make false claims of essential equivalence, just as one can make false claims about anything else.

Necessarily (John has a heart ≡ John has a liver)

is false because, as noted above, there are some possible worlds where

John has a heart ≡ John has a liver

is false. Now if 'Necessarily $(p \equiv q)$' is true, then '$p \equiv q$' is true in every possible world, including the actual world. So it is a rule of logic that 'Necessarily $(p \equiv q)$' entails '$p \equiv q$'. Following a common practice of logicians, I shall use a special symbol to express essential equivalence. The symbol I shall use is the double-headed hollow arrow '⇔'. Thus, hereafter I shall write

$p \Leftrightarrow q$

in place of

Necessarily $(p \equiv q)$.

The former expression, like the latter, can be translated 'In every possible world, p is materially equivalent to q' or 'In every possible world, p if and only if q' or 'p is essentially equivalent to q'.

We have seen that if two sentences are synonymous, that is, if they are intensionally equivalent, then they bear the interesting logical relationship to each other that I have dubbed 'essential equivalence'. But the converse does not hold. Some pairs of essentially equivalent sentences are not synonymous, and thus are not intensionally equivalent. Consider, for example, the two mathematical sentences '2 + 2 = 4' and '36 − 7 = 29'. Obviously, these do not mean the same thing, but they *are* essentially equivalent. Since each of them is a necessary truth, they are each true in every possible world. So, trivially, each has the same truth value as the other in every possible world. Indeed, any necessary truth is essentially equivalent to any other, for each has the same truth value as each of the others in every possible world. Another example of two statements that are essentially equivalent but not synonymous are 'This object has shape' and 'This object has size'.[14]

Thus of our three relations, intensional equivalence is the strongest, since it contains the other two, and extensional equivalence is the weakest, since it is contained in the other two. If a pair of sentences are intensionally equivalent, then they are also essentially equivalent, and if they are essentially equivalent, then they are also extensionally equivalent. Let me use the symbol '$=_{syn}$', where the 'syn' is short for 'synonymous', to express intensional equivalence. I translate '$p =_{syn} q$' as 'To say that p is to say that q'.[15] So each of the following entails the statement(s) below it and none entails the statement(s) above it:

$p =_{syn} q$

$p \Leftrightarrow q$

$p \equiv q$

The assertion project is the search for a sentence intensionally equivalent to 'x is true', and I have dubbed the search for a sentence extensionally equivalent to 'x is true' the 'extensional project'. The attempt to find a sentence essentially equivalent to 'x is true' will be called the essence project.

1.5 Natural Necessity

In addition to statements that are true in every possible world and statements that are true in only the actual world, there can be statements that are true in every world within this or that specified subset of worlds. Of particular interest is the subset of *naturally* possible worlds, which is the subset of worlds having all and only the same laws of nature as the actual world. This set includes worlds where Hitler was never born and worlds where your parents never met, but it does not include worlds where copper floats around weightlessly, since that would be a violation of a law of nature. Naturally possible objects or events are those that exist or happen in at least one naturally possible world, while naturally necessary objects or events are those that exist or occur in every naturally possible world. Similarly, a statement that is true in every naturally possible world is a naturally necessary truth; hence, the laws of nature are all naturally necessary truths. (This book takes no stand on the question of whether every naturally necessary truth should count as a law of nature.)

When a claim of extensional equivalence such as '$p \equiv q$' is true in every naturally possible world, then p and q are naturally equivalent. I shall express this relation using a double-headed (nonhollow) arrow like so: '$p \leftrightarrow q$'. I shall translate the latter sentence as 'p is naturally equivalent to q'. If p and q are equivalent in every possible world, then, of course, they are equivalent in every naturally possible world. So '$p \leftrightarrow q$' is true whenever '$p \Leftrightarrow q$' is true. And since the actual world is one of the naturally possible worlds, '$p \equiv q$' is true whenever '$p \leftrightarrow q$' is. So now we have the following four different types of equivalence relations, and each of the following sentences entails those listed below it, and none of them entails those listed above it.

$p =_{\text{syn}} q$

$p \Leftrightarrow q$

$p \leftrightarrow q$

$p \equiv q$

I shall call the attempt to find a sentence that is naturally equivalent to 'x is true' the naturalistic project.

1.6 Philosophical Analysis

When philosophers analyze a term, say 'morally right action', are they attempting to provide an intensional analysis or an extensional analysis or one of the two middling-strength sorts of analyses? Unhappily, I must report that most philosophers most of the time do not make clear which sort of analysis they are after. This is quite tragic because the difference between the various sorts of analyses is important. Consider the claim

An action is morally right
  ⟺ it maximizes the net happiness of the population.

Since this is a claim of essential equivalence, it is false if there is even one possible world where a happiness-maximizing action fails to be a right action. And since any event that is logically possible takes place in at least one possible world, all we need do to refute the claim is come up with a logically possible story in which a happiness-maximizing action is not a morally right action. So we can refute the claim by pointing out that it is logically possible that a given society could enslave 10 percent of its own population and that the increased happiness of the majority (via the material goods produced by all that free labor) would more than cancel out the increased unhappiness of the slaves. We need not claim that this has ever happened in the actual world or that it ever will. We need only note that it is logically possible; that is, we need only note that it is not a contradiction in terms to say that the increased happiness of the majority would more than cancel out the increased unhappiness of the slaves. But obviously the enslavement would be a morally wrong action. Thus the claim of essential equivalence is refuted. Recall now that a claim of intensional equivalence entails the corresponding claim of essential equivalence. Hence since

An action is morally right
  ⟺ it maximizes the net happiness of the population

is false,

An action is morally right
  $=_{\text{syn}}$ it maximizes the net happiness of the population

must be false as well. There is a general rule here: any counterexample that refutes a claim of essential equivalence will automatically also refute the corresponding claim of intensional equivalence. This is because, again, a logical requisite for two sentences being intensionally equivalent is that they be essentially equivalent.

But now consider a much milder claim:

An action is morally right
$\quad \equiv$ it maximizes the net happiness of the population

This only claims that in this, the actual world, the set of morally right actions is identical to the set of actions that maximize the net happiness of the population. The fact that there is some *other* world where the two sets are not identical is quite irrelevant to the truth or falsity of *this* claim. Thus, refuting this milder claim is much more difficult than refuting the earlier claim of essential equivalence. A merely logically possible counterexample will not do. We must instead produce an actual case from the history of the world (the *actual* world) in which a wrong action maximized the happiness of the population (or a right action failed to do so). This is a much harder conjuring. Because of the difficulty in measuring happiness, how could we ever know, for example, just how unhappy the slaves in antebellum America really were? And if we cannot know that, how could we have grounds for saying that more happiness was produced by their enslavement than unhappiness? The general lesson here is that claims of material equivalence are harder to refute than the corresponding claims of essential equivalence or intensional equivalence.

Why, then, would any philosopher ever want to produce an intensional or essential analysis of a term, since such analyses are so vulnerable to refutation? First, producing one of the stronger analyses is often easier because we have an extra set of tools available to us: our intuitions about what is possible, about how the world might have been. And for an intensional analysis we have our intuitions about the meanings of words. Second, the very fact that an assertion of extensional equivalence is relatively harder to refute is often a handicap in producing an extensional analysis, because it makes it harder to pick out a correct extensional analysis from among a group of competing analyses. Suppose, for example, we cannot come up with any actual, historical counterexamples to *either* of the following claims:

An action is morally right
$\quad \equiv$ it maximizes the net happiness of the population

An action is morally right
$\quad \equiv$ it conforms to a universalizable rule of behavior

Now we are in a quandary. Since we cannot refute either claim, how are we going to determine which, if either, is correct? Third and most important, one might be compelled to seek a stronger analysis of a term x (despite the high risk of refutation) simply because the broader philosophical problem one is working on requires one to find an expression that is essentially equivalent to, or even synonymous with, x. In such cases a mere extensional analysis will not do.

In sum, then, there are quite a number of factors one must take into account when determining which sort of analysis is appropriate for a given philosophical context. (It should now come as no surprise to the reader that refuting a claim of naturalistic equivalence does not require a counterexample from the actual world, but a merely logically possible scenario will not do either. What is required is a scenario from a naturally possible world.)

We can now return to the puzzle encountered earlier and reformulate it in light of our more recent results. For any statement p, each of the following entails the statements that follow it:

x is true $=_{\text{syn}} p$

x is true $\Leftrightarrow p$

x is true $\leftrightarrow p$

x is true $\equiv p$

But then it appears that an answer to the naturalistic project automatically provides an answer to the extensional project, and an answer to the essence project automatically provides an answer to both of the former projects, and an answer to the assertion project automatically provides an answer to each of the former three projects. So why are there *four* projects here? Is not the assertion project all we need? Well, the first thing to note is that few theorists of truth have shown any *explicit* awareness of the difference between the four kinds of projects. We can discover which sort of project any such theorist was in effect pursuing by means of the textual clues described in section 1.2. It just turns out that some theorists were pursuing the extensional project and others the naturalistic project and others the essence project and others the assertion project (and still others another subdivision of the speech-act project or the justification project). So the immediate answer to the question of why there are four projects here is that the philosophers pursuing one or another of these projects did not recognize the distinctions between them. As to the more interesting question about the apparent gratuity of the essence, naturalistic, and extensional projects, recall that there may be more than one statement that is materially equivalent to 'x is true'. The "correct" extensional analysis of the latter statement is the one that is most enlightening with respect to the intellectual problem or problems that motivated us to look for an analysis in the first place. For example, one school of thought in the philosophy of mind holds that there really are not any mental entities such as beliefs, hopes, and sensations, at least not if these are thought of as abstract, nonphysical entities. Any and all talk about such entities can, they claim, be translated into (or 'reduced to') talk about the neurons and states of the physical brain. Notice now that an *intensional* analysis of 'Emory has a belief that he is typing', that is, an analysis that fills the blank in

Emory has a belief that he is typing $=_{syn}$ ____,

could not even in principle be useful for this philosophical program, because only some expression with the same intension, that is, *connotation*, as 'Emory has a belief that he is typing' can correctly fill this blank. But no expression that refers only to neurons, brains, and other physical entities can possibly have the same connotation as this sentence. For it is quite possible that a person who had never heard of neurons could understand 'Emory has a belief that he is typing'. What physicalist theories of mind require is some analysis weaker than intensional equivalence. This point applies to any reductionist program. Despite the occasional tendency of reductionists to say that they want to cash the *meaning* of one category of terms via another category of terms, an intensional analysis is not only not needed, it is incompatible with such programs.

Similarly, there can be more than one correct answer to the naturalistic and essence projects. Thus the answer to the essence, naturalistic, and extensional projects that is automatically provided by an answer to the assertion project may not be the 'correct' answer in this sense. So if for some p, 'x is true $=_{syn} p$' is true, then 'x is true $\Leftrightarrow p$', 'x is true $\leftrightarrow p$', and 'x is true $\equiv p$' are true. But if $p \equiv q$, then 'x is true $\equiv q$' will also be true, and q may be a more enlightening extensional analysis of 'x is true' than p is. And if $p \Leftrightarrow r$ and $p \leftrightarrow s$, then 'x is true $\Leftrightarrow r$' and 'x is true $\leftrightarrow s$' will both be true, and r and s may well be more enlightening respectively essential and naturalistic analyses of 'x is true' than p is.

1.7   The Main Projects and Their Subdivisions

This section provides a more systematic description of the various projects that are implicitly present in the literature about truth. We shall also see in more detail why the sort of project descriptions quoted and paraphrased in section 1.1 are unacceptably vague or ambiguous. It is not possible in this section to provide realistic examples of any theories of truth, because even the presentation of such examples presupposes material to be covered in this and later chapters. On the other hand, *that* material presupposes the project descriptions I give in this section. My solution to this dilemma is to give a mostly abstract description of the various projects here, along with a few very brief and simple-minded examples. Accordingly, the project descriptions of this section will be best understood if read a second time after the entire book has been read through once.

The following outline provides the names and brief descriptions of the different truth projects that one or another philosopher was trying to fulfill in constructing a theory of truth, and it shows the genus-species relationships among them.[16] The descriptions here are too brief and oversimplified to be completely perspicuous. A fuller description of each follows.

I. *The metaphysical project.* This project attempts to identify what truth consists in, what it is for a statement (or belief or proposition, etc.) to be true. This project has three branches:
  A. *The extensional project.* This project attempts to identify the necessary and sufficient conditions for a statement (or belief or proposition, etc.) to be a member of the set of true statements. It attempts, in other words, to fix the *extension* (the reference, the denotation) of the predicate 'is true'.
  B. *The naturalistic project.* This project attempts to find conditions that, in any naturally possible world, are individually necessary and jointly sufficient for a statement being true in that world.[17]
  C. *The essence project.* This project attempts to find conditions that, in any possible world, are individually necessary and jointly sufficient for a statement being true in that world.[18]
II. *The justification project.* This project attempts to identify some characteristic, possessed by most true statements and not possessed by most false statements, by reference to which the probable truth or falsity of the statement can be judged.

III. *The speech-act project*. This project attempts to describe the locutionary or illocutionary purpose served by utterances that by their surface
grammar appear to ascribe the property of truth to some statement (or
belief, etc.), for example, utterances like 'Statement *s* is true'.

   A. *The illocutionary-act project*. This is just the speech-act project as
   pursued by those convinced that the utterances in question have no
   locutionary purpose. So this project attempts to describe what we
   are *doing* when we make this sort of utterance.

   B. *The assertion project*. This is just the speech-act project as pursued
   by those convinced that the utterances in question do have a
   locutionary purpose. So this project attempts to describe what we
   are *saying* when we make this sort of utterance. It attempts, in other
   words, to fix the *intension* (the sense, the connotation) of the
   predicate 'is true'.

      1. *The ascription project*. This is just the assertion project as
      pursued by those convinced that the surface grammar of such
      utterances is a safe guide to what we are saying when we make
      them.

      2. *The deep-structure project*. This is just the assertion project as
      pursued by those who are convinced that the surface grammar of
      such utterances is misleading.

There are several ways of describing the extensional project and these
are all, as we have seen, just different ways of saying the same thing:

• The project is to provide a noncircular specification of the set of all true
propositions (or true beliefs or true sentences or whatever).

• The project is to find an expression (possibly quite complex syntactically) that is *extensionally* equivalent to the predicate 'is true'.

• The project is to find a statement that materially implies, and is
materially implied by, a statement of the form '*x* is true'.

• The project is correctly to fill in the blank in

x is true $\equiv$ ____ .

Readers should keep all four descriptions in mind so as to heighten the
contrast with the other projects.

   It will help to distinguish the extensional project from the others by
noticing what sort of questions it is intended to answer and what sort it is

not intended to answer. It is supposed to answer such questions as the following: Is a proposition's (belief's, sentence's, etc.) correspondence with reality a necessary and/or a sufficient condition for its being true? Is a proposition's coherence with other propositions a necessary and/or a sufficient condition of its being true? Is a belief's usefulness to human beings a necessary and/or sufficient condition of its being true? It does *not* pretend to answer, For any given proposition, when and how are we *justified* in thinking that the proposition is (probably) true? What conversational *purpose* might expressions like 'such and such is true' have in our language?

If we conceive of the *definition* of 'truth' as a statement of the necessary and sufficient conditions for something's being true, then, of course, an extensional theory of truth does provide a definition of 'truth'. But on at least one other understanding of what a definition does, this type of truth theory does *not* provide a definition. For this type of theory does not answer the question What is the *meaning* of 'true', 'truth', and 'is true'? It does not attempt to find an expression that is *synonymous* with any of these terms.

Ideally, an extensional theory of truth is presented in a formula that makes use of the material-equivalence symbol. (I shall hereafter often refer to the material-equivalence symbol as the 'extensional-equivalence symbol.') The form of an ideally expressed extensional theory of truth, then, is this:

A proposition is true $\equiv$ it meets conditions x, y, z, etc.

An example might be

A proposition is true $\equiv$ it agrees with reality.

In this example only one condition is claimed to be both necessary and sufficient to make a proposition true; hence the right side of the equivalence sign is not a conjunction. Most theories will provide a list of jointly sufficient and individually necessary conditions.

Some philosophers have needed, or at least thought they needed, a theory of truth that does more than merely describe the set of statements that are true in this, the actual, world. Some have sought an analysis of truth that has the same degree of generality and universality as is possessed by scientific laws of nature. Such philosophers are in effect trying to produce a *scientific theory* of truth. This is what the naturalistic project attempts to provide. It tries to find some expression (possibly quite complex syntactically) that is naturally (not merely extensionally) equivalent to 'x is true'. It attempts, that is, to fill the blank in

x is true $\leftrightarrow$ ____ .

Filling this blank is a list of conditions that, in any naturally possible world, are requisite, individually, and sufficient, jointly, for the truth in that world of statement x.[19] (Note that while the analysis provided by a correct naturalistic theory of truth is true in every world with all and only the same laws of nature as this one, the analysis need not be a law of nature itself. Many theories about what a law of nature is put further constraints on what can count as such a law beyond just the requirement that the proposition in question be true in all naturally necessary worlds. Some would contend, for example, that only causal conditionals count as laws of nature. The naturalistic project per se is neutral about these issues.)

Like an extensional theory of truth, a naturalistic theory is not intended to answer questions about how we are to justify statements. Neither is such a theory supposed to tell us anything about the purposes, locutionary or illocutionary, for uttering truth ascriptions. Also, like the extensional project, the naturalistic project can be thought of as providing a definition, in *some* sense, of 'is true', but it cannot be thought of as providing the *meaning* of 'is true' or 'truth'.

The laws of logic are even more universal than the laws of nature, for the former are true in *every* possible world, not just every naturally possible world. Some philosophers have sought an analysis of truth that has this same degree of maximal universality. I have dubbed this the essence project because the features a thing, even an abstract thing like truth, has in every possible world are its *essential* features. The point here is to fill the blank in

x is true $\Leftrightarrow$ ____ .

Given the way I have defined '$\Leftrightarrow$', this means that the essence project wants an (possibly syntactically complex) expression that is equivalent, in every possible world, to 'x is true'. What would fill this blank is a list of conditions that, in *any* possible world, are individually requisite and jointly sufficient for the truth in that world of statement x.[20] Like the other two branches of the metaphysical project the essence project, can be thought of as providing a definition of truth in some sense of 'definition'.

Indeed, it is especially tempting to think that the essence project gives us the meaning of 'is true', but for reasons given in section 1.4, this temptation must be repressed. Also, like its brethren branches in the metaphysical project, a theory of the essence of truth has nothing to say about when we are justified in accepting a proposition or about what we are doing when we ascribe truth.

I use the term 'metaphysical project' to refer generically to all three of the above projects. All three are attempting, in some sense or other, to say what it is for a statement (or whatever) to be true. All three symbols '⇔', '↔', and '≡' are commonly translated with the phrase 'if and only if'. Hence the phrase is ambiguous.[21] Whenever 'p if and only if q' is true, we can say that q gives a necessary and sufficient condition for p. Thus the phrase 'necessary and sufficient condition' is ambiguous in a way that parallels the ambiguity of 'if and only if'. We can take advantage of this to describe, with deliberate ambiguity, the metaphysical project as the attempt to discover the conditions individually necessary and jointly sufficient for truth.

The goal of philosophers who pursue the justification project is to discover what sort of evidence or warrant can be used to determine whether or not a given proposition is *probably* true. Thus a theory that fulfills this project is one that tells us what sort of evidence and reasoning will entitle us to believe in the truth of a given proposition (with at least some degree of confidence, if not absolute certainty). For example, such a theory might say that if it seems to me that there is a blue typewriter in front of me and if I have no reason to think that I am the victim of an illusion, then it is *probably* true that there is a blue typewriter in front of me. More generally, it would say that visual experiences can be taken as *probably* accurate so long as there is no evidence of illusion present. The word 'probably' is important here, for a very sneaky magician could create the illusion that there is a blue typewriter here, and he might do it without my knowing he has; that is, he might leave no reason for me to believe that I am the victim of an illusion. So the fact that it seems there is a typewriter here and the fact that I have no reason to believe I am the victim of an illusion do not *guarantee* that there really is a blue typewriter here, At most, they only make it *probable* that there is.

On the other hand, what sort of evidence justifies me in believing that Tahiti is a paradise? Not visual experience, as was the case for the typewriter, for, alas, I have never seen Tahiti. The relevant evidence in this case would be what I have read or heard about it. So what counts as relevant evidence will vary from one type of proposition to another. Propositions about physical objects in this room have one sort of evidence, while propositions about far away objects have another, and propositions about abstract objects, like democracy or hate, will have still a third type of relevant evidence. Nevertheless, philosophers who pursue the justification project *usually* attempt to find what characteristic all kinds of evidence have in common, and they use this characteristic to construct a general theory of justification for all propositions. For example, a philosopher might contend that all kinds of evidence have the characteristic of showing that it is *useful to believe* the proposition in question.

So theories of justification answer questions like, For any given proposition (or belief or sentence, etc.), when and how are we justified in thinking that the proposition is probably true? It does *not* answer, What are the necessary and sufficient conditions for something's being true? And in no sense could a theory of justification be thought to provide a *definition* of truth.[22]

When theorists pursuing the justification project describe their theories, they often say that the theory provides a "criterion of truth," but this description tends to conflate the metaphysical and justification projects. The difference between the two kinds of criterion can be seen as a difference in practicality. The metaphysical project is not interested in providing a criterion we could *actually use* to determine if a proposition is true. This might seem surprising. Surely, in identifying the necessary and sufficient conditions for truth, we have *ipso facto* identified a set of criteria for determining whether or not a given statement is true. This, however, is not necessarily the case, for the necessary and sufficient conditions for truth may turn out to be very abstract conditions whose possession or nonpossession by a given statement is not something we can determine directly. We cannot, for example, directly apprehend whether or not a given proposition agrees with reality (except *possibly* in the case of certain small classes of statements such as those about our own sensations, e.g., 'I am in pain'). Hence, being told that agreement with reality is the sole necessary and sufficient condition for truth is of little help in deciding whether a given proposition is probably true. So while a theory fulfilling the metaphysical project may, in some sense, provide criteria of truth, the criteria it provides may not be of any practical use. It is the justification project that attempts to provide a practical criterion of truth. It attempts to identify some characteristic that, though it may not be among the necessary and sufficient conditions for truth, correlates well (though perhaps imperfectly) with truth and whose possession or nonpossession by a given statement can be determined with *relative* ease.

So a theory of justification is a conjunction of two claims: first, a certain characteristic potentially possessed by statements (or sentences or beliefs, etc.) correlates, perhaps imperfectly, with truth, and second, it is *relatively* easy to determine if a given statement (or sentence or belief, etc.) possesses the characteristic. Thus the theory of justification alluded to above is this:

Truth correlates positively with usefulness, and it is relatively easy to determine when a proposition (or sentence or belief, etc.) has this characteristic.

More generally, a theory of justification tries to fill the blank in the following:

Truth correlates positively with _____ and it is relatively easy to determine when a proposition (or sentence or belief, etc.) has this characteristic.

It should be clear that theories of justification are not really theories of truth at all. At least it is very misleading to call them theories of truth. They are not *about* truth. They are *about* justification. They do not *analyze* 'truth', 'true', or 'is true' in any way. They neither state the necessary and sufficient conditions for truth nor give the meaning of 'truth'. They provide a sufficient condition (or set of jointly sufficient conditions) for our being justified in believing a proposition.

Some philosophers have been interpreted as denying the distinction between truth and justification. Prominent among them are William James, Brand Blanshard, and Michael Dummett. It will be seen in sections 2.2 and 8.7, however, that many of the philosophers to whom this view has been attributed do not in fact deny the distinction. And as we shall see later in the book, the few who *do* identify truth and justification do not defend that claim very well. It might seem that those who equate truth with justification must also be denying the distinction between the metaphysical and justification projects. This is not the case, for to equate truth with justification is only to say that the correct answer to the question posed by one of the projects is the same as the correct answer to the question posed by the other. Consider that the following two questions have the same correct answer.

Who are my sisters?

Who are those two girls who grew up in the same home as I did?

Obviously, these are two *different* questions. The sort of theorist in question would use the same concept in filling the blank in *both* of the following:

x is true if and only if ____.

Truth correlates positively with ____, and it is relatively easy to determine when a proposition (or sentence or belief, etc.) has this characteristic.

For example, a theorist might claim both

x is true if and only if x is useful to believe,

and

Truth correlates positively with usefulness and it is relatively easy to determine when a proposition (or sentence or belief, etc.) has this characteristic.

Notice that these are two *different* claims. To use the same concept in fulfilling the two projects is not the same as denying that there is a difference between the two projects. Hence my distinction between the metaphysical and justification projects does not beg any questions against those who equate truth and justification or those who give the same answer to the two questions. Indeed, some philosophers in one or the other of these categories make explicit the distinction between the two projects just so it will be clear that they are not simply ignoring or failing to see the distinction (e.g., Blanshard 1941, 260).

As an example of the sort of philosophical twisting and turning that one is forced into by either a decision not to distinguish between a theory of truth and a theory of justification or by a failure to see the distinction, we have only to note the invocation of the "Intuitionistic Theory of Truth," by Nicholas Rescher, who made the mistake in question at one time. (He has rectified this in more recent writings.) In 1973 he offered what is, as I shall show below, a coherence theory of justification. But having convinced himself that he is defending a coherence theory of *truth* (indeed, he calls it a *definition* of truth), he must somehow evade the contradiction produced by the following facts:

a. The chief competitor of his theory is foundationalism; that is, they are both attempts to fulfill the same project.

b. Foundationalism is a theory of justification, not a theory of truth.[23]

Confronted with this, Rescher rejects (a). Instead of recognizing foundationalism as a competitor with his coherence theory, he supposes himself to have recognized a theory of truth that *is* a competitor with his theory. He calls it the intuitionistic theory and describes it thus: "According to the intuitionistic theory there are two sorts of truths (1) basic or primitive truths whose truthfulness is given immediately ... and (2) inferred truths that can be established by appropriate processes ... from those of the former group." [24] But this is either just a description of foundationalism (if the word 'truths' wherever it appears in the quotation is replaced with 'propositions'), or (if no such replacement is made) it is a description of a theory no one has ever held.[25] What Rescher should have seen (and did in more recent works) is that foundationalism *is* a competitor with his coherence theory and that this just means that his coherence theory is a theory of justification not truth. To show just how confusing things can get, Rescher drops the term 'intuitionistic theory of truth' later in the same book and replaces it with 'foundationalism' and recognizes that the latter is a competitor with his theory.[26]

Beyond questions about the necessary and sufficient conditions for truth and about the criteria for justification, we may ask about the conversational purpose served by utterances that ascribe truth to some statement (or some belief, or some proposition, etc.), or at least appear from their surface grammar to be ascribing truth to some statement. Among such utterances are 'Gödel's Theorem is true', '"Snow is white" is true', 'What Jan believes is true', and 'It's true, what Harry says'. That is, what are we *doing* when we make utterances of this sort? The speech-act project, which attempts to answer this question, naturally divides into two parts. One, the illocutionary-act project, attempts to describe what sort of illocutionary act is performed by an individual who makes such an utterance. (See below for an example of an illocutionary act.) The other, the assertion project, attempts to describe what we are saying when we make utterances of this sort. One who is convinced, as was P. F. Strawson in 1950, that we do not assert anything at all with such utterances, that their *only* purpose is to perform an illocutionary act, will regard the assertion project as wrong-headed through and through. Similarly, the illocutionary-act project will seem nonsensical to one who is convinced that the only thing we do with such utterances is assert something. One could, of course, hold that to make such utterances is both to assert something *and* to perform some illocutionary act. Strawson came to this position in 1964, (p. 68) and one suspects that others would endorse this view were the choice plainly put to them like this.

How can a word, phrase, or sentence be used to perform an illocutionary act? J. L. Austin (1956) has offered this example: in uttering 'I promise to repay you', a speaker is not describing herself as making a promise. She is, rather, actually making the promise. To make a promise *just is* to utter 'I promise...', and to utter 'I promise...' *just is* to make a promise. In making the utterance, one is not describing the act of promise making; one is *performing* the act. Austin calls utterances of this type "performative utterances." Another example of a performative utterance is the sentence 'I do' when uttered by a bride or groom at the appropriate moment in a marriage ceremony. When the bride says 'I do', she is taking the groom to be her lawful, wedded husband. She is *not*, according to Austin, *describing* herself as taking a lawful, wedded husband. She is not *saying* anything at all. Strawson's claim in 1950 is that when we utter expressions of the form 'Statement *s* is true', we are not asserting anything about *s*. We are not *asserting* anything at all. We are *doing* something. We are signaling our agreement with statement *s*. He does not mean that uttering '"The weather is beastly" is true' is the same as *saying* 'I agree that the weather is beastly'. He means that uttering '"The weather is beastly" is true' is a gesture or action roughly the same in its purpose as nodding one's head in agreement when someone else says 'The weather is beastly'. Just as nodding one's head is more a *doing* than a *saying*, so too, Strawson asserts, ascriptions of truth are more doings than sayings. It should be easy to see that Strawson would regard a list of the necessary and sufficient conditions for truth to be irrelevant to his project: one can signal one's agreement with a false statement as well as with a true one. Here, then, is an excellent piece of evidence that we must make distinctions beyond the one between theories of truth and theories of justification. Because we can agree with false statements as well as with true ones, there is no way to make sense of Strawson's theory if we do not see it as fulfilling a distinctly different project from both the metaphysical and the justification projects.

There are several ways to describe what the assertion project tries to do. They are all just different ways of saying the same thing:

• The project is to specify the informational content of the predicate 'is true'.

• The project is to find an expression (possibly syntactically complex) that is intensionally equivalent to 'is true', that is, an expression that is synonymous with 'is true'. The expression would therefore be one that could be substituted for 'is true' in any English sentence without changing the meaning or truth value of the sentence.

• The project is correctly to fill in the blank in both of the following (which mean the same thing):

x is true $=_{\text{syn}}$ ____.

To say that x is true is to say that ____.

I shall rely on the last of these descriptions most often. Thus, to sum up, the goal of the assertion project is to elucidate what we are *saying* when we ascribe truth to something (e.g., a belief, a proposition, etc.). For example, F. P. Ramsey (1927, 16–17) contended that the predicate 'is true' is vacuous: to ascribe truth to a statement is to do nothing more than assert the statement itself. For example,

'The weather is beastly' is true $=_{\text{syn}}$ the weather is beastly.

On the left side where the sentence appears within quotation marks, it is being *mentioned*, but on the right side the same sentence is being *used*. Once again, we translate the preceding formula thus: 'To say that "The weather is beastly" is true is to say that the weather is beastly'. More generally, Ramsey's theory is

's' is true $=_{\text{syn}} s$,

which says, 'To say that "s" is true is to say that s'.

The assertion project can itself be divided into two subprojects. For those who, like Ramsey, take the surface grammar of the utterances in question to be misleading, the assertion project becomes the deep-structure project. A theory fulfilling this project offers an expression that is not only synonymous with the utterance in question, but is so *by virtue of making plain the alleged deep grammatical structure* of the utterance. (In

Ramsey's case it is more a matter of making plain the vacuity of a part of the surface grammar.) J. L. Mackie, for example, contends that such utterances make a hidden reference to some state of affairs. His theory is this: "To say that a statement is true is to say that things are as, in it, they are stated to be. . . . To say that a statement is true is to say that whatever in the making of the statement is stated to obtain does obtain" (Mackie 1976, 50). Thus for Mackie, the predicate 'is true' is not vacuous. Utterances that appear to ascribe truth to a statement *do* say something about the statement besides merely asserting what the statement by itself would assert.

On the other hand, for those who have no quarrel with the surface grammatical structure of truth-ascribing utterances, the assertion project becomes the ascription project. For them, it is obvious what we are saying when we make such utterances. We are saying that there is some property called truth and that the statement in question possesses that property. The ascription project presumably embodies the ordinary (naive?) person's view of what we are saying when we make such utterances.[27]

1.8   Putting the Clues Together

I mentioned briefly above the sort of clues one can use to determine to which project a given theory of truth (or justification) belongs. Let us now examine those clues in more detail. As noted, the descriptions a philosopher gives of his own theory tend to be very poor clues. When philosophers who offer a metaphysical theory of truth describe their project, they tend to say that they wish to give the meaning of truth. Just as often they claim to be offering a criterion of truth. But the first phrase fails to distinguish the metaphysical project from the assertion project, and the second phrase fails to distinguish the metaphysical project from the justification project. The justification project is interested in providing a criterion that we could actually use. So when a philosopher's words indicate that it is a *practical* criterion she has in mind, we can take this as a clue that she is pursuing the justification project. Sometimes this type of theorist describes herself as offering a "test" for truth or a "mark" of truth. But to the extent that the terms 'test' and 'mark' are synonymous with 'criterion', then just to that extent they share its ambiguity. Assertion-project theorists tend to describe their project as the search for an analysis of the concept of truth or a definition of truth. But the former phrase could just as well describe the essence project, and the latter could well apply to any of the three divisions of the metaphysical project. It is also unfortunate that philosophers have chosen to use the English phrase 'if and only if' or its abbreviation 'iff' to express their theories of truth, for as noted already, this phrase is ambiguous as to whether it is extensional, naturalistic, essential, or intensional equivalence that is being asserted.

The criticisms that one philosopher makes about another's theory of truth are often a good clue as to what the first philosopher thinks a theory of truth should do. When a philosopher offering a metaphysical theory of truth fails to distinguish his project from those of other theorists, he is wont to complain of speech-act theories of truth that they do not provide a criterion of truth, and he is wont to complain of theories of justification that they are irrelevant to the concept of truth. Yet advocates theories of justification are apt to complain of metaphysical theories (and also speech-act theories) that they provide no *practical* criterion of truth, and speech-act theorists are liable to complain that metaphysical and justification project theories are irrelevant to the meaning of truth and/or the conversational *use* of 'is true'.

A characteristic of justification is that it comes in degrees: propositions with a lot of evidence in their favor are *more* probable than propositions with only a little. So if a philosopher of truth speaks of "degrees of truth" as though some propositions are "truer" than others, we can take this as a clue, though not a decisive one, that he or she is pursuing the justification project and that what he or she really means is that some propositions are more probable than others.[28] Notice also that evidence can sometimes be found for a proposition for which there previously was no evidence. This is what happened to the proposition that the world is round. Thus, sometimes an unjustified proposition *becomes* justified. So if a theorist speaks of propositions *becoming true*, as though truth happens to a proposition, we can take this as a clue, though not a decisive one, that he or she is pursuing the justification project and that he or she really means propositions can become justified as *probably* true.[29]

Textual evidence is not all that one must take into account when interpreting a philosopher, but it is the granite on which any good interpretation must be built. Let us pause here and see some concrete examples of how one should use textual clues to classify a theory of truth. Here, then, is *some* of the reasoning one would go through in trying to categorize the theories of Alfred Tarski, N. Rescher, and J. L. Mackie.

Tarski describes his work as a report on his "investigations concerning the definition of truth" (Tarski 1944, 13). This by itself could place him with either the metaphysical project or the assertion project, but it almost certainly indicates that he was not pursuing the justification project. This is confirmed by his denial that his theory of truth is "intended to establish the conditions under which we are warranted in asserting any given sentence" and his remark that "we may accept [my theory] without giving up any epistemological attitude we may have had" (1944, 33–34; see also Tarski 1969, 69). What we need, then, are clues for determining which of the other projects was his. We get no help from locating the connector he favors for expressing his theory, for it is the ambiguous phrase 'if and only if'. However, there are textual clues that place Tarski firmly with the metaphysical project and most probably with the extensional project. First, in discussing a characterization, of his theory as one that provides the necessary and sufficient conditions for truth, Tarski accepts the characterization, and yet he seems indifferent to the objection that his theory does not capture the essence of truth (1944, 34). Second, he suggests that his definition fixes the extension of the term 'true' (it identifies the set of all true sentences), which is exactly what is done by an extensional theory.[30]

Nicholas Rescher distinguishes the "definitional route" for explaining truth from the "criterial route." The latter, he says, is his project; the search for a "test" for truth (Rescher 1973, 1, 9–10). This remark eliminates the illocutionary-act project from consideration, since it is in no sense an attempt to provide a "criterion" or "test" for truth. Beyond this, his use of the terms 'criterion' and 'test' are not very helpful clues, for, as noted above, they can be used to describe either the metaphysical or justification projects. However, Rescher helps us out by distinguishing between "guaranteeing" and "authorizing" criteria. A criterion *guarantees* truth when a proposition's meeting the criterion *logically precludes* it from not being true. But if the criterion only gives "rational warrant" for thinking a proposition is probably true, then it is an *authorizing* criterion, and Rescher's project, he says, is to find an authorizing criterion for truth (1973, 4). This is an excellent clue for placing Rescher under the justification project, for the sort of criterion provided by either the metaphysical or assertion projects *is* a guaranteeing criterion.[31]

As I noted above, a philosopher who indicates he or she is looking for a *practical* criterion that could actually be used to determine whether or not a given proposition should be regarded as true is almost certainly pursuing the justification project. This provides a further clue for placing Rescher in the justification camp. His criterial approach, he says, is "decision-oriented." It is supposed to help us "implement and apply" the concept of truth (Rescher 1973, 2). A final clue for placing Rescher in the justification project is that he endorses the idea that truth comes in degrees: "In the context of a coherence analysis of truth, the prospect of degrees of truth is an inevitable fact: coherence being a matter of degree, so—on a coherence theory of truth—must truthfulness be also" (Rescher 1973, 198, 200).

Mackie uses the terms 'definition' and 'conceptual analysis of truth' as descriptions of his intentions (Mackie 1976, 40, 42). These terms are ambiguous between the metaphysical and assertion projects, but they rule out both the justification and illocutionary-act projects. He also says that he is not trying to provide a criterion of truth (p. 22), but he does not equate criteria of truth with theories of justification, for he says that instrumentalism and the coherence theory are acceptable as theories of justification but not as criteria of truth (p. 25). What *does* he mean by a "criterion of truth"? Our only clue is his belief that Tarski *is* offering a criterion of truth (p. 30). Since Tarski is trying to fulfill the metaphysical project, specifically, the extensional project, and since Mackie thinks that he (Mackie) is doing something different from what Tarski is doing, we have strong evidence that Mackie is not pursuing the extensional project and a strong suspicion that he is not pursuing any division of the metaphysical project. This is confirmed by his remark that he is providing an account of the *use* of the word 'true' (p. 50). This puts him clearly in some division or other of the speech-act camp, and since we have already eliminated the illocutionary-act project, the assertion project is the only one left that could be his. Finally, note that I suggested assertion theories are best expressed by means of the intensional-equivalence symbol and that the symbol is to be translated into English with 'To say that... is to say that...'. It is significant that in the unsymbolized formulations of his theory, he uses the very expression 'To say that... is to say that...' (p. 50). It is significant also that in the symbolized versions, Mackie uses the ordinary equal sign ' = ' instead of some logical connective, for the former is usually used by philosophers to express synonymy.

Mackie can also serve as an example of how textual evidence can be conflicting, for at one place he says that he is going to answer the question "What is it for something to be true?" (p. 17), which sounds as if he is pursuing some division or other of the metaphysical project. In this book I have chosen to take this as atypical and as outweighed by contrary evidence, but interpretations that categorize Mackie under the metaphysical project are possible.

So much, then, for examples of textual exegesis. When interpreting a philosopher, we must also be faithful to the principle of charity: when faced with a choice of interpretations of a given author, all else being equal, we ought to take the option that maximizes the intelligence and viability of the theory in question. This means, in most cases at least, that if a given theory seems plausible as an answer to one project but less plausible as an answer to another, we ought to interpret it as an answer to the former. And, of course, if a theory simply makes no sense as an answer to a particular project, we cannot interpret its author as so intending it. (Thus we cannot interpret Strawson's performative theory as an answer to any project except the illocutionary-act project.) Charity should be extended to the *critics* of a particular theory too, and herein a dilemma often lies, for it is frequently impossible to be charitable to every side of a debate. When views are incompatible, *someone* must be wrong and, I am afraid, occasionally we must interpret someone as *obviously* wrong. We can minimize the frequency of such occasions by making the principle of charity holistic. We confront a populous pool of philosophers who have had something to say about truth, and our goal should be to make as many of them seem intelligent and sensible as possible. This principle informs many of the interpretive decisions I make in this book.

For most of the philosophers to be discussed, I shall not provide in detail my evidence for categorizing them where I do. That would be a lengthy and tedious process more appropriate to a book on textual exegesis than a book on truth. (To a large extent, however, my evidence will become apparent when I discuss each of them in turn.) Anyone who steeps himself in the literature of a topic will develop certain intuitions about what how things fit together and about what this or that philosopher was trying to say when he wrote such and such. I too find my interpretations affected by such indistinct intuitions. This is not a claim of authority *ex cathedra*; rather, it is a confession that if asked why I made this or that interpretive decision, there would be times when I could say little more in answer than "It just seems right."

Table 1.1 below categorizes each of the theorists of truth I shall be discussing at any length in this book under the project (or projects) that I think he intended his theory to satisfy. Alternative interpretations are possible. Indeed, since it is hardly likely that I am right in all of my classifications, I strongly encourage all readers to stop now and then in reading this book and ask themselves if the theory under discussion might be better classified under a project other than the one under which I have placed it. (I do this explicitly a few times, but keeping the book to a manageable size requires that I not do it often.)

Here some cautionary remarks are in order: (1) In putting together the puzzle, we may *not* take as relevant clues the remarks about this or that theory of truth found in secondary sources, such as, introductory surveys of epistemology. These works were all written before most of the project distinctions of this chapter had been deployed. Not surprisingly, then, such works often describe theories of truth in language that readers of this book will recognize as ambiguous and often simply false. The general tendency in such works is to say that theories of truth are after the meaning of 'truth'. But this is inconsistent with the actual words of many theorists, and to the extent that it is not ambiguous, it falsely tends to put all theories into the assertion project. (2) Worse still, the oversimplifications found in such works have become part of the folklore of philosophy, by which I mean that philosophers now feel entitled to make *ex cathedra* pronouncements on the purposes of this or that theory of truth. But no one ought to take seriously question-begging dissents that presuppose a folklore, against which I argue in the remainder of the book. (3) Some readers may think that they can even now recall a remark or two from a primary source that would cast doubt on the propriety of my classification of the theories in question. Such readers are asked to do me the kindness of assuming, at least to the end of the book, that I am aware of the remark and that I believe I am in possession of evidence that outweighs it. Only when the book is read clean through would one be justified, even in principle, in concluding that I have left some pieces of the puzzle on the table.

It is worth pointing out that I nowhere suggest that the projects are disjoint in the sense that it is impossible for a theorist to intend that his theory fulfill more than one of them at the same time. Indeed, I have already mentioned examples of those who wish to give the same answer to more than one of the projects. To a surprising degree the clues do tend to place theories in one and only one camp; nevertheless, readers ought not feel browbeaten by my judgment on this issue, any more than on my basic classifications.

In Table 1.1, I have entered, to the right of each philosopher's name, the name of the type of truth theory he advocates according to the traditional way of dividing up theories of truth. (For some of the more recent theories I have coined a name.) Some philosophers not listed under the justification project have theories of justification as well as theories of truth. However, with the exception of foundationalism, which is listed for purposes of comparison, I include under the justification project only either (1) theories that are often mistakenly labeled (by their authors and/or critics) theories of truth or (2) the theories of those who give the same answer to the justification project as they give to the metaphysical project. Finally, in

Table 1.1
A categorization of theories of truth

I. The metaphysical project	
A. The extensional project	
Philosopher	*Theoretical school*
Alfred Tarski	Semantic theory
Saul Kripke	Semantic theory
B. The naturalistic project	
C. The essence project	
Philosopher	*Theoretical school*
C. S. Peirce	Pragmaticism
William James	Instrumentalism
Bertrand Russell	Correspondence theory
J. L. Austin	Correspondence theory
Brand Blanshard	Coherence theory
Paul Horwich	Minimal theory
II. The justification project	
Philosopher	*Theoretical shool*
F. H. Bradley	Coherence theory
Williams James (again)	Instrumentalism
Brand Blanshard (again)	Coherence theory
(Many others)	Foundationalism
III. The speech-act project	
A. The illocutionary-act project	
Philospher	*Theoretical school*
P. F. Strawson	Performantive theory
Huw Price	Darwinian theory
B. The assertion project	
1. The ascription project	
The ordinary (naive?) person	
2. The deep-structure project	
Philospher	*Theoretical school*
F. P. Ramsey	Redundancy theory
Alan White	Appraisal theory
C. J. F. Williams	Redundancy theory
D. Grover et al.	Prosentential theory

addition to those listed below, the views of Hartry Field, Donald Davidson, Michael Dummett, and several others will receive extended discussion, but for reasons that will become clear in the next section and
elswhere in the book, none of them really belong in this table. Also, of
course, many other figures will be briefly mentioned. No one is listed under
the naturalistic project only because none of those who are pursuing this
project claim to have produced a theory that satisfies the project (see
section 6.6).

1.9 Projects and Programs

Before leaving this chapter, I must note also the distinction between
projects and programs. Projects gain significance because solutions to
them can be put to use in broader philosophical enterprises. These broader
enterprises, often called programs, are more closely related to immediate
human problems and concerns than are the projects themselves. Or else
the program is nested within a still broader enterprise that is connected to
ordinary human concerns. There is no theoretical limit to the number
of nested layers one can find. We shall examine in this book several
of the most important of these broader programs in service to which
philosophers or linguists or logicians have wished to put this or that
answer to this or that project.

The failure to distinguish between projects and programs, like the
failure to distinguish between different projects, has confused.[32] It is often
said, for example, that Hartry Field, Donald Davidson, and Michael
Dummett have theories of truth. As we shall see, this is false. Field,
Davidson, and Dummett are pursuing broader philosophical programs,
and the work of each of them is concerned with whether or not *someone
else's* theory of truth can be put to work in the service of this or that
program.

These remarks suggest a further clue we ought avail ourselves of in
putting together the puzzle: if we can identify the broader program toward
which a given truth theorist is ultimately pointing and if we can determine
that only, say, assertion-project theories can possibly be put to use in
service of that broader program, then we have a superb clue that the
theory of truth in question ought be interpreted as an attempt to fulfill the
assertion project. To give an admittedly vague hint of things to come in
section 2.1, one of the reasons I classified Bertrand Russell's theory the

way I did in the previous section is that it comes in a work largely devoted to epistemology and thus seems intended to play a role in some epistemological program.

1.10 Chapter Summary

Many of the points I make in this chapter cry out for detailed examples, but examples of particular theories of truth cannot themselves be very clear until *after* I have made all the points of this and the next chapter. Let me renew a suggestion I made earlier: this chapter should be reread after the whole book has been gone through. In the meantime, let me summarize what has been said so far.

A book about theories of truth cannot begin with simple answers to questions like, What ought a theory of truth do? What problems ought a theory of truth solve? What questions ought a theory of truth answer? because there is a four-dimensional confusion surrounding these three questions. The confusion arises partly because previous writers on truth *have* given simple (and thus usually vague or ambiguous) answers to these questions. It also arises because too many past writers on truth have failed to notice that not all philosophers would give the same answer to these questions. It is difficult to evaluate or even understand a theory of truth until we know how its author would respond to these questions. Hence the four-dimensional confusion must be dissolved. The way to do this is analogous to fitting together a puzzle: we keep fiddling with the pieces until everything fits. In this case the pieces are textual clues relevant to how the various theorists would answer the three questions. The finished product is a list and accompanying description of each of the different kinds of truth-theory projects and a categorization of each theorist according to the project(s) he or she was attempting to fulfill. It turns out that we can make all the pieces fit with a scheme that postulates three different main projects (and certain subprojects).

What I have not done yet is to explain why anyone has any interest in accomplishing any of these projects. What broader programs motivate these projects? I shall turn to this question first in section 2.1 and return to it again many times, but first two small points about terminology are in order. In the relevant philosophical literature the phrases 'theory of truth', 'definition of truth', and 'analysis of truth' are treated as synonyms by the philosophical-linguistic community as a whole and, as often as not, by individual writers within the confines of their own writings. This is probably not a wise policy, but I have felt compelled to continue the practice anyway. One reason is that all three of the terms in question, 'theory', 'definition', and 'analysis' are ambiguous, and any decision on my part to assign them precise meanings is likely to seem misleading to some. A second reason is that in commenting on a quotation from the literature, I am bound to use the same choice from among the three terms in question as was used in the quotation. To do otherwise, I have found, incurs too heavy a price in loss of clarity and style. A second terminological concern is the common practice in the literature of interchangeably using the definite and indefinite articles when speaking of a generic category of truth theory. Thus one finds sentences like '*The* correspondence theory of truth has the implication that . . .' and other sentences like '*A* correspondence theory of truth implies that . . .'. In both cases the writer means '*All* correspondence theories (and thus any given one) imply . . .'. I too shall follow this practice, the reasons again having to do with clarity in context.

2 Justification and Truth Bearers

What questions should a theory of truth answer, and what intellectual worries should it assuage? The answer depends on what one wants to accomplish with a theory of truth. In this chapter I shall try to make clear just what intellectual worries motivate *epistemology* and why the metaphysical project and the justification project are important to the epistemological program. Other philosophical, linguistic, and logical programs will be introduced in later chapters.

2.1 The Epistemological Enterprise

There is little dispute that general skeptical worries are the historical motivation of interest in epistemology. For the purposes of this book, general skepticism shall be defined as the claim that none of our beliefs is objectively justified as any more likely true than its negation.[1] One implication of general skepticism, not often faced up to even by skeptics, is that all the activity of scientists, philosophers, and other persons intended to discover the facts of the matter or to justify this or that conclusion is but wasted time, because such activities are hopeless.[2] A second implication is that anyone's opinion is as good as anyone else's. And not just on matters of artistic merit but on *everything*. It is these alarming implications that philosophers have in mind when they speak of the *problem* of skepticism.

Everyone is a skeptic about *something*. Most of us are skeptics about the predictions of astrology; that is, we think that these predictions are no more objectively justified than their negations. Lots of people are also skeptics about evaluations of artistic merit. And, of course, there are people who believe that anyone's opinion on moral questions is as good as anyone else's. Usually the people who are skeptics in one or another of these three ways are also the very people who *do not care* (indeed, are often rather pleased) that astrological, artistic, or moral beliefs, as the case may be, are unjustified. But there are many kinds of belief whose justificatory status nearly everyone cares about. We care that our doctor's belief about how we should be treated when ill is justified. We care that the pilot's belief about how to fly the plane in which we are riding is more than just a guess. And most of all, we care about our own beliefs. It is important to us that we are *justified* in thinking that this road and not that other road will get us to London faster and that this ingredient and not that one will improve the taste of our salad dressing. If none of our beliefs is any more justified than its negation, then all of life becomes a perpetual guessing game. (If you are inclined to say at this point that we would soon learn the right roads, ingredients, etc. from experience, then you have not understood what a general skeptic is saying. One of the things he means when he says that no belief can ever be more justified than its negation is that experience does not provide such a justification. We are only kidding ourselves if we think it does. Exactly how he would make good on this remarkable claim is a story for another book.)

Perhaps most important of all, most of us care that we are justified in our moral beliefs. We do not want to think that our belief in the wrongness of murder is no more justified than the criminal's belief that murder is morally permissible. It is not just that we want to be correct in our moral decisions, we could guess at the right thing to do in every moral situation and by luck always guess correctly, but that would not satisfy us. At least not most of us. We want to believe that we can be *justified* in our moral beliefs, that we can, when facing a moral decision, gather evidence and find an answer that is at least more likely correct than a random guess, even if we cannot be *certain* that it is correct. The general skeptic does not deny that we can have *correct* beliefs. He will allow that we can, by luck. His contention is that we are never *justified* in any of our beliefs.

No one having studied the matter carefully would believe that it is *easy* to prove that general skepticism is wrong, not, at any rate, if we do not beg the question against skepticism by explicitly or implicitly presupposing that it is wrong in the very premises with which we argue against it. Just to the extent that we think it *might* be right, we begin to doubt the justificatory status of our other beliefs.

So it is the primary task of epistemology to discover whether our beliefs can be justified and, if so, how. Until we have learned how, say, a moral claim can be justified as more likely true than its negation; we shall not know what, in any given situation, is more likely the morally right thing to do. It is the task of a theory of justification to show us how our beliefs can be justified and, by virtue of doing so, to show that general skepticism is wrong. Thus the justification project is the most important task for epistemology. But as was pointed out in section 1.7, what fulfills the justification project is a theory of justification, not a theory of truth. Is there any reason for an epistemologist to be interested in a theory of truth per se? That is, would he have any interest in any of the other projects?

In fact, it is absolutely essential to any complete epistemology that it have an answer to the metaphysical project. Indeed, it is impossible to fulfill the justification project without having first fulfilled the metaphysical project. To see why this is so, we need to examine the structure of theories of justification.[3]

We saw in section 1.7 that the conditions for a belief's or proposition's being true need not turn out to be the sort of things that can be directly apprehended. We cannot just go look and see if they have been fulfilled. They just are not the sort of things one can see, even in a metaphorical sense. The best we can do is to have evidence that the truth conditions for a given proposition or belief are (at least *probably*) fulfilled. Hence the need for theories of justification.

So it is that a theory of justification identifies some characteristic that can be possessed by beliefs (or propositions, etc.) but that is easier to apprehend than the fulfillment of truth conditions and correlated with truth, albeit perhaps imperfectly correlated. So again the idea is to fill the blank in the following:

Truth correlates positively with ＿＿ and it is relatively easy to determine when a proposition (sentence, or belief, etc.) has this characteristic.

When a philosopher contends that the usefulness of a belief or proposition justifies it as probably true, he is saying, first, that it is relatively easy to determine if a belief or proposition is useful and, second, that usefulness is correlated with truth; that is, most useful beliefs are also true. (But unless the philosopher claims that usefulness is *perfectly* correlated with truth, a belief's usefulness is no guarantee that it is true.) Hence,

Truth correlates positively with usefulness, and it is relatively easy to determine when a proposition (sentence, or belief, etc.) has this characteristic.

Theories of justification that, like this one, hold that usefulness is the mark of truth are called instrumental theories of *justification* (not, I repeat, not instrumental theories of *truth*). This example is a very simple one. A theory of justification could contend that there is more than one mark of truth, in which case the name of the characteristic alleged to correlate with truth will be disjunctive. For example, a very simple version of a foundationalist theory of justification might look like this:

Truth correlates positively with being self-evident or being deduced from self-evident premises, and it is relatively easy to determine when a proposition (sentence, or belief, etc.) has either of these characteristics.[4]

What the first conjunct of the instrumental theory above says *in effect* is that usefulness makes it *likely* that *the necessary and sufficient conditions for a given belief's being true do obtain.*[5] Similarly, the foundational theory tells us what makes it likely that the necessary and sufficient conditions for a given belief's being true obtain.

Now at last we are in a position to see why a metaphysical theory of truth is so important to the construction of a theory of justification and hence why it is so important to epistemologists. Since theories of justification purport to tell us what characteristics signal that the necessary and sufficient conditions for truth are probably fulfilled with respect to a given proposition, we will have to know what those necessary and sufficient conditions are before we can evaluate any theory of justification. Which of the two theories of justification presented above, instrumental or foundational, is the correct theory of justification? Or are they both perfectly good, or is neither of them any good? Answering these questions requires an evaluation of the plausibility of the theories. But even in asking oneself whether either of these theories seems plausible, one fact becomes immediately obvious: we cannot begin to judge the plausibility of these theories unless we have some idea of what it is for a proposition to be true. And we cannot have such an idea unless we have an idea of what the necessary and sufficient conditions of truth are. But, of course, *metaphysical* theories of truth attempt to tell us what these conditions are. Therein lies their importance to epistemology: they make it possible to evaluate the plausibility of theories of justification. Thus, for epistemology, *the role of metaphysical theories of truth is a regulatory one. Relative to a given theory about the conditions for truth, some theories of justification will turn out to be very implausible and others very plausible.* The hope is that we can first discover the correct answer(s) to the metaphysical project and then use it (them) to help determine the correct answer(s) to the justification project.

In particular, which of the three subdivisions of the metaphysical project is the relevant one for an epistemologist? That will depend on whether the theories of justification she is evaluating are intended to be applicable only to the intelligent creatures of this world, to creatures of any naturally possible world, or to the creatures of any possible world. If, for example, the instrumental theory above is interpreted as claiming only that *in the actual world* usefulness correlates with truth, then we would need only a correct extensional theory of truth to evaluate it, for we would only need to know what conditions in this world are necessary and sufficient for truth. But if the instrumental theory is claiming that in *all* possible worlds usefulness correlates with truth, then evaluating its plausibility will require an idea of the conditions that, in every world, are necessary and sufficient for truth. She will need an essence theory to tell her that. Similarly, a correct answer to the naturalistic project will be required if the instrumental theory is interpreted as alleging that in all naturally possible worlds, truth correlates with usefulness.[6]

Hereafter when I wish, as I do in this chapter, to speak generically of all three divisions of the metaphysical project without burdening the reader or myself with long paragraphs, like the last one, referring explicitly to each division, I shall treat the metaphysical project as the attempt to fill the blank in

x is true iff ____,

where the connector 'iff' is shorthand for the ambiguous phrase 'if and only if'.

The theories of truth and justification we have seen so far have been relatively simple, but we shall see some rather more complex ones later in the book. To express these theories in a clear manner and make them easy to compare with one another, I have already made use of some special symbols from the language of logic. Quantifiers are another type of symbol needed to facilitate the goals of clarity and comparison. A *quantifier* is an expression used when a speaker cannot, or does not want to, specify exactly which individuals he is talking about but he can and does want to specify (to a degree) the quantity of individuals he is talking about. The terms 'some', 'all', 'every', 'most', 'many', 'few', and 'twenty-seven' in the following sentences are quantifiers.

Something went bump in the night.

All cats will go bump in the night.

Every dog stays quiet at night.

Most of the time, some of the people cannot be fooled.

Many are called, but few are chosen.

Some are called, but twenty-seven are chosen.

In this book I shall need only the quantifiers 'some' and 'all'.[7] The first of these is called the *existential quantifier*, and it is symbolized '$(\exists x)$'. 'Something went bump in the night' is written

$(\exists x)(x$ went bump in the night).

If we were to translate this sentence back into English in a literal minded way, it would read, 'There is at least one thing x such that x went bump in the night'. A little closer to natural English would be, 'There is at least one thing x such that it went bump in the night'. The fact that the second x in the first translation can be replaced by the pronoun 'it' illustrates something important. A variable like x works in a symbolic sentence very much like a pronoun works in an English sentence. It refers back to an individual previously introduced into the sentence. So the very first x in the symbolic sentence, the one inside the '$(\exists x)$', is in effect the antecedent of all the later x's that may appear in the sentence. In this very simple example there is only one later x, but symbolic sentences can have two or more, just as English sentences can have two or more pronouns referring back to the same antecedent.

'There is at least one thing x such that $x \dots$' is not the only way to translate the existential quantifier. It is often translated 'There *exists* an x such that $x \dots$', 'For some x, $x \dots$', 'Some $x \dots$', or just 'Something $\dots$'. So the quantified sentence above can also be translated into English as 'There exists an x such that x went bump in the night', 'For some x, x went bump in the night', 'Some x went bump in the night', and 'Something went bump in the night'. These all mean the same.

I shall not make use of the existential quantifier until a later chapter, but I shall immediately begin to make use of the quantifier 'all', which is more often called the *universal quantifier*, and it is symbolized '(x)'. Thus

$(x)($if x is a cat, then x goes bump in the night)

means 'For all x, if x is a cat, then x goes bump in the night'. This is, of course, just an oddly roundabout way of saying, 'All cats go bump in the night'. We can express this in a simpler, less roundabout way, provided we have specified (or the context makes clear) that *cats* are being talked about. When that specification is made, we can express 'All cats go bump in the night' with

$(x)(x$ goes bump in the night).

The category of things to which a variable in a quantified sentence refers is called the *range* of the variable. So the range of the variable in the preceding quantified sentence is the set of cats. We express this by saying that the variable "ranges over" cats. (When no range is specified for a variable, not even by the context, it should be presumed to range over everything in the universe.) It is often helpful to choose as a variable a letter that is mnemonic with respect to the range. Thus, let c range over cats. The new translation of 'All cats go bump in the night' is then

$(c)(c$ will go bump in the night).

There are many ways to translate a universally quantified sentence into English. Included among the correct translations of the last formula are

All cats go bump in the night,

Any and all cats go bump in the night,

All cats are such that they go bump in the night,

Every cat goes bump in the night,

For any cat, it goes bump in the night.

As you can see, a universally quantified sentence is used to assert that there is some characteristic that every member of a given category, i.e., range, has in common.

  A *truth bearer* is anything that can be true or false. There has been much disagreement in philosophy over what sort of things can be truth bearers, but this is a debate that is best postponed until sections 2.3 to 2.7. For now I shall simply take it for granted that beliefs, propositions, sentences, and statements can all be true or false. Because the motivation for epistemology is concern over whether and how our beliefs can be justified as true, it is the truth of beliefs with which an epistemologist is ultimately concerned. She is concerned with the truth of propositions, sentences, and statements only in so far as an explication of their truth will aid in explicating the truth of beliefs.[8] When we specify the necessary and sufficient conditions for true belief, we are in effect asserting that every member of the category of beliefs has a certain complex characteristic. For example, if we say that beliefs are true when and only when such and such conditions are fulfilled, we are in effect saying that all members of the category of beliefs have in common the characteristic that they are true if and only if such and such conditions are fulfilled. Symbolically, we write this as follows, where b ranges over beliefs:

(b)(b is true iff [such and such conditions] are fulfilled)

In English this says, 'For *any* belief, the belief is true if and only if [such and such conditions] are fulfilled.'

In practice, however, very few philosophers have *directly* explicated the truth of beliefs, as this formula does. Even those who think beliefs can be truth bearers are inclined to explicate the truth of propositions, sentences, or statements directly and then leave the truth of beliefs to be explicated in terms of either the proposition that is the belief's content or the sentence or statement that expresses the belief. Such theories need a two-tiered formula like this:

(b)(b is true iff any sentence that accurately expresses it is true)

(s)(s is true iff [such and such conditions] are fulfilled)

As you may have guessed, s is a variable ranging over all sentences. So the top tier gives a kind of *pro forma* (and circular) explication of true belief, while the bottom tier gives a more substantive explication of true sentence. The circularity of the top tier is not a problem, because the reference to truth is cashed out in the bottom tier. Only by a combination of the two tiers do we get a substantive explication of true belief. At least it will be substantive when we replace the placeholder phrase '[such and such conditions]' with a list of the necessary and sufficient conditions for a sentence's being true.

As an example, a very simple version of the correspondence theory of truth is the following:

(b)(b is true iff any sentence that accurately expresses it is true)

(s)(s is true iff s corresponds with reality)

The second of these reads, 'For any sentence, the sentence is true if and only if it corresponds with reality.'

2.2 Truth, Justification, and Warranted Assertibility

My description of the epistemological enterprise implies that justification must be defined or analyzed with reference to truth, or as it is sometimes said, the concept of justification presupposes the concept of truth. This is a very traditional way of viewing the relation between truth and justification, but it is not philosophically neutral. Some philosophers, if we take them literally, have claimed that truth must be defined or analyzed *in terms of* justification or one of its near synonyms, such as warranted assertibility. If that is correct, the description of the epistemological program in the preceding section has things backward: It is not the justification project that presupposes an answer to the metaphysical project. Matters are really quite the other way around.

There are a number of philosophical positions that have caused one or another thinker to say that truth is to be analyzed in terms justification, maximal justification, justification in ideal circumstances, or some near synonym thereof. Regrettably, those positions cannot be described here, because doing so presupposes matters not to be covered until later chapters, so I shall return to this issue later in the book. But a couple of points are worth making now even at the risk that they will not be entirely perspicuous yet to all readers.

First, as Richard Rorty (1979, 280) has noticed, the truth-as-justification thesis, as I shall call it, is often asserted as a roundabout way of expressing some *other* doctrine. Sometimes it is an odd way of expressing the thesis that there really is no legitimate philosophical program in which a theory of truth could play a role; hence, we really do not need a theory of truth, distinct from a theory of justification. At other times it is a metaphor for the thesis that truth is relative to a conceptual scheme. Sometimes too the truth-as-justification thesis is meant only to express the claim that truth is a vacuous concept while justification is not. Still others use it as a way of denying that truth is really the epistemic value our justificatory procedures succeed in obtaining for us. Finally and most oddly, the truth-as-justification thesis is sometimes asserted as a way of endorsing some or other particular answer to the metaphysical project. We saw in section 1.7 that it is possible to give the same answer to both the metaphysical and justification projects. To repeat the example given there, one could claim that usefulness is an accessible characteristic that positively correlates with truth *and* claim that being useful to believe is a necessary and sufficient condition for being true. This move, giving the same answer to both projects, was so common among the early advocates of what I shall call Nonrealist answers to the metaphysical project (section 3.1) that it has come to be taken by many as the defining characteristic of Nonrealist theories of truth. And thus some who seem to endorse the truth-as-justification thesis mean only to endorse some particular Nonrealist answer to the metaphysical project.[9] On the other hand, we should not conclude that no one really believes that truth should be defined in terms of justification. John Dewey almost certainly believed just that. Here is one of his many expressions of the view: "Men have slowly grown accustomed in all specific beliefs to identifying the true with the verified. But they still hesitate to recognize the implication of this identification and to derive the definition of truth from it."[10]

Second, the various philosophical positions that might lead one to endorse the truth-as-justification thesis all involve some fundamentally different attitude toward the problem of skepticism than the one I took in the last section. This is no surprise. Since the epistemological program, on my traditional account, has its roots in the problem of skepticism, we would expect to find that those who either deny the need for such a program or reject my description of it will not see the problem of skepticism in the traditional way. In particular, some of the philosophical positions in question, such as Hilary Putnam's (1981), include ontological doctrines in the context of which the problem of skepticism simply cannot arise. Other philosophers, like Rorty, have concluded that skepticism is irrefutable and for just that reason conclude that the traditional epistemological program is self-destructive and that we should abandon it in favor of programs that have some hope of solving their own problems. Third and most dubious are the views that hold we are entitled just to assume that skepticism is wrong and thereafter give it no further thought (e.g., M. Williams 1986, 223–242).

Further discussion of the issues raised in the last two paragraphs will have to wait until later chapters. In the meantime I offer the following argument against the claim that truth can be analyzed in terms of justification. It is part of the meaning of 'justified', 'verified', and 'warranted' that nothing is justified or verified or warranted *simpliciter*. These participles require as a complement a prepositional phrase beginning with 'as'. If a law is justified, then it is justified as fair and useful. If a business expense is justified, then it is justified as likely to lead to better long term profits. (Context usually allows us to leave the prepositional phrase implicit, and this no doubt has contributed to misunderstanding.) But what are statements or beliefs justified *as* or warranted *as*? 'As *true*' is the answer *vénérable*. Let us assume for the moment that the venerable answer is correct. The immediate implication of this is that to equate 'true' with 'justified' or to analyze truth even partly in terms of justification is at best a hopelessly circular analysis and at worst an unintelligible one that turns '*s* is true' into the infinitely long piece of nonsense '*s* is justified as justified as justified as ... '.

Some have tried to evade this consequence by suggesting that statements are warranted "as assertible," but this will not do. In one sense of 'assertible', any statement is assertible if it is *physically capable* of being asserted. But no one would claim all such statements are true. In the other sense of 'assertible', roughly analogous to 'honorable', an assertible statement is one that can be *justifiably* asserted, just as an honorable man is one who can be justifiably honored. (Not merely one who is capable of being honored. All persons, even criminals, are capable of being honored.) But on this sense of 'assertible', the phrase 'warranted assertibility' is a redundancy that avoids coming to grips with the fact that a statement can be justifiably asserted only when it is justified *as* (probably) possessing some value or other, and the venerable view, which I am assuming for the moment, identifies that value as truth. Thus by this maneuver the circularity is postponed only momentarily. Nor does it help any to equate 'true' with 'justified within a system' or 'justified within a conceptual scheme'. For again, I ask, Justified as *what* within the system? On this view, '*s* is true' (or '*s* is true within a system') is circularly explained as meaning '*s* is justified *as true* within a system', or else it is equated with something unintelligible like '*s* is justified as justified within a system within a system'.

All of this follows on the venerable answer to the the question, What are statements or beliefs justified *as*? But suppose we reject that answer. Suppose, instead, we take it that when a statement or belief is justified, it is justified as having explanatory power, predictive power, coherence with our other beliefs, simplicity and/or some pragmatic value. By itself, this is a suggestion with much merit, but when married to the claim that truth is to be analyzed in terms of justification, it turns the latter thesis into a pointlessly roundabout and metaphorical way of rejecting truth as an epistemic value. What is really being suggested by this nonvenerable answer is that we should stop seeing truth as the value we are (and/or ought to be) aiming at when we engage in inquiry and the justification of belief and confirmation of theory. Rather, we should see ourselves as trying to build a coherent world view that helps us explain and predict the course of experience and helps us, in Rorty's phrase, *cope with* the world (Rorty 1982, xliii). But again, as Rorty usually sees, it is just a muddle to then go on and equate truth with this other (set of) epistemic value(s) (Rorty 1982, xxv, xxviii) with or without an intervening stop at justification. Those who try to make such an identification are behaving as though there is some statute mandating that we use the string t^r^u^t^h to label the ultimate epistemic value or collection of values, *whatever* it turns out to be. (One cause of this sort of muddle is the belief that somehow it ought to be built into the very definition of truth that truth is valuable. I argue against this idea in section 3.4.)

In point of fact, we are taught what these other values are partly by *contasting* them with truth. It is pointed out, for example, that false propositions can sometimes have a lot of explanatory power and true ones sometimes fail to have any. Closely related to this is our need to distinguish different kinds of reasons for belief. Consider Pascal's reason for believing in God: the consequences of not so believing if one turns out to be wrong are horrendous, eternity in hell, but the consequences of believing in God if there is not one are minor. Part of the reason we have a concept of truth is to allow us to say, Pascal has a pragmatic reason to believe in God, but it gives him no justification for thinking 'God exists' is *true*. Moreover, the logic of truth is different from the logic of these other values. For example, anything deduced from a true statement must itself be true, but not everything deduced from a statement with, say, explanatory power will itself have explanatory power. To put the same point another way, equating truth with explanatory power conflicts with our intuitions about which rules of interference are truth-preserving: if it is true that $p \, \& \, q$, it is true that p, but this rule no longer holds when 'is true' means 'has explanatory power'. Hence, equating truth with some other value(s) threatens to make a mockery of logic.

It seems, then, that regardless of whether we give the venerable answer or some new-fangled answer to the question 'Justified as *what*?' the truth-as-justification thesis turns out at best to be a muddled metaphor for a very different thesis and at worst to produce a circular and/or unintelligible analysis of truth. The only way to save the thesis is to reject the opening premise of my argument, the claim that 'justified' is shorthand for 'justified as *v*' for some value *v*. Such a rejection seems to require one or the other of three tacks. The first tack is to insist that 'justified' (or 'assertible') is a primitive term whose meaning is understood intuitively and is not further analyzable. The second tack is a variation of the first in that it allows that 'justified' can be analyzed in terms of being derived *via* certain rules or principles of justification. But the second tack insists that the correctness of these rules cannot itself be cashed out in terms of their being truth-preserving or as likely to lead to beliefs with explanatory or predictive power or some other value. Rather, the correctness of the rules is supposedly just intuitively recognizable independently of any reference to values. At least some members of the intuitionist school in the philosophy of mathematics can be interpreted as saying this. They equate the truth of mathematical statements with *provability*, and the latter notion is cashed in terms of certain rules of deduction whose correctness is somehow just *seen*. The third tack, a variation of the second, allows that the correctness of the rules of justification can be further analyzed, but not in terms of their ability to produce conclusions that possess some value or other. Rather, they are "correct" *only* in the sense that they are traditional and conventionally accepted within our culture.

In reply, I note that the third tack leaves us with absolutely no way to explain why our rules of justification are so successful, why, for example, our technology keeps getting better. If the response is that our rules have evolved to be what they are precisely *because* they are so successful, then advocates of the third tack are really surrendering unconditionally, for to say this is to admit that the correctness of the rules of justification ultimately consists in the fact that they enhance our ability to obtain certain epistemic or pragmatic values. To advocates of the second tack, we might fairly ask why it is that *we* do not have an intuition that, say, *modus ponens* is a correct rule, *antecedently of our recognition that it is truth-preserving*. As for the first tack, I do not know how we could convince someone that he does not possess an irreducibly primitive concept of justification if he insists that he does, but neither do I see how he could convince us that we do possess such a concept if we are certain that we do not.[11]

Equating truth with justification also has the counterintuitive implication that the truth value of a statement may change when more relevant evidence becomes available (Davidson 1990, 307–308). This consequence is avoided if truth is equated with *maximal* justification or justification in ideal circumstances. But neither of these moves helps with the larger problem: equating truth with maximal justification still leaves us asking, Maximally justified *as what*? Nor (contra Putnam 1982) can the major problem be evaded by identifying truth with justification in ideal circumstances. On the contrary, no sense can be given to the notion of ideal circumstances unless we have first made some choice of value at which justification is to aim. Else what reason could there be for thinking that observation through smudged eyeglasses is less ideal than observation through clean ones?

Attempts to analyze truth in terms of *probability* or maximal probability (as, e.g., in Reichenbach 1931) suffer from precisely the same problems, because for a statement or belief to be probable is for it to be probably *true*. (See section 8.7 for a longer discussion of the attempt to define truth in terms of probability.)

2.3   Confusion about Truth Bearers

The problem of truth bearers is the problem of figuring out what *sort* of thing can have truth value, that is, what sort of thing can be true or false. Among the candidates are beliefs, propositions, judgments, assertions, statements, theories, remarks, ideas, acts of thought, utterances, sentence tokens, sentence types, sentences (unspecified), and speech acts. Even if all philosophers reached sufficient agreement to identify by name the one right bearer of truth, our problems would hardly be at an end, for there is also disagreement about the nature of the things named by each of these terms. One person's idea of a sentence may be different from the next person's.

On the other hand, varying terminology may hide identity of conception. Philosopher *a*'s notion of sentence type might be what philosopher *b* calls a statement. Philosopher *c*'s definition of utterance makes utterances sound an awful lot like sentence tokens, given philosopher *d*'s definition of the latter, and both look suspiciously compatible with *e*'s description of a speech act, which itself looks a lot like an assertion except when an assertion looks like a statement. Sometimes even *one* philosopher's description of two candidates can make the two seem indistinguishable: Haack, for example, defines a statement as "what is said when a declarative sentence is uttered or inscribed." It is the *content* of the sentence. Two utterances make the same statement when they say the same thing. A proposition, she says, is what is common to a set of synonymous declarative sentences. Two sentences express the same proposition when they have the same meaning (Haack 1978, 76–77). But then, to my way of thinking, there is no difference between statements and propositions. Of course, even if two philosophers agree on both the name and the appropriate description of the correct truth bearer, they may very well disagree about *why* it should be considered the correct bearer of truth. Finally, many philosophers, particularly those pursuing some of the subdivisions of the speech-act project, are of the opinion that *nothing* bears truth value, that is, there are no truth bearers.

What we have here is a conceptual mess that one should venture into only with a patient mind and a wary eye. Armed with both, let us sample some of the things that have been said about various candidates for the title of 'truth bearer'. When a name appears in parentheses following a statement, the philosopher named endorses the view. Other views listed have been attributed by commentators to other, unnamed philosophers.

- Sentence tokens are physical objects (Haack 1978, 76–77).
- Sentences (whether type or token is unspecified) and *statements* are material objects (O'Connor and Carr 1982, 171).
- A statement is an *act* of uttering a sentence; it is a dated event (Platts 1979, 38).
- A statement is the *content* of a declarative sentence (Haack 1978, 75–76).
- Sentence types are classes of similar tokens or a pattern that similar tokens exemplify (Haack 1978, 75–76).
- Sentence types are *sets* of sentence tokens whose members play identical roles in the language in which they occur. They need not look alike (Sellars 1963b).
- Propositions are mental entities.[12]
- A proposition is the *content* of a saying (Platts 1979, 38). (Compare the fourth item on this list.)
- Propositions are the meanings of sentences *and* the objects of states of consciousness (O'Connor and Carr 1982, 171).
- A proposition is what is common to a set of synonymous declarative sentences (Haack 1978, 75–76).
- Propositions are timeless, wordless entities.[13]
- Propositions are what expressions in different grammatical moods have in common. They are described with gerunds: 'Tom's shutting the door' is

the proposition held in common by 'Tom shut the door' (declarative mood), 'Has Tom shut the door?' (interrogative mood), 'Tom! Shut the door!' (imperative mood).[14]
• Propositions are numerically identical with facts (Armstrong 1973, 113; Chisholm 1977, 88).

A rehearsal of the arguments, pro and con, concerning the various viewpoints sampled here would be counterproductive and would double the length of the book. Instead, I offer here stipulated definitions of the most important kinds of entities that have been alleged by one person or another to possess truth values. These definitions are, however, as close as one is likely to get to anything that could be appropriately called "the standard definitions."

A *sentence token* is a physical entity. A written sentence token is made up of molecules of chalk on a blackboard or molecules of ink or graphite on paper or some such. A spoken sentence token is made up of sound waves. Different inscriptions (or verbalizations) of the same idea, e.g.,

Snow is white,

Snow is white,

are distinctly different sentence tokens because the molecules (or sound waves) of which they are constructed are numerically distinct. These two tokens do, of course, have something in common. They are both members of the same sentence *type*. Traditionally, a *sentence type* is a set of identical or very similar sentence tokens. This is not very useful, however, since it means that the sentence tokens

Snow is white,

It's white; snow, that is,

La neige est blanche

are not members of the same sentence type as, intuitively, they should be. I prefer, therefore, the definition of sentence type due to Wilfred Sellars: a *sentence type* is a set of sentence tokens each of which plays the same role as does each of the others, that is, each of which means the same thing. The advantage of this definition is that it makes sentence types into translinguistic items. For example, both 'Snow is white' and 'La neige est blanche' are members of the same sentence type. It also allows us to escape disconcerting questions arising from the lack of similarity between printed, handwritten, and spoken tokens of what intuitively should count as the same sentence type. A further disadvantage of the traditional definition that is avoided by Sellars's definition is that, on the former, two tokens of 'The horse is an animal' count as being members of the same type even when in one 'the horse' refers to a particular horse and in the other it refers to the species. I shall use the word 'sentence' only when the distinction between types and tokens is not important.[15]

A *proposition* is an abstract entity. It is the informational content of a complete sentence in the declarative mood. It is also the thing named by the noun clause of statements predicating mental attitudes. For example, 'that snow is white' in 'John believes that snow is white' refers to a proposition. Readers familiar with the notion of a platonic form or universal may find the following analogy helpful: a proposition is to a declarative sentence as a platonic form is to a predicate. To speak somewhat metaphorically, whatever abstract "stuff" platonic forms are made from, thence too propositions. Propositions are not identical to sentence types, because a sentence type is not anything more than the collection of its members, while a proposition would still exist even if it had never beeen expressed with a sentence token. But propositions have in common with sentence types the feature of being translinguistic. Just as

Snow is white,

La neige est blanche

are both members of the same type, so too they express the same proposition. (This definition/description is not intended to presuppose one way or the other the question of whether there really are such things as propositions, it is meant only to describe what they are if they exist.)

An *utterance* is an action. It is the act of creating a sentence token, whether for locutionary or illocutionary purposes. A sentence token is thus the product of an utterance. An *assertion* is one kind of utterance; specifically, it is an utterance that creates a declarative sentence token for the locutionary purpose of communicating information. Since there is an utterance for every sentence token, utterances, and thus assertions, are not translinguistic entities. (One can speak of types (that is, sets) of utterances and types of assertions, but it will not be necessary to do so in this book.) In contexts where the distinctions among assertions, sentence types, and sentence tokens are not important (or must be dodged for one reason or another) I shall reserve the term 'statement' as a deliberately ambiguous term covering all three of these entities.

A *belief* is a mental entity. (I take no stand in this book as to whether or not beliefs can be reduced to physical entities or states of physical entities. Nor do I assume one way or another the question of whether beliefs are states or actions.) A type/token distinction can be made with respect to beliefs too: one can speak of *John's* belief that snow is white or of *the* belief that snow is white, where the latter is the set of all particular beliefs in snow's whiteness held by various people in the world. The distinction, however, will not normally matter in this book. So, save where the contrary is explicitly stated, I leave 'belief' with its ordinary ambiguity with respect to this distinction.

Now to the more central question of what sort of thing or things can possess truth values. Again, there is a selection of viewpoints:

- Beliefs are truth bearers (Russell 1912, 128–129).

- Statements are truth bearers (Austin 1950, 121–122).

- Beliefs and statements are truth bearers (Hamlyn 1970, 113).

- Sentence types are truth bearers (Tarski 1933, 156 n. 1).

- Sentence tokens are truth bearers (Tarski 1969, 63, 68).

- Ideas are truth bearers (James).[16]

- Judgments are truth bearers (Blanshard 1941, 264, 270–271).

- Beliefs, assertions, and sentence tokens can all bear truth (Chisholm 1977, 89).

- Belief-state types, thought-episode types, and assertion-act types can all bear truth (Armstrong 1973, 113–114).

- Nothing is a truth bearer (Ramsey, Strawson, C. J. F. Williams, and various others).[17]

It would serve no purpose to slog through all the arguments for and against the various positions sampled here (although the last view listed will be discussed in section 2.7 and several sections of chapter 10). Instead, I shall be content with a general argument to the conclusion that there are in fact very few restrictions on what can count as a truth bearer, followed by a more detailed defense of sentence tokens as truth bearers.

2.4   A Tolerant Attitude about Truth Bearers

One good turn the debate has taken in recent years is an increasing suspicion of the dogma that only *one* sort of thing can really bear truth values and that all the other candidates can be true or false only metaphorically. I suggest that we ought to go even farther round this good turn. It is a mistake to think that there is only one kind of entity or only a very small class of kinds of entities that can bear truth values, for there are no restrictions *in principle* on what kinds of entities can possess truth or falsity. If this is right, there is no "correct" answer to the question of what kind of thing can possess truth values. The matter is one of *choice*, not discovery. In any philosophical drama where the concept of truth is a principle character, we may cast any sort of thing we please in the role of truth bearer. To be sure, our choice will be guided by the goals of the theoretical enterprise at hand. For a given philosophical program it will be more useful to regard this sort of entity rather than that one as the bearer of truth values. For a different program it may turn out that the reverse decision is the wiser one. But the key word here is 'useful', for when we rule out some entities as an inappropriate choice of truth bearers, we ought to do so only when *in the context at hand* the choice would make it difficult for the theory under construction to do what we want it to do. We should never find ourselves rejecting a proposed truth bearer on the grounds that it is impossible for the kind of entity in question to ever be true or false. There is no sort of entity that cannot in principle bear truth values. In particular, and contrary to the thoughts of many, sentence tokens are useful truth bearers.

Let me note a practical constraint, applicable in all of the most important philosophical contexts, on what could count as a useful choice of truth bearer. There are a great number of things that are true and a great number that are false, so the kind of entity chosen as truth bearer would have to come in great quantity, or, failing that, it would have to be of such a kind that new members of the kind can be created with ease (e.g., sentence tokens). The members of the chosen kind must be numerous enough or easy enough to create that there will be one of the kind available, so to speak, for any state of affairs anyone has expressed, pondered, or believed in, or might someday express, ponder, or believe in. So it is easy to see why, historically, the list of candidates for the title of truth bearer has been short relative to the number of different kinds of entities in the world: they all seem to be either entities that can be created at will (like sentence tokens) or entities that come in great numbers (like propositions). It would be an advantage if the class of chosen entities was infinite or potentially so, but this is not necessary. Think, for example, of the extensional project. Suppose it is a contingent fact about human history, including future history, that there are only a finite number of states of affairs that will ever be expressed, pondered, or believed in by anyone. If so, then in principle there is no harm done to the project by choosing a finitely large class of truth bearers.

On the other hand, some philosophical enterprises would be impossible to fulfill, given a finitely sized class of truth bearers. Consider the Davidson Program, the enterprise of constructing, for some natural language, a theory of meaning for every actual and potential declarative expression of the language by setting out the truth conditions for all such expressions. (This program will be explained in much greater detail in sections 8.1 and 8.2. The characterization given here will do for now.) There is no limit to the number of declarative expressions that can be created for a natural language. So if the theory of meaning is to cover the potential declarative expressions as well as the actual ones, we shall need an infinitely large class of truth bearers. The natural choice here would be just the set of potential declarative utterances, but if this choice should prove problematic for some reason, we have other options. We could take propositions as truth bearers. The meaning of the declarative utterances of the language could then be cashed *immediately* in terms of the propositions they express and *mediately* in terms of the truth conditions of these propositions. Yet while the Davidson Program requires that we regard some infinite class of entities as truth bearers, other enterprises, as noted above, do not, and we do not have to choose the same kind of entity in every philosophical context. If this commits us to the view that more than one kind of entity possesses truth values, then so be it. There is no reason in principle why this should not be so.

It should be kept in mind that this restriction on choice of truth bearers, that the set of them be large, is motivated entirely by practical, not logical or metaphysical, considerations. The epistemological program and the Davidson Program just will not fly without a sufficiently large class of truth bearers. The restriction is *not* required by any considerations having to do with the nature of truth or the logic of statements containing 'true' or 'truth'. As we shall see below, there are some possible worlds where the corresponding philosophical programs do not require this restriction.

With this practical restriction in mind, let us now see if there are any logical or metaphysical restrictions on what could count as a truth bearer. As positive evidence for the claim that there are not, consider some possible worlds where very odd but not inappropriate choices of truth bearers have been made. First, a possible world in which there are an enormous number of teddy bears. There are so many and in such variety of size and color that the people of this world have chosen to use teddy bears to express themselves. Imagine also that the people of this world have worked out semantic rules correlating each size of teddy bear with some type of object in the world and correlating each color in which teddy bears are found with some property. Whenever one person wishes to assert something to another, he simply hands the corresponding teddy bear to his interlocutor. For every state of affairs that anyone in this world has ever wished to assert, there has been a teddy bear close at hand with just the right size and color to express the state of affairs. Why could not the teddy bears be considered the bearers of truth in this world? I can find nothing in the concept of truth that would make this impossible. Contrast truth with an empirical property like three-dimensionality. There are certain kinds of entities, like emotions, that cannot be three-dimensional. Our notion of dimension is such that it makes no sense, save metaphorically, to say that anger has dimension. But is there anything in the notion of truth that makes it senseless to say that (in the hypothetical world described above) a teddy bear is false or true? It might *sound* peculiar (to us, not to the people of the hypothetical world), but it is not a contradiction in terms. Truth is not too big a burden for a bare bear to bear.

Teddy bears are linguistic objects in the world described, and this may suggest to some that being a linguistic object is a necessary condition for being a truth bearer. But there is reason to resist the suggestion. Imagine a teddy bear world in which there are also an enormous number of flowers, enough so that for every state of affairs that anyone in that world has ever wished to express, there has been a flower available with just the right shape and color to correlate with the purported fact. In that world, flowers could also be the bearers of truth. The point is that in that world there is more than one kind of entity that can be true or false, and the creatures who live there have a choice. There is no question of their being right or wrong to choose teddy bears over flowers, if that is their choice, because it is not a matter of rightness or wrongness; it is a matter of simple decision.[18] More to the immediate point, they do not have to choose as truth bearer the same kind of entity with which they choose to communicate. They could, e.g., choose to communicate with teddy bears but nevertheless choose to regard flowers as the bearers of truth. That is, they take the flowers to be the things that are correlated with states of affairs and the teddy bears to be mere linguistic substitutes for flowers in much the same way that some philosophers in our world contend that propositions are the bearers of truth and that sentences are merely expressions of propositions. Here too there is no question of their being right or wrong to separate in this way the medium of communication from the bearer of truth; it is simply a matter of decision. And, of course, they could choose to communicate with spoken and/or written symbols, as we do, and they could *still* choose to regard flowers or teddy bears (or both) as truth bearers.

Consider now a world where there are only twenty teddy bears but where it happens to be a contingent fact that there are only twenty states of affairs that anyone in the world ever has or will express, ponder, or believe in. The choice of teddy bears as carriers of truth value would not be a roadblock in such a world to the construction of a theory of truth. One could imagine, e.g., a theory claiming that any of the twenty teddy bears is true if and only if it corresponds with a fact. There are, of course, more than twenty *states of affairs* in the world in question, and it is not *impossible* for the inhabitants to express, ponder, or believe in one of the others. But *as it happens*, none of the inhabitants ever has done so, and none will ever do so. So the fact that a theory of true teddy bears cannot "handle," so to speak, the additional states of affairs does no harm to the explanatory power of the theory. It explains anyway the truth or falsity of anything they ever think about. And it would do this regardless of whether or not they use teddy bears as the medium of communication and/or as the immediate object of belief. They could, for example, regard propositions as the immediate object of belief and correlate propositions with teddy bears.

Abstract objects can be truth bearers as well. There is some possible world where the inhabitants choose to correlate *locations* on the surface of the planet, specified by latitude and longitude, with states of affairs, and they choose to regard locations as bearers of truth. It is not even necessary that the set of truth bearers be of a single *kind*. Consider a world where nothing ever changes its physical location. If locations have been correlated with states of affairs in the manner described above, the people of this world could choose to take the *objects* at the various locations as the truth bearers rather than the locations themselves. In such a world a theory of truth could hold that a stone will be true if the state of affairs with which its location is correlated obtains. A plant will be false if the state of affairs with which its location is correlated does not obtain.

We can take the fact that in principle the class of teddy bears, the class of flowers, the class of locations, and classes of disparate objects can all bear truth to be strong inductive evidence for the claim that the members of *any* class of entities can in principle possess truth value. Hence, many sorts of things can bear truth values, including beliefs (whether thought of as acts or as mental states), propositions, sentence tokens, numbers, and others. We have a *choice* of which to use. The choice is guided by our purposes in constructing those philosophical theories within which some direct or indirect reference to truth bearers must be made. Moreover, different philosophical contexts will impose different practical constraints on our choice, so we need not choose the same class of entities in every context. It would not seem to be essential to the Davidson Program to include beliefs as truth bearers. But as we saw in section 1.1, because epistemology is ultimately concerned with whether and how our *beliefs* can be justified as probably true, an epistemologist will have to include beliefs on his list of truth bearers. Recall from the same section that it is not necessary for the epistemologist to regard beliefs as the *only* things that can possess truth values. If it proves theoretically convenient, she may define true belief in terms of the truth of the sentence expressing the belief and then go on to provide a more substantive definition of true sentence. In this case she takes two things, beliefs and sentences, as truth bearers.

2.5 Sentence Tokens

Here are some practical philosophical advantages of choosing sentence tokens as truth bearers:

• Unlike some truth bearers, such as propositions, there is no dispute that sentence tokens exist.

• Unlike beliefs, there is no ontological dispute about what kind of thing sentence tokens are. It is agreed on all sides that they are material objects.

(Or at least *physical* objects if we do not want to count the sound waves of spoken sentence tokens as material.)

• Unlike beliefs and most other truth bearers, there is no dispute over what the *parts* of a sentence are. It is agreed on all sides that the parts are clause tokens, phrase tokens, word tokens, and letter tokens. (In another sense of 'part' it is agreed that the parts of a written sentence token are the molecules of ink or chalk or whatever.)

• There is no dispute on the criterion for individuating numerically distinct sentence tokens. If I state in writing that I am hungry and my father states in writing that his son is hungry, are there two *statements* here or only one? The answer is a matter of some dispute. On the other hand, it is agreed on all sides that there are *two* sentence tokens here, because the molecules of ink that make up my token are numerically distinct from the molecules that make up my father's.

George Pitcher alleges that the claim that sentence tokens can have the property of truth implies that one can discover the truth value of a sentence by examining the sentence to see if it has this property, as opposed to examining its relation to the facts of the matter or its relation to other sentences, and manifestly one cannot discover the truth value of a sentence by examining it (Pitcher 1964, editor's introduction, 3). But the possession by some object of a relational property cannot be determined by examining the object itself. For example, I have the property of being employed by the state of Oklahoma, but you could never discover that just by examining me. You would need payroll records, the testimony of my boss, perhaps observation of my behavior, or some such. So Pitcher's implicit assumption is that truth is not a relational property, and he gives no argument for this assumption.

Another objection of Pitcher's is that the reason a sentence is true has to do with what it says, and since two sentence tokens can say exactly the same thing, it must be something they have in common, not the sentence tokens themselves, that possess truth values (Pitcher 1964, 5). But this is a non sequitur. The two tokens say the same thing, but each one says it independently. Why could not *each* of the sentence tokens be true because of what *it* says? The implied restriction Pitcher wants to put on truth bearers seems to be this: no two members of the class of truth bearers may have exactly the same truth value for exactly the same reason. If they seem to, then they are not really truth bearers at all. Rather, something they have in common bears truth. But I can see no logical or metaphysical reason for imposing such a restriction and it is not a principle that applies generally. Consider the property of being my sister: there are two women in the world who possess this property, and it is not something they have in common that "really" possesses the property, they each have it. There is not *one* thing that is my sister, there are *two*.

Another popular objection to sentence tokens as truth bearers is that some sentence tokens are neither true nor false. (Hamlyn 1970, 128). The hidden assumption behind this objection is that *every* member of the sort of thing that *can* bear truth value *must have* a truth value. But this assumption is plainly false. Not every woman has the property being my sister, but obviously it does not follow that women are not the *kind* of thing that can have this property. Hence, the fact that some sentence tokens do not have truth values does not prevent sentence tokens from being the *kind* of thing that *can* have truth values.

Hamlyn gives another popular objection to sentence tokens as truth bearers (1970, 128). This is that some sentence tokens change truth values from one context to another or from one time to another. Here the hidden assumption is that truth is eternal in the sense that no individual truth bearer can ever change its truth value. This assumption is puzzling. Perhaps it comes from the fear that if truth values are not eternal, we might wake up some day to discover that Napoleon *won* the battle of Waterloo, not in the sense that we might discover we had always been wrong about that, but in the sense that we *had* been right but somehow the historical facts themselves (not just what we *took* to be the facts) have changed. But this is not the sense in which sentence tokens change truth values. A token like 'Napoleon lost at Waterloo' can change truth value only if it somehow ceases to express the state of affairs that Napoleon lost at Waterloo and comes instead to express some nonobtaining state of affairs or comes not to express any state of affairs at all.[19] Suppose the former happens. Is there anything absurd in saying that in such a case the token has changed truth value? After all, this would not imply that the *facts* have changed. Indeed, if the token has somehow come to mean that snow is purple, it had better be the case that its truth value has changed. I would think it is an advantage of sentence tokens that they conform to our intuitions in this respect. None of this is to say that *only* sentence tokens can bear truth values. It is simply not an *objection* to sentence tokens as truth bearers that their truth values can change. It may be that there is something *expressed* by a token (e.g., a belief) that does not ever change truth value. But this too is not an objection to *also* taking sentence tokens as truth bearers. And there are advantages to doing so, as noted above.

Another common objection to sentence tokens is expressed by Anil Gupta: "The objects of truth are sentences. A more nominalistic construal of truth bearers, such as their identification with sentence tokens, is not plausible because of the obvious difficulty that there are unexpressed truths, just as there are many unnamed objects" (1982, 4). But here again the objection is based on an arbitrary restriction on what can count as a truth bearer. It is agreed that there are unexpressed *facts*. But it follows from this that there are unexpressed *truths* only on the additional assumption that there must be a truth for every fact. So the restriction implied by Gupta's argument is that a kind can count as a class of truth bearers only if there is at least one member of the kind for every fact, including unexpressed facts. Now it is not at all unlikely that there will be philosophical contexts in which there are practical advantages to allowing the existence of unexpressed truths. In such contexts it would not be practical to count sentence tokens as the *only* kind of entities that can bear truth. But Gupta errs in treating the restriction as a logical or metaphysical demand imposed by the very nature of truth and operative in every context. Suppose that it has been a fact for some millions of years that the interior of Venus is molten gold, and suppose further that until this moment no one has ever expressed, pondered, or believed in this fact. It does not contradict these suppositions in the least to add that until this moment it was *not* a *truth* that the interior of Venus is molten gold. If this seems odd at first, note that this last claim is perfectly compatible with the claim that *if* someone had expressed the fact that the interior of Venus is molten gold, he *would* have expressed a truth, because, under the view being defended here, he *would* have created a true sentence token by making the utterance in question.

There may even be philosophical contexts in which it is advantageous to discard ordinary usage and take sentence tokens as the only truth bearers. In the study of the model theory of systems of formal logic, for example, it is at least prima facie plausible to suggest that all we are really interested in are the logical relations between sentence tokens of a formal language, as distinct from the logical relations between beliefs.[20]

2.6   Truth versus Truth-in-L

Finally, it has been suggested by Tarski and many others that a sentence token may express something true in one language and at the same time express something false or meaningless in another language. We would then have to say that the sentence token was both true and not true at the same time, which is a plain contradiction. (Being meaningless is one way of being not true, being false is another.) One could, for example, *create* two artificial languages and give the token 'Grooble noop dak' the meaning in one language, call it language A, that there is a blue typewriter here and the meaning in the other language, call it language B, that there is *not* a blue typewriter here. It is agreed, however, that this is a roadblock to taking sentence tokens as truth bearers only if we suppose that truth is a translinguistic property. But we do not have to so take it. We can simply relativize our definitions of truth to particular languages. That is, we do not attempt to define truth *simpliciter*, we define true-in-English, true-in-French, true-in-language-A, etc. This solves the immediate problem because while 't is true' and 't is not true' contradict each other, 't is true in English' and 't is not true in French' do not. Thus, the problem is easily finessed (Chisholm 1977, 90; Platts 1979, 39–40; Tarski 1944, 14).

There may be good reasons why a theory of truth for sentence tokens would have to be relativized to languages in this way (see sections 5.5, 6.3, and 9.3 for more on this issue). But the argument of the preceding paragraph is not a good one. The claim that a token can be true in one language and not true in another at the same time depends on the assumption that there is some intelligible way that a sentence token can be "in" two different languages at once. In fact, the assumption is even stronger than that, for the relativization of theories of truth to particular languages is not required unless there is some logically possible situation in which we *must* construe a particular token as being in two languages at once, in one of which it is true and in the other of which it is not true. As long as one can, for any possible situation or circumstance, reasonably construe the token involved as being in only one language at a time, there is no need to relativize truth to language (the reasons alluded to at the top of this paragraph aside).

Is there any way that a token can be *in* two languages at once? It is not easy to see how, especially when it is remembered that sentence tokens are physical objects. One can certainly imagine a paragraph of language *A* in which a token of 'Grooble noop dak' appears and a paragraph of language *B* in which another token of 'Grooble noop dak' appears, but these are two different tokens, not one token in two languages. Suppose we take scissors and cut out the token from language *A* and paste it into the paragraph of *B*. Now the same token that was in *A* is in *B*, but not at the same time. Its truth value has changed, but at no time has it been both true and not true.

Next consider a book in English washed up on the shores of France. In what sense are its tokens *in* the French language? Granted, the tokens in the book would be meaningless to a non-English-speaking Frenchman. But this does not mean the tokens are meaningless *in* French; it means they are meaningless *to* a Frenchman *just because* they are *not in* French. Similar reasoning holds for a token of English dropped into a conversation otherwise conducted in French. Not only is the token not in French (contra Grover, Camp, and Belnap 1975, 103), it is precisely because it is not in French that it is incomprehensible to any non-English speaker in the conversation. And in general, for any logically possible situation in which, allegedly, a token is true in one language and meaningless in another, the evidence offered in support of the claim that the token is meaningless in one of the languages would *eo ipso* serve as evidence that the token is not *in* that language.

Suppose now we imagine Smith to be standing between two people to one of whom he wishes to lie and to the other of whom he wishes to speak only the truth. Suppose further that one speaks only language *A* and the other speaks only language *B*. So he says "Grooble noop dak," intending it to be in both languages at once. One listener takes it to mean there is a blue typewriter here, and the other listener takes it to mean that there is not. I suppose we *could* construe this to be a genuine case of a token appearing in two languages at once.

But we are *not compelled* to do so. It is not unreasonable to construe it as a case in which the token is in only, say, language *A*, and the *B*-speaking person who took it to be in language *B* (as Smith intended him to) was simply mistaken to so take it. His mistake was akin, in some ways, to the mistake one would make in thinking that the murmuring one hears from the next room is in one's own language when it is not. Against this it will be protested that Smith *intends* his token to be in language *B* (as well as *A*). Admittedly, the speaker's intentions do count for something in determining to just what language a token belongs. But nevertheless, I do not think it is *unreasonable* to construe it as a case in which both the *B* speaker *and* Smith were mistaken in thinking that the token is in language *B*, a case, that is, in which Smith failed to make good on his intentions. Admittedly too, there may be no nonarbitrary way of deciding which language Smith's token is in, but it would not follow from this that it is in *both*. What I say here about 'Grooble noop dak' applies as well to a spoken token of the German 'Harvey liebt', which would sound to an English speaker like 'Harvey leaped'. I do not deny that there are situations in which we have the *option* of construing a token as being in two languages at once. But we are forced to relativize the truth of tokens to languages only if there is some logically possible situation in which a token cannot reasonably be taken as *not* being in two languages at once.

Note that the language-relativity problem does not arise for translinguistic entities like propositions, belief types, and sentence types (on the Sellarsian definition), since they are not in *any* language, let alone in more than one. On the other hand, it has been contended that individual belief tokens *are* in language. We think and believe, so it is said, in a kind of inner "Mentalese." Even on the assumption that this is correct, no one belief token is in *two* inner languages, true in one and false in the other. Assertions, being actions, are individuated by reference to the different sentence tokens they produce. Since there is no case in which we must take a given sentence token as being in two languages at once, neither are we ever compelled to so construe the assertion that produced it. However, there is one kind of entity to which the language-relativity objection is well taken: sentence types *on the traditional definition*. On the latter construal of sentence types, they are sets of similar tokens. So a language-*A* token of 'Grooble noop dak' and a language-*B* token of 'Grooble noop dak' are both members of the same sentence type. Hence that sentence type is both true and not true. This gives us good reason not to *choose* sentence types (traditionally defined) as truth bearers. (That choice is not already ruled out because sentence types are sets. Recall the lesson of section 2.4: any domain of objects, including objects that are themselves sets, *can* be truth bearers.)

2.7   An Objection to the Concept of a Truth Bearer

C. J. F. Williams has argued that there is no such thing as a truth bearer. This view is shared by all who accept what I shall call the deflationary thesis, which is the claim that there are no such properties as truth and falsity. If there are no such properties, then nothing can bear truth values. Further discussion of the deflationary thesis will have to wait until chapter 10. In the meantime, let us consider a clever argument from Williams that does not require that he first establish the deflationary thesis.

He takes the position that 'What sort of thing bears truth?' ought to have the same answer as 'To what sort of thing is truth being ascribed in ascriptions of truth?' (I continue to use 'ascriptions of truth' to refer to utterances whose surface grammar makes them appear to be ascriptions of truth.) But the most common ascriptions of truth found in our language are not, according to Williams, ascriptions in which some *particular* sentence, statement, belief, proposition, or what have you is explicitly identified, as one is in '"The table is purple" is true'. Rather, our most common ascriptions of truth are "blind" ascriptions, like 'What Percy says is true', in which the speaker does not specify exactly what it is that Percy says. But 'what Percy says', despite being the grammatical subject of the sentence, does not *name* anything anymore than does 'what the postman brought' in 'What the postman brought is on the mantel'. Both 'what Percy said' and 'what the postman brought' are incomplete symbols, much like 'something'. The latter can also serve as the grammatical subject of a sentence, but it does not name anything. In support of this contention, Williams notes that 'something', 'what Percy says', and 'what the postman brought' can all be negated (into 'nothing', 'what Percy does not say', and 'what the postman did not bring', respectively) but names cannot be negated (Williams 1976, xii, 33). (What would be the negation of 'Joseph'?)

So the answer to the question 'To what is truth being ascribed in ascriptions of truth?' is simply 'Nothing'. Nothing *is* true or false. Nothing *has* or *possesses* a truth value. Accordingly, the answer to the question 'What sort of thing bears truth?' is also 'Nothing'. Or, as Williams prefers to say, the question "does not arise."

Since '"The table is purple"' in '"The table is purple" is true' is indisputably a name, Williams's argument depends crucially on disregarding such nonblind ascriptions. Presumably, he would insist that since blind ascriptions are the most conmmon kind, we must treat nonblind ascriptions as misleading variations from the fundamental form of ascriptions. But suppose we do not make the assumption that the most common form of a given type of discourse is also the most fundamental. Suppose, instead, we take the peculiarity of the fact that, while 'what Percy says' is the subject of a sentence, it lacks some features of names as evidence that blind ascriptions of truth are clumsy deviations from the fundamental form of truth ascriptions. *Nonblind* ascriptions, in which the subject of the sentence is clearly a name, are the fundamental form of truth ascriptions on this way of viewing things.

Even if we assume that Williams's analysis is correct, there is a questionable assumption about philosophical methodology in his argument: if the analysis of ascriptions of truth reveals that nothing in them is the name of an entity that possesses a truth value, then it follows that no entity possesses a truth value. It is as simple as that. The matter is settled.

This kind assumption about how to discover metaphysical truths has a venerable history in philosophy, but most of those who have relied on it implicitly would cough nervously at seeing it laid out baldly like this, and for good reason. Linguistic analysis is an important tool for philosophy, but it rarely settles a metaphysical question (or prevents one from arising). Our irresistible intellectual concerns and problems, like those motivating epistemology, and our solutions to those problems have as much claim to determining our ontological commitments as does our language. In other words, we are committed to those entities we need to postulate for the purpose of constructing adequate explanatory theories. If we need to postulate the existence of truth bearers to fulfill the epistemological program, the Davidson Program, or some other program, and if the grammatical subject of ascriptions of truth are not names of objects, it is no less reasonable to conclude that language *hides* the identity of truth bearers than it is to conclude that language *reveals* that there are no truth bearers. Perhaps the most that could be concluded from Williams's analysis of truth ascriptions, if it were correct, would be that our language does not *presuppose* that there are entities that bear truth values, but it does not eliminate the possibility that there are.

Perhaps the point will be clearer if we contrast the present issue with a problem that really can, in principle, be dissolved by linguistic analysis. Our language contains names, such as 'Hamlet', of nonexistents, but this raises a puzzle. If Hamlet does not exist, how can 'Hamlet' *refer* to anything? But suppose we discover, after patient analysis of the deep grammatical structure of sentences in which names of nonexistents appear, that such expressions are only shorthand for sentences in which no such nonreferring terms appear. Then we can truly say that we have dissolved the problem, since it was only the apparent presence of such names in our language that created our puzzlement in the first place. Now if our puzzlement over what, if anything, can be a truth bearer arose *only* because we found expressions in our language that seemed to presuppose the existence of such entities, then it would be appropriate in principle to dissolve the problem by showing that such expressions are misleading and really do not presuppose the existence of truth bearers. But this is *not* how our questions about truth bearers arise. Our interest begins with a certain value choice: we value having justified beliefs, and that choice makes skepticism a problem, and solving the problem of skepticism leads us to the justification project, and that, in turn, requires a solution to the metaphysical project, at which point the question of what sort of thing can bear truth arises or, more correctly, at which point we *postulate* that certain kinds of entities can be true or false. At no point do we *presuppose* that there are truth bearers and/or that truth ascriptions refer to them. Hence Williams's sort of project cannot, even in principle, either solve or dissolve our problem. (See section 10.7 for a further discussion of this issue, and see section 10.5 for a further discussion of Williams's views.)

2.8   Chapter Summary

We have now seen one very important program in service to which the metaphysical project can be put. It is the epistemological program of evaluating the plausibility of theories of justification. Moreover, we have seen that attempts to reverse the order of priority here and define truth in terms of a previously arrived at notion of justification are either (1) circular, (2) unintelligible, (3) rest on the dubious claim that we possess a primitive, unanalyzable concept of *justification* or *correct principle of justification*, or (4) are just metaphorical ways of rejecting truth as a value.

Also in this chapter we saw how there is as much confusion about truth bearers as there is about truth in general. Indeed, we saw an example of a philosopher, C. J. F. Williams, who claims that there is no such thing as a truth bearer. I argued that identifying the "correct" truth bearer is a matter of decision and in particular that the objections made to taking sentence tokens as truth bearers are based on easily refuted assumptions.

We shall examine several other programs later in the book. In the meantime, let us now turn our attention to some of the historically important attempts to fulfill the metaphysical project.

3 Nonrealist Theories

3.1 Realist and Nonrealist Theories of Truth

Answers to one or another of the three branches of the metaphysical project may be divided into two broad categories: Realist, which includes most (but not all, as we shall see in sections 4.6 and 6.4) of the theories historically called correspondence theories, and Nonrealist, which includes the theories historically called coherence, pragmatic, pragmatistic, and instrumental theories. A Realist theory holds that among the conditions individually necessary and jointly sufficient for the truth of a belief (proposition, sentence, or whatever) is a condition to the effect that a certain state of affairs must obtain. I use the term 'state of affairs' in its philosophical (nonordinary) sense: 'State of affairs' is not a synonym for 'fact' or 'situation', because *potential* but nonactual facts are states of affairs as well. Indeed, even impossible facts count as states of affairs, although these states of affairs never obtain even in any possible world. Perhaps the best way to define 'state of affairs' is to say that anything whose obtaining can be asserted (truly or falsely) with a declarative sentence counts as a state of affairs and nothing else so counts.[1] Thus for each of the following sentences there is a state of affairs that is asserted to obtain by the sentence: 'Snow is white', 'Snow is pink', 'There is a round square on my table'. A *fact*, then, is a state of affairs that obtains in the *actual* world.[2] A further condition for a theory counting as a Realist theory of truth is that the fact in question must be *mind-independent*, that is, neither its existence nor its nature depends on the existence of any mind, nor on the thoughts of any mind, nor on the conceptual scheme of any mind, nor on the epistemic capacities, limitations, or achievements of any mind. (This requirement will be modified somewhat below.) The class of minds includes the minds of God, the World Spirit, or the Absolute, if there be such things (see below). So a mind-independent fact is independent of these minds in addition to being independent of my mind, your mind, and every other mortal's mind. Moreover, to count as mind-independent, a fact must not itself be a mental entity. It must not be an idea or thought in anyone's mind. (This is not to say that no mind has thoughts *about* the fact, but the fact itself must not be a thought, a mental entity.)

Thus a Realist theory of truth imposes a certain *ontological* condition on the truth of a truth bearer. Ontology (literally, the study of being) is a network of philosophical issues centering on the question of what kinds of things really exist and what kinds of things are only myths or illusions. And from among the kinds of things that really exist, ontology also wants to know which kinds exist in their own right and which kinds, by contrast, *depend* for their existence on the prior (temporal or logical) existence of some other kind of thing. The typical person in a modern industrial society does not believe that witches, goblins, or unicorns exist. She believes in the existence of macroscopic physical things (such as my desk), numbers, beliefs and other mental entities, atoms, and perhaps God. Moreover, she believes that the macroscopic physical things are made up out of atoms, so the existence of the former is dependent on the existence of the latter. Philosophers usually agree with the person in the street about the nonexistence of witches, goblins, and unicorns, but many philosophers find the average person much too generous in what she believes. For example, many philosophers would say that numbers are really mythical things; fictions, albeit *useful* fictions. Even when a philosopher agrees with the ordinary person that many different kinds of things exist, the philosopher may insist that the average person fails to recognize just how few kinds of things exist in their own right. Some would say, for example, that only physical things exist in their own right. The things we call mental entities, such as beliefs, desires, and intentions, are only states or activities of the neural cells in our brains. Others insist that only mental entities really exist in their own right. The latter school of thought has two branches: A solipsist believes that everything in the universe is simply an idea or sensation (or a combination of ideas and/or sensations) in his own mind. Even physical objects, like you and me and, for that matter, his own body, are just ideas or sensations in his mind. The other branch is called absolute idealism. An absolute idealist, like a solipsist, holds that the universe is entirely constituted by some mind and its ideas and sensations, but he does not identify that mind with his own. Rather, he regards his mind and yours and mine as subsets of the ideas and sensations in some one gigantic mind, which he usually calls the Absolute or the World Spirit or, more familiarly, God. On the other hand, a realist ontology (note the lowercase 'r') holds that there is at least one kind of thing that exists in its own right and is not a mental entity. (There is disagreement among realists about just which kind of thing this nonmental kind of thing is.)

Realism and realism are two different things. The former is a doctrine about truth, not about what exists. It holds that for a belief (or sentence or whatever) to be true, a certain state of affairs must obtain independently of mind. But in principle its possible to be a Realist (about truth) and some kind of antirealist (ontologically). For example, an absolute idealist denies that any states of affairs obtain mind-independently, but he could still be a Realist. If he were, he would be saying that one condition for the truth of a belief (or sentence or whatever) is never met, so there are no truths. This would be an odd position to take, but not an inconsistent one.

Exactly which state of affairs must obtain for a given belief or statement to be true? It is the state of affairs that the statement asserts or the state of affairs believed. Thus on a Realist theory of truth, the belief that snow is white is true only if snow *is* white in the extramental world (not *if and* only if snow is white, for a Realist theory may hold that there are other conditions necessary to the belief's being true). If snow is white *only* in the sense that the believer's conceptual scheme requires that snow be classified as white, then one necessary condition for the belief being true is not fulfilled. Hence the belief, on a Realist theory, is not true. Similarly, the belief is not true if snow is white *only* in the sense that 'Snow is white' would be a warranted assertion, given the believer's conceptual scheme.

Note that a theory of truth may appear to be Realist without actually being so. Suppose a theory entailed

'Snow is white' is true iff snow *is* white.

But suppose that the ontological beliefs of the author of the theory are such that to assert that snow is white as the right-hand side of this formula does is not to say that there is a mind-independent world and that in it snow is white. Rather, his ontological beliefs are such that to assert that snow is white is to assert only that we cannot help but *perceive* snow as white, because of the way our perceptual faculties, our mind, and/or our conceptual scheme are organized. In this case the theory is not Realist, for while it does hold that snow's being white is a necessary condition for the truth of the sentence 'Snow is white', it does not require that snow's being white be a fact in a mind-independent world. Thus, we must distinguish between theories that are Realist and those that are merely quasi realist. The latter are those that hold that the facts of the matter are what determine truth. To put it another way, quasi-realist theories hold that one of the necessary and sufficient conditions for a statement's or belief's being true is that a state of affairs must obtain. But some quasi-realist theories are not Realist because they do not require that the state of affairs in question obtain mind-independently.[3] (For examples of such theories, see sections 3.2 and 3.3, and see section 4.6 for a discussion of a closely related matter.) So some quasi-realist theories are Nonrealist, but every Realist theory is quasi realist.

Suppose, for the preceding example, we have no idea what the theory's author's ontological beliefs are. Then the theory itself will be ambiguous in a crucial way: we shall have no way of categorizing it as Realist or Nonrealist. Thus, to avoid ambiguity, a quasi-realist theory must be accompanied, at least implicitly, by an ontological interpretation of facts. Not in the sense that the interpretation must describe the *structure* of facts, for that issue can be left fuzzy without harming our ability to classify the theory of truth along the Realist/Nonrealist divide. But we ought to be told whether or not the facts the theory supposes to be necessary conditions for truth are mind-independent.[4]

As things stand so far, a Realist theory of truth is one that holds as necessary conditions for the truth of a belief (or statement, etc.) that (1) a certain state of affairs obtains, (2) it is the same state of affairs that the belief is a belief in (or the statement expresses, etc.), and (3) it obtains mind-independently. But a modification of this is in order.

The modification is motivated by sentences like 'John has a mind' and 'John thinks there is a book on the table', which may very well be true, even on a Realist theory, although they describe facts that are *not* independent of mind in at least one sense of that term. The modification is also motivated by the existence of certain facts that appear mind-independent but nevertheless depend on the mind in one sense. Take the fact that there is a Ford Mustang parked on my street. This fact would not have obtained had some engineer at Ford Motor Co. not had certain thoughts around 1962 about designing a new car model. So the existence of the fact that a Mustang is now parked on my street is partially dependent on the existence of, and the thoughts within, a mind. But there are other senses in which, *on a realist ontology*, the existence of the fact is not dependent on any mind: It is not necessary for anyone to believe there is a Mustang parked on my street for that fact to obtain. It is not necessary that anyone's conceptual scheme be structured in some particular way, and it is not necessary that anyone be justified in asserting the Mustang is parked there for it to be a fact that it is parked there. Similarly, it can be a fact, on a realist ontology, that John has a mind even if no one, not even John, believes he does or is warranted in asserting that he does. And it can be a fact on a realist ontology that John thinks there is a book on the table even if no one, not even John, believes or is warranted in asserting that John thinks there is a book on the table (e.g., if John has this thought only subconsciously and hence is not aware that he has it). The trick is to formulate ontological realism in such a way that it allows the sorts of facts in question even though they in *some* sense depend on a mind. Various attempts have been made. One example is C. S. Peirce in one of his more realist moments:

Thus a dream, meaning what is dreamed, is not real because, for example, if it be true that the dream was about hen's eggs, it is because the action of the dreamer's mind made it to be true. But the *fact* that a given person did dream of hen's eggs, if it be true *is* true whether he remembers dreaming it, or thinks he dreamed it or not. It in truth depends on the action of his mind, but does *not* depend upon any attribution by his mind to the *fact* that he dreamed, which is now that whose reality is in question. (Peirce 1966, 419)

William Alston tries:

Whatever there is is what it is regardless of how we think of it. Even if there were no human thought, even if there were no human beings, whatever there is other than human thought (and what depends on that, causally or logically) would still be just what it actually is. (Alston 1979, 779)

J. N. Findlay essays:

Subjective attitudes [are] irrelevant to mathematical and other propositions, unless such propositions concern these as constituents or denotata. (Findlay 1984, 43)

Finally, Ralph C. S. Walker, while speaking for the Realist, suggests,

Truths about beliefs can hardly be independent of the beliefs that make them true. They may however be independent of anything that may be believed about those beliefs themselves. (Walker 1989, 3)

It is not clear that all of these will handle the sort of tricky cases mentioned above, and even if they do, there are still trickier cases. Suppose Smith has the belief expressible with the sentence 'My brain is now in brain state 438', and suppose further that people's brains are in state 438 when and only when they are having belief tokens of the type 'My brain is now in brain state 438'. Now it is a fact that Smith is in brain state 438 *only because he believes he is*, yet that his physical brain is in state 438 is something that even an ontological realist will want to count as a fact.

I can do no better than my predecessors at defining ontological realism in just the right way, so I shall not try. Instead, I shall call the sense in which, even on a realist ontology, the fact about the Mustang *is* dependent on a mind 'derivative dependence'. And I shall call the senses of mind dependence in which, on a realist ontology, it is *not* dependent on a mind 'full-blooded dependence'. Similarly, the states of affairs expressible with 'John has a mind' and 'John thinks there is a book on the table' are derivatively dependent on a mind, but they are not, on a realist ontology, full-bloodedly dependent. Here, then, is a modification of my earlier account of Realist theories of truth. A theory will still count as Realist even if the fact whose existence it includes among the necessary conditions for truth is allowed to be derivatively dependent on a mind. But it will not count as Realist if it allows the fact to be full-bloodedly dependent. So the definition of a Realist theory of truth is this:

A theory of truth, T, is a Realist theory if and only if T says that any given belief (statement, or whatever) is true only if the very same state of affairs that the belief is a belief in (or that the statement expresses) obtains either independently of any mind or with only derivative dependence.[5]

I hope that this in conjunction with the preceding discussion and quotations will make things clear enough to do the job, even if it leaves some unusual, puzzling cases. The definition is rather long and stylistically displeasing, so hereafter I shall make use of short slogans like 'Realist theories hold that truth depends on the facts of the matter' or even briefer references to extramental facts or some such. All such slogans and references should be taken as shorthand for the definition given here.

A Nonrealist theory is any theory that is not Realist, and it is with these that we shall be occupied in the remainder of the chapter. Since a Realist theory of truth is a combination of quasi realism about truth and ontological realism, Nonrealism about truth is any theory that denies one or the other of these. So all Nonrealist theories have in common the view that extramental reality or 'the (extramental) facts' (if there be such) have nothing to do with truth or falsity. That is, it is *not*, repeat *not*, a necessary or a sufficient condition for the truth of, say, the belief that snow is white that snow actually be white in an extramental world. Whether or not it is an extramental fact that snow is white, or whether or not there even is an extramental world, has nothing to do with the truth of the belief that snow is white. All Nonrealist theories, *if they are consistent* and if they acknowledge the existence of an extramental world at all, insist that it is at least theoretically possible for the belief that snow is white to be false even if it is an extramental fact that snow is white, and also that it is theoretically possible for it to be true even if it is not an extramental fact that snow is white. Indeed, precisely this characteristic is the most serious potential weakness of plausibility for Nonrealist answers to the metaphysical project. A Nonrealist about truth who denies the existence of an extramental reality, who is either a solipsist or an absolute idealist, seems to escape this implausible consequence. However, solipsism and absolute idealism themselves are difficult doctrines to defend.

3.2   Charles S. Peirce's Pragmaticism

Charles S. Peirce first called his theory 'pragmatism' and later changed its name to 'pragmaticism' when the former term was appropriated by John Dewey, F. C. S. Schiller, and William James to label their very different sort of theory (5.414).[6] Peirce and James are notorious for the inconsistency of their remarks about truth.[7] Various attempts to impose some consistency on them have been made (e.g., Almeder 1985). Many commentators have tried to make them not only self-consistent but also consistent with each other as well. 'The pragmatic theory of truth' is the title usually given by such commentators to the *one* theory they believe they have discerned in the works of both men (and Dewey and Schiller as well). It is certainly possible to interpret the two in this way, but it can only be done if one is willing to ignore some passages in their writings as atypical or as "not what he meant." Indeed, this process of pruning away inconsistent remarks is necessary even to make each of them self-consistent within his own writings. Note, for example, these passages from one interpreter of James as she rules out certain of his remarks as atypical:

There are passages in which James claims that the truth of a belief is the same as the actual process of verification.... But these are overstatements on his part. (Suckiel 1982, 96)

There are several unusual instances when James... opts for an extreme relativism.... Given the extensive development of James's account of objective truth, it seems reasonable to discount these infrequent subjectivist passages. (Suckiel 1982, 166 n. 33)

See, for example, those passages... in which [James] deviates from his main intent and overplays the meaning psychological and other empirical considerations have in his account. (Suckiel 1982 167 n. 60)

My way of dealing with the many inconsistencies is, first, to disdain the term 'pragmatism' and with it any thought of making the pragmatists seem consistent with each other. Second, I shall not even attempt to make coherent sense of the inconsistencies within the writings of each of Peirce and James. Instead, I shall attribute to James a simple but consistent instrumental theory of truth, and I shall attribute to Peirce the consensus theory he called pragmaticism. (James would also embrace an instrumentalist answer to the justification project. See section 7.3.) Thus there are certain of Peirce's remarks on truth that I am going to ignore: In at least three places he seems to endorse a Jamesian instrumentalism (1.344; 5.375 n. 2; Peirce 1966, 381). In at least one place he identifies truth with what is verified by experimental method, but in most cases he regards this sort of theory as a theory of justification (especially in science) or a theory of "approximate truth" or both (5.569, 2.142, 2.776, 5.170). Finally, he suggested at one time that truth means "that at which inquiry aims" (5.557). Since there can be little dispute that Peirce regards relief from doubt as the goal of inquiry (5.372–375), this would make truth equivalent to relief from doubt, but the latter claim is precisely what Peirce later repudiates (6.485). So let us pass on to the theory with which Peirce is most famously associated.

Peirce asks us to notice a fact, or what he took to be a fact, about the conclusions reached by persons using different methods and/or pools of evidence to explore the same question or make sense of the same event: with enough persistence in their investigations, they will all reach the same conclusion. Imagine ten scientists, each using a different method for investigating the speed of light. "They may at first obtain different results, but, as each perfects his method..., the results will move steadily together toward a destined center" (5.407). To take a more down-to-earth example, "Suppose two men, one deaf, the other blind. One hears a man declare he means to kill another, hears the victim cry; the other sees the murder done..., the one having, for example, the idea of a man shouting, the other of a man with a threatening aspect; but their final conclusions, the thought remotest from sense, will be identical and free from the one-sidedness of their idiosyncrasies" (8.12). So the general point is this: "Let any human being have enough information and exert enough thought upon any question, and the result will be that he will arrive at a certain definite conclusion, which is the same that any other mind will reach" (7.319).

But it is not just that different minds tend to agree. By itself that would imply only that either all the minds reach the same correct conclusion or they all reach the same *in*correct conclusion. Peirce, however, claims that the common conclusion reached by all the minds is always the *true* conclusion: "Human opinion universally tends in the long run to... the truth.... There is, then, to every question a true answer, a final conclusion, to which the opinion of every man is constantly gravitating" (8.12, compare 7.319).

By itself, this is no more than a statement of intellectual optimism, but Peirce means more than that. He claims that *by definition* the final conclusion is true.[8] A proposition is true if and only if it would be agreed to by everyone who investigates the matter with which it concerns itself:[9]

The opinion which is fated to be ultimately agreed to by all who investigate is what we mean by truth. (5.407)

Truth, what can this possibly mean except it be that there is one destined upshot to inquiry with reference to the question in hand. (3.432)

The truth of the proposition that Caesar crossed the Rubicon consists in the fact that the further we push our archaeological and other studies, the more strongly will that conclusion force itself on our minds forever—or would do so, if study were to go on forever. (5.565)

Truth is that concordance of an abstract statement with the ideal limit towards which endless investigation would tend to bring scientific belief, which concordance the abstract statement may possess by virtue of the confession of its inaccuracy and one-sidedness, and this confession is an essential ingredient of truth. (5.565)

As a measure of how serious Peirce is about this, note that in principle it does not matter how the final consensus opinion is arrived at. It is true no matter how it came about: "If a general belief... can in any way be produced, though it be by the faggot and the rack, to talk of error in such belief is utterly absurd" (8.16).

As a *matter of fact*, Peirce does not believe that any method save scientific method can succeed in attaining (and sustaining indefinitely) a consensus of opinion. Other methods can at best achieve only a temporary agreement. Still, it is important to remember that a consensus conclusion is not true *because* it was arrived at by experience and scientific method. Rather, it is true because it is agreed to universally. In the final analysis, what makes experience and scientific method good ways to get at truth is not that they effectively reveal reality (although he thinks they do) but rather that they are effective at producing agreement. If some other method, say mass hypnosis (or "the faggot and the rack"), were as effective at producing consensus, then it would be every bit as good a method for attaining truth as is scientific method. (And indeed, as we shall see, in Peirce's eyes it would be every bit as good at revealing reality.)

Why is Peirce so confident that all investigators will come to agree, and why does he think that scientific method is so good at doing this? No one can sustain a belief if the people around him disagree, so the only method that will bring about agreement is one that affects the beliefs of the whole community (5.378). To do this, the method must make use of something public and external to the individual minds of the community (5.384; Peirce 1966, 398). Scientific method will do this because it is based on the experience of an objective reality. The method works like this: Reality affects us through our perceptions. The reality is objective because we cannot control our perceptions. In any given situation I find myself in, reality determines what I see and do not see, what I hear and do not hear. It is not up to me whether or not I see my bulletin board when I look up from this desk. If, in reality, there is a bulletin board on my wall, I shall see it; if not, not. And the reality of the bulletin board will affect everyone else in a similar way. Thus everyone who investigates will come to the same conclusion: that there is a bulletin board on my wall (2.138, 2.141-142, 2.775). Similarly in the case of the scientists studying the speed of light, the reality of the actual speed of light determines the experimental results of the ten different experiments and leads all ten scientists to the same conclusion. And in the murder case, the reality of the murder ensures that the blind man will hear the report of a gun and the deaf man will see the shooting. So although reality affects them in different ways, it leads them both to the same conclusion: that there has been a murder. It is still possible, of course, for the two men to reach different conclusions. The blind man may conclude that his friends are playing a trick on him, trying to fool him into thinking he has heard a murder. But further perceptions will make this belief increasingly unlikely. The sound of screaming bystanders, the sound of a police siren approaching, such will drive him away from his original judgment and toward the view that a real murder has taken place. If he continues to have such perceptions and if he aggressively seeks out more perceptions relevant to the situation (which is essentially what Peirce's scientific method involves), he will conclude that no amount of cleverness could produce a deception so elaborate. So it is that objective reality, by its power to give us perceptions we can neither control nor suppress, drives us progressively closer to conclusions that accurately reflect that reality. As Peirce put it, "The conception of truth gradually develops..., reaching the idea of truth as overwhelmingly forced upon the mind in experience as the effect of an independent reality" (5.564). Since there is just one objective reality and it is driving all of us to beliefs that accurately reflect it, we are *ipso facto* driven to agree with one another.

There is one big complication to be introduced, but consider what Peirce's theory looks like so far. A true proposition is one to which everyone would eventually agree if they each had enough of the experiences relevant to the proposition. But the only propositions to which everyone would agree are those that accurately reflect reality. Hence, 'is true' is equivalent to 'accurately reflects objective reality'.[10] But curiously, Peirce turns his attention away from this equivalence and focuses instead on what would otherwise seem to be an incidental and uninteresting equivalence between 'is true' and 'would eventually be agreed to by everyone with sufficient relevant experiences'. To put the same point another way, Peirce's theory of truth is plausible only because it is parasitic on another, hidden theory of truth: truth as correspondence with reality. So why doesn't Peirce simply offer the latter as his theory of truth?

The explanation for Peirce's seemingly misplaced focus of attention becomes clear when we examine his concept of reality in more detail. So far it has seemed that reality is independent of mind for Peirce, and indeed, he seems at times anxious to say just that: "There are real things, whose characters are entirely independent of our opinions about them" (5.384). "This theory is also highly favorable to a belief in external realities.... 'The real' means that which is independent of how we may think or feel *about it*" (8.13; compare 5.430). "Reality is that mode of being by virtue of which the real thing is as it is, irrespectively of what any mind or any definite collection of minds may represent it to be" (5.565; compare 5.384). But these remarks turn out to be misleading. Reality is independent of any *one* mind and of any proper subset of minds, but it is not independent of all minds. Reality is whatever is *said* to exist or to be the case in the propositions to which everyone (with sufficient relevant experiences) would agree:

Reality is independent, not necessarily of thought in general, but only of what you or I or any finite number of men may think about it.... On the other hand, though the object of the final opinion depends on what that opinion is, yet what that opinion is does not depend on what you or I or any man thinks. (5.408; see also 5.257, 7.336)

My social theory of reality, namely, that the real is the idea in which the community ultimately settles down. (6.610)

Everything, therefore which will be thought to exist in the final opinion is real, and nothing else. (8.12)

This theory involves a phenomenalism. But it is the phenomenalism of Kant, and not that of Hume.... It was the essence of [Kant's] philosophy to regard the real object as determined by the mind.... It was to regard the reality as the normal product of mental action. (8.15)

So reality is not mind-independent after all. It is independent of any individual mind (so it counts as "objective" in Peirce's eyes), but it is not independent of the human community's mind. What is real is determined by, constituted by, the minds in the community. *Now* it is clear why Peirce is so uninterested in the equivalence between 'is true' and 'reflects reality', for this equivalence is merely incidental: 'Reflects reality' itself means no more than 'would be agreed to, given sufficient relevant experiences'.

But this move by Peirce seems to be the Achilles heel of his entire enterprise regarding truth. The plausibility of his intellectual optimism rests on an image of reality forcing people to have perceptions (and thus ultimately conclusions) that they can neither control nor suppress. And the plausibility of his theorized equivalence between truth and consensus opinion rested on the plausible equivalence between truth and correspondence with reality. But the latter equivalence turns out to be but a misleading rewording of the former. Peirce's justification for his theory circles back on itself, and as a result, the plausibility of the theory collapses.

If this is not clear enough already, notice how destructive Peirce's ontological doctrine is to the proffered image of reality controlling our perceptions. The latter idea is plausible, indeed commonsensical, on a Realist ontology: mind-independent objects interact (via other sorts of mind-independent entities like light waves and sound waves) with our sense organs to produce perceptions, and since we cannot control what objects are out there, we cannot control what we perceive. But on Peirce's ontology, the objects that supposedly control our perceptions are a peculiar sort of idealist object. (Just how peculiar we shall see in a moment.) An idea in the minds of those who have had sufficient relevant experiences somehow forces other people, those who have not had all these experiences, to have certain perceptions. Even more puzzling, consider the people who have had sufficient relevant experiences and have reached the "final conclusion." Peirce would have us believe that the very perceptions that caused this group to reach the final conclusion were forced on them, *in a reverse-chronological direction*, by the final conclusion, which, at the time they had the perceptions, they had not reached. And some of the perceptions you and I are having right now are forced on us by an idea which, if we have it at all, we will only have at some future time.

Peirce tries to defend himself by referring to a Humean analysis of cause and effect:

At first sight it seems no doubt a paradoxical statement that, "The object of final belief which exists only in consequence of the belief, should itself produce the belief"; ... there is nothing extraordinary ... in saying that the existence of external realities depends upon the fact, that opinion will finally settle in the belief in them. And yet that these realities existed before the belief took rise, and were even the cause of that belief, just as the force of gravity is the cause of the falling of the inkstand—although the force of gravity consists merely in the fact that the inkstand and other objects will fall. (7.340-344)

But the analogy here is faulty, even if we accept the analysis of cause implied therein. First, gravity is not *the* cause of the inkstand's falling, it is only *one* necessary condition to the inkstand's falling. Another is that someone knocked the inkstand off the table, and the event of someone's knocking the inkstand off the table does not "depend upon," nor is it a "consequence of," the inkstand's falling. Indeed, the relation of dependency and consequence is quite the other way round. Second, gravity is not a consequence of *this* inkstand's falling. Thus even if we did allow that gravity is the cause of the inkstand's falling, to say this is not to assert that an event can be the consequence of one of its own effects. The existential dependency here is *not* reciprocal. Third, gravity, on the Peirce's Humean analysis, *is* a consequence of the fact that things *tend* to fall. But neither gravity nor the tendency are events in time. Hence, to assert that the former is both a cause and consequence of the latter is not to assert the possibility of reverse-chronological causation. But coming to believe the final conclusion, on the one hand, and the occurrence of the perceptions that bring about that belief, on the other, *are* events in time, and they came at different times. Hence, to assert that the chronologically earlier of these is caused by the chronologically later is to assert something not at all analogous to any causal relations involving the inkstand. Fourth, even the apparent reciprocal existential dependency between gravity and the tendency of objects to fall is delusive. On the Peirce's Humean analysis of cause, the relationship between these two is one of *identity*: 'gravity' and 'the tendency of things to fall' are just two names for the same thing.

The problems in Peirce's account go even deeper than this. The entity supposed to produce our present perceptions is not even an idea that will *actually* exist at some future time. Instead, it has a kind of hypothetical existence. The final conclusion is one that *would* be reached by anyone *if* he had sufficient relevant experiences. Although Peirce sometimes speaks as if the final conclusion is fated or destined, on those occasions in which he self-consciously considers whether this conclusion will ever be actually reached, he is much more cautious:

> We cannot be quite sure the community will ever settle down to an unalterable conclusion upon any given question..., nor can we rationally presume any overwhelming *consensus* of opinion will be reached upon every question. (6.610)

> I do not say that it is infallibly true that there is any belief to which a person would come if he were to carry his inquiries far enough. I only say that that alone is what I call Truth. I cannot infallibly know that there *is* any truth. (Peirce 1966, 398)

So the causal action of the final conclusion on our present actual perceptions is not only reverse-chronological, it is also action *from* within a hypothetical domain *to* the actual domain. This view is not only implausible; I think we can seriously question whether it is even intelligible.

Put into the standard form for essence theories, Peirce's theory looks like this:

$(x)(x$ is true $\Leftrightarrow$ everyone who has sufficient relevant perceptions will be compelled to agree to $x)$

The variable x ranges over propositions.[11] Peirce is claiming that there is just one condition that is both necessary and sufficient for the truth of any proposition. It must be such that it will be agreed to by everyone who has sufficient relevant perceptions. *It does not matter whether or not x expresses a fact in a mind-independent world.*

Peirce's theory is what I called in section 3.1 a quasi-realist theory: he thinks that what would be agreed on determines what the facts are, that is, he claims,

Snow is white iff everyone who has sufficient relevant perceptions will be compelled to agree to 'Snow is white'.

Hence, since he also equates truth with what would be agreed to, he would also accept,

'Snow is white' is true iff snow *is* white.

But although his theory is quasi realist, it is not Realist, because he does not regard the 'Snow is white' on the right-hand side of the 'iff' as expressing a mind-independent fact. Rather, snow is white only because the collection of minds would agree to it. What sort of equivalence is being asserted with the 'iff' in the last two formulas? If Peirce would allow that there are some possible worlds with no minds, and hence no minds that could come to agreement, then he could not claim that in every possible world reality is created by community agreement. In that case, the 'iff' could be no stronger than naturalistic equivalence, and it might even be mere extensional equivalence if Peirce would allow worlds with the same laws of nature as the actual world but that contain no minds. On the other hand, it is not inconceivable that Peirce would insist that there is no possible world without a collection of minds whose agreement on the facts makes the world what it is. In this case he would be claiming that 'There are minds' is a *necessary truth*, and the 'iff' would express *essential* equivalence.

3.3   William James's Instrumentalism

The first thing we can say about William James is that between his novelist brother Henry and himself, William has the clearer prose. The second thing is that the first thing is not saying much: clarity and consistency were not James family traits. Part of the problem is that James philosophically grew up in the later nineteenth century, an era in which ambiguity, indirection, and rococo encrustations of metaphor were standard features of philosophical expression. Also, if a characteristic feature of much twentieth-century Anglo-American philosophy is the making of distinctions between things the ordinary man identifies, an equally common theme of the prior era was the conflation of things the ordinary man thinks distinct, the True and the Real being notable examples. Argumentation that preceding and succeeding generations would count as textbook indulgence in the fallacy of equivocation was elevated to a philosophic method in the world of James's intellectual upbringing. James's views never recovered from this intense early irradiation of nonsense. His was a mind capable of asserting, within a few pages, two definitions of truth enjoying not a word in common, without so much as acknowledging the difference, let alone explaining it $(MT, 141, 142)$.[12] He could embrace extreme subjectivism $(MT, 129)$ and yet, when indicted for that sin, insist with wounded innocence that he was an objectivist $(MT, 105)$. In one bizarrely guileless passage he refers to himself as a relativist and proclaims that relativism does not involve a denial of absolutism $(MT, 142–143)$. Although he complained repeatedly that his critics misunderstood him, sometimes referred to their objections as "slanders" $(MT, 147)$, and once attributed to them "an inability almost pathetic, to understand the thesis which they seek to refute" $(MT, 10)$, there were times when he grudgingly conceded that some of the fault might lie with his own careless expression and/or intrinsic flaws in his philosophy itself. At such moments, however, he as often as not retreated into special pleading so outrageous as to strike the reader as comical. There are the places, for example, where he dismisses proofs of the contradictoriness of his views as mere technicalities $(MT, 38, 39, 41–42)$. Then too there is the remarkable passage where he complains that his critics abuse him by attending to the content of his philosophy instead of its spirit $(MT, 99)$.

There is hardly any theory of truth James did not endorse at one time or another, including the correspondence theory $(P, 96)$, the coherence theory $(P, 34–37, MT, 104–105)$, and a Peircean consensus theory $(MT, 142–143)$. As already noted, we can deal with such a philosopher profitably only by being prepared to ignore some of his remarks as "not what he meant" and by offering some explanation and integration that the original author does not provide.[13]

To begin with, then, James insists many times that he happily accepts the dictionary definition of a true belief or statement[14] as one that "agrees with reality" (*MT*, 104, 117–118; *P*, 96). But he insists that this phrase is doubly ambiguous: it does not tell us what sort of relation could constitute agreement in this context, and it does not tell us what is meant by 'reality'. To take second things first, James believed that reality, or at least the reality to which true ideas must agree, depends on the mind:[15] "An experience, perceptual or conceptual, must conform to reality in order to be true. ... By 'reality' humanism [one of James's names for his philosophy] means nothing more than the other conceptual or perceptual experiences with which a given present experience may find itself in point of fact mixed up" (*MT*, 59; also see *MT*, 64, 74–75, 115, for other statements of his antirealism besides those quoted below).

As to whether there is any such thing as a reality independent of mind, he was usually neutral:[16]

That this drift of experience itself is in the last resort due to something independent of all possible experience may or may not be true. There may or may not be an extra-experiential 'ding an sich'[17] that keeps the ball rolling, or an 'absolute' that lies eternally behind all the successive determinations which human thought has made.

... And we are not required to seek [truth] in a relation of experience as such to anything beyond itself. (*MT*, 45)

But whether the Other, the universal *That*, has itself any definite inner structure, or whether, if it have any, the structure resembles any of our predicated *whats*, this is a question which humanism leaves untouched. For us, at any rate, it insists, reality is an accumulation of our own intellectual inventions, and the struggle for 'truth' in our progressive dealings with it is always a struggle to work in new nouns and adjectives while altering as little as possible the old. (*MT*, 43)

Experience comes in two kinds. Most simply, there is what James calls "acquaintance" with simple objects:

Let us next pass on to the case of immediate or intuitive acquaintance with an object. ... The thought-stuff and the thing-stuff are here indistinguishably the same in nature ..., and there is no context of intermediaries or associates to stand between and separate the thought and thing. ... But if our own private vision of the paper be considered in abstraction from every other event ..., then the paper seen and the seeing of it are only two names for one indivisible fact. ... The paper is in the mind and the mind is around the paper, because paper and mind are only two names that are given later to the one experience, when, taken in a larger world of which it forms a part, its connexions are traced in different directions. *To know immediately, then, or intuitively, is for mental content and object to be identical.* (*MT,* 35–36)

He adds a footnote:

What is meant by this is that 'the experience' can be referred to either of two great associative systems, that of the experiencer's mental history, or that of the experienced facts of the world. Of both of these systems it forms part, and may be regarded, indeed, as one of their points of intersection. (*MT,* 36)

But if our experience consisted of nothing but discrete intuitions of simple objects, it would be chaotic and unintelligible. We must be able to see the *relationships* between objects and be able to categorize them. Thus, our minds organize and structure experience by means of our most basic categories and concepts. These concepts "are now a part of the very structure of our mind. ... No experience can upset them" (*MT,* 42). However, unlike Kant, he does not seem to think that these things are built into our mind. They are inductive discoveries of our ancestors. (And presumably he would say that we are *taught* to use them.) The concepts in question include "the notions of one Time and of one Space as single continuous receptacles; the distinction between thoughts and things, matter and mind; between permanent subjects and changing attributes; the conception of classes with sub-classes within them; the separation of fortuitous from regularly caused connexions" (*MT,* 42). There is something misleading, however, in James's description of these notions as inductive discoveries. In the context at hand, it would be more accurate to say that our precivilized forebears *decided,* in a subconscious, unintentional manner, that the mind-dependent world would have one Time and one Space, that it would have regular causal laws, that it would have a class of fruit with subclasses of apples and oranges. They *made* the world this way by so conceiving of it. Why did they choose to structure the world with these features and not some other features? James's answer, to get ahead of ourselves a bit, is that they found it more *useful* to organize the world in this manner. The last quotation continues,

Surely all these were once definite conquests made ... by our ancestors in their attempts to get the chaos of their crude individual experiences into a more shareable and manageable shape. They proved of such sovereign use as *denkmittel* that they are now a part of the very structure of our mind. We cannot play fast and loose with them. No experience can upset them. On the contrary, they apperceive every experience and assign it to its place.

To what effect? That we may the better foresee the course of our experiences, communicate with one another, and steer our lives by rule. Also that we may have a cleaner, clearer, more inclusive mental view. (*MT*, 42)

Philosophers who make truth a matter of agreement with mind-dependent reality are usually motivated by skeptical worries, and James was no exception. If truth consists in agreement with reality *in*dependent of mind, then we can never be justified in thinking that any of our beliefs are at least probably true. Our contact with a mind-independent world, if there is such a thing, is mediated by our perceptual organs and the concepts with which we organize perceptual experience. There is no way to step out from behind these organs and this conceptual scheme to see if the ideas and sensations they produce really do agree with the mind-independent reality:

How does the partisan of absolute reality know what this orders him to think? He cannot get direct sight of the absolute; and he has no means of guessing what it wants of him except by following the humanistic clues. The only truth that he himself will ever practically *accept* will be that to which his finite experiences lead him of themselves....

All the *sanctions* of a law of truth lie in the very texture of experience. Absolute or no absolute, the concrete truth *for us* will always be that way of thinking in which our various experiences most profitably combine. (*MT*, 46–47)

I shall discuss the question of whether this is a viable way of dealing with the problem of skepticism in section 3.6.

So much, then, for James's ontology. There is a second ambiguity in the bromide that a true idea must agree with reality:

Ordinary epistemology contents itself with the vague statement that the ideas must 'correspond' or 'agree'; the pragmatist insists on being more concrete, and asks what such 'agreement' may mean in detail. (*MT*, 105)

The "intellectualistic" position ... is that ... the truth-relation ... means, in Mr. Pratt's words, merely "this simple thing, *that the object of which one is thinking is as one thinks it.*"[18]

... I now formally ask Professor Pratt to tell what this "as"-ness in itself *consists* in. ...

I myself agree most cordially that for an idea to be true the object must be "as" the idea declares it. (*MT*, 92–94; compare *P*, 96)

James, it turns out, believes that there is more than one way in which an idea can "agree with" reality in a manner that makes it true, not all of them applicable to every type of belief or proposition. In the first place, he wants to concede to Realist theories of truth that *one* way a truth bearer can agree with reality is by *copying* some part of reality: "Our true ideas of sensible things do indeed copy them. Shut your eyes and think of yonder clock on the wall and you get just such a true picture or copy of its dial" (*P*, 96; compare *P*, 140).

It is questionable just how seriously we ought take this concession, because the sorts of ideas that he says can *copy* reality, those of "sensible things" and "phenomenal fact," are precisely the ideas of intuitive acquaintance that he elsewhere says are *constitutive* of reality (see the quotations above). And things are not copies of *themselves*. One thing is not a copy of another if they are numerically the same object. At any rate, James does not think that it is possible for most ideas to agree with reality in the sense of copying part of it:

> From the frequency of copying in the knowledge of phenomenal fact, copying has been supposed to be the essence of truth in matters rational also. Geometry and logic, it has been supposed, must copy archetypical thoughts in the Creator.... [But] the whole notion of copying tends to evaporate from these sciences. Their objects can be better interpreted as being created step by step by men, as fast as they successively conceive them. (*MT*, 51–52)

> When you speak of the "time-keeping function" of the clock, or of its spring's "elasticity," it is hard to see exactly what your ideas can copy. (*P*, 96)

So what are the other ways that a truth bearer might agree with reality? *By proving useful to those who believe it* is James's famous answer:

> Those thoughts are true which guide us to *beneficial interaction* with sensible particulars as they occur, whether they copy these in advance or not. (*MT*, 51)

> To "agree" in the widest sense with a reality *can ... mean ... to be put into such working touch with it as to handle either it or something connected with it better than if we disagreed....* Any idea that helps us to *deal,* whether practically or intellectually, with either the reality or its belongings, that does not entangle our progress in frustrations, that *fits,* in fact and adapts our life to the reality's whole setting [is true]. (*P*, 102)

> The possession of true thoughts means everywhere the possession of invaluable instruments of action. (*P*, 97)

> Messrs. Schiller and Dewey appear with their pragmatistic account of what truth everywhere signifies.... It means ... *that ideas ... become true just in so far as they*

help us to get into satisfactory relations with other parts of our experience, to summarize them and get about among them by conceptual shortcuts. . . . Any idea that will carry us prosperously from any one part of our experience to any other part, linking things satisfactorily, working securely, simplifying, saving labor; is . . . true *instrumentally*. (*P*, 34)

Interpreted as an essence-project theory of truth, instrumentalism in a very simple form says,

(*b*)[*b* is true ⇔ (*b* copies a part of reality or *b* is a useful belief to have)],

where *b* ranges over beliefs.[19] What exactly would usefulness mean in such a context? As James is stingy with concrete examples, we shall have to make of them what we can:

Thus, for my statement 'the desk exists' to be true of a desk recognized as real by you, it must be able to lead me to shake your desk, to explain myself by words that suggest that desk to your mind, to make a drawing that is like the desk you see, etc. (*MT*, 117–118)

The idea, for example, may be that a certain door opens into a room where a glass of beer may be bought. If opening the door leads to the actual sight and taste of the beer, the man calls the idea true. (*MT*, 129)

My idea is that you really have a headache; it works well with what I see of your expression, and with what I hear you say. (*MT*, 98)

There are several overlapping senses of usefulness at work here. The first remark notes that one way a belief can be useful is if it helps us to manipulate the objects of the world. This seems reasonable enough, for it would seem that being able to manipulate things would be an essential means to obtaining one's goals in life, no matter what those goals be. Another thing suggested by the first remark is that beliefs are useful when they allow successful communication with our fellows. Perhaps James would identify this as the sense in which rules of grammar and definitions can be useful, and hence true. The second remark implies that a belief can be useful if it leads to accurate predictions. This is confirmed by his remark, "We live in a world of realities that can be infinitely useful or infinitely harmful. Ideas that tell us which of them to expect count as true" (*P*, 98). The third remark implies that another way that a belief can be useful, or "work," as James frequently puts it, is by *explaining* other occurrences: I see your knitted brow, see you rub your temples, hear you utter "Owwooo." The hypothesis that you have a headache would explain these three events. If we replace the vague reference to usefulness in our instrumentalist formula with explicit references to these more specific types of usefulness, we get this:

(b)[b is true ⟺ (b copies a part of reality
        or the assumption of b helps with the manipulation of
            objects
        or communication is facilitated by the assumption of b
        or predictions based on b have been successful
        or b explains other occurrences)].

There are further complications to be introduced, but it is best to see them as motivated by objections and counterexamples to what we have so far.

Suppose you have an appointment at 8:00 one morning and your watch reads 7:50. You believe your watch is working correctly, and acting on this belief, you leave for your appointment and arrive precisely on time. But suppose, unbeknownst to you, your watch had stopped at 7:50 the previous evening. It is just by coincidence that you looked at it exactly twelve hours later. So your belief that your watch was working was false. *Or was it?* According to instrumentalism, your belief was *true* because it proved to be a useful one. The fact that your watch was not working has nothing to do with whether or not your belief that it was working was true. The facts of the matter are irrelevant. What counts is the usefulness of the belief. To this sort of counterexample James responds that when he speaks of usefulness, he means useful over the long term and when all things are considered: "'*The true,*' *to put it very briefly, is only the expedient in the way of our thinking, just as 'the right' is only the expedient in the way of our behaving. Expedient in almost any fashion; and expedient in the long run and on the whole of course; for what meets expediently all the experience in sight will not necessarily meet all farther experiences equally satisfactorily*" (*P*, 106).

Modifying instrumentalism so as to equate *long-term* usefulness with truth forestalls many counterexamples, but not all. Your belief that your watch is working will cease to be useful the first time you look at it when the time is not 7:50. On the other hand, it might be useful *throughout Jones's life* for him to believe that he is better at his job than anyone else (e.g., because the increased confidence it gives him pays huge dividends).

But this can be the case even if he is not in fact better at his job than anyone else.

Not surprisingly, then, James has another answer to counterexamples of this sort. He denies that there is any case in which a belief fails to express a fact when it is true by his account of truth:

The definition claims to be exact and adequate, does not it? Then it can be substituted for the word ..., can't it? ...
   The particular application of this rigoristic treatment to my own little account of truth as working seems to be something like what follows. I say "working" is what the "truth" of our ideas means, and call it a definition.... It follows that whoso calls an idea true, and means by that word that it works, cannot mean anything else... but that it does work.... "According to the pragmatists," Mr. Russell writes,[20] "to say 'it is true that other people exist' *means* 'it is useful to believe that other people exist.' But if so, then these two phrases are merely different words for the same proposition."...
   But may not real terms, I now ask, have accidents not expressed in their definitions?... Truth has its implications as well as its workings. If anyone believe that other men exist it is ... an implication of its truth, that they should exist in fact. (*MT,* 148-149)

I think I hear some critic retort as follows: "If satisfactions are all that is needed to make truth, how about the notorious fact that errors are so often satisfactory? And how about the equally notorious fact that certain true beliefs may cause the bitterest dissatisfaction? Isn't it clear that not the satisfaction which it gives but the relation of the belief *to the reality* is all that makes it true?" ...
   The pragmatist calls satisfactions indispensable for truth-building, but I have everywhere called them insufficient unless reality be also incidentally led to. If the reality assumed were cancelled from the pragmatist's universe of discourse, he would straightway give the name of falsehoods to the beliefs remaining, in spite of all their satisfactoriness. (*MT,* 105-106)

A horse may be defined as a beast that walks on the nails of his middle digits. Whenever we see a horse we see such a beast, just as whenever we believe a "truth" we believe something expedient. Messrs. Russell and Hawtrey, if they followed their anti-pragmatist logic, would have to say here that we see *that it is* such a beast, a fact which notoriously no one sees who is not a comparative anatomist. (*MT,* 152)

That these ideas should be true in advance of and apart from their utility, that, in other words, their objects should be really there, is the very condition of their having that kind of utility. (*MT,* 112)

Interpreting these remarks is hazardous because the distinctions described in chapter 1 of this book between extensional, naturalistic, essential, and intensional equivalence had not been fully deployed when James wrote. His terminology in some of these remarks, particularly "accidents" and "incidently," suggests to modern ears that he regards usefulness as the *essence* of truth, and he thinks that it just so happens that all beliefs that are useful in this, the actual, world express facts. On the other hand, the last of the above remarks could be interpreted in the opposite way: James may be saying that it is the essence of a true belief that it express a fact but it just so happens in this world that all such beliefs are useful. There are other possible interpretations, but rather than survey them all, let us ask how James could think that there is even an extensional coincidence between useful beliefs and beliefs that express facts. The answer lies in his ontology: what the facts of the matter are is determined by our conceptual scheme. The broadest and most basic features of that scheme, and thus of reality, are handed down to us by our primordial predecessors. The more middling-level features are derived from our particular culture and scientific epoch. "Ptolemaic astronomy, euclidean space, aristotelian logic, scholastic metaphysics, were expedient for centuries, but human experience has boiled over those limits, and we now call these things only relatively true ..." (*P*, 107).

Finally, the most particular facts, such as that there is a bulletin board here now, are determined, subject to the constraint that they be consistent with the basic and middling features of our inherited scheme (*P*, 34–37), by what we each individually find useful to believe. If it is true that there is a bulletin board here now, it is so because my overall ability, over the long term, to achieve my goals is enhanced by my so believing. And so it is that James too can accept the quasi-realist equivalence

'Snow is white' is true iff snow is white.

But for James, as for Peirce, the right-hand side of the equivalence does not assert a mind-independent fact. At any rate, James's answer to the counterexample involving Jones's confidence in his own superiority is that in the possible world described, Jones really *is* better at his job than anyone else. This is *made* to be a fact by the overall long-term usefulness of Jones's belief that he is.

This ontological answer to the counterexample commits James to the view that truth, and indeed reality itself, is relative; for suppose that Jones's coworker Smith believes that *he* can do Jones's work better than Jones. If this belief is beneficial to Smith overall and for the long term, then it is true *for Smith* that Smith is better at the job in question, while it is true *for Jones* that Jones is better. James did not shy away from this implication:[21]

Truth may vary with the standpoint of the man who holds it. (*MT*, 135)

Dr. Pratt perplexes me again by seeming to charge [pragmatism] with an account of truth which would allow the object believed in not to exist, even if the belief in it were true. "Since the truth of an idea," he writes, "means merely the fact that the idea works, that fact is all you mean when you say the idea is true" (p. 206). "*When you say the idea is true*"—does that mean true for *you*, the critic, or true for the believer whom you are describing? The critic's trouble over this seems to be come from his taking the word 'true' irrelatively, whereas the pragmatist always means 'true for him who experiences the workings'. (*MT*, 97)

[My critics] forget that in any concrete account of what is denoted by 'truth' in human life, the word can only be used relatively to some particular trower. Thus, I may hold it true that Shakespeare wrote the plays that bear his name, and may express my opinion to a critic. If the critic be both a pragmatist and a baconian [one who believes that Francis Bacon wrote the plays attributed to Shakespeare], he will in his capacity of pragmatist see plainly that the workings of my opinion, I being what I am, make it perfectly true for me, while in his capacity of baconian he still believes that Shakespeare never wrote the plays in question. But most anti-pragmatist critics take the word 'truth' as something absolute. (*MT*, 147–148)

Thus what is true for Smith is not always what is true for Jones. James is not so much offering a theory of truth as he is offering a theory of a binary relation called *true-for*, which has statements or beliefs as one relatum and people as another. In light of this and the requirement that usefulness be thought of in a holistic, long-term sense, I reformulate James theory thus:

$(b)(s)[b$ is true for $s \Leftrightarrow (b$ copies a part of s's reality

or all things considered and over the long-term, acceptance of b helps s explain, predict, and manipulate his world and communicate with others better than if s did not accept $b)]$,

where s ranges over people.

Many an invalid "rebuttal" of relativism depends on conflating relativism with subjectivism and, correspondingly, absolutism with objectivism, but the relative/absolute distinction is not the same as the subjective/objective distinction. Individual subjectivism about truth (IST) is

$(s)(x)(x$ is true for s iff s believes $x)$,

where x ranges over propositions. Individual relativism about truth (IRT) can be defined thus:[22]

The truth value of propositions varies from person to person.

Notice that IST does not *quite* entail IRT, although it would in conjunction with the undisputed additional premise that people do not all believe the same things. More important, IRT does not entail IST. Consider the following theory of truth:

$(s)(x)(x$ is true for s iff the longest hair on s's head is longer than the shortest printed expression of x in s's language).

This theory, in conjunction with the undisputed premise that hair length varies from person to person, entails IRT, but it does not involve IST in any way. Quite the contrary, this peculiar theory makes truth a matter of *objective* properties of people, specifically the length of their longest hairs. For similar reasons, James's theory does not commit him to IST. Whether or not x is true for Jones does not depend on whether or not Jones believes it; it depends on whether or not it is useful for Jones to believe it. Thus arguments against IST do not stand muster as arguments against IRT in general or James's theory in particular.[23] Hilary Putnam, for example, argues against relativism with the premise that "the relativist cannot, in the end, make any sense of the distinction between *being right* and *thinking he is right*" (1981, 122). And on the following page he says that antiobjectivism is the "defining characteristic" of relativism. Clearly, he has conflated relativism with subjectivism.[24] Note in particular that it is perfectly possible on James's theory for Jones to be wrong though he thinks he is right. This would happen every time he believed something that is not useful, overall and for the long-term. One objection of Putnam's relevant to relativism is his claim that a consistent relativist would have to say that his own theory of truth is itself only relatively true, true *for* the relativist but perhaps not for everyone else; and if the relativist does concede this, then, says Putnam, "our grasp of what the position even means begins to wobble" (Putnam 1981, 121). James's answer to this sort of objection is as follows:

A correspondent puts this objection as follows: "When you say to your audience, 'pragmatism is the truth concerning truth,' the first truth is different from the second. About the first you and they are not to be at odds; you are not giving them liberty to take or leave it according as it works satisfactorily or not for their private uses. Yet the second truth, which ought to describe and include the first, affirms this liberty. Thus the *intent* of your utterance seems to contradict the *content* of it." ...

The pragmatist's idea of truth is just such a challenge. He finds it ultrasatisfactory to accept [pragmatism], and takes his own stand accordingly. But, being gregarious as they are, men seek to spread their beliefs, to awaken imitation, to infect others. Why should not *you* also find the same belief satisfactory? thinks the pragmatist, and forthwith endeavors to convert you. ... What there is of self-contradiction in all this I confess I cannot discover. The pragmatist's conduct in his own case seems to me on the contrary admirably to illustrate his universal formula. (*MT*, 107–108)

By this remark James might intend to bite the bullet and concede that his theory is only relatively true while denying that there is anything unintelligible in such a position. On the other hand, he might mean that while his theory makes the necessary and sufficient conditions for truth relative to individuals, it just so happens that some propositions, including his theory itself, are useful for *everyone* to believe and are thus true for everyone.

James often noted the objection that instrumentalism cannot acknowledge the existence of theoretical truths, truths with no practical value at all (*MT*, 58, 101, 111). Here is his most specific and concretely worded attempt to answer it:

With the past, tho we suppose ourselves to know it truly, we have no practical relations at all. It is obvious that, altho interests strictly practical have been the original starting-point of our search for true phenomenal descriptions, yet an intrinsic interest in the bare describing function has grown up. We wish accounts that shall be true, whether they bring collateral profit or not. The primitive function has developed its demand for mere exercise. This theoretic curiosity seems to be the characteristically human *differentia*. ... A true idea now means not only one that prepares us for an actual perception. It means also one that might prepare us for a merely possible perception, or one that, if spoken, would suggest possible perceptions to others, or suggest actual perceptions which the speaker cannot share. (*MT*, 53)

The references to true descriptions in the first part of this passage are difficult to reconcile with the general thrust of James's theory. Perhaps he is again thinking, that one way in which a proposition can agree with reality is by copying it, but we saw above that this notion is difficult to make sense of in light of his antirealist ontology. There is, however, a credible answer to the objection lurking in the second part of the passage: our desire for *explanation and prediction* (not description) is originally motivated by practical interests, but an intrinsic interest in the explaining and predicting functions has developed. Being able to explain and predict our world has become part of the human idea of the good life. They have become not just means to a goal but are among our goals themselves. So it is that having beliefs that explain and predict help us to achieve our goals and thus are useful, even if they have no other, practical value, even, that is, in cases where the only goals they help achieve just are the ability to explain and predict.

James thought that his instrumentalist theory told us not only what truth is but also what justification, or *verification*, as James preferred to call it, is (e.g., *MT*, 91, 94, 109). At times he even seemed to want to *analyze* truth *in terms of* verification, which, as we saw in section 2.2, where I called it the truth-as-justification thesis, is a position of dubious intelligibility. ("True ideas are those that we can assimilate, validate, corroborate and verify" [*P*, 97].) Fortunately, in contexts where he is trying especially hard to be precise, such as when he is answering objections or clearing up misunderstandings, it is clear that he does see the difference between what I call the metaphysical and justification projects and he simply wants to give more or less *the same answer* to both:

Sixth misunderstanding: Pragmatism explains not what truth is, but only how it is arrived at.
In point of fact it tells us both, tells us what it is incidentally to telling us how it is arrived at. (*MT*, 108)

James does not really define truth in terms of verification so much as he defines them both in terms of some third thing: the values of explanation, prediction, and manipulation of the world. It is possible to interpret James as meaning that 'verified for *s*' should be analyzed with exactly the same formula as is 'true for *s*'. If so, then a *side effect* of this is that 'true' and 'verified' are equivalent. This would explain those Jamesian remarks in which he seems to equate the two, which remarks have had a bad influence on the course of philosophy, since they tend to confer respectability by precedent on the notion that truth can be analyzed in terms of justification. But it is not very sympathetic to James to so interpret him, to interpret him, that is, as meaning that one can produce a correct analysis of justification simply by substituting 'justified for *s*' for 'true for *s*' in the formulation of his theory of truth above. Consider again the case of the watch that stopped at 7.50. In lucky circumstances the assumption that the watch is working proves useful anyway. To avoid having to say that in such cases it is true that the watch is working, James insisted that truth be cashed in terms of what is useful, *all things considered and over the long term*. But there are two reasons why James would not want to put these constraints on justification, as distinct from truth. First, it would mean that nothing is justified for me until the end of my life, at which point I could look back and see which beliefs had proved useful overall and for the long term. Second, there is no need for the holistic, long-term constraints when justification rather than truth is at issue: the case of the stopped watch is not a counterexample to the idea that justification can be cashed in terms of narrow, short-term usefulness. At most what the case shows is that evidence, justification, is sometimes misleading. Sometimes a false proposition is justified. But it is no objection to a theory of justification that it has this implication. Quite the contrary, one ought be suspicious of a theory that implied that this could never happen. Thus it is more sympathetic to attribute to James the view that each occasion in which a belief proves immediately useful in one of the more precise ways described above stands as a piece of evidence that the belief is probably, if not certainly, true. It stands as evidence, that is, that the belief is probably going to be useful overall and for the long term.

3.4   Truth and Value

James, then, is one of those philosophers, alluded to in section 2.2, who want to equate truth with a set of *other* values, and the criticisms made there against this position apply to him: First, part of the reason that we have a concept of truth is so that we can *contrast* it with other values, like explanatory power, predictive power, and the ability to manipulate the world. We need truth to be different from other values to account for the fact that, for example, Pascal has a reason for believing in God but his reason is different from the sort of reason possessed by one who has evidence that God exists. Second, the logic of truth is different from the logic of these other values. For example, anything deduced from a true statement must itself be true, but not everything deduced from a statement with explanatory power will itself have explanatory power.

Before leaving the instrumentalist theory of truth, I want to suggest that the thesis that James and many of those influenced by him, were groping toward is not the claim that truth is reducible to, or analyzable in terms of, other values. Although, as a matter of accurate history, we must attribute just that claim to James, there is lurking in the *spirit* of instrumentalism a very different, and much more defensible and intriguing, idea. This other idea is not a theory about what truth *is*; rather, it is a thesis about values. Specifically, it is the thesis that the property of agreeing with, or corresponding to, a reality independent of mind is not *intrinsically* a particularly valuable property for our beliefs to have. On the contrary, what we are seeking, and what we are getting when we succeed in being rational, are beliefs that collectively maximize our overall, long-term ability to explain, predict, and manipulate our world for the furtherance of our goals. That something like this lies behind instrumentalist theories of truth is almost made explicit by those instrumentalists, like Brian Ellis, who reject contrary theories of truth precisely because they "cannot account for the value of truth" (Ellis 1988, 422–423). But questions about what a thing is should be kept distinct from questions about whether or not it is valuable. Much mischief and no good can come from trying to build it into the very concept of a thing that the thing is valuable. Among other disasters, such a procedure would deprive us of the freedom to change our minds about the value of a thing. Consider the silliness of defining a buttonhook as a *valuable* tool for fastening button-down shoes instead of just as a tool for fastening button-down shoes. Dummett has also claimed that somehow it should be built into the very definition of truth that truth is valuable.[25] He argues (1959, 2–3) that just as it is part of the concept of winning a game that one aims to win, so too it is part of the concept of truth that truth is desirable. But this argument from analogy is faulty: winning is not what one aims at when, say, one's opponent is a small child suffering from undernourished self-esteem. A defender of Dummett may be inclined to say here that in cases like this, one is really playing a different game, a game in which winning is constituted by seeing to it that the child is victorious, so winning is after all always something one aims at. But on this way of thinking, 'winning' is just a synonym for 'achieving one's goals', so Dummett is really attempting to draw an analogy between truth and achieving one's goals, and his assertion that these are analogous just begs the question at issue.

Now the thesis that it is not intrinsically valuable that there be a correspondence between beliefs and mind-independent reality is compatible with

1. the claim that beliefs that correspond to mind-independent reality are valuable as a means to the end of having beliefs with these other properties and

2. the claim that a belief's having these other properties is evidence that the belief probably corresponds to mind-independent reality.

(But the thesis would be incompatible with the claim that these other properties are valuable *because* they are evidence that the belief corresponds. So on the thesis being outlined here, claim (2) is incidental and rather uninteresting.) Both claims (1) and (2) assume a correlation between, on the one hand, the property of corresponding with reality independent of mind and, on the other, such properties as explanatory and predictive power. I suspect that establishing such a correlation without begging any questions against skepticism would be very difficult, but the point being made here is independent of all these issues. The point is rather that there is no law requiring us to use the string t ̂r ̂u ̂t ̂h as our word for the property or set of properties we think it most important for our beliefs to possess. We are free to accept the pretheoretical notion of truth as correspondence with a reality independent of mind and also accept, without inconsistency, that truth is not a particularly valuable property. Such a viewpoint captures everything of philosophical substance in instrumentalism while escaping the objections mentioned in the last two paragraphs. Instrumentalism might thus be more usefully thought of as a doctrine about what we care about rather than a doctrine about how to analyze truth.

There is some textual evidence that it is really issues about values other than correspondence with, or copying, mind-independent reality with which James is wrestling and that he is confusing with the question of what truth is:

A priori, however, it is not self-evident that the sole business of our minds with realities should be to copy them. (*MT*, 50)

If our symbols *fit* the world, in the sense of determining our expectations rightly, they may even be the better for not copying its terms. (*MT*, 51)

The suspicion is in the air nowadays that the superiority of one of our [beliefs] to another may not consist so much in its literal "objectivity" as in subjective qualities like usefulness, its "elegance" or its congruity with our residual beliefs. (*MT*, 41)

Up to about 1850 almost everyone believed that sciences expressed truths that were exact copies of a definite code of non-human realities. But the enormously rapid multiplication of theories in these latter days has well-nigh upset the notion of any one of them being a more literally objective kind of thing than another.

There are so many geometries, so many classifications, each one of them good for so much and yet not good for everything, that the notion that even the truest formula may be a human device and not a literal transcript has dawned upon us. (*MT*, 40)

Theoretic truth, truth of passive copying, sought in the sole interests of copying as such, not because copying is *good for something* ... seems, if you look at it coldly, to be an almost preposterous ideal. Why should the universe, existing in itself, also exist in copies? ... And even if it could, what would the motive be? (*MT*, 57)

It is worth noting too that James's agnosticism regarding the existence of a world independent of mind fits well the view that correspondence with such a world is not a particularly valuable property, for certainly one who placed little value on beliefs that depict a mind-independent world would have little interest in whether there is any such world.

3.5   Brand Blanshard's Coherence Theory

The term 'coherence' as used by coherence theories has never been very precisely defined. The most we can say by way of a general definition is that a set of two or more beliefs are said to cohere if and only if (1) each member of the set is consistent with any subset of the others and (2) each is implied (inductively if not deductively) by all of the others taken as premises or, according to some coherence theories, each is implied by *each* of the others individually.

Many defenders of coherence theory, if they were made aware of the distinction between the various projects, would identify the justification project as the one they intend their theories to satisfy. But Brand Blanshard is one defender of coherence theory who indisputably intended it to be *both* a theory of justification *and* an answer to one of the three branches of the metaphysical project, specifically, the essence project. Nor does his intention result simply from a failure to distinguish the two kinds of theory, for, just as there is for James, there is textual evidence that Blanshard knows the difference: "Coherence is the sole criterion of truth. We have now to face the question whether it also gives us the nature of truth. ... One may reject coherence as the definition of truth while accepting it as the test" (Blanshard 1941, 260). However, having accepted the coherence theory of justification, Blanshard felt compelled to accept the coherence theory as a theory of truth. Let us start with his reasons for endorsing the coherence theory of justification and then examine his claim that one must accept the same theory for both justification and truth.

Blanshard believed that if reality is something completely external to human minds, then no theory of justification would ever work. We would never have knowledge, except by dumb luck, and would therefore be forced to accept general skepticism; "If thought and things are conceived as related only externally, then knowledge is luck" (p. 261). The way to avoid this, he suggested, is to postulate that the thoughts in our minds are really not completely distinct from the things in the world we think about. When I think about a chair, I actually have the chair itself in my mind in a sort of undeveloped state: "To think of a thing is to get that thing itself in some degree within the mind. To think of a colour or an emotion is to have that within us which if it *were developed and completed*, would identify itself with the object" (pp. 261–262). So with the additional assumption that the world is coherent, it seem to follow that our beliefs are probably true to the extent that they cohere. Accordingly, he endorses the claim that the coherence of beliefs is evidence of their truth.

But many philosophers who endorse a coherence theory of justification do not feel compelled to endorse a coherence theory of truth as well.[26] Why does Blanshard feel compelled? What does he think is the problem in marrying a coherence theory of justification to, say, a correspondence theory of truth? We find the answer in the following remarks: "Would the mere fact that such elements as these are coherently arranged prove that anything precisely corresponding to them exists 'out there'? I cannot see that it would.... And this difficulty is typical. If you place the nature of truth in one sort of character and its test in something quite different, you are pretty certain, sooner or later, to find the two falling apart. In the end, the only test of truth that is not misleading is the special nature or character that is itself constitutive of truth" (p. 268).

The key word here is 'prove'. Blanshard seems to think that a test of truth must be such that whatever passes the test would thereby be *proven* to be true. He does not seem to recognize the possibility that there might be value in a test that makes it *probable* that a belief is true. At any rate, because he thought justification must *prove* a belief true and because he endorses the coherence theory of justification, he is forced to equate truth with whatever quality a belief is proven to have when it coheres with other beliefs. But the only thing the coherence of a belief *proves* about the belief is that it coheres. Thus, Blanshard concludes, truth must consist in coherence.[27] So Blanshard's motivation for giving the same answer to the justification and essence projects is the same as James's and most others who give the same answer to both: fear of skepticism. Blanshard, however, wants to evade not only the strong kind of skepticism that says none of our judgments is justified as even a little more likely true than its negation but also the rather mild kind of skepticism that asserts that none of our judgments can be *proven* true.

Let us proceed to Blanshard's explication of truth. *Pure* truth, he says, is a fully coherent set of beliefs. And "fully coherent knowledge would be knowledge which in every judgment entailed, and was entailed by, the rest of the system. Probably we never find in fact a system where there is so much of interdependence" (p. 264). Shortly afterward he makes an even stronger claim about the entailment relations between the members of the system: "No proposition would be arbitrary, every proposition would be entailed by the others jointly and even singly" (p. 265). Since a self-contradictory judgment or pair of inconsistent judgments would trivially entail anything and everything, and since presumably Blanshard does not want that kind of entailment to be a truth making relation, there is an implied condition of consistency on any system of judgments that is to count as true. Although we never actually achieve the standard of individual mutual entailment in our set of judgments, we sometimes come close: "It is perhaps in such systems as Euclidean geometry that we get the most perfect examples of coherence that have been constructed" (p. 265). But not just *any* coherent system of beliefs counts as true. Blanshard does not want to say that two such systems, each coherent within itself but inconsistent with the other, are *both* true. So which coherent system is the true one? It is, says Blanshard, the one "in which everything real and possible is coherently included" (p. 276). In other words, the purely true system is one that gives us a complete picture of the universe. A mere self-consistent novel would be just as fictional on coherence theory as on any other theory of truth, because even the longest novel in history would, Blanshard thinks, fall far short of a complete picture of the world. So Blanshard's theory of pure truth would be formulated like this:

(b)(b is purely true ⇔ b is a member of a consistent set of beliefs that together give a complete picture of the world and individually entail each of the others).

The first point that needs to be made here is that the word 'entail' is standardly defined by means of the word 'true': p entails q iff q cannot be false at the same time that p is true. So on the standard conception of entailment, Blanshard's definition is implicitly circular. Some coherence theorists try to avoid this consequence by defining entailment in terms of a certain set of rules of derivation: p entails q iff q can be derived from p via one or more of the rules in R, where R is a standard set of rules of inference whose members refer only to the syntactic structure of propositions, not to their truth values. One such rule, called *modus ponens*, reads "From a proposition of the form 'if p, then q' and the proposition p, one may derive the proposition q." But this maneuver rescues the coherence theory of truth from circularity only at the price of losing whatever plausibility it might have had. This becomes clear if we consider another set of rules one of whose members is the rule, call it *modus goofus*, "From a proposition p, one may derive the proposition not p." Now suppose someone were to claim that a set of propositions that are mutually "entailing" via this second set of rules are, for that reason, true. No one would take seriously such a theory of truth, and the reason why no one would is not far from reach: *modus goofus* is not a *correct* rule. So the plausibility of the syntactic definition of entailment and a coherence theory of truth using that sense of 'entailment', rests on the implicit assumption that the term 'standard' in the definition is being used as a synonym for 'correct'. But what would 'correct' mean here? What does *modus ponens* have that *modus goofus* does not have? The obvious answer is that the former is *truth*-preserving, and the latter is not. But this answer is not available to a coherence theorist, who wants to avoid circularity in his analysis of truth, for it restores an implicit reference to truth into the definition of entailment, and thus into the analysis of truth. It seems, then, that the coherence theorist must fall back on the claim that we possess a primitive, unanalyzable notion of a correct rule of inference, or he must define 'correct rule of inference' as a rule that is traditionally and commonly accepted in the human culture, or he must define correctness here in terms of values other than truth. The first option is not likely to be convincing to those of us who are convinced we have no such primitive concept. The second option leaves the coherence theorist with no way to explain why and how our traditionally accepted rules have been so successful. The third option may well be viable in the end, but it faces serious difficulties. For one thing, the rules that classical logic takes to be correct are generally *not* preserving of values other than truth. It is not the case, for example, that q has explanatory power whenever p and 'if p then q' do. Also, the third option makes the coherence theory collapse into a kind of instrumentalism with all the problems attendant therein, including the aforementioned problem that 'truth' is used in our language as a name for something distinct from these other values. (See sections 2.2 and 3.4.) Even a coherence theory that makes no use of the concept of entailment will be circular, since all coherence theories define truth partly in terms of consistency, and this too is a concept that can only be defined in terms of truth: two or more statements are consistent if they can both be *true* at the same time.

A second objection to the coherence theory is that it seems at least theoretically possible that there could be two complete pictures of the world each of which is coherent in the requisite sense but that are inconsistent with each other. Unfortunately, Blanshard's response to this objection involves a *non sequitur*: "If the systems differ neither in facts nor structure, they are not two systems but one. If, with the same facts, they are to differ at all, they must differ in structure, but then there will be at least one fact which each of them must omit, namely, the fact that the other possesses the particular structure it does" (p. 277). But this, as I said, just does not follow. Why cannot system A include the fact that system B is structured thus and thus, and why cannot system B include the fact that system A is structured so and so? Moreover, to get to the heart of the objection, Blanshard ignores the possibility that the two systems could "differ in facts," that is, that they could each give completely different pictures of the world.

But since Blanshard does not think that pure truth has ever been attained anyway, let us move on to his doctrine of degrees of truth.[28] There are two senses of 'degrees of truth' that Blanshard insists he does not have in mind. The first of these is the sense used when we say of two wrong answers to a question that one is closer to the truth (truer) than the other. Second, he rejects a sense of 'degrees of truth' in which we take note of the fact that every assertion has a number of implications and some of these may be false and some true. The more of them that are true, the truer the assertion. For example, 'This is a blue typewriter' has the following implications among others: 'This is a writing tool', 'This is a machine', 'There is something blue here', etc. The more of these that are true, the truer the original assertion. One might wonder, however, whether there is in fact any such sense of 'degrees of truth'. It seems that an assertion is wholly false if *any* of its implications is false. At any rate, if there is such a sense of 'degrees of truth', Blanshard rejects it as the sense he wants to use, because each of the implications is treated as either absolutely true or absolutely false. In other words, this sort of degrees of truth reduces to the absolute truth of the constituent implications of the assertion. Blanshard is seeking a sense of 'degrees of truth' that is not reducible in this way to absolute truth (pp. 305–307).

So in what sense are some beliefs "truer" than others? His first statement of the sense he has in mind is this: "A given judgment is true in the *degree* to which its content could maintain itself in the light of a completed system of knowledge, false in the *degree* to which its appearance there would require transformation" (p. 304). There is something puzzling in this. On one sense of 'content', a belief may be said to have as its *content* all of its implications. If this is what he means by 'content' in the preceding quotation, then a belief (or judgment, as he would prefer to call it) is truer in proportion to how many of its implications are part of the purely true system. But each implication would individually be either a part of the purely true system or not a part of it. So the truth of each implication is not a matter of degree. But this would make degrees of truth reducible to the absolute truth of the constituent parts of the belief, which is just the sense of 'degrees of truth' that Blanshard rejects. So what does he mean by 'content' here if not the implications of the belief? "The same words as uttered by different persons or by the same person at different times, bear contracted or expanded meanings which will therefore embody truth in varying degrees" (p. 313). So the content of a belief involves its meaning in some sense of 'meaning' that includes more than just the implications of the belief. What else does it include? He gives as an example the difference in meaning of a child's assertion that Napoleon lost at Waterloo and an historian's assertion of the identical fact: "Similarly it is clear about the school-boy that even if his ultimate subject and his form of words are the same as the historian's, his judgment is *not* the same. ... When he says that Napoleon lost Waterloo, what he is really thinking is perhaps that a plucky little fighter in a cocked hat and riding a big white horse had to gallop off at top speed to get away from pursuing red-coats. ... This meaning has been ... deeply infected by childish feelings, tastes and fancies" (p. 308).

It must be acknowledged straight away that Blanshard's usual clarity has deserted him here. The things Blanshard identifies as what the school-boy is "really thinking" are just *other beliefs*. Are *these* a part of the meaning of his belief that Napoleon lost at Waterloo? Moreover, what is wrong with these other beliefs is not that they are childish, it is that they are false, absolutely false. So again we have truth degrees reduced to absolute truth or falsity.

Blanshard makes one more attempt to make clear what he means by the 'content' of a belief: "To think of anything is to think of it in essential relations" (317). We cannot, for example, think of an aorta without thinking of the other body organs to which it connects or serves. Similarly, we cannot conceive of a chair apart from the purpose for which it was designed. Nor the number 3 apart from the numbers than which it is greater or lesser. Nor, finally, the color blue apart from the other colors of the spectrum. But I cannot see how this would connect up with the notion of degrees of truth except that we can be right or wrong in our belief about to what the aorta is connected to, about the purpose of a chair, etc. If this is what he has in mind, then once again 'degrees of truth' turns out to be only a handy way of talking about the absolute truth or falsity of each of a large number of beliefs. It seems, therefore, that Blanshard is unable to make any sense of the notion that truth comes in degrees except insofar as that notion is but a metaphor or a conversational shortcut. It is interesting to note, however, that in response to the objection that his theory entails that even truths of mathematics, like '2 + 2 = 4', and truths of logic, like the Law of the Excluded Middle, are only true to a degree. Blanshard was prepared to bite the bullet and insist that these kinds of beliefs are indeed only true to a degree.

Let me give such formulation as I can to Blanshard's theory of truth other than pure truth:

(b)[b is true to degree $n \Leftrightarrow n\%$ of the content of b would be present in a purely true system of beliefs],

where n is a number from 0 to 100.

The chief weakness of the coherence theory of truth is its lack of initial plausibility. It does not seem that a truth bearer's relationship to other truth bearers, as distinct from its relations with the world, could have anything to do with its truth value. Because of this lack of initial plausibility, it is vital that coherence theorists provide positive arguments for it (as distinct from attacks on the correspondence theory or attempts to refute attacks on the coherence theory), but such positive arguments are hard to find in the literature. Blanshard's only positive argument, as noted above, depends on (1) his apparent failure to recognize that justification does not have to necessitate the truth of a justified belief, and (2) his coherence theory of *justification*, which itself depends on his idealist ontology. If we believe that there is a world independent of our thoughts, then no proposition that purports to describe that world can be considered true if it is inconsistent with that world, no matter how well it coheres with other propositions. And if it does express that world accurately, then it cannot be false, no matter how much it fails to cohere. Hence on a realist ontology it is hard to deny that coherence is neither a necessary nor a sufficient condition for truth. Simon Blackburn generalizes this to cover all Nonrealist theories: "Our judgment that a cat is in the garden is made true, if it is true, by the cat's being in the garden. The issue of how other people would judge it is no part of this truth condition. Nor is the question of whether the belief that it is would enter into any proposed system of belief. We don't, as were, look sideways, either to other people or to systems of belief. We look at the cat and look round the garden" (1984, 247–248).

None of this constitutes an argument against idealism, but since the coherence theory of truth derives whatever plausibility it has from an idealist or some kind of nonrealist ontology, the difficulties facing such ontologies become difficulties for the coherence theory.

It is not clear whether Blanshard's theory is quasi realist. It is not clear, that is, whether he can accept equivalences on the pattern of

'Snow is white' is true iff snow is white.

Certainly for Blanshard the right-hand side of this statement does not assert a mind-independent fact. The world is mind-dependent in his view, but it is not clear exactly how it depends on mind. Specifically, it is not clear whether or not Blanshard would say that for it to be a fact that *p just is* for the belief that *p* to be a member of a consistent set of beliefs that together give a complete picture of the world and individually entail each of the others. *If* he agreed to the latter claim, then on his view the right-hand side of the above equivalence claim asserts that the belief that snow is white is a member of just such a set, and thus he could accept the equivalence as a whole. But an idealist as such, even one who endorses the coherence theory of truth, need not suppose that reality is determined by which beliefs are and which are not members of a coherent set. As Ralph Walker notes, "One might hold that although the nature of the world entirely depends upon mind, it depends upon some other aspect of mind than the propositions it accepts. ... What would determine truth would not be beliefs, but mental states of some other kind" (1989, 39). This is an important point to keep in mind, if only to combat the common allegation that *every* Nonrealist is a quasi realist and that *everyone* can accept such quasi-realist equivalences as the one above. (See section 6.4 for a discussion of this issue.)

3.6   Skepticism and Nonrealist Theories

We have seen that skeptical worries are the chief motivation behind Nonrealist theories of truth. It is very hard, impossible, some would say, to ever be justified in believing that this or that is a mind-independent fact. Our subconscious minds so thoroughly filter and modify observational input that what we take to be facts have no resemblance to the mind-independent facts. (That is, phenomenal facts have no resemblance to mind-independent facts.) Thus if we make the existence of a mind-independent fact a necessary condition for the truth of a belief (sentence, or whatever), we would never be justified in thinking that *any* belief is true. Accordingly, the theory of truth would entail skepticism.

I believe that this worry is misplaced, and I mean 'misplaced' in the literal sense, not as a synonym for 'illegitimate', for the problem of skepticism is a genuine intellectual problem. But a theory of truth is not the place to engage the problem of skepticism. It is the job of theories of *justification* to tell us whether and when our beliefs are probably true. But a philosopher makes it too easy on himself if he defines truth in terms of phenomenal, or nonrealist, facts. For then, of course, it would be very easy to show that we are usually justified in our beliefs. But this would not be a satisfying rebuttal to skepticism. By this maneuver we are told in large print that we have adequate justification for most of our beliefs about the world, but simultaneously the small print tells us that this "world" we believe in consists largely of mental constructs and may not resemble the mind-independent world in the slightest. However sincere the philosophers who have made this move may have been, there is an unintended element of pretense or self-delusion involved. For the problem of skepticism is the concern that our beliefs may not be justified as accurate reflections of the mind-independent world. The problem cannot be solved by pretending our concerns are different than they really are. Davidson makes the point thus: "[Such theories] are skeptical in the way idealism or phenomenalism are skeptical; they are skeptical not because they make reality unknowable, but because they reduce reality to so much less than we believe there is" (1990, 298). Thus nonrealists, in effect, if not in intention, *redefine* truth so as to make it more attainable.[29] They define it in such a way that it becomes easy to have beliefs justified as probably true. Thus a Nonrealist cannot even begin to deal with the problem of skepticism and the worries it produces unless he first convinces us that there really is no external world.

One must be especially on guard against the common sort of Nonrealist who makes it appear that it is the skeptic who is doing something unusual and that consequently the burden of proof should fall on him. Specifically, the Nonrealist proffers an image of the skeptic pointlessly postulating an extramental world and then arguing that we do not have knowledge of that world. Barry Stroud has detected the misunderstanding behind this move:

If an imperceptible "reality," as it is called on this picture, is forever inaccessible to us, what concern can it be of ours? ... This response to philosophical scepticism ... is probably based on misunderstanding. It depends on a particular diagnosis or account of how and why the philosophical argument succeeds in reaching its conclusion. The idea is that the "conclusion" is reached only by contrivance. The inaccessible "reality" denied to us is said to be simply an artifact of the philosopher's investigation and not something that otherwise should concern us. (1984, 34–35)

But as Stroud points out, a skeptic's inquiry is not different in kind from the sort of ordinary situation in which we might inquire as to whether we really know this or that proposition. A skeptic differs only in that the reasons he discovers for thinking he does not know, say, that he is sitting by the fire with a piece of paper in his hand are applicable to nearly all propositions, and thus his conclusion is more sweeping than what an ordinary person would reach. But the world and the knowledge the skeptic is talking about are the same world and knowledge the ordinary person is talking about:

I can ask what I really know about the common cold ..., and ... I can go on to discover that I do not really know what I thought I knew. In such ordinary cases there is no suggestion that what I have discovered is that I lack some special, esoteric thing called "real knowledge," or that I lack knowledge of some exotic, hitherto-unheard-of domain called "reality." (Stroud 1984, 35)

We have every reason to think that [the skeptic] has revealed the impossibility of the very knowledge of the world that we are most interested in and which we began by thinking we possess. (Stroud 1984, 35)

But suppose, it will be suggested, that we analyze truth in terms of mind-independent fact and then when we turn our attention to theories of justification and give them an honest and thorough evaluation, it turns out that, on a Realist theory of truth, no theory of justification succeeds and there is no way to justify our beliefs in some vital area of discourse as probably true. Or worse, what if it should turn out that *none* of our beliefs is justified as probably true? What shall we do then? What we should do, I think, and this will come as a shock to some, for it is not a popular suggestion, is to face up to our own conclusions with all the intellectual honesty we can muster and say "Well, it appears then that skepticism in such and such area of discourse (or globally, if that's how it turns out) is correct. Our beliefs are not justified after all." The implications of skepticism, even global skepticism, may well turn out to be less tragic than appears, for I think there are important senses of epistemic rationality according to which it is not a necessary condition for being epistemically rational that one's beliefs be justified as probably true. This suggestion will be taken up in more detail in section 8.7.

The outright surrender to skepticism has been thought to be unacceptable, even psychologically impossible, by many. So unacceptable that in doing epistemology, it is contended by some that we must *assume* right from the start that skepticism is wrong. The only question is where it goes wrong. This attitude has always struck me as dogmatic and question-begging. Moreover, even if the attitude is correct, what it suggests is not that we should delude ourselves by redefining truth but that we should conclude that something went wrong in our evaluation of theories of justification or in whatever arguments led us to believe that we cannot possibly get around the filter of our own minds to gain knowledge of a world independent of mind

3.7   A Regress Problem for All Nonrealist Theories

Suppose that the proposition p is true. Then according to the coherence theory, it coheres with the most comprehensive system of beliefs whose members imply each other. But what about *this* proposition, the one that says that p coheres with the designated set? Its truth, on a coherence theory, also consists in its coherence with the designated set. Similarly, the truth of "'p coheres with the designated set' coheres with the designated set" consists in *its* coherence with the designated set. But for *any* proposition p, there is a set of propositions on this pattern:

p

p coheres with the designated set

'p coheres with the designated set' coheres with the designated set

etc.

For example, p might be the proposition that the moon is made of green cheese. The implication of this is that the coherence theory really cannot distinguish the set of true propositions from any random set of propositions. "Granted," a coherence theorist will be tempted to say, "there exists a proposition reading '"The moon is made of green cheese" coheres with the designated set.' But that proposition is *false*; 'The moon is made of green cheese' really does not cohere with the designated set. True propositions, I hold, are those that really do cohere with the set." Such a reply misses the point. What would it mean on a coherence theory to say that p "really does" cohere with the designated set? It would mean simply that the metalevel proposition expressible with 'p really does cohere with the designated set' coheres with the designated set, it would *not* mean that it is a mind-independent *fact* that p coheres with the designated set. The only escape for the coherence theorist is to stop the regress by picking out some proposition in the chain and saying of it, "The truth of *this* proposition is grounded in the *mind-independent fact* that it coheres with the designated set." The coherence theorist, in other words, must concede that coherence is not the nature of truth for *every* kind of proposition. He must concede that for propositions of a certain metalevel (or meta-meta- or meta-meta-meta-, etc.) some sort of Realist theory is correct. (Compare Walker 1989, 144–145 192–193.)

It does not help a coherence theorist to put additional restrictions on what counts as the designated set. In particular, it does not help (contra Dauer 1974) to insist that the set must contain some or most or all of the *observational* beliefs *actually* held by some person or set of persons. For again, the truth of the claim that p coheres with a set containing most of the observational beliefs actually held by the specified person(s) amounts, on a coherence theory, to just the claim that 'p coheres with a set containing most of the observational beliefs actually held by the specified person(s)' coheres with a set containing most of the observational beliefs actually held by the specified person(s).

The problem described here is applicable not just to the coherence theory but to any Nonrealist theory. On Peirce's theory, for example, the truth of 'p will be agreed to by all who have sufficient relevant experiences' itself consists in the truth of '"p will be agreed to by all who have sufficient relevant experiences" will be agreed to by all who have sufficient relevant experiences'.

3.8 Local Nonrealism

The regress problem faces any Nonrealist who wants to apply his theory to metalevel statements such as 'p coheres with the designated set' and meta-metalevel statements such as '"p coheres with the designated set" coheres with the designated set' and meta-meta-metalevel statements, and so on for every level. The only way to avoid this if one is going to be a Nonrealist about truth at all is to pick a level and declare that for it and all higher-level statements, truth is defined by some Realist theory. This sort of mixed position on truth can be called a local Nonrealism, since it embraces Nonrealism for some but not all statements. But one can, and many do, hold to a local Nonrealism for reasons independent of the regress problem. Indeed, it has not been uncommon for philosophers to argue that truth consists in different things according to the subject matter of the truth bearer in question. It has been claimed, for example, that the truth of moral statements, statements that one *ought* to do such and such, is properly analyzed along coherence lines, while descriptive statements should receive a Realist analysis. Others who are Realists about present-tense statements are Nonrealists about statements asserting things about the distant future or past. H. B. Acton has endorsed a local Nonrealism about the laws of logic: "Not *all* true propositions are true because they correspond to facts. Such propositions as 'two contradictory propositions cannot both be true' do not correspond to facts. . . . Thus, the theory I have been examining must hold that 'true' is ambiguous, and that propositions in logic are true in a different sense from other propositions" (Acton 1935, 191).

For two reasons I shall continue, for the most part, to write as though one has no option but to embrace a single theory of truth for all truth bearers, regardless of their subject matter. First, there is the purely practical consideration that the book would become too long were I to evaluate each theory of truth separately for each of the many topics humans think and talk about. Second, when a philosopher endorses a given theory of truth T for one particular subject matter, the reasons he offers for this endorsement are usually just variations of the reasons *other* philosophers have for endorsing T with respect to *all* subject matter. An example will illustrate. We saw in the last section that fear of skepticism is often the motivation for endorsing a Nonrealist theory of truth. The same point applies to those who advocate Nonrealism only for statements about this or that subject. Many who are unconvinced by skeptical arguments concerning our (lack of) justification for everyday descriptive beliefs *are* nevertheless convinced that, on a Realist theory of truth, none of our *moral* beliefs would be justified as any more likely true than their denials. Still others are skeptical only about *mathematical* statements. Very often, then, such philosophers embrace a Nonrealist theory of truth for, as the case may be, moral or mathematical statements, while remaining Realists about all others. The arguments for and against such local Nonrealist theories would precisely parallel the pro and con arguments about global Nonrealism and thus need not be explicitly repeated.

Although I shall rarely do so explicitly, readers will nevertheless find it instructive to stop now and then to consider whether a theory under discussion might be defensible for beliefs (or statements, etc.) about a some particular subject matter, even if it is not *universally* so.

It is also possible to hold that beliefs or statements within a particular subject matter, say moral beliefs or statements, simply have no truth value. The term 'antirealism' is often used to label such views, as in 'so and so is an antirealist about moral statements', but this is doubly misleading. On the one hand, such "anti-"realists do not necessarily reject Realist theories of truth for the subject matter in question. Quite the contrary, they usually endorse global Realism about truth. What they reject for the statements of a particular class is the principle of bivalence, which holds that no statement can be neither true nor false. But one can reject this principle and still embrace a Realist theory of truth. One could hold, for example, that a necessary and sufficient condition for a statement's being true is that it correspond to a state of affairs that obtains independently of mind, and a necessary and sufficient condition for a statement's being false is that it correspond to a state of affairs that does not obtain independently of mind.

Such a theory is compatible with the claim that statements of a particular class do not correspond to *any* state of affairs and thus fail to be either true or false. (See the last paragraph of section 5.8.) For example, many "anti-" realists about moral statements hold that moral discourse is not fact-stating discourse at all; rather, moral statements are expressions (not descriptions) of the speaker's emotions and hence do not correspond in the intended sense to any state of affairs. (See the next chapter for more on correspondence relations.) But such emotivists, as they are called, are *not* rejecting Realism as the definition of truth; they simply think that the definition is never instantiated by any moral statements. A second reason that the term 'antirealist' is misleading is that it is often used generically to refer to both those who deny that the statements in a particular class have any truth value and also to local Nonrealists.

For a longer and helpful discussion of the issues of this section, see Vision 1988, 1–24.

3.9   Chapter Summary

In this chapter I have described the difference between Realist and Nonrealist answers to the metaphysical project. The former all hold that one among the individually necessary and jointly sufficient conditions for the truth of a sentence is that the very fact expressed by the sentence must obtain in a world independent of mind. Nonrealist theories do not require such a condition, and *that*, as it turns out, is their chief potential weakness. It is nearly impossible, given a Nonrealist theory of truth, to provide a genuine rebuttal to skepticism unless the theory is married to a rejection of realist ontology and that rejection is persuasively defended. Moreover, it seems that a *pure* Nonrealist theory cannot really distinguish the set of true propositions or beliefs from any other random set of propositions.

The three Nonrealist theories described here each suffer from additional, more specific problems. The internal intelligibility of Peirce's theory is shaky at best. James's theory seems most viable when treated not as a theory of truth at all but as a theory about what makes a belief valuable (although that would not be a historically accurate *interpretation* of James). Blanshard does not succeed in answering some of the classic objections to the coherence theory, such as that it is circular, since it uses the concepts of consistency and entailment and these are defined in terms of truth.

4 The Correspondence Theory

4.1 Two Kinds of Correspondence

We come now to that most venerable of all kinds of theories of truth: correspondence theories, of which there are two types: correspondence as correlation and correspondence as congruence. The first of these, put very simply, says that every truth bearer is correlated to a state of affairs. If the state of affairs to which a given truth bearer is correlated actually obtains, then the truth bearer is true; otherwise it is false. What the correspondence-as-correlation theory does *not* claim is that the truth bearer mirrors, pictures, or is in any sense structurally isomorphic with the state of affairs to which it is correlated. A truth bearer *as a whole* is correlated to a state of affairs *as a whole*. On the other hand, correspondence as congruence *does* claim that there is a structural isomorphism between truth bearers and the facts to which they correspond when the truth bearer is true. Like the two halves of a torn piece of paper, the parts of the truth bearer fit with the parts of the fact (Pitcher 1964, editor's introduction, 10). Indeed, it is precisely because of this isomorphism, say the defenders of correspondence as congruence, that the fact and the truth bearer can be said to correspond with each other. The structure of beliefs (propositions, sentences, or whatever is taken to be the truth bearer) mirrors or pictures the structure of facts much in the way in which a map mirrors the structure of that portion of the world of which it is a map. Defenders of correspondence as correlation, however, deny that there is anything natural about the correlation between beliefs (or whatever) and facts. The correlation is a result of linguistic conventions, which are themselves the result of the historical development of the language. It just happened that 'Tahiti is a paradise' is the string of letters and spaces we use to assert the fact that Tahiti is a paradise. In another language, or in English if it had had a different history, a different string would express the same fact. And that different string of letters and spaces may have more or fewer parts than does the English sentence 'Tahiti is a paradise'.

Aristotle offered the first correspondence-as-correlation theory with his famous remark 'To say that [either] that which is is *not* or that which is not *is*, is a falsehood; and to say that that which is is and that which is not is not, is true' (*Metaphysics* 1011b26). And Plato may have been suggesting a correspondence-as-congruence theory at *Sophist* 262E–263D, which is too long to quote here. I shall jump ahead to more modern formulations of the theories.

4.2 Bertrand Russell's Theory of Correspondence as Congruence

Let us examine first the correspondence as congruence theory of Bertrand Russell.[1] A belief, says Russell, is a relationship between four different things. First is the *subject*, the person who has the belief. Second and third are two *object terms*. One of these is roughly analogous to the subject of a sentence; it is the thing thought by the believer to be doing something to something else. The other object term is roughly analogous to the object of a sentence; it is the thing thought to be having something done to it. Fourth is the *object relation*, which is roughly analogous to the verb of a sentence. It is the relation that holds between the two object terms. So Othello's belief that Desdemona loves Cassio is a complex relation between Othello, the subject; Desdemona, an object term; Cassio, another object term; and loving, the object relation (Russell 1912, 124–125, 129).

The complex relation of belief also has what Russell calls *direction*, which is why Othello's belief that Desdemona loves Cassio is different from his belief that Cassio loves Desdemona, although both beliefs have the same four terms. In the former belief the direction is from Othello to Desdemona to loving to Cassio, in the latter it is from Othello to Cassio to loving to Desdemona (pp. 126–127).

So what makes a belief true?

> When a belief is true, there is another complex unity, in which the relation which was one of the objects of the belief relates the other objects. ... On the other hand, when a belief is *false*, there is no such complex unity composed only of the objects of the belief. ... Thus a belief is *true* when it *corresponds* to a certain associated complex, and *false* when it does not. ...
> This complex unity is called the *fact corresponding to the belief.* (Pp. 128–129)

Russell is saying that truth involves a congruence between two complex relations. The first is the four-term relation of belief holding between Othello, Desdemona, Cassio, and loving. The second is a three-term relation called "a fact" involving only Desdemona, Cassio, and loving. If there is such a three-term relation and its direction is the same as the four-term relation of Othello's belief, then his belief is true. If there is no three-term relation with the same terms and direction, then the belief is false. In other words, if in the extra mental world Desdemona really does love Cassio, then Othello's belief that she does is true.

A diagram may help to clarify things here. On the left of figure 4.1 is Othello's belief that Desdemona loves Cassio with its four terms. The vertical arrow symbolizes its direction. On the right is the fact that Desdemona loves Cassio with its three terms and a vertical arrow showing its direction. (The large equal signs indicate identity.) The two relations (the belief and the fact) can be said to fit because each of the two object terms, Desdemona and Cassio, appear in *both* relations, and the object relation, loving, appears in both, *and* the belief and the fact have the same direction. If any of these conditions were not met, the belief and the fact would fail to fit, and the belief would be false. Thus the belief would be false if the direction of the fact were different (if Cassio loved Desdemona) or if one of the object terms were different (if Desdemona loved Ralph) or if the object relation were different (if Desdemona hated Cassio).

Formulating Russell's theory requires the use of some new symbols. The first of these is the existential quantifier, '($\exists$)'. The meaning of this symbol was discussed in section 2.1. Another new symbol is the identity symbol, '$=$', which can be variously translated as 'is identical to', 'is the same thing as', or simply 'is'. Also, we need variables 'x' and 'y' to range over

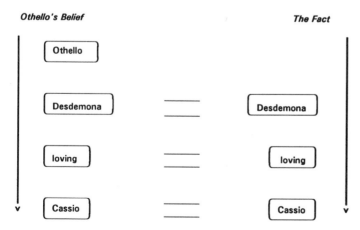

Figure 4.1
Russell's theory of true belief

object terms and a variable. '*R*' to range over what Russell calls 'object relations.' The '*b*', as always, ranges over beliefs, while '*B*' ranges over believers (what Russell calls 'subjects'). To assert the direction of a fact requires no special symbols, since logic has a word-order syntax, just as English does. To assert that object o_1 bears a certain relation F to object o_2, we simply write '$o_1 F o_2$', and this says something different from '$o_2 F o_1$'. Thus the order of the symbols used to express a fact effectively conveys the direction of the fact asserted. How, then, do we name a belief so as to convey the proper order of its object terms and relation term? Since the belief, for Russell, is a relation that includes the believer himself (the subject term), the name of a belief will have to include a symbol that names the person who has the belief as well as symbols naming the object terms and the object relation. So if '*J*' is the name of a believer and he has a belief about o_1, o_2, and F, then the name of this belief will include the symbols '*J*', 'o_1', 'o_2', and '*F*'. But those symbols cannot come in just any order. Each belief has direction, so the name of a belief will have to express its direction in some way. The standard way to do this is to use sequence brackets '⟨' and '⟩'. So '⟨J, o_1, F, o_2⟩' names J's belief that o_1 bears relation F to o_2. The significance of the sequence brackets is that they convey the idea that the order of the items that appear between them must be exactly what it is. Reversing the placement of o_1 and o_2 would create a name of a *different* belief. But again, we do not need to explicitly express the direction of the corresponding fact, because this is implied by the syntax of the formal assertion.

These tools enable us to put Russell's theory, interpreted as an answer to the essence project, into the following formula:[2]

$$(b)[b \text{ is true} \Leftrightarrow (\exists B)(\exists x)(\exists y)(\exists R)(b = \langle B, x, R, y \rangle \ \& \ xRy)]$$

Translated into something more or less resembling English, this formula says, 'For any belief b, b is true if and only if there is a believer B, objects x and y, and a relation R such that b is B's belief that x bears relation R to y, and x *does* bear relation R to y.' A relatively more natural rendering would read, 'Any belief is true if and only if the belief holds that an object x bears a certain relation to another object y, *and x really does* bear that relation to y.'[3]

One problem with Russell's analysis is that if we take him at his word, then it is the real Desdemona and the real Cassio, *not* Othello's idea of them, that are terms in the complex relation of Othello's belief. But what if there is no such person as Cassio and Othello only thinks there is? At first glance it would seem that this entails merely that Othello's belief is false, for if there is no Cassio, it certainly cannot be a fact that Desdemona loves Cassio. But if the belief that Desdemona loves Cassio includes the real Cassio as one of its terms, then if there is no Cassio, there could be no such belief. So it is not that Othello's belief is false, it is that, on Russell's analysis of belief, Othello cannot have such a belief. (Compare Horwich 1990, 113.) But obviously he can. For he could mistakenly believe that there is such a person as Cassio and that Desdemona loves that person. So Russell's analysis allows that one can have false beliefs, but only in the sense that the objects of the belief are not related in the way one thinks they are. On Russell's analysis, one *cannot* have a false belief in the sense that one or more of the objects one thinks to be related simply do not exist. For if it does not exist, one cannot have the belief at all. And there is something terribly wrong in this. Children *do* believe that Santa Claus has a white beard. The fact that there is no Santa Claus does not prevent them from having this belief. Hence, it seems that if belief is a relation, it cannot be a relation between really extant objects. There must be room for *ideas* of nonexistent objects to be terms in the relation. Russell might try to deal with this problem by invoking his theory of descriptions, according to which sentences with nonreferring terms, e.g., 'Santa Claus', are really abbreviations of sentences that contain no such terms. On this theory, 'Santa Claus has a white beard' is just a paraphrase for the existential generalization 'There is something that has the property of being Santa Claus and that has a white beard.' The latter sentence, and thus the former too, is false because nothing has the property of being Santa Claus. But there are some difficulties Russell would have to overcome to make good on this strategy. First, whatever the merits of his theory of descriptions for *sentences*, it is not clear that it would be applicable to beliefs. Could the mental state (or brain state, if you prefer) of believing that Santa Claus has a white beard really be *identical* to the state of believing that there is something that has the property of being Santa Claus and that has a white beard? Second, on Russell's analysis, 'Santa Claus has a white beard' comes out false, but intuitively, it seems to be *true*.[4]

But abandoning Russell's analysis of belief would not require us to abandon the whole of his theory of truth. It simply would requires us to cut out of the formula those elements necessary only to his theory of what a belief is.[5] What is left behind is his theory of truth per se. The latter contains two conditions for truth. One of these asserts that a certain fact exists, the other connects the belief with this fact:

(b){b is true ⇔ (∃x)(∃y)(∃R)[(b is the belief that xRy) & xRy]}

In quasi English this says, 'For any belief, the belief is true if and only if there are some object x, some object y, and some relation R, such that the belief is the belief that x has relation R to y, and x *does* have relation R to y.' The fact xRy is a mind-independent fact in Russell's view (1912, 129–130), and thus his is a Realist theory of truth.

4.3   J. L. Austin's Theory of Correspondence as Correlation

J. L. Austin suggests that truth is *not* a matter of the congruence between a truth bearer and a fact: "There is no need whatsoever for the words used in making a true statement to 'mirror' in any way, however indirect, any feature whatsoever of the situation or event" (1950, 125). The correspondence between the truth bearer and the world is "*absolutely and purely conventional*" (p. 124). It is true, he concedes, that certain expressions in a well-developed language may mirror the features of the world. But the advantages of such mirroring are purely matters of linguistic efficiency. They make the language more adaptable and learnable. But they do not make its expressions any more capable of being true. A correspondence as congruence theory cannot account, Austin insists, for the fact that in rudimentary languages that use a single word to assert that a situation is the case, these single word statements can have truth values despite the fact that, owing to their simple structure, they are not isomorphic to the situations they assert (p. 125). The Latin 'Sum' is one such one-word sentence.[6]

Michael Pendlebury points up another problem for the theory of correspondence as congruence, even as applied to simple subject-predicate sentences. Such a theory seems committed to the view that every predicate, even a vague predicate like 'is bald', stands for a property. Either an individual has a property or it does not, so 'John is bald' would have to be either determinately true or determinately false. But arguably at least, sentences with vague predicates are neither, because baldness is a matter of degree (Pendlebury 1986, 187).

As an alternative to the correspondence-as-congruence theory, Austin proposes that truth involves a single four-term relation between statements, sentences, states of affairs, and types of states of affairs. A statement, for Austin, is the assertion made by, or information conveyed by, a declarative sentence. A sentence is the medium in which a statement is made, much as a block of marble is the medium for a statue.

The meaning of declarative statements is, according to Austin, a matter of two kinds of conventions that have evolved in our language. First, there are descriptive conventions correlating *sentences* with types of states of affairs. Second, there are demonstrative conventions correlating *statements* to historic (read 'particular') states of affairs. So "a statement is said to be true when the historic state of affairs to which it is correlated by the demonstrative conventions (the one to which it 'refers') is of a type which the sentence used in making it is correlated by the descriptive conventions" (Austin 1950, 121–122). A statement is false when it misdescribes the particular state of affairs to which it is correlated by demonstrative conventions. That is, a statement is false if and only if the sentence used to make the statement describes a type of state of affairs that is not the type to which the indicated particular state of affairs belongs (p. 129 n. 1). Figure 4.2 depicts the four-cornered relation present when a statement is true.

Take, for example, the sentence 'The cat is on the mat.' This sentence describes a certain type of situation; namely, those situations in which a cat is on a mat. If I use this sentence to make the statement that the cat is on the mat, then the statement is correlated by demonstrative conventions to a particular state of affairs. Which state of affairs? One is tempted to say the state of affairs of the cat's being on the mat. But it cannot be as simple

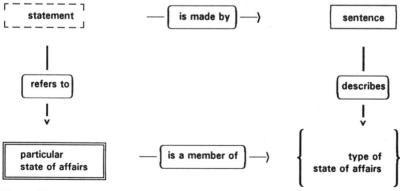

Figure 4.2
Austin's theory of true statement

as this. If we identify the state of affairs referred to by a statement by looking to see what *type* of state of affairs is described by the sentence used to make the statement, then we shall end up concluding that *all* statements are true. But some statements are false. I could have made the statement that the cat is not on the mat. The sentence used in making this statement describes the type of situation in which there are no cats on the mat. One of these two statements has got to be false. There must be some sense in which both of these statements can refer to the same particular state of affairs, one correctly describing it, the other incorrectly describing it. So we cannot indiscriminately use the very words of these sentences to identify the one state of affairs to which they both refer. Presumably, the state of affairs referred to in any ordinary context in which one might say 'The cat is on the mat' or 'The cat is not on the mat' is the here and now state of affairs in which speaker and hearer find themselves along with a cat and a nearby mat. So if the present state of affairs in which I am located includes a cat on a mat, my statement is true, for the present state of affairs *is* of just the sort described by my sentence 'The cat is on the mat.'[7]

In his paper Austin is primarily interested in such subsidiary issues as the nature of truth bearers and whether or not truth ascriptions are performative utterances. (The former issue was discussed in sections 2.3 to 2.7, and the latter will be taken up in section 10.1.) But the issue that concerns us here, the character of his truth theory per se, receives surprisingly brief treatment by Austin. As Strawson points out, and as Austin for the most part acknowledges, Austin's theory raises at least as many questions as it answers. Little is said, for example, about how the theory would apply to existential statements and generalizations, which do not *appear*, at least, to make use of demonstrative conventions or to refer to particular states of affairs (Strawson 1950, 36–37, 51). (Note Austin's acknowledgement of the omission at Austin 1950, 123 n. 4.) Austin also leaves rather vague the notion of a *type* of state of affairs (p. 122 n. 2). Most crucially, he gives not a clue as to the nature of the demonstrative and descriptive conventions. Just what are these conventions, and how do they work? After all, the only things that seem to be referred to by the statement that the cat is on the mat are a cat and a mat. Exactly how does a statement, in particular, a statement expressed with a one-word sentence, refer to a state of affairs?

There are two other matters left implicit in Austin's account that I want to bring into relief. Falsity, for Austin, is the failure of the bottommost arrow in figure 4.2 to hold good: the particular state of affairs is not a member of the "right" type of state of affairs. One might wonder, then, about the other arrows in figure 4.2. Can these fail to hold good? Can a statement fail to refer to *any* state of affairs? Can a declarative sentence fail to describe *any* type of state of affairs? Can a statement be made other than in the medium of a sentence? If so, what effect would such failures have on the truth value of the statement? Austin's implicit answer, I think, is that these other relations can never fail. Look again at his definition of truth quoted above. The definition does not so much assert as it *presupposes* that any statement is correlated to a particular state of affairs, that any sentence is correlated to a type of state of affairs, and that if a statement is made at all, it is made with a sentence. In other words, Austin is taking it that a statement, *by definition*, is correlated by demonstrative conventions to some particular state of affairs: anything that is not so correlated just does not count as a statement. Similarly, an utterance does not count as a (declarative) sentence unless it is correlated by descriptive conventions to a type of state of affairs. And statements, by definition, are made with declarative sentences.

The second point I want to clarify concerns the nature of the particular states of affairs to which statements refer. Not all states of affairs are facts (see section 3.1). There are nonactual states of affairs. There is, for example, the state of affairs of a round square being on the mantel. Could a statement be correlated with (refer to) *this* particular state of affairs? If so, then it would seem that the statement made by the sentence 'The round square is on the mantel' could be *true*! After all, the (nonobtaining) state of affairs to which the statement is correlated *is* a member of the type described by the sentence. I think, therefore, that we must take Austin as presupposing that only actual states of affairs can be correlated to statements by the demonstrative conventions. (He may have been trying to express this presupposition by his use of the word 'historic' in the definition of 'true statement'.) Thus a further implicit condition on truth is that the state of affairs be actual, that it obtain in the actual world.

In the formula below I make explicit the conditions on truth that Austin presupposes. With '*s*' as a variable ranging over statements, '*t*' ranging over sentences, '*x*' ranging over states of affairs, and '*r*' ranging over types of states of affairs, Austin's theory is formulated like this:

$(s)[s$ is true $\Leftrightarrow (\exists x)(\exists r)(\exists t)(t$ is used to make $s)$
$\qquad\qquad\qquad$ & $(s$ refers to $x)$ & $(t$ describes $r)$
$\qquad\qquad\qquad$ & $(x$ is of type $r)$ & $(x$ obtains$)]$.

Austin spends much of his paper arguing against those speech-act theories that deny that truth ascriptions say anything about the statements to which they seem to ascribe truth. In particular, he argues against Strawson's illocutionary-act theory, which denies that truth ascriptions *say* anything at all. These issues will have to wait until chapter 10, but note that Austin apparently thought at the time that his arguments against these latter two kinds of theories constituted a kind of negative defense of his own theory. He thought, that is, that these theories were competitors with his. But they are not: his theory of truth (quoted above) is an answer to the metaphysical project (specifically, the essence project, on my interpretation). It tells us what it is for a statement to *be* true. It has nothing to say about the locutionary or illocutionary purposes of truth ascriptions. Taken literally, it gives the essential conditions for when "[a] statement is said to be true." But as we saw in section 1.7, Austin was acutely aware of the fact that sentences sometimes have illocutionary purposes. Austin would be the very last to recklessly assume that the fact that certain conditions must obtain before one can make a certain utterance is a sign that to make the utterance is to *say* that those conditions obtain. Indeed, he would not even have regarded it as a sign that the utterance *says* anything at all. (Certain conditions must hold before one can properly say 'I promise...', but Austin did not regard such utterances as asserting that those conditions obtain.) So his theory of truth as such does not tell us what we are saying or doing when we utter truth ascriptions. To be sure, Austin, as noted, had opinions about these purposes, and he expressed them in his paper (mostly negative opinions about others' theories, as distinct from a detailed positive doctrine of his own). But his *theory* is logically compatible with the very speech-act theories he argues against. Suppose that the necessary and sufficient conditions for a statement's *being* true are just what Austin says they are: the particular state of affairs to which the statement is correlated must be, etc. It does not follow that what we are *saying* when we *say* 'That statement is true' is 'The particular state of affairs to which that statement is correlated must be, etc.' We might be saying something else. There is no contradiction in this set of suppositions. Now Austin, to repeat, may well have had excellent reasons for rejecting the speech-act theories at issue here. The point is that these theories do not contradict his own metaphysical project theory, as he thought they did. Hence, his arguments against them provide no defense of his theory. Here we have another case of a theorist not distinguishing the different kinds of truth projects.[8] (He later came somewhat uncertainly to see the difference. See Austin 1954, 154.)

It is important to keep straight what is and what is not being said in the preceding paragraph. It is not being claimed that everything any speech-act theorist ever said in his or her writings on truth is compatible with everything that Austin said in his work on the same topic. On the contrary, to take just one example, Strawson had views about the nature of facts that are incompatible not only with Austin's view of facts but with Austin's theory of truth as well. What is being claimed is that Austin's theory of truth, of what truth is, is not per se incompatible with a speech-act theory about what we are doing when we make utterances apparently ascribing truth. One cannot derive a contradiction from the conjunction of the two of them.

Austin's theory as so far presented tends to hide an interesting similarity it has to Russell's theory (and to the semantic theory I shall present in section 5.8). What Austin offers is a kind of theory of meaning for statements and a theory of truth for statements combined into one, much as Russell's is a theory of belief and a theory of truth combined into one.[9] Suppose we "squeeze together" all of the conjuncts in the Austin formula having to do with this theory of meaning into a single conjunct declaring that s must mean that x. We thus get

$$(s)\{s \text{ is true} \Leftrightarrow (\exists x)[(s \text{ means that } x) \& (x \text{ obtains})]\}.$$

What is interesting about this is how much it looks like the simplest formulation of Russell's theory at the end of section 4.2 (which itself squeezed out Russell's theory of belief).[10] It has just two conditions for truth. One declaring that a certain fact exists and the other connecting the truth bearer with the fact. The nature of the connection is different in the two cases because the type of truth bearer is different: for Russell it is beliefs; for Austin statements. But the essential pattern is identical. Would Austin want to modify the 'obtains' with 'mind-independently' or 'mind-dependently'? "Neither one" would be his explicit answer, for Austin regarded all ontological disputes as just confusions about language. Indeed, he disdained the very idea of an ontological theory and always insisted that he did not have one of his own. However, the view of reality that he thinks is revealed when the confusions in question are cleared away is the view that the everyone else has always called commonsense realism. Accordingly, it seems that he wants the state of affairs x to obtain independently of mind, and so I classify his theory as a Realist theory of truth.[11]

4.4 Some Technical Problems

Since we are going to see quite a number of truth theories with essentially the same formal structure as we found lurking in both Russell's and Austin's theories, it is in order here to note some interlocking disputes over the proper way to formalize such theories. There are some who would prefer to formalize Austin's theory (the simpler version) with a propositional, or sentential, variable p instead of an object variable x ranging over states of affairs. But since p stands in the place of a sentence, not a name, the 'obtains' should be dropped, for to concatenate a predicate to a sentence is to produce an unintelligible expression. '"It is raining" obtains' is perfectly grammatical, but 'It is raining obtains' is nonsense. Accordingly, this school of thought would formalize Austin thus:

$(s)\{s$ is true $\Leftrightarrow (\exists p)[(s$ means that $p)$ & $p]\}$

So a p all by itself, call it a lonely p, is allowed to be a complete conjunct in the formula. On the other hand, *this* formula is controversial in a number of respects. First and most seriously, it seems at least on the face of it as if the p is being used as two different kinds of variables within the same formula: only a sentence would be an appropriate substitutend for the lonely p, but arguably, at least, the p in the quantifier is senseless unless it ranges over objects of some sort, in which case only *names* would be appropriate substitutends for it. The point can be put like this: If the preceding formula is intelligible, then so too is

$(\exists p)p.$

But it is far from clear what the latter would mean. The strangeness of formulas like the last one lead conservative philosophers of logic to reject the whole idea of quantifying over propositional variables. But antitraditionalists see no mystery here. The last formula means simply that "there are facts" (Prior 1971, 25) or "something or other is the case" (Williams 1976, 49). They defend quantification over propositional variables as a variety of the kind of logic, called second-order logic, that allows for quantification over predicates. For example, the formulas for Russell's theory in section 4.2 are second-order statements because they quantify over the predicate variables R or ϕ. A propositional variable, according to this school of thought, is just a special kind of predicate variable.[12]

Further complexity is added to the controversy by those who would prefer to replace the s with a quoted p as in

$(p)['p'$ is true $\Leftrightarrow ('p'$ means that $p)$ & $p]$

or, more commonly,

$(p)('p'$ is true $\Leftrightarrow p)$.

These have special problems of their own. To mention just one, the usual use of quotation marks is to help form a name for the linguistic entity they enclose. So the left-hand side of the preceding formula seems to be predicating truth of the *letter* 'p'. Finally, some have chosen to do without quantifiers at all and to make do with a certain kind of incomplete sentence called a schema or open sentence. (The concept of an open sentence is explained in section 5.4.)

A further discussion of the various issues arising from the formalization of theories of truth would take a lot of space and would quickly take us very far from the central concerns of this book. So although I discuss some of them in the next chapter and they come up again in section 10.7, I shall otherwise leave them aside. In the remainder of the book I shall use the symbolic idiom favored by the particular philosopher under discussion, and I shall assume that all such formulas are intelligible at least at some level. By following this practice, however, I do not mean to take any stand vis-à-vis the issues noted in this section, nor do I want my readers to make the mistake of thinking that these technical issues are "merely" technical, for all of them connect to significant philosophical issues. If, when discussing a philosopher who did not make use of the symbolic apparati of logic at all, I think it advantageous to provide a formal expression of his or her theory, I shall use the symbolic mode that seems most compatible with the letter and spirit of the theory at hand.[13]

4.5 The Essence of the Correspondence Theory

I have already noted the similarity between Russell's theory of truth when stripped of his theory of belief and Austin's when stripped of his theory of meaning:

(b){b is true $\Leftrightarrow (\exists x)(\exists y)(\exists R)[(b$ is the belief that xRy) & xRy]}

(s){s is true $\Leftrightarrow (\exists x)[(s$ means that x) & (x obtains)]}

Both of these can be thought of as instantiations of different sorts of the following schema:[14]

(t){t is true $\Leftrightarrow (\exists x)[(tRx)$ & (x obtains)]},[15]

where t ranges over some unspecified class of truth bearers and x over states of affairs. 'R' is a placeholder for some relation appropriate for the purpose of correlating bearer and state of affairs. The relation in question varies with the choice of truth bearer. For beliefs, 'R' would be 'is a belief that'. For linguistic entities, like sentences, 'says that' or 'expresses', 'asserts', or 'means that', would be more appropriate choices. If propositions are the bearer in question, then the appropriate relation would depend on how one defines 'proposition'. (The remaining differences between Russell's simplified theory and the schema are attributable to Russell's conviction that the belief must be isomorphic to the corresponding fact.) Although I interpret both Russell and Austin as offering answers to the essence project, there is no reason why one could not offer a correspondence theory as an answer to either the extensional or naturalistic projects; so let me generalize the schema still further by replacing the '$\Leftrightarrow$' with the ambiguous 'iff', thereby producing what I shall call schema (C):

(t){t is true iff $(\exists x)[(tRx)$ & (x obtains)]}   (C)

Although many others besides Russell and Austin have proposed correspondence theories, I think I am relatively safe in concluding that schema (C) captures the essence of the correspondence theory, for Russell's theory is *the* (original modern) correspondence-as-congruence theory of truth, and Austin's theory is *the* (original modern) correspondence-as-correlation theory of truth. If there were a theory traditionally classified as correspondence that did not instantiate schema (C), then precisely because Russell and Austin are paradigmatic, all that would follow is that the theory in question is *not* a correspondence theory after all. The alternative conclusions would be either (1) that Russell's or

Austin's theory is not a correspondence theory, which is as silly as saying that the Wright brothers did not invent the airplane but only something easily confused with an airplane, or (2) that there is not any common denominator for correspondence theories, which would leave the term 'correspondence theory' bereft of any connotation at all.

I do not mean to suggest either that the above simplified versions account for everything Russell and Austin were trying to do, or that the differences between the two are unimportant. But the purpose of this section is to find what common element, if any, transcends the varying philosophical and historical contexts in which these two theories were proposed. Hence, complaints to the effect that the trimmed versions of Russell's and Austin's theories are oversimplified are quite true. And quite irrelevant.

Perhaps it is worth noting that the theories of many other self-avowed correspondence theorists are also instantiations of schema (C). Roderick Chisholm offers this:

T is a sentence token that is true in $L =_{\text{def}} T$ is a sentence token and there is a state of affairs h such that (1) T expresses h in L and (2) h obtains.[16]

(The phrase 'there is' on the right-hand side of the formula is just the existential quantifier, and Chisholm's connector ' = def.' is translated into English with the phrase 'is defined as'. The 'L' is the name of some language.) George Bealer (1982, 204) offers the following:

x is true iff$_{\text{df}}$ x corresponds to a condition that obtains.

('Condition' is Bealer's word for state of affairs.)

4.6 Nonrealist Correspondence Theories

Historically, most correspondence theories, like Russell's and Austin's, have been Realist theories; but contra Vision (1988, 29), Forbes (1986, 37–38), and Davidson (1990, 308), correspondence theories are not intrinsically Realist. Schema (C) commits one only to quasi realism; it requires that a certain state of affairs x obtains, but not that it obtain independently of mind. It is perfectly possible to hold that truth consists in correspondence with facts and to hold also that facts are mind-dependent entities. This is precisely the position taken by the early twentieth century idealist J. M. E. McTaggart, who explicitly embraces a correspondence theory of truth: to be true, a belief must correspond to the facts. But facts are, for McTaggart, ideal entities or, as he puts it, spiritual substance (1921, 10–37). Specifically, his theory is a correspondence-as-correlation theory, since he rejects the idea that the correspondence relation is one of copying (pp. 12–13) and, indeed, insists that the relation is indefinable (p. 11). So for McTaggart, the 'R' in schema (C) is replaceable with an indefinable 'corresponds to'. D. W. Hamlyn also offered a Nonrealist correspondence theory (1970, 140–141), although in 1962 he had rejected the very possibility of such a theory. D. J. O'Connor may also endorse such a theory (1975, 78–88, 128–136), but his thoughts on the point are not entirely clear. Nor are Wilfred Sellars's, who may also have been putting forth such a quasi-realist, but Nonrealist, theory in 1963a. In light of his overall theory, Kant's remarks at 1782, A58, may indicate that he too would endorse such a theory.

4.7 Objections to the Correspondence Theory

Traditionally, the correspondence theory has been described as the claim that truth involves a relation between truth bearers and reality. Thus it has been supposed that there are three kinds of criticisms that can be directed against any particular correspondence theory. First, one can object, about what the theory identifies as the truth bearer (beliefs, propositions, statements, etc.), that such things cannot possibly, for this or that reason, be truth bearers. Second, one may object, about whatever slice of reality (facts, situations, states of affairs, etc.) is identified by the theory as the correspondent of the truth bearer, that such things cannot, for this or that reason, serve as the correspondents. Third, one can object to the alleged relation between truth bearers and reality on the grounds that there is no such relation or that its nature has not been clearly explained by the theory. Issues about truth bearers were discussed in sections 2.3 to 2.7. Here I deal with criticisms of the second and third sorts.

Objections to the correspondence relation
Correspondence theories are often generically summed up with the slogan 'A true statement (belief, or whatever) corresponds with the facts', and this naturally leads us to think that there is some new, special, and previously

unheard of, relation being postulated by correspondence theories. This in turn leads some philosophers to criticize particular correspondence theories as mysterious when they do not find contained therein the sort of extended explication that new and special relations are thought to deserve. But the objection tends to invest the word 'correspondence' with more significance than it really has. 'Correspondence' serves as nothing more than a handy summing up of a theory in which no such special relation makes any appearance. Consider again the quotation from Russell:

> When a belief is true, there is another complex unity, in which the relation which was one of the objects of the belief relates the other objects. . . . On the other hand, when a belief is *false*, there is no such complex unity composed only of the objects of the belief. . . . Thus a belief is *true* when it *corresponds* to a certain associated complex, and *false* when it does not. (1912, 128)

Note that the term 'corresponds' does not appear in the first statement of the theory. It comes a few sentences later, introduced by the word 'Thus', as a sort of *summing up* of the theory. The same can be said of Austin's theory, as he himself says: "I gave (somewhat qualified) support to the common English expression that a true statement is one which 'corresponds with the facts'. I professed not to like this, in its own way doubtless unexceptionable, terminology, and preferred some jargon of my own, in which 'facts' and 'corresponds' do not occur at all. . . . 'Corresponds with the facts' is a mere idiom, as it were a 'fused' idiom, not to be taken at all at its apparent face-value" (1954, 154–155). A. N. Prior has reached a similar conclusion. It is appropriate, he says, to use the word 'correspondence' in describing truth, although the word does not appear in his own definition of truth: "To say that X's belief that p is true is to say that X believes that p and (it is the case that) p. There seems no reason to see any more in 'correspondence with fact' than this" (Prior 1971, 21–22). D. W. Hamlyn makes the same point:

> If one wished to generalize this and say what are the necessary and sufficient conditions of any assertion being judged true, it is difficult to know what else one could say other than that the assertion must correspond to the facts. But nothing turns on the use of the word 'corresponds' here. All that is meant is that wherever there is a true statement there is a fact stated by it and wherever a fact a possible true statement which states it. . . .

Hence, the claim, sometimes heard, that the Correspondence Theory agrees with our ordinary remarks to the effect that something that has been said fits or is in agreement with the facts, is of doubtful relevance. The assertion that a statement is true if and only if it corresponds to the facts is a philosophical assertion of the highest generality.[17]

A correspondence theorist's description of the connection between truth bearers and facts is largely dictated by his choice of truth bearer anyway. If the truth bearer is a linguistic entity like statements or sentences, then the connection will have to be described with a verb like 'means that', 'says that', or 'expresses'. If beliefs are the truth bearers, then the connection is described with 'is the belief that'. These familiar, albeit hard to define, notions are in no way new or special. It is quite possible that two correspondence theorists who are agreed that, say, statements are the bearers of truth may disagree about the proper definition of 'means that', so at some level there is a genuine dispute over of the nature of the connection between truth bearer and fact that cannot be reduced to a dispute about the identity of the truth bearer. But definitions of 'means that' and 'is the belief that' are projects of, respectively, the philosophy of language and the philosophy of mind. So it is at best misleading to treat a dispute at this level as if it were some special problem arising from the postulation of correspondence theories of truth. At worst, it leads observers to think that the very existence of such disputes constitutes an objection to correspondence theories.

Max Black, among others, has made the closely related objection that a theory of truth that uses philosophically loaded concepts (specifically, the concepts expressible with 'expresses', 'says that', or 'means that') to analyze truth is incomplete and unclear because that such concepts are as in need of analysis as truth (1948, 52). But charges of incompleteness are dubious in any philosophical context precisely because it is difficult to imagine any theory against which the same objection could not be made: philosophically important topics tend to link with one another, and it seems unreasonable to think that one cannot solve *any* problem unless one solves *every* problem. In fact, we do know enough about 'says that' to know what a given sentence says and to know which sentences express which facts. Some progress is made by reducing 'truth' to 'saying' or 'expressing'. It is true that philosophy will eventually want an analysis of 'says that', 'believes that', etc., but it does not follow that in the meantime an analysis of truth per se that uses such a concept is incorrect, unclear, or even incomplete. It is not necessary for a theory of truth, *as such*, to provide definitions of these terms. Indeed, it is often misleading to plug such a *definiens* into a theory of truth. The similarity of Russell's and

Austin's theories to each other was hidden until I substituted the simpler 'is the belief that' and 'means that' for, respectively, Russell's theory of belief and Austin's theory of meaning in their theories of truth.

Another venerable objection to the idea that truth can be cashed in terms of a correspondence relation, one most recently voiced by C. J. F. Williams, is that doing so, on any conception of correspondence, prevents one from having an intelligible analysis of *falsehood*: "If truth were a relational property of this sort, to say that something was true would be to say that it stood in a given relation to a given object, and to deny that it was true would be to deny that it stood in that relation to that object" (Williams 1976, 75). The key word here is the next to the last one, 'that'. This word entitles Williams to complain: "If 'Toby sighed' is true it would, on this view, fit, or otherwise be related to, the fact that Toby sighed. But if 'Toby sighed' is false there is no fact for it to fail to fit" (p. 75). It is to be admitted that correspondence theories have occasionally been worded in such a way as to make them subject to this objection. Here is one example: "According to [my correspondence] theory, a true proposition corresponds or agrees with, and a false proposition fails to correspond or disagrees with, *its* fact" (Ratner 1935, 142; emphasis mine). But it is clear from the rest of Ratner's paper that he does not literally mean the absurdity that each false proposition has its own fact (to which it fails to correspond); and the only clear example Williams can cite (p. 75) is a brief passage from Russell 1924, a work that is not, as a whole, about truth. At any rate, a correspondence theory has available to it a perfectly sensible and natural analysis of falsehood. Consider again the simplest formulation of Russell's theory:

$(b)\{b$ is true $\Leftrightarrow (\exists x)(\exists y)(\exists R)[(b$ is the belief that $xRy)$ and $xRy]\}$

The formula naturally suggests that a Russellian explication of falsehood would be:

$(b)\{b$ is false $\Leftrightarrow$ is not the case that
$(\exists x)(\exists y)(\exists R)[(b$ is the belief that $xRy)$ and $xRy]\}.$

That is, if truth is analyzed with an existential claim, then falsehood ought to be analyzed with the negation of that same existential claim, and this is precisely what we find in the quotation from Russell: falsehood is explicated with the denial of the same existential claim used to explicate truth. Note in the second sentence the phrase 'there is no such ...'.

When a belief is true, there is another complex unity, in which the relation which was one of the objects of the belief relates the other objects. ... On the other hand, when a belief is *false*, there is no such complex unity composed only of the objects of the belief. ... Thus a belief is *true* when it *corresponds* to a certain associated complex, and *false* when it does not. (Russell 1912, 128–129)

Russell does not say that a belief is false when a specified fact exists and the belief fails to correspond to just *that* fact. Rather, he says that a belief is false when it fails to correspond to any actual fact; that is, when *there is no fact* to which it corresponds. There is thus no shortage of facts for 'Toby sighed' to fail to fit when it is false. It fails to fit any of them. (Compare Prior 1971, 21, 98–99.)

Objections to facts

Strawson (1950) and most recently Davidson (1990, 302–305) and many others in between have rejected the very notion of a *fact* as some nonlinguistic entity existing in the world.[18] Facts, they say, are not really anything different from true sentences. To think otherwise is just a muddle based on the assumption that every linguistic entity, of whatever size and type, must name something. Once this assumption is made, the objectors explain, we are forced to postulate facts to be the things named by true sentences. The evidence for the claim that 'fact' is just another name for 'true sentence' is supposed to be this: we cannot individuate and identify any particular fact save by using the very same words that we use to individuate and identify its corresponding sentence.

There are, however, good reasons for resisting this line of thought: (1) Facts can enter into causal relations in a way that true sentences cannot. There is a sense of 'cause' in which the fact that the memo was derogatory caused Ralph to lose his job, but in that same sense of 'cause' the true sentence 'The memo was derogatory' cannot cause Ralph to lose his job. (2) One of the constituents of the fact that the memo was derogatory is a certain memo, but no memo (distinct from the *word* 'memo') can be a constituent of the true sentence 'The memo was derogatory.' (3) It should be no surprise that we cannot specify a given fact save by means of the sentence to which the fact corresponds, because it could not possibly be otherwise. Suppose our language contained a series of nouns ('fact$_1$', 'fact$_2$', etc.) each referring uniquely to a different fact. We could then use these nouns to identify particular facts, *but we could also use these terms to make statements*, even if they were not intended for that purpose when coined. 'Fact$_1$' would be a one-word sentence as well as a noun, whether we liked it or not. *Any* expression that could be used to identify facts *could* be used to make statements.

On the other hand, some who would accept the existence of atomic facts would still object to the correspondence theory of truth on the grounds that while there are many true beliefs (statements, or whatever) that are disjunctive, conditional, or negative, there is no such thing as a disjunctive, conditional, or negative fact.[19] But this view is unconvincing for two reasons. First, it is not at all clear why there cannot be facts of these sorts. Perhaps on some technical, philosophical sense of 'fact' there are none, but then so much the worse for the technical sense of 'fact'. Surely it is not incorrect English (contra Acton 1935, 189) for an ordinary person to say, 'It is a fact that either the train gets here on time or I shall be late' or 'It is a fact that if the price of corn does not rise, then I shall go broke' or 'It is a fact that I'm not going to make it.' (Compare Srzednicki 1966, 391–392.) Second, even if there are no facts of these sorts, this would be of relevance only to correspondence-as-congruence theories. On a correspondence-as-correlation theory, the fact referred to by a true disjunctive statement need not itself be a "disjunctive entity," whatever that could be.

There is another way for a defender of a correspondence theory to avoid, if he desires, commitment to conditional, negative, or disjunctive facts. It would simply require modifying the correspondence theory in question so as to provide a *recursive* analysis of the truth of nonatomic sentence tokens. I describe this technique in section 5.3. In sum, then, not all correspondence theories commit one to the existence nonatomic facts, and anyway, there is no reason to doubt the existence of nonatomic facts in one perfectly ordinary sense of 'fact'.

4.8   Chapter Summary

We are not yet finished with the survey of Realist answers to the metaphysical project, but let us pause here to see where we have been. One of the traditional terms under which theories of truth have been cataloged is 'the correspondence theory'. It appears that all correspondence theories have in common the claim that one of the individually necessary and jointly sufficient conditions for the truth of a belief (proposition, or whatever) is that the very fact that the belief is a belief in (or the very fact that the proposition expresses) must obtain. But a correspondence theory need not require that the fact exist independently of mind. Thus a correspondence theory can be Nonrealist. Two correspondence theories that are Realist, however, are Russell's and Austin's. The similarities between them are hidden at first, because Russell embeds a theory of belief in his theory of truth and Austin embeds a theory of meaning in his theory of truth. When these extraneous matters are removed, it is clear that both theories hold that there are two jointly necessary and sufficient conditions for truth. First, a fact (or state of affairs) must exist independently of mind. Second, the truth bearer must be connected to the fact. (How it is connected depends on what is chosen as the truth bearer.)

After noting some of the technical issues relevant to the expression of theories of truth, we examined some of the most common objections to correspondence theories, and none were found to be particularly telling.

5 Alfred Tarski's Semantic Theory

5.1 Tarski's Goals

Alfred Tarski, 1902-1983, one of the great logician-mathematicians of this century, was writing mathematical papers of great importance before his twenty-second birthday, and by his twenty-eighth he had invented the first formal semantics for quantified predicate logic, the logic of all reasoning about mathematics.[1] The heart of this great accomplishment is his theory of truth. It has been called the semantic theory of truth, but Tarski himself never uses this label, preferring instead 'semantic *conception* of truth', which he believes is the conception of truth that is the essence of the correspondence theory (Tarski 1933, 153; Tarski 1969, 63). So in his own eyes, he is a correspondence theorist. I shall discuss in section 5.8 whether Tarski is right in thinking that his is a correspondence theory. In the meantime I shall follow conventional practice and call it a semantic theory of truth.

He calls truth a *semantic* concept because it can be defined in terms of other semantic concepts, especially, the concept of *satisfaction* (about which more below). Semantic concepts, like satisfaction, definition, and designation, deal with the relations between expressions and objects (Tarski 1944, 17). Indeed, one of Tarski's principal goals in analyzing truth was to secure the foundations for what he called "scientific semantics."[2] He wanted, in other words, to establish the study of semantics as a scientifically respectable discipline (Tarski 1944, 36). To accomplish this, he needed, or at least thought he needed, to provide a guarantee that the discipline of semantics does not presuppose the existence of any abstract entities whose existence is not already presupposed by physical science. The Logical Positivist school of philosophy, which was in its heyday at the time (the late 1920s), disparaged most abstract entities as at best useless postulations or as at worst mysterious and "metaphysical" objects, belief in which is hardly more intellectually respectable than belief in ghosts and goblins. Under the influence of this school, Tarski embraced the doctrine of physicalism (1944, sect. 21, passim; 1936, 406). Physicalism can be defined in a rough way as the belief that all intellectually respectable concepts can be defined ultimately and entirely in terms of the concepts of logic, mathematics, and physical science. (I give a more detailed explication of physicalism in sections 6.6 to 6.8.) Thus, to ensure that semantics conforms to the dictates of physicalism, Tarski needed to reduce all semantic concepts to physical and/or logicomathematical concepts. His strategy was to define all semantic concepts, save satisfaction, in terms of truth. Truth itself is then defined in terms of satisfaction, and finally, satisfaction is defined in terms of physical and logicomathematical concepts alone (Tarski 1933, 153, 194). (I explain the concept of satisfaction in section 5.4.) This strategy, if successful, also ensures that two of Tarski's other goals are met. No semantic term need be taken as primitive (i.e., undefined), and semantic terms do not have to be defined circularly in terms of one another.

Tarski also wanted his theory of truth to show how the grammatical structure of a sentence affects its truth value. Readers familiar with propositional logic will realize that the truth tables are a kind of (incomplete) graphic definition of truth that accomplishes just this task for the compound sentences of that logic.[3] Before Tarski, no one had done this effectively for quantified predicate logic, so he set it as one of his goals. This logical program is nowadays often called model theory, so we may say that Tarski's second program, besides physicalism, was to create a model theory for quantified predicate logic.

In section 2.1 we saw one broader philosophical program in service to which an answer to the metaphysical project can be put. It was the epistemological program of evaluating competing theories of justification. Now we are introduced to two other philosophical programs in service to which Tarski wants to use an answer to the metaphysical project (specifically, as I interpret him, the extensional project): physicalism and model theory. Each of these programs puts special criteria of adequacy on answers to the extensional project above and beyond the general demand that any answer to that project accurately describe the extension of 'is true'. The epistemological program, as we saw, requires that we treat beliefs as truth bearers (although not necessarily as the only kind of truth bearer). As we shall see shortly, the physicalist program effectively requires that a theory of truth make a detour, so to speak, through the concept of satisfaction, and the model theory program effectively requires the use of a technique of definition called recursion (described in section 5.3). Accordingly, what counts as the "correct" answer to the extensional project will depend on the philosophical context. A theory that serves perfectly well for one program may fail to meet the special adequacy criteria of another. The point to be kept in mind is that it is not necessary that any one answer to the extensional project be useful for all of these programs. In principle, there would be no cause for objection if Tarski had created two different extensional definitions of truth, one each for his two broader programs. Presumably, he would want these two definitions to be consistent with each other, but since both theories would be extensional, consistency would only require that what appears on the right-hand side of the ' ≡ ' symbol in one of the definitions be extensionally equivalent to what appears on the right-hand side of the ' ≡ ' in the other. In technical lingo, the *definiens* (literally, the "defining part," the part on the right-hand side of the ' ≡ ' symbol) of one of the two definitions must be extensionally equivalent to the *definiens* of the other.

Tarski had at least two other goals for his theory. First, he wanted it to be immune from refutation by the Liar Paradox. This paradox and Tarski's method of avoiding it are discussed in sections 9.1 and 9.3. Those details of his theory relevant primarily to his solution of the paradox will not be mentioned in this chapter. Second, Tarski wanted a theory that would meet what he called the material adequacy condition. I shall have much to say about this condition later in this chapter and in section 6.1, but a brief characterization is possible here. The condition asserts simply that any good theory of truth has to *entail* all sentences on the pattern of the following:

'The wall is red' is true ≡ the wall is red

'Snow is slippery' is true ≡ snow is slippery

'Bob ran around the track' is true ≡ Bob ran around the track

'Grass is red' is true ≡ grass is red

For every sentence of the language for which truth is being explicated, there is an equivalence in which the sentence is mentioned on the left side and used on the right side. It is easy enough to formulate the pattern of all these equivalences, and Tarski does so with a formula that has variously been called "form T," "schema T," and "convention T":

X is true if, and only if, p.

We shall call any such equivalence (with 'p' replaced by any sentence of the language to which the word "*true*" refers, and 'X' replaced by a name of this sentence) an "*equivalence of the form (T)*."[4]

It is not hard to see why Tarski thought a minimal condition on any adequate theory of truth is that it entail all T-sentences (i.e. sentences that instantiate convention T): the T-sentences are obviously true (if we keep in mind that the equivalence asserted by a T-sentence is extensional not intensional), so any theory that is incompatible with them would be false. (In this regard, notice that one can accept the T-sentences but insist that the sentence on the right-hand side of the ' $\equiv$ ' expresses a mind-*de*pendent state of affairs.) But a theory of truth can be mighty implausible and still be compatible with the T-sentences (see section 6.1). This is why Tarski's material adequacy condition (hereafter, MAC) requires that a theory of truth actually *entail* the T-sentences.

One disputed issue in Tarskian exegesis concerns his attitude toward other theories (or, as he would put it, other conceptions) of truth. Some interpreters have attributed to Tarski the very tolerant view that his is only one of many conceptions of truth and that other conceptions (e.g., coherence, pragmatic) are not necessarily wrong, they are just different. Others have thought that Tarski meant to reject other conceptions of truth as just plain wrong. Unfortunately, the textual evidence is ambiguous. He never quite explicitly pronounces on the rightness or wrongness of other theories. There are passages in which he seems to take the tolerant attitude, as he does in the very generous passage in which he allows that if we were ever to coin different names for the concepts defined by the different conceptions, he would not mind if 'true' were given to some other conception and 'frue' were given to his (Tarski 1944, 27–28). And at one time he explicitly denied that he was trying to capture the ordinary meaning of 'true' (Tarski 1933, 153). But he grew bolder later in life and was then prepared to make just this claim and to reject the other theories for failing to capture the ordinary meaning of truth.[5] It is worth noting that besides thinking that the semantic conception is the preferred conception for logic, mathematics, semantics, and physicalism, Tarski also commended his theory to epistemologists (1933, 267). It is hard to see, then, what remaining value he could possibly have seen for other conceptions.

5.2 Tarski's Theory

Tarski says that 'true' expresses a property, or names a class, of sentences, so it is sentences that he regards as truth bearers.[6] What we need is a formula of the form

$(s)(s$ is true $\equiv$ ____$)$,

with 's' ranging over sentences. Let me begin this examination of Tarski's theory by seeing how it would apply to a very simple language with a finite number of sentences. Let us say that the language has only the following five sentences and that it provides no way to produce any new sentences:

The table is round.

The carpet is purple.

John loves Mary.

Bob is a noodle-brained fool.

Napoleon is alive.

So we want a theory that entails all five of the following T-sentences:

'The table is round' is true $\equiv$ the table is round

'The carpet is purple' is true $\equiv$ the carpet is purple

'John loves Mary' is true $\equiv$ John loves Mary

'Bob is a noodle-brained fool' is true $\equiv$ Bob is a noodle-brained fool

'Napoleon is alive' is true $\equiv$ Napoleon is alive

One theory, if we can call it that, that would meet the latter condition is a conjunction of all of the T-sentences. Tarski recognizes this fact in saying that each of these T-sentences is a "partial definition" of truth, and a complete definition would be a "logical conjunction" or "logical product" of all of them (1944, 16; 1933, 187). By 'logical conjunction' Tarski means something logically equivalent to a conjunction of the T-sentences. The following is just such a logical conjunction:

$(s)[s$ is true $\equiv$ either $(s = $ 'The table is round' and the table is round)
　　　　　　　or $(s = $ 'The carpet is purple' and the carpet is purple)
　　　　　　　or $(s = $ 'John loves Mary' and John loves Mary)
　　　　　　　or $(s$ $= $ 'Bob is a noodle-brained fool' and Bob is a
　　　　　　　　　noodle-brained fool)
　　　　　　　or $(s = $ 'Napoleon is alive' and Napoleon is alive)$]$[7]

The preceding extensional analysis of 'is true' is completely satisfactory from Tarski's point of view (on the assumption that such terms as 'fool' and 'alive' can be reduced to physical terms) for the simple language in question. All other semantic terms can now be defined in terms of truth, and there is no need, for this simple language, to make use of the concept of satisfaction at all.

5.3   Recursion

But the definition only works because the language in question has a finite number of sentences. If it had an infinite number, the definition of truth would have to be infinitely long, which is impossible (Tarski 1933, 188). So let us now imagine a language with an infinite number of sentences. It includes all five of the sentences in the last language, but it also has the truth-functional operators 'not', 'and', 'or', and 'if ... then', with which new sentences can be built from old ones. Thus the language includes among its sentences the following:

The table is not round.

If the carpet is purple, then Bob is a noodle-brained fool.

John loves Mary, and Napoleon is alive.

The carpet is purple, or John loves Mary and Napoleon is alive.

John loves Mary; and the carpet is purple, or John loves Mary and Napoleon is alive.

Note that in the last of these sentences 'John loves Mary' appears as a clause more than once, and the operator 'and' appears more than once. There is no limit to how many times a given atomic sentence can appear as a clause in a larger sentence, and there is no limit to how many times a given operator can be applied to build a still bigger sentence. This is why the language contains an infinite number of sentences. Obviously, then, the definition of truth cannot have a separate clause for each sentence in the language.

How, then, do we define truth for such a language? Tarski's answer is that we must make use of a technique called "recursive definition" (1969, 68–69; 1933, 189). The technique is used to create an extensional analysis of terms whose extension (the set of things to which the term applies) is infinite. The set we are interested in is the set of all true sentences of the language, but let us first practice the recursive technique on the terms 'train segment' and 'train'. I begin with the following recursive definition of a train segment:

$(g)(g$ is a train segment $\equiv g$ is an engine, or g is a dining car,
or g is a freight car, or g is a sleeping car,
or g is a sitting car,
or a and b are train segments
and g is a coupled to $b)$

The first thing to notice about this definition is that it is disjunctive. This is because train segments come in different lengths and are made up of different kinds of railroad cars. But notice that we do not have to have a separate disjunct in the definition for every train segment there ever was or will be. Instead, we have one disjunct for each of the most basic kinds of train segments, those that are only one car long. If there were only one kind of railroad car, we would need only one basis clause reading 'g is a railroad car'. But since there are different kinds of one-car train segments, we need a separate disjunct for each. The last clause in the definition simply says that any coupling of train segments is itself a train segment. So if a is a sleeping car and b is a dining car, then a coupled to b is a train segment. And if c is a freight car, then c coupled to the ab segment is a three-car train segment. If de is a two-car segment, then de coupled to abc is a five-car segment. Thus the last clause of the definition gathers into the set of train segments *all* segments other than the five types of basic segments. The definition also ensures that only a segment of one or more railroad cars will count as a train segment. We are assured of this because the ' $\equiv$ ' is translated 'if *and only if* '. Another point to make about the definition is that the term being defined, 'train segment', *recurs* (i.e., reappears) in the last clause of the definition. The definition is not viciously circular, however, because the earlier clauses cash out the reference to train segments in the last clause. By this I mean that one could successfully use the definition to determine, for any object in the world, whether or not that object is a train segment. If the object does not consist of parts coupled together, then one simply checks to see whether it is one or another of the five kinds of railroad cars. If it is, the object is a train segment; if not, not. Suppose the object does consist of two or more parts coupled together. Then one must mentally divide it into two sections along one of the couplings. Next one must examine each of the sections following the same recipe. If one of the sections turns out to consist of two or more parts coupled together, then one must mentally divide it into two subsections. No matter how many elemental parts the object originally has, one would eventually examine each elemental part to determine whether or not it is a railroad car. If all the elemental parts are railroad cars, the object is a train segment. If any of them are not, the object is not a train segment.[8]

Now let us define 'train' recursively. We start with

$(t)(t$ is a train $\equiv$ ____$)$.

The hard part is filling in the blank. The first clause must define the most basic type of train, which is simply an engine by itself. Thus

$(t)(t$ is a train $\equiv t$ is an engine, or ____$)$.

All other trains can be built up by coupling train segments to the back of engines or other trains. Thus we need only one more clause in our definition.

$(t)(t$ is a train $\equiv t$ is an engine,
        or a is a train segment and b is a train
        and t is a coupled to the back of $b)$

Notice again the characteristic features of a recursive definition: one or more clauses noncircularly defining the most basic members of the set being defined, followed by one or more recursive clauses defining how other members of the set are built out of the more basic members. In both of the examples, there was only one recursive clause. This is not always the case. If there is more than one way to build up nonbasic members, there will have to be a separate recursive clause for each method. Consider the following definition, with its three recursive clauses:

$(x)(x$ is in John Doe's family $\equiv x$ is John Doe,
        or a is in Doe's family
        and x is married to a
        or a is in Doe's family
        and x is born to a
        or a is in Doe's family
        and x is adopted by $a)$.

The recursive method works so long as there are only a finite number of types of basic members of the set in question and there are only a finite number of ways in which nonbasic members can be built up or added.

Before going further, the reader is encouraged to test her or his understanding of recursive technique by defining the set of tree branches. Hint: basic branches grow directly out of a tree trunk, while other branches grow out of branches.

To return to the problem of defining truth for a language with an infinite number of sentences, I note first that there are five atomic sentences and four ways to build compound sentences from them: negation, disjunction, conjunction, and conditionalization. Recall that 'not p' is true whenever it is false that p, that 'p or q' is true if either it is true that p or it is true that q, that 'p and q' is true when both it is true that p and it is true that q, and that 'if p, then q' is true when either it is false that p or it is true that q.[9] Accordingly, the recursive definition of truth is the following:

$(s)[s$ is true $\equiv$ either $(s =$ 'The table is round'
　　　　　　　and the table is round)
　　　　　or $(s =$ 'The carpet is purple'
　　　　　　　and the carpet is purple)
　　　　　or $(s =$ 'John loves Mary'
　　　　　　　and John loves Mary)
　　　　　or $(s =$ 'Bob is a noodle-brained fool'
　　　　　　　and Bob is a noodle-brained fool)
　　　　　or $(s =$ 'Napoleon is alive'
　　　　　　　and Napoleon is alive)
　　　　　or $(s =$ 'not p'
　　　　　　　and it is not true that p)
　　　　　or $(s =$ 'p or q'
　　　　　　　and either it is true that p or it is true that q)
　　　　　or $(s =$ 'p and q'
　　　　　　　and it is true that p and it is true that q)
　　　　　or $(s =$ 'if p, then q'
　　　　　　　and either it is not true that p or it is true that q)]$

This definition also meets the material adequacy condition, because it entails all the T-sentences for the language. Consider, for example, the sentence

(1) 'Bob loves Mary, or the table is round and the carpet is purple.'

The definition tells us that this sentence is true if and only if either

(2) 'Bob loves Mary' is true,

or

(3) 'The table is round and the carpet is purple' is true.

The definition further tells us that (2) is true if and only if Bob loves Mary and that (3) is true if and only if

(4) 'The table is round' is true,

and

(5) 'The carpet is purple' is true.

But (4) is true if and only if the table is round, and (5) is true if and only if the carpet is purple. So

'Bob loves Mary, or the table is round and the carpet is purple' is true
  $\equiv$ Bob loves Mary, or the table is round and the carpet is purple.

This, of course, is one of the T-sentences.

5.4   Satisfaction

But Tarski wants to define truth for languages even more complex than the last one. Specifically, he wants a truth definition for the language of quantified predicate logic, which is the logic of all reasoning about numbers, sets, angles, vectors, matrices, and other mathematical objects and topics. In addition to the truth-functional operators, this language has quantifiers and variables. Because this language has an infinite number of sentences, we shall have to make use of the recursive technique again, but there is an extra little wrinkle in this language that complicates matters. In the last language we looked at, all the sentences were either basic sentences or built up from basic sentences, but in a quantified language it is possible to build new sentences by combining two expressions *neither of which is itself a sentence* (1933, 189). The two kinds of expressions are open sentences and quantifiers. An open sentence is an expression that is grammatically complete just like a sentence except that it has a variable in one or more of the places where one would expect to see a noun. Each of the following is an open sentence:

x is a noodle-brained fool.

x is the father of John.

x is the father of y.

x is between Sam and Mary.

Bob is between y and z.

x is between y and z.

x is black, and either z includes y or y is a fool.

The term 'open sentence' is misleading in that it implies that an open sentence, is a kind of sentence. It is not. An open sentence is not a sentence, because it really does not say anything. An expression that does not say anything does not, of course, say anything true or false. Thus an open sentence is neither true nor false. We can turn an open sentence into a genuine sentence by closing it. There are two ways to do this: replace the variables with names, or bind the variables with quantifiers. (The logic needed for mathematics can get along with just the existential and universal quantifiers.) Binding the variables in an open sentence, and thereby creating a genuine sentence, is simply a matter of quantifying over each variable in the open sentence. There is only one quantifier per variable even if some of the variables appear more than once in the sentence. Hence the following are all genuine sentences:

$(x)(x$ is a noodle-brained fool$)$

$(x)(\exists y)(x$ is the father of $y)$.

$(x)[x$ is black and $(y)(\exists z)(y$ is between x and z or z loves $x)]$

Note that if even a single variable is left unbound in an expression, the expression still counts as an open (nongenuine) sentence.

There are an infinite number of quantified sentences. In itself this might not seem to be a problem. Why not just treat these like other sentences? Give each noncompound quantified sentence its own clause in the definition of truth, and define the truth of compound quantified sentences recursively. This option, however, is not available, because some compound quantified sentences are not built up from other genuine sentences. Quantified sentences, again, can be made by affixing appropriate quantifiers to an open sentence, one quantifier for each variable in the open sentence. But there are an infinite number of open sentences because *open sentences can be compounded with the truth-functional operators* just as well as can genuine sentences. (For an example, see the last member of the list of open sentences given above.) Thus all of the following are genuine sentences.

$(\exists x)(x$ is red)

$(\exists x)(\exists y)(x$ is red and y is red)

$(\exists x)(\exists y)(\exists z)($if x is red, then either y is red and z is red or z is not red)

So there are an infinite number of quantified sentences, none of whose parts is itself a sentence. And the preceding examples show that this holds even for languages with only one predicate and only one kind of quantifier. Since the open sentences that are the parts of these quantified sentences have no truth value, *we cannot recursively define the truth of such sentences in terms of the truth value of its parts.* And again, since there are an infinite number of such sentences, we cannot give them each its own clause in the definition of truth. Therein lies the dilemma that Tarski solved.[10]

Tarski's great insight is this: since the property of truth is not possessed by open sentences we must find some *other* property with the following characteristics:

• It can be possessed by both open sentences and genuine sentences.

• The possession or nonpossession of the property by a given quantified sentence is completely determined by the truth-functional operators in the sentence and by the possession or non-possession of the property by the uncompounded open clauses contained within the overall sentence.

• It is possible to define truth in terms of genuine sentences' possessing or not possessing the property so that the resulting definition of truth will entail all of the T-sentences.

The first two characteristics ensure that we can define the property in question recursively and thus that we can apply our definition to languages with an infinite number of sentences. The third characteristic ensures that the definition of truth will meet the material adequacy condition (Tarski 1933, 189).

'Satisfaction' is the name Tarski gave to the property he discovered that has all the requisite characteristics. A more correct name would be 'satisfaction by a sequence of objects'. I shall define this property in a moment, but first, note how simple the resulting definition of truth becomes: "A sentence is true if it is satisfied by all [sequences of] objects, and false otherwise" (Tarski 1944, 25; compare Tarski 1933, 195). This will remain a bit mysterious until I present Tarski's explication of the concept of satisfaction, but first let me formalize what he has given us so far:

$(s)(s$ is true $\equiv s$ is satisfied by all sequences of objects),

where 's' ranges over sentences. Now what we need is a definition of satisfaction that will ensure that this definition of truth will entail all the T-sentences. Satisfaction is, Tarski says, a relational property, a relation between a sequence of objects on the one hand and a sentence or open sentence on the other. (Since satisfaction is a relation between expressions and parts of the world, it counts as a semantic concept.) For the moment, let me simplify by leaving sequences and genuine sentences out of account and talking only of what it means for an individual object to satisfy an open sentence. Let 'x is purple' be the open sentence, and let my table be the object. So how does the table satisfy 'x is purple'? By being painted purple, of course, or by being constructed out of a purple-colored material. So an object satisfies an open sentence if and only if it possesses the property expressed by the predicate of the open sentence (Tarski 1933, 190). The essence of Tarski's theory is already beginning to emerge: the table satisfies 'x is purple' when the table is purple. So the *facts of the matter* are important; Tarski's theory is at least a quasi-realist theory. (I shall argue in section 6.5 that it is most usefully interpreted as a Realist theory.)

It will come as no surprise now to learn that the table satisfies 'x is purple and x is round' if and only if it satisfies 'x is purple' and it satisfies 'x is round'. So the table satisfies the compound open sentence if and only if it is both round and purple. The table satisfies 'x is purple *or* x is round' if and only if it satisfies 'x is purple' *or* it satisfies 'x is round'. It satisfies 'x is *not* purple' if and only if it *fails to satisfy* 'x is purple'. Finally, it satisfies 'if x is purple, then x is round' if and only if it either fails to satisfy 'x is purple' or it satisfies 'x is round'.

What about the open sentence 'x loves y'? Shall we say that the table satisfies this when it loves itself? Or should we say instead that only a set of two objects can satisfy an open sentence with two variables? And if we say the latter, under what circumstances will the table and the chair satisfy 'x loves y'? Must they love each other, or is it only necessary that one love the other, and if so, which must love which? These are the sort of questions that forced Tarski to resort to sequences of objects (1933, 191). A sequence of objects is a lot like a set of objects except that, unlike a set, the *order* of the objects is important when dealing with sequences. The following sets are all identical to each other; in other words, these are really not different sets but are different ways of naming the same set:

{the table, the chair, democracy}

{democracy, the chair, the table}

{the chair, the table, democracy}

But the following are all *different* sequences:

⟨the table, the chair, democracy⟩

⟨democracy, the chair, the table⟩

⟨the chair, the table, democracy⟩

When you change the order of the objects in a sequence, you have changed the sequence. Note that sequences, like sets, can be infinite in size (e.g., the sequence of natural numbers) and can have abstract objects as members. Note also that an object can appear more than once in a sequence. So the following are also sequences:

⟨the table, the chair, democracy, the table, Bulgaria, ... ⟩

⟨the table, the table, the table, the table, ... ⟩

When Tarski speaks of *all* infinite sequences, he means to include these funny looking sequences as well. Finally, there are no limits on what order objects can come in. So for all the objects in the world and each possible ordering of them, there is some sequence that has just *that* ordering. An implication of this is that for any object in the world, there is some sequence that has just that object in the fourth place, and there is a sequence that has just that object in the sixteenth place, and there is a sequence that has just that object in both the fourth and sixteenth places.

Another implication is that for a given sequence, say

$\langle$ the table, the chair, democracy, the table, Bulgaria, ... $\rangle$,

there is another sequence that is just like this one except that it has the table in the fifth place. And there is another just like this one except that it has Downing Street in the fifth place. In general, for *any* object, there is a sequence just like this one except that it has just *that* object in the fifth place. (The same implication holds, of course, for all the other places in the sequence.) The fact that this is so will turn out to be highly significant for our recursive definition of satisfaction.

One other complication is necessary before we can understand how an open sentence with more than one variable is satisfied. Since there is no limit to how big a compounded open sentence can be, there is also no limit to how many variables it can have. So we must replace our x, y, and z with the variables x_1, x_2, x_3, x_4, ... Now instead of talking of a single object satisfying an open sentence, we talk of an infinite sequence of objects satisfying an open sentence. The open sentence 'x_1 is purple' is satisfied by an infinite sequence of objects if and only if the first member of the sequence is purple. It does not matter what the other members of the sequence are, and it does not matter whether these other objects satisfy 'x_1 is purple'; they are irrelevant. Because the variable in the open sentence is the first variable, only the first member of the sequence matters. An infinite sequence satisfies 'x_2 is purple' if and only if the second member of the sequence is purple. An infinite sequence satisfies 'x_1 loves x_2' if and only if the first member of the sequence loves the second, but unless the second also loves the first, the sequence will *not* satisfy 'x_2 loves x_1'.

The truth-functional operators will continue to work as they have. Thus an infinite sequence will satisfy 'if x_{13} is purple, then x_2 loves x_{735} or x_{46} is round' if and only if either the sequence fails to satisfy 'x_{13} is purple' or it does satisfy 'x_2 loves x_{735} or x_{46} is round'. It will satisfy the latter if and only if either it satisfies 'x_2 loves x_{735}' or it satisfies 'x_{46} is round'. So the original open sentence is satisfied by the sequence if and only if either the 13th object in the sequence is not purple or the 2nd object loves the 735th or the 46th object is round. (Hereafter when I use the word 'sequence', I refer always to an *infinite* sequence.)

So much for satisfaction as applied to open sentences. How, then, does a sequence satisfy a quantified sentence? We know that if the definition of truth is to entail all the T-sentences, then a universally quantified sentence, say '$(x_4)(x_4$ is round)', had better turn out to be true when and only when *everything* in the world is round. Tarski ensures this by setting two conditions that must be met for a sequence, call it sequence S, to satisfy a universally quantified sentence such as '$(x_4)(x_4$ is round)':

1. S must satisfy the open sentence that would be created by deleting the quantifier. So in this case it must satisfy 'x_4 is round'. (Thus whatever object S has in the fourth place must be round.)
2. This same open sentence must also be satisfied by *every* sequence that is just like S except that it has a different object in the fourth place.

Recall from above that for every object in the world, there is some sequence just like S except that it has just that object in the fourth place. So, since condition (2) tells us that *all* of these sequences must satisfy 'x_4 is round', the condition says, in effect, that everything in the world other than the object in the fourth place of S must be round. Between them (1) and (2) are saying that *every* object must be round. Thus '$(x_4)(x_4$ is round)' is satisfied by a sequence S if and only if everything in the world is round. And what goes for sequence S goes for any other sequence as well. The universally quantified sentence is not satisfied by some sequence unless everything in the world is round. And if it is satisfied by some sequence, then everything in the world is round. Thus, so far as universally quantified sentences are concerned, we might just as well define a true sentence as a sentence that is satisfied by *some* sequence. The resulting definition would entail all the T-sentences corresponding to each universally quantified sentence of the language. It would entail, for example,

$(x_4)(x_4$ is round)' is true $\equiv$ everything is round.

As it will turn out, this conclusion applies to existentially quantified sentences as well and to nonquantified sentences like 'Ralph is short'. Since a definition of truth as satisfaction by *some* sequence works perfectly well, why did Tarski define truth as satisfaction by *all* sequences? The answer is that, as a practical matter, the two definitions amount to exactly the same thing. As noted above, the condition that must be met for S to satisfy '$(x_4)(x_4$ is round)' is exactly the same condition that any sequence must meet to satisfy this sentence, namely, everything must be round. So if the sole condition for S's satisfying this sentence is met, then *eo ipso* the sole condition for the satisfaction of this sentence by all the other sequences is also met. So if one sequence satisfies the sentence, they all do. If one fails to satisfy the sentence, that could only be because not everything is round, in which case none of the other sequences would satisfy the sentence either (Tarski 1933, 194). The same point, as we shall see, applies to all other genuine sentences: to be satisfied by one sequence is to be satisfied by them all. Thus it matters not whether we define truth as satisfaction by some sequence or as satisfaction by all sequences.

Some technical points before we go on. First, conditions (1) and (2) can be combined into a single condition requiring that the open sentence created by deleting the universal quantifier be satisfied by all sequences differing from S in *at most* the fourth place. Second, we can generalize the new combined condition so that it does not matter which variable appears in the sentence. Let k be any integer. Then any expression of the form '$(x_k)(x_k$ is round)' is satisfied by a sequence S if and only if the open sentence created by deleting the universal quantifier is satisfied by all sequences differing from S in at most the kth place. Third, we can further generalize the condition so that it applies to any universally quantified sentence, no matter what open sentence follows the quantifier. Let ϕ range over all open sentences. Then any expression of the form '$(x_k)\phi$' is satisfied by a sequence S if and only if ϕ is satisfied by all sequences differing from S in at most the kth place.[11]

The T-sentence for an existentially quantified sentence has this form:[12]

'$(\exists x_k)\phi$' is true $\equiv (\exists x_k)\phi$.

So if the definition of truth must entail all the T sentences, it had better turn out that '$(\exists x_k)\phi$' is true when and only when something ϕs. And since 'true' just means satisfied by some sequence, it had better turn out that '$(\exists x_k)\phi$' is satisfied by a sequence when and only when something ϕs. The following condition ensures that this will be so:

An expression of the form '$(\exists x_k)\phi$' is satisfied by a sequence S if and only if *some* sequence differing from S in at most the kth place satisfies ϕ.

But as we saw above, for every object, there is *some* sequence just like S except that it has just that object in the kth place. So the condition will be met when and only when something in the world ϕs. Notice here too that if one sequence satisfies the existential claim, they all do.

The language for which I shall define 'satisfaction' has just two predicates 'is red' and 'loves'. Following Tarski, I shall allow no names of objects in our language, at least to begin with. This means that the only genuine sentences in the language are quantified sentences. Also following Tarski (1933, 168), I shall have only two truth-functional operators: 'not' and 'or'. There is no point to complicating the language with any others, because 'and' and 'if ... then' can be defined in terms of 'not' and 'or'. The language also has the infinite set of variables described above. In the following definition, 'θ', 'ψ', and 'ϕ' all range over both genuine sentences and open sentences, 'j', like 'k', ranges over integers. The '$\neg$' means 'not' or 'it is not the case that ...'. So the official definition of satisfaction is:

$(\theta)[\theta$ is satisfied by an infinite sequence S
  $\equiv (\theta = $ 'x_k is red' for some k, and the kth object in S is red)
    or ($\theta = $ 'x_k loves x_j' for some k and j, and the kth object in S loves the jth object in S)
    or ($\theta = $ '$\neg \phi$', and S does not satisfy ϕ)
    or ($\theta = $ 'ψ or ϕ' and either S satisfies ψ or S satisfies ϕ)
    or ($\theta = $ '(x_k) ϕ', and *every* sequence that differs from S in at most the kth place satisfies ϕ)
    or ($\theta = $ '$(\exists x_k)$ ϕ' and *some* sequence that differs from S in at most the kth place satisfies ϕ)].[13]

And the definition of truth, once again, is

$(s)(s$ is true $\equiv s$ is satisfied by all [or some] sequences).

5.5   Names and Natural Languages

One outstanding characteristic of Tarski's account is that the definition of satisfaction must have a separate clause for each predicate in the language for which we are defining truth; that is, one clause explicates what it means for a sequence to satisfy 'is red', and then another clause explicates what it means for a sequence to satisfy 'loves', and so on for every predicate in the language. The reason these many different clauses are required is that the necessary and sufficient conditions for an object's satisfying a given open sentence are *different* from the conditions necessary and sufficient for that object to satisfy any *other* open sentence. As I noted above, for the table to satisfy 'x is purple', it is necessary and sufficient that the table be colored purple, but for the table to satisfy 'x is round', it is necessary and sufficient that the table be round.[14] So for Tarski, 'satisfaction of "x is purple"' turns out to be a *different* concept from 'satisfaction of "x is round"'. This fact was partly hidden in Tarski's presentation of this theory because he used as his example language a language of set theory that has only one predicate, 'is included in' (1933, 165–169). Textbooks in metalogic, model theory, and formal semantics also tend to hide this fact by replacing all the clauses for the various predicates with a single *schema* clause for all predicates. Such schemas typically use a variable like 'P' to range over all predicates in the language. Such a schema clause (for a language whose predicates are all one-place) might look like this:

(z = 'Px_k', for some k, and the kth member of S is an element of the set denoted by 'P')

But a schema is an open sentence (no quantifier binds the 'P') and is thus not a genuinely complete clause. Strictly speaking, it is senseless. We are to read it not as a real clause in the definition but only as a space-saving stand-in for a whole, possibly infinite, series of clauses, one for each predicate of the language.

The implication of the fact that the definition of satisfaction must have a separate clause for each predicate in the language is that Tarski's method only works for languages with a finite number of predicates. (Compare Putnam 1978, 10.) This is no hindrance for the languages of mathematical reasoning, which are the languages that interested Tarski, but natural languages have an infinite number of predicates. Think of the series of predicates 'is the first in line', 'is the second in line', 'is the third in line', etc. Of course, all lines are finite, but this only means we would eventually get to predicates that cannot be truly predicated of anything. It would not mean that such predicates do not exist. Thus, without modification Tarski's technique of defining satisfaction and hence truth is not applicable to a natural language.[15] This is an especially disappointing result for epistemologists. They wish to define truth ultimately for beliefs, and it is important that the definition apply to *any* belief someone might have. But for any predicate in the language, there is a potential belief in which just that predicate figures. Someone might someday have the belief that Ralph is first in line, and someone might believe that Ralph is second in line and so forth, for all the predicates in the series gestured to above. On the other hand, descriptions like 'the first in line', 'the 36th in line', 'the 1,557,823rd in line', etc. are built up from a *finite* stock of words. So if, as Donald Davidson believes, it is possible in principle to change (and complicate) the definition of satisfaction so as to handle all forms of adverbial or other predicate modification, then it may be possible in principle to create a roughly Tarski-like definition of truth for natural languages after all. This issue will be discussed in detail in section 8.1.

Tarski does not try to define satisfaction or truth for any languages with names. Let us see what would happen if we tried. Suppose we added a couple of names, say 'Ralph' and 'Mary', to the language and thereby added six unquantified but genuine sentences: 'Ralph is red', 'Mary is red', 'Mary loves Mary', 'Mary loves Ralph', 'Ralph loves Mary' and 'Ralph loves Ralph'. Now we must change the definition to ensure that it will entail the following T-sentences:

'Ralph is red' is true $\equiv$ Ralph is red

'Mary is red' is true $\equiv$ Mary is red

'Mary loves Mary' is true $\equiv$ Mary loves Mary

'Mary loves Ralph' is true $\equiv$ Mary loves Ralph

'Ralph loves Mary' is true $\equiv$ Ralph loves Mary

'Ralph loves Ralph' is true $\equiv$ Ralph loves Ralph

To accomplish this, we first take 'n'' and 'n'''' as variables ranging over names in the language and then add this:

($z =$ 'n' is red' for some n',
       and the object denoted by 'n'' is red)
or ($z =$ 'n' loves n'''' for some n' and some n'',
       and the object denoted by 'n'' loves the object denoted by 'n'''')

This has become the standard way of adding names to a language for which truth is being defined, but it would be unacceptable to Tarski as it stands because it makes 'satisfaction' defined partly in terms of the semantic concept of denotation.[16] To salvage the project of defining all semantic terms ultimately in terms of nonsemantic terms, we would have to supplement the definition of 'satisfaction' with a definition of 'denotation' having a separate clause for each primitive name in the language:

$(x)(y)[x$ denotes y
     $\equiv (x =$ 'Ralph' and $y =$ Ralph or $x =$ 'Mary' and $y =$ Mary)].

There are a variety of other ways one could create a roughly Tarski-like set of definitions for languages with names, but all of them require that we have *at least* (see section 8.3) one clause each for every name in the language. This result is general. Not only does each primitive predicate and each primitive name require a separate clause, so too does every primitive term of any kind in the language.

W. V. O. Quine suggests that we can have a language without names but with all the advantages of one that does have names. Instead of introducing names like 'Ralph' and 'Mary', we introduce the predicates 'Ralphizes' and 'Maryizes'. Instead of 'Ralph is red', the language will have a sentence reading '$(\exists x)(x$ Ralphizes and x is red)' (Quine 1970, 25). We would have to add a clause to the definition, on the pattern of the clause for 'is red', for each such new predicate. It is questionable whether Tarski would consider this a friendly amendment. He insists that all terms that appear on the right side of the equivalence sign be absolutely clear in their meanings, and one must wonder how well we really understand what 'Ralphizes' means; especially since we are not allowed to cash in its meaning in terms of denotation or any other semantic concept.

Tarski did not believe it was possible to define truth for natural languages, as distinct from the artificial languages of logic and mathematics (Tarski 1969, 68). He gave several reasons for this. One of them is that there is no *systematic* way of determining for a natural language which of its expressions count as grammatically complete sentences and which do not (Tarski 1969, 65; Tarski 1933, 164). But the most important reason is that natural languages are, he thought, hopelessly paradoxical because they are what he calls "universal" or "semantically closed" languages. A semantically closed language is one that has the power to describe the semantic characteristics of its own elements. We can say in English, for example, 'That verb is unclear', 'The noun at the beginning is plural', and 'That sentence is true'. We can also say 'This sentence is false', where 'this' refers to the very sentence in which it appears. But as we shall see in section 9.1, the very fact that there is such a sentence will, in conjunction with a theory of truth for the language, entail a contradiction. We shall see in section 9.3 how Tarski ensures that the artificial languages for which he defines truth will be semantically *open* (1933, 164; 1944, 20–21; and 1969, 65–68).

The fact that each predicate is listed separately in the definition of satisfaction means that languages with different predicates will have different definitions of satisfaction and hence of truth. So on Tarski's system there is not any *one* theory of truth, there is a different one for every language. (Tarski acknowledged this, but for the wrong reason. He claimed that this limitation results from the alleged fact that a sentence token can be true in one language and false or meaningless in another [1933, 153; 1944, 14; 1969, 64]. I argued in section 2.6 that Tarski is mistaken in this last claim; no sentence token true in one language is false or meaningless in another.) We can, however, make explicit in the definition of truth the fact that the definition applies to only one language by explicitly naming, in the definition, the language, call it L_1, for which truth is being defined:

$(s)(s$ is true in $L_1 \equiv s$ is satisfied in L_1 by all sequences)

For a different language, call it L_2, the definition of truth is

$(s)(s$ is true in $L_2 \equiv s$ is satisfied in L_2 by all sequences).

So there is not one theory of truth. Indeed, we really do not even have two theories of truth here. What we have is one theory of 'true-in-L_1' and one theory of 'true-in-L_2'. In the end, Tarski has defined not truth but truth-in-this-language and truth-in-that-language. The question of whether this characteristic is a serious *objection* to Tarski's work is taken up in section 6.3.

5.6   Programs and Special Adequacy Conditions

I noted in section 5.1 that each of the different programs in whose service an answer to the metaphysical project can be put imposes special restrictions on what will count as a good answer to the project, but no *one* answer to the project has to be relevant to every such program and thus no one theory of truth need meet all of these special restrictions. An epistemologist must acknowledge beliefs as (one kind of) truth bearer, but neither a model theorist per se nor a physicalist per se have any particular need to allow beliefs as truth bearers. Neither an epistemologist nor a model theorist per se has need for a theory that reduces truth to physical phenomena, and so there is no need to avoid defining truth in terms of other semantic concepts.[17] (Thus, as noted above, contemporary textbooks of metalogic or model theory no longer avoid using the semantic concept of denotation in the definition of satisfaction and hence of truth.) It does not seem that a physicalist per se must make use of recursive techniques. Does an epistemologist? Would, for example, Russell's and Austin's nonrecursive theories of truth serve the epistemologist's program of evaluating theories of justification (the special objections made to each of them in the last chapter aside)?

In Austin's case I think the answer is yes. This is clear if we keep in mind that in the formula for his theory,

$(s)[s$ is true $\Leftrightarrow (\exists x)(\exists r)(\exists t)(t$ is used to make $s)$
$\qquad \& \ (s$ refers to $x) \ \& \ (t$ describes $r)$
$\qquad \& \ (x$ is of type $r) \ \& \ (x$ obtains$)]$,

s ranges over *all* statements and t ranges over *all* sentences, however compounded, quantificationally complex, and/or syntactically complex they may be, and that states of affairs (over which x ranges) and thus types of states of affairs (r) can be as complex as you please. This is controversial. As we saw in section 4.7, it has been said that there are no disjunctive facts, conditional facts, or negative facts. I have defined a fact as a state of affairs that obtains. So on this view, either there are no disjunctive, conditional, or negative states of affairs, or there are but they never obtain. Either way, the implication is that on Austin's theory of truth, all disjunctive and conditional statements will come out false, and so too will all negations. But this view was unconvincing for two reasons. First, it is not at all clear why there cannot be facts of these sorts. Second, even if there are no facts of these sorts, it is not clear what relevance this has, precisely because it is not the case that disjunctive, conditional, and negative statements must be taken as referring to disjunctive, conditional, and negative states of affairs. Why must we assume that the states of affairs (and, if they obtain, the facts) must mirror the structure of the statements (sentences) that we use to refer to (describe) them? Indeed, it is part of Austin's point that statements are not isomorphic to states of affairs.

We saw in section 4.2 that the formulation of Russell's theory,

$(b)[b$ is true $\Leftrightarrow (\exists B)(\exists x)(\exists y)(\exists R)(b = \langle B, x, R, y \rangle \ \& \ xRy)]$,

only accounts for beliefs about two-place relations. But the techniques alluded to in note 3 of chapter 4 allow us to extend Russell's theory, without use of recursion, to beliefs of any degree of complexity. It appears, then, that neither a correspondence-as-correlation nor a correspondence-as-congruence theory need make use of recursion to be applicable to all statements or beliefs. So Russell's and Austin's theories can be used in the epistemological program of evaluating theories of justification, or at least the fact that they are not recursive poses no special problems in this regard. But notice that neither of them could be put to use in Tarski's program of constructing a model theory for quantified predicate logic (see section 5.1), because neither makes it possible to see how the truth value of a statement (belief) is affected by the quantifiers contained therein.

5.7   The Essence of Tarski's Notion of Truth

Tarski often complained that his critics confused his MAC, specifically his schema T,

X is true if and only if p,

with his definition of truth. Schema T cannot be a definition of truth, because it has unbound variables and thus is an open sentence. This means that it does not really entail *anything*, so it would not entail the equivalences matching its own form, and thus it would not itself meet the MAC. Moreover, simply binding the variables in the schema would not produce a definition of truth consistent with Tarski's intentions. We can see why this is so by recalling the instantiation conditions that Tarski embedded in his text after the displayed schema:

X is true if, and only if, p.

We shall call any such equivalence (with 'p' replaced by any sentence of the language to which the word "*true*" refers, and 'X' replaced by a name of this sentence) an "*equivalence of the form (T)*."[18]

The reason this caveat is needed is that the MAC would not be credible as a criterion of adequacy for a theory of truth unless it is specified that the sentence of which truth is being predicated be the *same* sentence that asserts that the state of affairs p obtains. So Tarski wants his theory to say that there is one *particular* state of affairs that, if it obtains, makes 'the table is purple' true. Which state of affairs? The state of affairs of the table's being purple, of course. Thus for any given true sentence, the fact that makes it true is the fact that the sentence expresses. So the instantiation conditions for schema T specify the way in which X and p must be coordinated. But if the T-sentences would be ridiculous when X and p are not coordinated in this way, this just means that *p's coordination with X is an additional necessary condition to X's being true* (in addition, that is, to

p's obtaining). A definition of truth consisting of just a quantified version of schema T would not express Tarski's insistence that the X and the p be coordinated in this way. The easiest way to get this point into a quantified formula is to make it explicit. One way of doing that would be with this formula:

$(X)\{X$ is true $\equiv (\exists p)[(X$ says that $p)$ and $p]\}$

Those who blanch at quantification over propositional variables might prefer

$(X)\{X$ is true $\equiv (\exists y)[(X$ expresses $y)$ and y obtains]$\}$,

where y ranges over states of affairs. (The attentive reader ought have a sense of *deja vu* here. This theory looks strikingly similar in structure to the formula for Russell's theory and the simpler formulations of Austin's. This is not a coincidence, but I postpone further discussion of this matter until section 5.8.) This theory, however formulated, does not entail the T-sentences by itself, but in conjunction with certain undisputed extensional facts, it does.[19] The extensional facts are expressed by what are called M-sentences, examples of which are the following:

'Snow is white' means that snow is white.

'Bob is a noodle-brained fool' means that Bob is a noodle-brained fool.

'The table is purple' means that the table is purple.

In other words, M-sentences are any sentences instantiating the following schema:

X means that p,

where p is replaced by a sentence and X by the name of that very sentence.

W. V. O. Quine, Donald Davidson, A. N. Prior, Arthur Pap, D. J. O'Connor, and Keith Lehrer[20] have all made the point that the coordination of truth bearer to the obtaining state of affairs is an necessary condition for truth. As Davidson says, "What Convention T, and the trite sentences it declares to be true, like "'Grass is Green" spoken by an English speaker, is true if and only if grass is green', reveal is that the truth of an utterance depends on just two things: what the words as spoken mean, and how the world is arranged" (Davidson 1986, 309). O'Connor puts it this way: "Suppose that P is the proposition 'There are six protons in the carbon atom.' What is then required for P to be true further than that there are in fact six protons in a carbon atom? And if nothing further is required how does asserting that P is true differ from asserting that P?... There does appear to be something more required for the truth of P, namely, that the words used in stating P should have the meanings that they have in English and that the syntax of English is such that those words, in that order, convey the information content of P."[21]

But Quine, Davidson, Prior, Pap, O'Connor, and Lehrer do not intend to imply that T-sentences are false. Recall from section 1.3 that there can be more than one correct extensional analysis of an expression, and recall further that, as odd as it sounds, this entails that a necessary condition for the application of the expression need not show up on all correct lists of the necessary and sufficient conditions for the application of the expression. What *is* implied by O'Connor's remark is that *one* correct extensional analysis of "'There are six protons in the carbon atom" is true' is

'There are six protons in the carbon atom' is true
$\equiv$ 'There are six protons in the carbon atom' means in English that there are six protons in the carbon atom, and indeed there are six protons in the carbon atom.

It just so happens that in the actual world 'There are six protons in the carbon atom' *does* mean in English that there are six protons in the carbon atom.[22] But this fact plus the preceding equivalence entails (by ordinary propositional logic) that the following is also true:

'There are six protons in the carbon atom' is true
$\equiv$ there are six protons in the carbon atom

This, of course, is just one of the T-sentences. The same argument could be made for all the other T-sentences. So the T-sentences are true. Again, this is just because in the actual world, which is the only world with which claims of extensional equivalence are concerned, English sentences have the meanings that they do. Thus it just so happens that in the actual world 'There are six protons in the carbon atom' is true whenever there are six protons in the carbon atom. John Etchemendy has made the same point in an enlightening way:

There is a substantive difference between the propositions expressed, for example, by the following two sentences:

(a) Snow is white

(b) 'Snow is white,' is true.

The first of these makes a claim that depends only on the color of snow; the second claim, on the other hand, depends on both the color of snow and the meaning of the sentence 'Snow is white.' For this reason the states of affairs described can vary independently: 'Snow is white' might have been false, though snow was still white; if, for instance, 'snow' had meant *grass*. And conversely, snow might not have been white, though 'Snow is white' was still true; say if 'snow' had meant *vanilla ice cream*. (Etchemendy 1988, 61)

Note the modal word 'might' in Etchemendy's remark. "'Snow is white' *might* have been false" is another way of saying that there is some *possible world* where 'Snow is white' *is* false. When he says the two states of affairs can vary independently, this means that they vary *across possible worlds*. He does not mean that in this, the actual, world 'Snow is white' can be false when snow *is* white.[23]

We encountered above a theory of truth that bears a striking structural similarity to the formula for Russell's theory and the simple formulation of Austin's:

$$(x)\{x \text{ is true} \equiv (\exists p)[(x \text{ says that } p) \text{ and } p]\},$$

or in the less technically controversial version,

$$(x)\{x \text{ is true} \equiv (\exists y)[(x \text{ expresses } y) \text{ and } y \text{ obtains}]\}.$$

For ease of reference, let me call this theory S. Tarski does briefly consider two theories like S. His reasons for not endorsing them are instructive:

I mean a definition which we can express in the following words:

(1) *a true sentence is one which says that the state of affairs is so and so, and the state of affairs indeed is so and so.*

... To make this intention more definite, and to give it a correct form, is precisely the task of a semantical definition. (Tarski 1933, 155)

The complaints here about indefiniteness and incorrect form are the only explicit complaints Tarski has about (1). He does not say that it is an incorrect analysis of truth. Indeed, he says that sentences conforming to the T schema are "completely in accordance with" it (1933, 157). Moreover, unlike those versions of the correspondence theory whose vagueness he complains about, (1) is not something handed down to him by other philosophers. It is his own statement of the essence of his own intentions. We ought to take this as a striking piece of evidence that it would capture the essence, if not all the details or the proper form, of his conception of truth per se. (The 'per se' will be explained below.)

Although he does not make them explicit here, Tarski has two main complaints about the form of (1). First, it has the semantic term 'says that' in the *definiens* for 'is true'. Second, it does not show how the grammatical structures of sentences affects their truth values. But beyond his physicalist and model-theoretic ambitions, Tarski has no other genuine reason for not embracing (1). The other theory like S in structure that Tarski considers is this: "For all x, x is a true sentence if and only if, for a certain p, x is identical with 'p', and p" (1933, 159). He rejects this because of certain problems concerning the interpretation of the symbol "'p'". The ordinary interpretation of single quotation marks is that they form the *name* of some expression that appears in between them. Hence on the ordinary interpretation, "'p'" is *one* word, a name. The 'p' inside "'p'" is no more a proper part of the "'p'" than the letter t is a proper part of the word *true*. So the "p" that appears between the single quotation marks in the last quotation cannot be the *variable* "p" that appears elsewhere in the formula. What the formula is really saying, as Tarski points out (1933, 160), is that the letter "p" is the only true sentence, which is absurd. Tarski next considers treating the quotation marks as a function from sentences to names of sentences. Under such an interpretation the "p" in the single quotation marks in the formula is a proper part of the expression "'p'", and it is the same variable as the "p" that appears elsewhere in the formula. While Tarski does *not* decisively reject such a theory, he does complain that naming is a semantical notion, so such a naming function would introduce a semantical concept into the *definiens* of the theory and thereby spoil his plans.[24]

So it seems that the ways in which Tarski's final theory deviates from an S-like theory are motivated entirely by his physicalist and model-theoretic ambitions. If we eliminate those features of his theory and technique relevant only to these programs, the theory and the recursive definition of satisfaction on which it rests would turn into something more or less like the formal version of S. This is what is meant in saying that (1) captures the essence of Tarski's idea of truth per se.

So it is that Tarski, like Russell and Austin, hid the essence of his notion of truth by tacking onto it features motivated solely by ambitions that, though closely related, are not strictly necessary to the fulfillment of the metaphysical project as such. (Tarski's case doesn't parallel that of Russell and Austin in one respect. Instead of adding doctrinal matter to a theory based on schema (C) [see section 4.5], he simply imposes special restrictions on the formulation of the theory: the 'R' of schema (C) is not to be a semantic relation, and the whole theory must show how the truth value of a compound sentence is affected by the truth values of its clauses.)

Two other points need to be made about theory S. First, it does not have to relativize truth to particular languages. This is because, unlike the theory with which Tarski eventually ended up, theory S does not need a separate clause defining truth (or some other concept, like satisfaction) separately for each sentence (or predicate). Thus theory S, which expresses the essence of Tarski's notion of truth, captures the translinguistic concept of truth. Since it was his physicalist program—eliminating semantic terms in favor of logicomathematical and physical terms—that forced Tarski to reject theory S, it is this program that requires him to define truth separately for each language.

Second, theory S does not entail the principle of bivalence. The latter holds that every declarative sentence is either true or false; no sentence can be neither. The reason theory S does not entail this principle is that it holds that there are two conditions necessary for the truth of a given sentence: the sentence must express a certain state of affairs, and that state of affairs must obtain. Thus, theory S allows that there are two ways a sentence might fail to be true, two ways it can be not true. It may express a state of affairs that fails to obtain, in which case it is false (and thus not true). Or it may fail to express *any* state of affairs, in which case it does not *say anything*, so it does not say anything true or anything false, so it is neither true nor false (and thus it is not true). But the definition of truth with which Tarski ended up does at least appear to entail the principle of bivalence, at least when the principle is taken to be a thesis concerning only sentences about this, the actual, world, for Tarski's definition satisfies the MAC, and the latter at least seems to presuppose that every declarative sentence in the actual world is either true or false. Again, then, Tarski's commitment, if he is so committed, to the principle of bivalence (taken to concern only sentences about the actual world) is a side effect of the extra programmatic goals that forced him to abandon theory S. (See section 6.1 for a discussion of whether the MAC, and hence Tarski's theory, really does entail the principle of bivalence.)

5.8   Is the Semantic Theory a Correspondence Theory?

There is ongoing dispute in Tarskian interpretation about

1. whether he intended his theory to be a correspondence theory of truth
2. whether, aside from his intentions, his theory *is* a correspondence theory.

J. L. Mackie, Susan Haack, and Herbert Keuth defend negative answers to these questions,[25] while Donald Davidson,[26] Karl Popper, Wilfred Sellars, and Mark Platts answer them in the affirmative.[27] Gerald Vision gives a no to (2), while Hartry Field and A. J. Ayer answer it yes.[28]

I side with the yea-sayers on question (1) because the following remarks by Tarski do not leave room for doubt that he thought of his theory as a correspondence theory: "We regard the truth of a sentence as its 'correspondence with reality'" (1936, 404). Elsewhere he says that he "aims to catch hold of an old notion" (1944, 13). What old notion? "I shall be concerned exclusively with grasping the intentions which are contained in the so-called *classical* conception of truth ('true—corresponding with reality') in contrast, for example, with the *utilitarian* conception ('true—in a certain respect useful')" (1933, 153).

We should like our definition to do justice to the intuitions which adhere to the *classical Aristotelian conception of truth*—intuitions which find their expression in the well-known words of Aristotle's *Metaphysics*:

To say of what is that it is not, or of what is not that it is, is false, while to say of what is that it is, or of what is not that it is not is true.

... We could perhaps express this conception by means of the familiar formula:

The truth of a sentence consists in its agreement with (or correspondence to) reality.

(For a theory of truth which is to be based upon the latter formulation the term 'correspondence theory' has been suggested.) ... We could possibly use for the same purpose the following phrase:

A sentence is true if it designates an existing state of affairs. (Tarski's italics)[29]

Later he confirms that the difference between the latter two italicized formulas in the preceding quotation and his theory is simply that they are vaguer than his, *not* that they say something different. All of this establishes that Tarski thought of himself as offering a more precise correspondence theory. Haack believes that Tarski meant to reject the "old notion" as "ambiguous, and even doubtfully coherent" (Haack 1978, 100, 112). But Tarski does not make either charge.[30] To call a theory imprecise is not at all the same thing as charging it with dubious coherence (senselessness) or with ambiguity (more than one meaning); still less is it to *reject* the theory. Indeed, why would Tarski express the desire to capture "*the* actual meaning" of a conception he thought to be meaningless or multiply sensed? At one place Tarski concedes that he is less than certain he has captured the intuitions behind the correspondence theory, precisely because he is less than certain that *it* is intended to express the Aristotelian conception, which he is sure he *has* captured. But even here Tarski seems to think it is at least probable that the latter is expressed, albeit vaguely, by modern correspondence formulations and hence that his is a correspondence theory (1944, 31–32).

Haack also notes that Tarski says he is not surprised to learn that most nonphilosophers responding to a questionnaire rejected the claim that truth is correspondence with reality while most accepted the claim that 'It is snowing' is true if and only if it is snowing. But it is clear that he regards this outcome as only further evidence of the vagueness of the traditional correspondence formulation, not as relevant evidence to the question of whether the semantic and correspondence conceptions are the same conception of truth (Tarski 1944, 32).

But Tarski might well have failed in his own intentions, so my affirmative answer to question (1) does not entail an affirmative answer to question (2). Is Tarski's theory a correspondence theory? As we saw in section 4.5, the essence of the correspondence theory is captured in schema C:

$$(t)\{t \text{ is true iff } (\exists x)[(tRx) \text{ and } (x \text{ obtains})]\} \qquad (C)$$

Accordingly, a correspondence theory is any theory that instantiates schema (C) by specifying what sort of truth bearer t ranges over, replaces the 'iff' with some equivalence symbol appropriate to the project at hand, and replaces the 'R' with some relation appropriate to connecting truth bearers of the specified kind with states of affairs.

Does Tarski's theory instantiate schema (C)? Well, theory S (section 5.7), which expresses the essence of Tarski's notion of truth per se, certainly does. Specifically, it makes R the semantic relation of *expressing* or *saying*. But, of course, it was precisely for this reason that Tarski was forced to reject theory S. Does the theory he actually ended up with instantiate schema (C)? Strictly, it does not, since a Tarskian definition of truth is relativized to a particular language, while schema (C) is not. Still, it might be thought that this feature of Tarski's work should not be allowed to affect what generic category his definition (strictly, definitions) are placed in. We should perhaps allow that a theory counts as a correspondence theory if it instantiates a language-relative version of schema (C):

$(t)\{t$ is true-in-L iff $(\exists x)[(tRx)$ and $(x$ obtains$)]\}$,

where t is a sentence, statement, utterance, or some other sentencelike linguistic item and the 'R' holds the place of some language-relative relation appropriate to connecting the linguistic item to a state of affairs. But I think that in the end it is unlikely we will ever establish that Tarski's definition instantiates even this narrower version of the schema, because when the truth bearer is a sentence, it would seem that R has to be some kind of semantic relation, and that is precisely what Tarski cannot allow, given his ambition to eliminate semantic concepts from the *definiens* of a definition of truth. Hence Tarski has to define truths so as not to make explicit the relation between a true sentence and an obtaining state of affairs. And this in turn means that he must, in the case of simple languages without quantifiers or open sentences, list each sentence of the language in question separately and simply *assign* it to a state of affairs. Of course, we recognize that he assigns to each sentence just the state of affairs *expressed* by the sentence, but this is not made explicit in his definition. (This last point will become more evident in section 6.3, where I point out that if confronted with a Tarski-like definition of truth for a language that we do not understand, we *cannot* tell that it assigns to each sentence just the state of affairs expressed by that sentence.) For more complex languages that have quantifiers and open sentences, he must separately list, in the definition of satisfaction for the language, each predicate of the language and assign it a property. Again, if the language is one we understand, we can recognize that he has assigned to each predicate just the property *named* by the predicate, but this semantic relation is not made explicit in the definition.

So whether we classify Tarski's theory of truth as a correspondence theory depends on whether we are talking about his notion of truth per se, theory S, or about the theory to which he was forced to resort, given his extra physicalist and model-theoretic ambitions. The former is a correspondence theory, but the latter is not. Even the theory he ended up with, however, is not a *competitor* with the correspondence theory in the sense that it conflicts with the latter. They are quite compatible. The differences between them are simply that theory S, a correspondence theory, is not relativized to particular languages and is unsuitable for the physicalist and model-theoretic programs.

5.9   Chapter Summary

Understanding Tarski's theory requires an understanding of the broader programs in service to which he wished to put it. He wants to reduce all semantic concepts to physical and logico-mathematical concepts and, by doing so, to make semantics a science. This goal forces Tarski to reject any definition of truth in which an unreduced semantic term appears in the *definiens*. This in turn effectively requires that he define truth in terms of satisfaction, which is itself separately defined for every predicate of the language for which truth is being defined. Thus there must be a separate definition of truth for each language, and the worry arises that he can define truth only for artificial languages with a finite number of predicates. Tarski was not bothered by this, but it is very bothersome for those who would put the metaphysical project to work in the service of epistemology. For no language with only a finite number of predicates could ever express every belief that someone or other might have in the future, and it is the truth of beliefs that are of ultimate concern to epistemologists. Another side effect of his banishment of semantic terms from the *definiens* is that his definition, for any given language, cannot explicitly capture the essence of his own notion of truth per se. Finally, we saw that the question of whether Tarski's theory should be thought of as a correspondence theory depends on exactly what we are referring to with the phrase 'Tarski's theory': theory S or the theory with which Tarski finally ended up.

  I turn now to some of the major objections that have been made to Tarski's theory.

6 Objections to Tarski's Theory

6.1 Objections to Tarski's Material Adequacy Condition

Susan Haack has complained (1978, 101–102) that the MAC does not rule out bizarre theories of truth like

$(p)(p$ is true $\equiv p$ is asserted in the Bible),

which is consistent with all instances of schema (T). But she is forgetting that the MAC requires that a theory *entail*, not merely be compatible with, all the T-sentences, and the Bible theory does not by itself entail them.

Haack's second objection concerns the principle of bivalence, which says that every meaningful declarative sentence is either true or false, none is neither. This principle has been denied. There are those who say that some sentences are "indeterminate" in their truth value, and others say that some sentences simply have no truth value. In either case, the sentences in question are neither true nor false. So there are, on these views, at least two ways a sentence can fail to be true: it can be false, or it can be neither true nor false. Haack's objection is that the MAC presupposes the principle of bivalence and thereby too hastily rules out any theory of truth that denies the principle. It certainly does appear that the MAC has this effect, since it requires that a theory of truth for a language entail, for *every* sentence s of the language, a T-sentence of the form

s is true $\equiv p$,

where p is the state of affairs expressed by s. And for any state of affairs expressed on the right-hand side of a T-sentence, it seems that either it obtains or it does not. There does not seem to be any third possibility. So it would seem that for any sentence s mentioned on the left-hand side of a T-sentence, either it is true or it is false. There does not seem to be any third possibility, any way it can fail to be true other than by being false.

This is a weak objection at best. For one thing, the T-sentences are assertions of mere extensional equivalence, so if the MAC presupposes the principle of bivalence, it does so only when that principle is interpreted as the claim that *as a matter of contingent fact*, every sentence is either true or false. It does not presuppose the principle when the latter is taken to be the claim that it is *impossible* for a sentence to be neither true nor false. Moreover, since the denial of the principle is itself highly controversial, it is not much of an objection to merely note the incompatibility of that denial with the MAC.

It is debatable whether the MAC really does presuppose the principle of bivalence anyway. Suppose one holds, as many do, that there are such things as vague states of affairs, which I define as a state of affairs such that it is indeterminate whether or not the state of affairs obtains. (Note that in calling a state of affairs indeterminate, I do not mean merely that it is impossible *to tell* whether or not it obtains. Rather, I mean that its ontological status is itself indeterminate.) An example of such a state of affairs might be the state of affairs expressed by 'John is not yet an adult', where 'John' names someone in his teens (Walker 1989, 32–33). Anyone holding such a view and accepting the MAC would be committed to accepting the T-sentences for all sentences of the language in question, including

'John is not yet an adult' is true ≡ John is not yet an adult.

Would this be a consistent position to hold? Gerald Vision argues that it is not. If we assume that the principle of bivalence does not hold, there is an argument showing that the preceding T-sentence is false. If the state of affairs of John's being not yet an adult is indeterminate, then the right-hand side of the preceding T-sentence and the sentence *mentioned* on the left-hand side are neither true nor false, and thus not true. But then the whole of the left-hand side is false, so the left- and right-hand sides have different truth values, so the T-sentence as a whole is false (Vision 1988, 115).

But this conclusion is too strong. The standard definition of the ' ≡ ' says,

'$p \equiv q$' is (a) true when both 'p' and 'q' are true or when both are false, and (b) false when one is true and the other false.

The standard definition says nothing at all about cases where either 'p' or 'q' or both are indeterminate. It leaves truth and falsity undefined for such biconditionals. Hence the biconditional above is not false, as Vision concludes, but neither false nor true. On the other hand, in contexts where the principle of bivalence is being denied, it is usual to modify the definition of '$\equiv$' so that it will cover biconditionals containing an indeterminate antecedent or consequent or both. Suppose Vision is assuming some such modified definition. What would it be? To get the conclusion that '$p \equiv q$' is false when 'p' is false and 'q' is indeterminate, it seems that the second clause of his modified definition (corresponding to clause (b) in the standard definition) must be:

(b') false whenever 'p' and 'q' have different truth values (including the case where one is false and the other indeterminate).

I don't know how to argue against one who finds this definition intuitively satisfying, but I will note that (so far as I can discover) *all* of the logicians who have developed three-valued logics, where the "third value" is 'indeterminate', 'meaningless', 'paradoxical', or 'not known whether true or false', have found (b') implausible. To them, it is intuitively compelling that when 'p' is false and 'q' is indeterminate, '$p \equiv q$' is indeterminate as well. (See Haack 1974, 47–72, for a discussion and references to the relevant literature.)

Maybe the weaker conclusion, that the biconditional is neither true nor false, is all that Vision needs to make his point anyway. After all, we normally say that one who embraces a theory T is committed to the *truth* of all of the logical consequences of T. If that rule holds in this context, then one who denies bivalence (because of the existence of indeterminate states of affairs) cannot accept the MAC, because it entails something that is not true (or false). I have no steady intuitions on whether the normal rule should apply in a context where it is being assumed (for the sake of argument at least) that bivalence does not hold, so I shall take no final stand on Vision's argument, but I do not find it inconceivable that where bivalence doesn't hold, one who embraces T is committed only to the nonfalsity of the implications of T, not to their truth. If that weaker rule is the appropriate one in such contexts, then it is not inconsistent to embrace the MAC and deny bivalence.

6.2 The Semantic Theory and the Justification Project

It will be useful here to dispense with a common but misguided objection to Tarski's theory based on a failure to distinguish theories of truth from theories of justification. O'Connor states the objection as clearly as anyone has, and he is aware of the distinction it overlooks, but he does not seem aware of just how significant the distinction is:

> How do we know that, for example, snow satisfies 'x is white' without already knowing that the sentence 'snow is white' is true[?] ... Indeed it is obvious that we cannot identify the individuals that satisfy an open sentence without knowing the truth value of the closed sentences resulting from substituting in it the names of the individuals for the unbound variable. That being so, is not an explanation of truth and falsity in terms of satisfaction plainly circular?
>
> To this objection, a defender of the semantic theory of truth will reply that the theory is designed simply to give a clear and precise *definition* of truth. It does not pretend to offer a method for determining which particular sentences are true and which are false. The reply is justified but it does point to a feature of the theory that seriously limits its philosophical interest. It might be thought to be a strange kind of definition which was no aid to identifying members of the class defined. (O'Connor 1975, 107).

But Tarski's definition of truth provides all the aid in identifying members of the class it defines as does any other definition of any other concept. To identify the members of the class of horses, one needs first a definition of 'horse' setting out the necessary and sufficient conditions for being a horse. But one must then go out and *look* at various objects in the world to see whether or not, for any given object, it meets the conditions. The definition aids by telling us what we should look for. Similarly, to determine whether or not a given sentence is true, we need two things: a definition of truth telling us what to look for and a method of observation or justification by means of which we do the looking. Notice that without a definition of truth we would have no idea whether we should go look at snow and determine its color, whether we should look to see if the sentence 'Snow is white' coheres with other sentences expressing our beliefs, or whether we should try to determine what everyone with sufficient relevant experiences will eventually agree to with respect to the color of snow. The proof that Tarski's theory gives all the aid that any other definition of any other concept gives is that his theory tells us which of these things we should do (the first). The proof that it gives us no *more* aid than any other definition is that if we are really in doubt about the truth value of 'Snow is white', we would still have to go look at snow and determine its color.

6.3   The Relativity Objection

We saw in section 5.5 that Tarski does not so much define truth as he defines truth-in-L_1, truth-in-L_2, etc. Many regard this as a serious defect.

As Simon Blackburn words the objection, Tarski's work is no more revealing of the nature of truth than definitions of the series of concepts proper-legal-verdict-on-Wednesday, proper-legal-verdict-on-Thursday, etc. would be revealing of the nature of a proper legal verdict (Blackburn 1984, 266–267). To simplify my discussion of this objection, let me return to the simple kind of language described in section 5.2, which has no truth-functional operators like 'not', 'and', 'or', or 'if... then'; no quantifiers; no variables; and hence no open sentences. (The points to be made apply equally well to the more complex kinds of languages.) Let L_1 and L_2 be two such languages where L_1 consists only of the sentences 'The table is round', 'The carpet is purple', and 'John loves Mary', and L_2 consists only of the sentences 'Bob is a noodle-brained fool' and 'Napoleon is alive'. Tarski-like definitions of true-in-L_1 and true-in-L_2 are respectively the following:

$(s)[s$ is true-in-L_1

$\equiv (s = $ 'The table is round' and the table is round)

or $(s = $ 'The carpet is purple' and the carpet is purple)

or $(s = $ 'John loves Mary' and John loves Mary)]

$(s)[s$ is true-in-L_2

$\equiv (s = $ 'Bob is a noodle-brained fool'

and Bob is a noodle-brained fool)

or $(s = $ 'Napoleon is alive' and Napoleon is alive)][1]

Now it might seem that we can discern a common element in the definitions of true-in-L_1 and true-in-L_2 and, by extension, in the Tarski-like definition for any language. If, for example, the sentence 'Kendall is tall' were added to L_1, we would have no difficulty discerning that the proper way to correct the above definition of true-in-L_1 is by adding the clause

or $(s = $ "Kendall is tall" and Kendall is tall).

Similarly, given a language L_3 consisting only of the sentences 'Emory is blond' and 'Collin is sweet', we could easily discern enough of a pattern in the above two definitions to realize that the correct Tarski-like definition of true-in-L_3 is

$(s)[s$ is true-in-$L_3 \equiv (s = $ 'Emory is blond' and Emory is blond)

or $(s = $ 'Collin is sweet' and Collin is sweet)].

The common element we seem to discern is that a sentence in *whatever*
language is true if and only if *a certain state of affairs obtains*, specifically,
the state of affairs expressed by the sentence. Hence we are tempted to
think that, implicitly at least, Tarski has given us the essence of translinguistic truth after all.

But our intuitions here are deluded. To see why, suppose a language,
call it L_4, consisting of only the sentences '∈ □ Δ' and '∅ ◇ ⊢'. And
suppose I, who understand this language, define 'true-in-L_4' thus:

$(s)[s$ is true-in-$L_4 \equiv (s =$ '∈ □ Δ' and snow is white)
          or $(s =$ '∅ ◇ ⊢' and snow is green)]

Now if I were to inform you that a new sentence in this mysterious
language had been discovered, '⊢ ∴ ¬', and I asked *you* to extend the
definition to cover the new sentence, you would be completely unable to
do it. Similarly, you would be unable to create a definition of 'true-in-L_5' if
L_5 is a language consisting only of the sentences 'Γ ∪ ∩' and ' ∧ ⊨'. You
could not do either of these things because you do not understand L_4 or
L_5, you do not know what their sentences mean.

Or suppose I coin the term 'rotdeeple' to name a certain property I have
in mind and I define 'rotdeeple' for language L_6 consisting of only the
sentences 'Snow is white' and 'Snow is green':

$(s)[s$ is rotdeeple-in-L_6
   $\equiv (s =$ 'Snow is white' and snow is white)
   or $(s =$ 'Snow is green' and snow is green)]

Again, if it were discovered that L_6 had a third sentence, 'Blue is the sky',
you would be unable to extend the definition of 'rotdeeple-in-L_6' to cover
the new sentence because you do not know what concept 'rotdeeple'
expresses. One possibility is that it is a synonym for 'true', in which case
the proper additional clause would be

or $(s =$ 'Blue is the sky' and blue is the sky).

But 'rotdeeple' might not be a synonym for 'true'. For all you know it
might be a synonym for 'contains a word that names the color of snow', in
which case the proper additional clause would be

or $(s =$ 'Blue is the sky' and snow is blue).[2]

For similar reasons, you cannot create a definition of 'rotdeeple' for any of the other languages, including English.

The implication of all this is that our ability to extend the definition of true-in-L_1 and to create a definition of true-in-L_3 depends on more than just our acquaintance with the definitions of true-in-L_1 and true-in-L_2. Our ability also depends on (1) the fact that we *understand* L_1, L_2, and L_3, we know the meanings of their sentences; and (2) our knowledge of what properties 'true-in-L_1', 'true-in-L_2', and 'true-in-L_3' name, our knowledge, that is, that they are meant to conform to our pretheoretical notion of truth. (Compare Davidson 1977a, 217, and Davidson 1990, 286–287.) If we did not have the latter piece of knowledge, then for all we would know 'true-in-L_1' might mean 'true in L_1 and does not assert that Kendall is tall or false in L_1 and asserts that Kendall is tall', in which case the proper extension of the definition would not require, as we thought, the clause

or (s = 'Kendall is tall' and Kendall is tall).

Rather, it would require

or (s = 'Kendall is tall' and Kendall is *not* tall).

So when we detect the pattern in the definitions of 'true-in-L_1' and 'true-in-L_2' that allows us to extend the definition of the former and to create similar definitions for other languages (that we understand), what we are detecting is, first, that the two definitions conform to the principle that a sentence is true just when it says that p and p obtains; they conform, that is, to what I called theory S in section 5.7, and second, that they manage to do this not by using the semantic term 'says that' but rather by simply naming each sentence of the language and pairing it off with the state of affairs that we *independently* recognize as the very state of affairs expressed by the sentence. If we knew nothing else about Tarski's goals, we might wonder why such an odd technique is used, but the point here is that a Tarski-like definition of truth-in-L, for whatever L, does not *express* (even implicitly) our pretheoretical, translinguistic notion of truth; it *presupposes* it. (Compare Bealer 1982, 200–202.)

On the other hand, we ought not let the relativity objection drive us to Putnam's conclusion that the Tarskian properties truth-in-L_1, truth-in-L_2, truth-in-the-language-of-set-theory, etc. have nothing to do with our translinguistic notion of truth (Putnam 1985, 64). Such a conclusion misses the significance of the fact that for languages we understand, we can recognize that Tarski-like definitions do conform to theory S, and hence they do capture something in our translinguistic notion. Specifically, each such definition captures part of the *extension* of translinguistic truth. Moreover, each of them does this without using any semantic terminology. And for languages with truth-functional operators and quantifiers, the recursive clauses in a Tarski-like definition of satisfaction for the language tells us how the presence of such terms in a sentence affects the truth value of the sentence. In short, then, Tarski-like definitions do exactly what Tarski wanted them to do.

So the force of the relativity objection can only be measured from the perspective of some goal. If what is sought is an expression of the essence of our translinguistic notion of truth, then the objection shows that Tarski-like definitions just will not do. To fulfill this goal, we have to turn to something like theory S. But if the goal is to show how to describe the extension of the truth predicate without using semantic terms, then the objection is irrelevant. It should not be surprising that matters should turn out this way: as we saw in section 5.7, theory S need not be relativised to languages. But although theory S expressed the essence of Tarski's notion of truth per se, Tarski had to reject it because it uses a semantic concept in its *definiens*. Hence it is Tarski's physicalist program that forces him to relativize his definitions to particular languages. More correctly, it is his desire to eliminate semantic terms that has this effect; the fact that the particular nonsemantic vocabulary he is aiming at consists of physical (and logicomathematical) terms does not itself require him to abandon theory S. (His solution to the Liar Paradox also requires him to make truth language-relative, but not in the sense of 'language-relative' at issue in this section. See section 9.3.)

6.4 The Vacuity Objection

Perhaps the most devastating objection to Tarski's theory, if it holds up, is that the theory is vacuous in the sense that it does not contradict any of its competitors. There is a legitimate line of reasoning that leads to a moderate version of this conclusion, but the objectors often put the conclusion in an exaggerated form and often supplement (or conflate) the legitimate line of reasoning with arguments resting on one or another or a combination of the following mistakes:

1. A tendency to confuse an analysis of 'is true' that makes *use* of the symbol ' $\equiv$ ' or the more ambiguous 'if and only if' (or its abbreviation 'iff') with an analysis of ' $\equiv$ ' or 'if and only if'.
2. A tendency to forget that the MAC requires that a theory of truth entail, not merely be compatible with, all the T-sentences.
3. A failure to distinguish the various projects described in chapter 1.
4. A tendency to equate Tarski's theory with Ramsey's redundancy theory.
5. A desire to conclude, on shaky evidence, that Tarski intended his theory to be *ontologically* neutral, that is, that he intended it to be compatible with both ontological realism and all forms of ontological nonrealism. (See section 3.1.)

Let us look quickly at these mistakes and then examine the legitimate argument for the objection to see just how potent is the conclusion thereby supported. (Note that some of those who make what I am calling the vacuity objection, particularly many of those who make mistake (4), think it is a point in Tarski's favor, not an objection, that it is vacuous in this way. I postpone further discussion of this until chapter 10.)

Although I have seen it in print only once (Keuth 1978, 425), I have heard mistake (1) made in conversation often enough to convince me that it must be mentioned here. The argument goes like this: An advocate of an instrumental theory of truth could accept Tarski's schema T (and thus all the T-sentences) in the sense that he regards a belief represented by the expression on the left side of the 'iff' operator, '"Snow is white" is true', to be *equally useful* for a believer as the belief represented by the expression on the right side, 'Snow is white'. The instrumentalist, in other words, can give an instrumentalist interpretation of the 'iff' operator. He can translate it as 'is as useful to believe as'. Similarly, a coherence theorist is free to point out that the expression on the left-hand side coheres or fails to cohere to just the same degree as the expression on the right-hand side. The coherence theorist can thus take 'iff' to mean 'has the same degree of coherence as'. So *if* Tarski were trying to analyze the 'iff' operator, then his analysis would be vacuous. But he was not trying to do that. Tarski was taking the 'iff' operator as a primitive (1944, 28–29), while he *interpreted* the predicate 'is true'.[3]

We saw in section 6.1 that if the MAC required that a theory of truth be only logically *compatible* with the T-sentences, it would not rule out even exotic theories like the Bible theory of truth:

$(p)(p$ is true $\equiv p$ is asserted in the Bible)

But again, since the MAC requires that a theory *entail* all the T-sentences, it does rule out the Bible theory. The tendency to forget what the MAC actually demands seems to be at least *part* of Wilfred Sellars's and Max Black's motivation for endorsing the vacuity objection:

As has often been noted, the formula

'Snow is white' (in our language) is true $\equiv$ Snow is white

is viewed with the greatest equanimity by pragmatist and coherentist alike. (Sellars 1963a, 197)

Adherents of the correspondence, the coherence, or the pragmatist, "theories" of truth will all indifferently accept the schema S [Black's version of schema T]. They would all be prepared to agree that

'It is snowing today' is true iff It is snowing,

'London is a city' is true iff London is a city,

AND SO ON.

And insofar as the semantic definition of truth has such consequences as these *and no others*, the philosophical dispute stays unsettled. The philosophical disputants are concerned about what *in general* entitles us to say "It is snowing" or "London is a city" *and so on*. (Black 1948, 60–61)

But to repeat, even if it is true that advocates of other theories can view T-sentences "with the greatest equanimity" and "indifferently accept" schema T, it is irrelevant; for the MAC requires more than this. It is worth noting, however, as a hint about the nature of the *legitimate* argument for the vacuity objection, that if an instrumentalist about truth also holds to an instrumentalist ontology, that is, an instrumentalist theory of what it is for a state of affairs to obtain (as does James, for example; see section 3.3), then the *combination* of his ontology and his theory of truth *will* entail the T-sentences. By this I mean that the conjunction of

(1) 'Snow is white' is true iff it is useful to believe that snow is white

and

(2) Snow is white iff it is useful to believe that snow is white

entails

'Snow is white' is true iff snow is white.

So the conjunction of a theory of truth that entails all sentences on the pattern of (1) and an ontological theory that entails all sentences on the pattern of (2) would entail all T-sentences. A similar example could be given in terms of the coherence theory of truth and a coherence theory of what it is for a state of affairs to obtain. For that matter, I suppose one could hold that what it is for a fact to exist, that is, for a state of affairs to obtain, is simply that it be asserted in the Bible. That is,

Snow is white iff 'Snow is white' is asserted in the Bible.

This too, *in conjunction with* the Bible theory of truth, would entail all the T-sentences. I shall have more to say on the significance of this below, but the point here is that neither an instrumental theory of truth *by itself* (independent of any ontological doctrine) nor a coherence theory of truth *by itself* will entail the T-sentences, and thus neither meets the MAC.[4]

Now defenders of either the instrumental or coherence theories of *justification*, as distinct from theories of *truth*, can accept a Tarski-like theory of truth with indifference, but if they do, this just means that they are accepting a *Tarski-like* theory of *truth*; that is, they are saying that the relation of a sentence to other sentences (or its usefulness) is evidence indicating that it probably expresses a fact. Thus a failure to distinguish the two kinds of projects could lead one to think that advocates of instrumental or coherence theories of truth can also accept Tarski's theory with indifference. That this mistake is part of Black's motivation for embracing the vacuity objection is indicated by the last sentence of the quotation from him, for disputes about what *entitles us to say* that it is snowing are disputes about what *justifies* us in thinking that it is probably true that it is snowing. They are *not* disputes about what the necessary and sufficient conditions for a sentence's being true are.

The common but reckless tendency to identify Tarski's theory with F. P. Ramsey's redundancy theory also lends undeserved credence to the vacuity objection. The latter holds to claims of the pattern

'Snow is white' is true $=_{syn}$ snow is white,

which is translated as either 'To say that "snow is white" is true is to say that snow is white' or with '"'Snow is white' is true" is synonymous with "Snow is white"'. If one recklessly assumes that the 'if and only if' in schema T and the T-sentences is to be identified with the '$=_{syn}$' of assertion project theories, and if one forgets that Tarski's theory is not the same thing as the T schema (which is used by Tarski to express an *adequacy condition* on theories of truth), then one will fail to see any difference between Tarski's and Ramsey's theories. One will conclude, in other words, that Tarski is offering a theory about what we are *saying* when we ascribe truth, and so, of course, his theory will seem quite compatible with the coherence and instrumental theories, which are themselves about what truth *is*. But for the reasons given in section 1.8 and chapter 5, it is virtually certain that Tarski did not mean to express synonymy with his 'if and only if' or to give a theory about truth ascribing utterances. And Tarski himself gave reasons why his theory cannot be considered a redundancy theory (Tarski 1944, 30–31). Nevertheless, a conflation of Tarski with Ramsey seems to be at least one of the reasons why the vacuity objection is endorsed by W. V. O. Quine (1960, 24), Hilary Putnam (1981, 128–129), and Arthur Pap (1949, 350).[5]

Although he does not mention Ramsey by name, Sellars seems to make essentially the same mistake in the following remark: "Needless to say, the pragmatist and the coherentist have had to pay a price for this seeming trivialization of their once worthy opponent. For they can no longer claim, if they ever did, that 'truth' *means* successful working or that 'truth' *means* coherence. ... But what comfort can the correspondence [read 'semantic'] theorist take in a victory which ... reduces his claim to a formula which ... has, according to his erstwhile antagonists, nothing to do with the philosophical problem of truth" (Sellars 1963a, 197–198). So Sellars recognizes at least two projects. The first looks for the meaning of 'true', and he thinks that the semantic theory is the correct answer here. But this project is trivial, according to Sellars. The second project, the one he thinks is important, is to solve "the philosophical problem of truth." Tarski had already noted objections like this and complained that none of the objectors had ever been able to explain what "the philosophical problem of truth" is (1944, 34). It would come as no surprise to Tarski, then, to learn that Sellars also does not explain what he conceives the problem to be. In fact, the phrase 'philosophical problem of truth' is vague enough to be applied to any of the projects. But we should not get involved in this section with the questions of which project was Tarski's and whether that project is important. The vital point here is that even by Sellars's lights, the semantic theory can be accepted with equanimity by pragmatists and coherentists only because they are working on a different project.[6] But this no more makes semantic theory trivial than nominalism as an ontological theory is made trivial because it is compatible with every theory of morality. A theory is not trivial because it can be accepted by everyone who is pursuing a *different* project than the one the theory addresses. It is only trivial or vacuous if its competitors (other theories pursuing the same project) are all compatible with it.

The more legitimate argument for the vacuity objection, as Blackburn recognizes, centers on the ambiguity in quasi-realist theories of truth. What exactly is the ontological status of the fact asserted on the right-hand side of a T-sentence? Is it mind-dependent or not?[7] If Tarski's theory is ontologically neutral, that is, compatible with both ontological realism and nonrealism (see section 3.1), then the door is open for, say, a coherence theorist to accept the T-sentences, provided he rejects ontological realism. Michael Dummett has made the point with respect to an ontological doctrine called mathematical intuitionism. In this context we may take the latter as the simple claim that mathematical entities exist when *and only when* they are proved to exist and that mathematical states of affairs obtain when, only when, and *because* they are proved to obtain (so mathematical statements are true when and only when they are proved). Dummett says,

[For intuitionism] there seems no obstacle to admitting the correctness of schema (T). Of course, in doing so, we must construe the statement that appears on the right-hand side of any instance of the schema in an intuitionistic manner. ... '598017 + 246532 = 844549' is true just in the case in which 598017 + 246532 = 844549. We may ... discover that 598017 + 246532 does indeed equal 844549: but does that mean that the equation was already true before the computation was performed, or that it would have been true even if the computation had never been performed? The truth definition leaves such questions quite unanswered. (1975a, 233)

But is semantic theory really ontologically neutral? Mark Platts, using 'realist' with a lowercase 'r' to mean what I have meant by 'quasi realist', suggests that semantic theory can be given a "realist reading" implying that "what makes it the case that 'Grass is green' is true ... is the obtaining of the state of affairs specified by the right-hand side" (1979, 12). Platts is understating the case when he says the formula *can* be given a quasi-realist reading. In fact, Tarski did give it just that reading, although admittedly he did not emphasize the point or make it *quite* as explicit as it could be made, for he says in two places that a vague *but not inconsistent statement* of the same conception of truth he is trying to analyze would be, "A sentence is true if it designates an *existing state of affairs*" (1944, 15, 32; 1969, 63).

(Read 'obtaining' for 'existing' in Tarski's remark.) But as Blackburn and Dummett would be quick to point out, this remark of Tarski's does not really solve the problem, for there is still the question of what it means for a state of affairs to obtain. A coherence theorist may say, and many of them *would* say, that what it is for the fact that snow is white to exist is just that the Absolute, or God, or the World Mind, has the *idea* that snow is white. Moreover, what it is for the Absolute to *have an idea* is just that the idea is a member of a perfectly coherent system of ideas. In other words, the coherence theorist is claiming that 'being true', 'expressing a state of affairs that obtains', 'expressing an idea of the Absolute', and 'being a member of a perfectly coherent system' are all extensionally equivalent to one another. Hence *if* Tarski's theory says nothing that would conflict with any of these equivalence claims, his theory can be accepted with equanimity by the this sort of coherence theorist. Similarly, an instrumentalist can, as James does, embrace an instrumentalist account of reality, of what it is to be a fact, of what it is for a state of affairs to obtain: it is a fact that snow is white just when it is useful to believe that snow is white. Such an instrumentalist can accept Tarski's claim that 'being true' and 'expressing a state of affairs that obtains' are extensionally equivalent because he insists that 'expressing a useful belief' is extensionally equivalent to both of them.

This means that just as a Nonrealist correspondence theory is possible (see section 4.6), so too is a Nonrealist semantic theory. *If* Tarski did not specify whether or not the state of affairs expressed by the right-hand side of the T-sentences obtains mind-dependently or mind-independently, his theory straddles the great divide between Realist and Nonrealist answers to the metaphysical project. And even if Tarski *did* specify that the states of affairs in question are to be thought of as obtaining mind-independently, it would be perfectly possible for one to offer a theory just like Tarski's, save that it specifies that the states of affairs obtain mind-*dependently*, or save that it refrains from giving any ontological characterization to them at all. Thus a semantic theory can be 'realist' in the sense that Platts uses above but still not be 'Realist' as I have defined the term.[8]

Keep in mind, however, that, contra Black and Sellars, the problem is *not* that the semantic theory is compatible with Nonrealist theories of truth per se. In fact, as we saw earlier in this section, the latter theories are in the same position relative to the MAC as is the Bible theory of truth: they are compatible with the T-sentences but do not entail them and thus do not meet the MAC. The problem, if you can call it that, is that a semantic theory that provides no doctrine of what it is for a state of affairs to exist is compatible with the *combination* of the coherence theory of truth *and* a coherence theory of reality, and it is compatible with the *combination* of an instrumentalist theory of truth *and* an instrumentalist theory of reality, and so on for other Nonrealist theories.[9]

Just how vacuous is a semantic theory that maintains an ontological neutrality? That such a theory would be compatible with all Realist theories is not in dispute, so the question about its vacuity turns on whether it is also compatible with Nonrealist theories. In the rhetoric of those who make the vacuity objection, it is *utterly* vacuous because it is compatible with *any* other theory of truth. But the legitimate argument for the objection, which I have just rehearsed, does not support such a dramatic conclusion. To be sure, an ontologically neutral semantic theorist should concede at the very least that his theory is compatible with a great many of the actual Nonrealist theories that have been offered. Specifically, it is compatible with any Nonrealist, but quasi-realist theory, including those of Peirce, James, and McTaggart, for an ontologically neutral semantic theory of truth (at least when stripped of extra ambitions connected with model theory and physicalism) does not amount to more than an endorsement of quasi realism. But it is not clear that such a theory would be compatible with *all* Nonrealist theories, precisely because it is not clear that all such theories are quasi realist.

A theory of truth of interest in this context is that of Samuel Alexander, who, it is often said, was an ontological realist but who nevertheless endorsed a *coherence* theory of truth (Alexander 1920, 247–272). Alexander's remarks on truth are so muddled that one would be foolish to attribute any theory to him with any confidence. Among other things, he represents a truly extreme case of failing to distinguish the metaphysical and justification projects. One possible interpretation of him is to see him as accepting the existence of a mind-independent world but denying that what goes on in that world has anything to do with which propositions are true: a proposition is true when it coheres with other propositions. Recall that Realism is a combination of quasi realism about truth and ontological realism about the nature of reality. So a Nonrealist theory of truth is one that rejects *either* quasi realism or ontological realism. Peirce, James, and McTaggart reject the latter. Blanshard rejects the latter and possibly the former as well (see below). Alexander, under the current interpretation, rejects only quasi realism. Thus his is a Nonrealist theory that is not compatible with even an ontologically neutral semantic theory. We saw in chapter 3 that there are compelling counterexamples to theories that, like this one, allow that 'Snow is white' can be false even if it is a mind-independent fact that snow is white and that 'Snow is white' can be true even if it is a mind-independent fact that snow is not white. Thus if our object were to give a sympathetic interpretation to Alexander, we would want to say that he really *means* to endorse a Realist theory of truth and either a coherence theory of *justification* or the thesis that coherent belief sets are more epistemically valuable than belief sets that correspond to the mind-independent world. But the object here is to establish that it is quite *possible* to have a Nonrealist theory of truth incompatible with an ontologically neutral semantic theory and that, indeed, Alexander's may be an *actual* case of such a theory.

Suppose, then, that the vacuity objector retreats to the somewhat milder claim (made, for example, by Field 1986, 71) that Tarski's theory is compatible with every actual and possible theory of truth not easily refuted by counterexample. This is probably right, but let me offer some highly speculative thoughts to the effect that we should not be absolutely confident of even this milder claim.

Recall from section 3.5 that it is unclear just what sort of account of reality Blanshard would endorse. It is not clear, in other words, how he would fill in the blank in

The state of affairs expressed by 'Snow is white' obtains iff ____ .

That he would reject an ontologically realist analysis is not to be disputed. The crucial question is whether he would fill out the blank above with *something at least extensionally equivalent* to what he would use to fill the blank in

'Snow is white' is true iff ____ .

Let's assume, for the sake of argument, that Blanshard would not. Since the two blank fillers are not extensionally equivalent, the left-hand sides of these two statements will not be extensionally equivalent either. This is another way of saying that some T-sentences count as false on Blanshard's theory so interpreted. Hence his theory would involve a rejection of quasi realism and thus be incompatible with even an ontologically neutral semantic theory of truth. Does this ensure that his theory, under this interpretation, is easily refutable by counterexamples? He would be committed, to be sure, to the claim that 'Snow is white' *could be* false, even if it is a fact that snow is white. But the fact in question would be mind-*dependent*. Specifically, it would depend on some feature of mind *other than* the coherence of the belief with other beliefs, and this other feature of a mind, whatever it is, can vary independently from the coherence of the mind's beliefs. Suppose it turns out, on some such theory, that there are relatively few cases where some sentence is false even though it expresses a fact (and few where some sentence is true even though the state of affairs it expresses fails to obtain). And suppose further that those few cases are explained (or at least explained away) by reference to the way in which the coherence of the mind's beliefs and that other feature of the mind vary independently. Then it might not seem implausible, indeed, it might seem quite natural, that the set of true sentences and the set of sentences expressing facts should be disjoint to some extent. And thus the overall Blanshardian view might be plausible, despite the fact that it contradicts quasi realism. Of course, vacuity objectors will rightly insist that we need some account of what this mysterious other feature of mind is before we can be said to have made good on the preceding speculations. But our ignorance here cuts both ways. Until it is shown that one cannot make good on these speculations, we ought to be at least a little hesitant to accept even the milder version of the vacuity objection.

Note another implication of my discussion of Alexander and of McTaggart in section 4.6: the set of ontological realists is not identical to the set of correspondence theorists or the set of Realists about truth, and thus, contrary to a recent trend that seems to originate with Dummett (see section 8.4 and note 5 of chapter 3), the debate about truth cannot be reduced to a debate about ontology. Arguing about theories of truth is not just a roundabout way of arguing about ontology, nor is the latter debate a roundabout way of arguing about the proper theory of truth. Walker 1989, 2–3, 21–24, is a typical example of how Dummett's misleading picture is now frequently just taken for granted. Since Walker thinks that the dispute is a purely ontological one and that Tarski is ontologically neutral, he ends up concluding that Tarski does not have a theory of truth at all (Walker 1989, 23–25).

So our conclusion should be that *if* Tarski's theory is ontologically neutral, then it is compatible with a great many of the Nonrealist theories that have actually been defended, but even if it is ontologically neutral, it is not compatible with every possible Nonrealist theory of truth and may not even be compatible with every actual, every possible plausible, or every actual plausible Nonrealist theory of truth. This still leaves unanswered the question of whether Tarski's theory is ontologically neutral and, if it is, whether it is possible to construct a Tarski-like semantic theory that is indisputably Realist. For if it is possible, then there would not be much interest in the fact that *one* version of the semantic theory (Tarski's) is vacuous.

It is in fact easy to have a Realist, Tarski-like theory of truth. One could, for example, have a convention or stipulation that the adverb 'mind-independently', used as an operator on sentences (or clauses), means that the sentence so modified alleges a mind-independent fact. Then, creating a Realist, Tarski-like theory of truth is as simple as embedding 'mind-independently' into the second conjunct of each of the basis clauses of Tarski's truth theory:

$(\theta = $ 'x_k is red' for some k,
   and *mind-independently* the kth object in S is red)
or $(\theta = $ 'x_k loves x_j', for some k and j,
   and *mind-independently* the kth object in S loves the jth object in S)

And the MAC would be rewritten to say that an adequate theory of truth must entail all sentences on the pattern of

'Snow is white' is true $\equiv$ *mind-independently* snow is white.

But it would not be necessary to resort to this stratagem. Russell, after all, did not include any explicit proclamation of his ontological realism in his theory of truth, but no one disputes that it is a Realist theory, as I define that notion, because Russell made it clear in his other writings (of that era) that he thinks that facts are mind-independent things. By the same token, one who made clear one's ontological realism somewhere in one's corpus could embrace Tarski's theory and his MAC exactly as they are, and the resulting theory would have to count as a Realist one. (If a vacuity objector balked at this, then it would be his duty to explain this great mystery: why, in 78 years as of this writing, has no one accused *Russell's* theory of vacuity?) Indeed, I will go further and suggest that should anyone (including Tarski) assert Tarski's theory and not explicitly *re-nounce* ontological realism, the theory thereby asserted is a Realist one. In other words, the default interpretation of any philosopher who utters a declarative clause (such as the second conjunct of the basis clauses of Tarski's definition or the right-hand side of the T-sentences) is to take him or her as referring to a mind-independent world unless and until we are given convincing reason not to do so.

The fact that there can be a Realist, and thus nonvacuous, Tarski-like theory of truth has considerable significance, for the contrary assumption is a plank in the platform of a number of recent philosophical movements. First, Nonrealist answers to the metaphysical project have enjoyed renewed popularity in the last few years partly because of the perception that there is no correct nonvacuous alternative. Others have contended that the metaphysical project is itself ill-conceived in some way because there is *no* answer to it (not even a Nonrealist one) that is both correct and nonvacuous. Putnam often seems to say this (e.g., 1981, chap. 6). Finally, the contention that there cannot be a nonvacuous Tarski-like theory of truth is a key premise in Rorty's argument that we ought to abandon philosophy in favor of a "post-philosophical culture" (Rorty 1982, preface, esp. xxiii-xxix).

6.5   Is Tarski Ontologically Neutral?

All of the arguments mentioned in the last paragraph are ruined by the mere possibility of a Realist semantic theory, and the question of whether the *first* semantic theory, Tarski's, was Realist, which is the topic of this section, is only of interpretive and historical interest. It will be of interest to historians of logic and philosophy, but others may skip this section. I do not think any of the following arguments are decisive, but I think that they are at least strong enough to put the burden of proof on those who interpret Tarski as ontologically neutral.

The *only* textual evidence ever offered in support of the claim that Tarski intended his theory to be ontologically neutral is the following oft quoted claim: "We may remain naive realists, critical realists or idealists, empiricists or metaphysicians—whatever we were before. The semantic conception is completely neutral toward all these issues" (Tarski 1944, 34). Even this small piece of evidence evaporates when we see the *whole* remark, in which it is clear that Tarski uses these terms to label epistemological, not ontological, views: "Thus, we may accept the se-mantic conception of truth without giving up any *epistemological* attitude

we may have had, we may remain [etc. as in the preceding quotation]"
(emphasis mine). This judgment is reinforced when it is recalled that in the
Logical Positivist era, in which Tarski was writing, 'naive realism', 'critical
realism', and even 'idealism' were as much names of theories of perception
or justification as names of ontological doctrines. For example, 'naive
realism' denoted the view that sense data are numerically identical to the
surfaces of physical objects, and 'idealism' labeled the view that sense data
are entirely the constructions of our minds. This, for example, is how H. H.
Price used these terms in his book *Perception* (1932, esp. 1–17, 26), written
in this era. 'Metaphysician' would have denoted, for Tarski, anyone who
accepted nonempiricist methods in their conception of justification. He
says as much himself (1944, 35). So Tarski is saying only that his theory is
not a theory of justification, that it is not meant to be an answer to the
justification project.[10] This becomes even clearer when we examine the
entire passage from which this remark comes. I hope my readers will
indulge me in this long quotation. I am being very thorough because the
primary piece of evidence on this issue of interpreting Tarski is the
structure and content of this quotation.

It has been claimed that—due to the fact that a sentence like 'snow is white' is
taken to be semantically true if snow is *in fact* white (italics by the critic)—logic
finds itself involved in a most uncritical realism.

If there were an opportunity to discuss the objection with its author, I should
raise two points. First, I should ask him to drop the words '*in fact*', which do not
occur in the original formulation and which are misleading, even if they do not
affect the content. For these words convey the impression that the semantic
conception of truth is intended to establish the conditions under which we are
warranted in asserting any given sentence, and in particular any empirical
sentence. However, a moment's reflection shows that this impression is merely an
illusion; and I think that the author of the objection falls victim to the illusion
which he himself created.

In fact, the semantic definition of truth implies nothing regarding the conditions
under which a sentence like (1):

(1) *snow is white*

can be asserted. It implies only that, whenever we assert or reject this sentence, we
must be ready to assert or reject the correlated sentence (2):

(2) *the sentence 'snow is white' is true.*

Thus, we may accept the semantic conception of truth without giving up any
epistemological attitude we may have had; we may remain naive realists, critical

realists or idealists, empiricists or metaphysicians—whatever we were before. The semantic conception is completely neutral toward all these issues.

In the second place, I should try to get some information regarding the conception of truth which (in the opinion of the author of the objection) does not involve logic in a most naive realism. I would gather that this conception must be incompatible with the semantic one. Thus, there must be sentences which are true in one of these conceptions without being true in the other. Assume, e.g., the sentence (1) to be of this kind. The truth of this sentence in the semantic conception is determined by an equivalence of the form (T):

The sentence 'snow is white' is true if, and only if, snow is white.

Hence in the new conception we must reject this equivalence, and consequently we must assume its denial:

The sentence 'snow is white' is true if, and only if, snow is not white (or perhaps: *snow, in fact, is not white*).

This sounds somewhat paradoxical. I do not regard such a consequence of the new conception as absurd; but I am a little fearful that someone in the future may charge this conception with involving logic in a 'most sophisticated kind of irrealism.' At any rate, it seems to me important to realize that every conception of truth which is incompatible with the semantic one carries with it consequences of this type. (Tarski 1944, 33–34)

Tarski begins by noting an ontological objection to the effect that the semantic theory involves an uncritical realism. But instead of dealing with this objection immediately, he postpones his rebuttal in order to deal with a misunderstanding of the semantic theory that he sees lurking within the objection. His discussion of the *misunderstanding* begins with the word 'First' in the fifth line. His answer to the *objection* does not begin until the words 'in the second place' in the fifth paragraph. Thus the fourth paragraph, part of which is so often cited as evidence of Tarski's ontological neutrality, is a part of his attempt to clear up a misunderstanding. The misunderstanding is the belief that "the semantic conception of truth is intended to establish the conditions under which we are warranted in asserting any given sentence" (lines 8–9). In fact, says Tarski, the semantic theory takes no stand on questions of warrant. And *that* is the point of the fourth paragraph.[11] When in the fifth paragraph Tarski gets around to actually dealing with the objection, *he does not deny that his theory involves what his critics call "a most naive realism."* Instead, he seems to concede that it does but to insist that any theory that did not would entail dubious, almost paradoxical results. Thus, far from asserting an ontological neutrality, Tarski seems to be embracing a naive or uncritical ontological realism. He does, of course, rebel against these *labels* for his view. That seems to be the point of the sixth paragraph, in which he sarcastically implies that his opponents are indulging in name-calling. He would not have reacted this way if the view in question were not his, because in that case he would not object to its being characterized as "naive" or "uncritical"; he would have simply denied that it was his view. Had he ever worked out his ontological views, Tarski would probably have found that commonsense realism, at least about the physical world, and possibly scientific realism were the doctrines to which he really subscribed.

So in sum, Tarski is in effect saying to his critics, "If by 'naive' or 'uncritical' realism you are referring to the theory of justification or perception known by that name, you have misunderstood, for my theory is neutral about epistemological issues. But if you are referring to an ontological doctrine by these terms, you are right to attribute it to me, but you are only resorting to name-calling instead of making a genuine objection."

6.6 Hartry Field and the Physicalist Program

As we saw in section 5.1, one of Tarski's broader enterprises, in the service of which he wants to put his answer to the extensional project, is the program of physicalism (Tarski 1936, 406). Physicalism was roughly described there as the thesis that all intellectually respectable concepts can be defined ultimately and entirely in terms of the concepts of logic, mathematics, and physical science. (Compare Field 1986, 109 n. 22.) Any concepts not so definable are, like witches and unicorns, mythical beasts. So according to physicalism, the fact naturally expressed with the words 'Quine believes he is writing about Tarski' can be expressed, at least in principle, with a sentence that contains no nonphysical terminology (i.e., a sentence without the word 'believes' or any other mental term), or if it cannot, then it is not a fact that Quine believes he is writing about Tarski, in which case the statement is meaningless. (Presumably, if this conclusion were reached, it would be reached because the physicalist decided that beliefs are irreducibly nonphysical and hence mythical. Because of the very strong intuitions we all have that there is such a thing as a belief, the physicalists will strive mightily and for many generations to reduce belief to physical concepts before they give in and declare them mythical [Field 1972, 93].) Neurath states the view thus: "Physicalism is the form work in unified science takes in our time. Whatever else is said in pronouncements is either 'meaningless' or merely a means to emotion, 'poetry.' For physicalism as it is represented here quite strictly, everything that was put forward as philosophy by scholastics, Kantians, phenomenologists, is *meaningless* except that part of their formulations that can be translated into scientific, that is physicalist, statements" (1931a, 56–57). Thus, to ensure that semantics conforms to the dictates of physicalism, Tarski needed to reduce all semantic concepts to physical and/or logicomathematical concepts. Or to put it another way, Tarski wants to make semantics into a physical science.

Hartry Field (1972, 93) shares Tarski's ambitions, but he thinks that Tarski was only partially successful in carrying out the physicalist program as it applies to semantics. In reducing the concept of truth to the concept of satisfaction, Tarski, according to Field, made a valuable first step, and he made a valuable second step with the recursive clauses of his definition of satisfaction, since these have the effect of reducing satisfaction for complex sentences to satisfaction for simple sentences. However, Field claims (1972, 82, 94–95), the basis clauses of Tarski's definition of satisfaction do not, as Tarski thought they did, *reduce* the semantic concept of satisfaction for simple sentences in a manner that is successful from the standpoint of the physicalist program. This seems to be a surprising charge on the face of it, since there certainly are *not* any terms, save logicomathematical and physical terms, in the basis clauses of Tarski's definition. For example, the basis clauses of a Tarskian definition of satisfaction for a language with (only) the predicates 'is red', and 'is round', and 'is included in' are these:

$(\theta = {}'x_k$ is red' for some k, and the kth object in S is red)
or $(\theta = {}'x_k$ is round' for some k, and the kth object in S is round)
or $(\theta = {}'x_k$ is included in x_j' for some k and j,
    and the kth object in S is included in the jth object in $S)^{12}$

Field does not deny this (p. 89), but he insists that a physicalistically acceptable *reduction* of semantic concepts to logicomathematical and physical concepts requires more than a mere *translation* of semantic terms into logicomathematical and physical terms. Tarski, he says, takes the following three conditions to be jointly sufficient as well as individually necessary for a physicalistically acceptable definition of truth:

1. In the definition, say, $(s)[s$ is true iff ___], the blank is filled with a well-formed formula (i.e., a grammatically correct expression) in which no semantic terms appear.
2. The 'iff' in the definition represents *extensional* equivalence; that is, it is synonymous with ' $\equiv$ '.
3. The definition is correct; that is, it entails all instances of schema T.[13]

Field agrees that (1) to (3) express necessary conditions for a physicalistically acceptable definition, and if they expressed jointly sufficient conditions, then Tarski's definition would be physicalistically acceptable, since it certainly meets all three. However, in Field's view, (2) as it stands is not as demanding as it should be. It should require that the 'iff' in a truth definition represent an equivalence relation that is *stronger* than extensional. To *reduce* one set of concepts to another requires more than a merely extensionally correct definition. On the other hand, it would be going to far to insist that the 'iff' represent *intensional* equivalence, for that would mean that a definition cannot be physicalistically acceptable unless the right-hand side of the 'iff' expresses conditions that are *in every possible world* necessary and jointly sufficient for truth, but there are many successful reductions that do not meet this very demanding standard. So what we need, Field says (p. 95), is an equivalence relation that is stronger than extensional equivalence but weaker than intensional equivalence. Field is suggesting that a genuine *reduction* of semantic terms to logico-mathematical and physical terms requires a definition in which the 'iff' represents, in the terminology of this book, *natural equivalence* and thus is synonymous with ' $\leftrightarrow$ '. (See section 1.5.) Hence, on Field's view, the right-hand side of the 'iff' in a physicalistically acceptable definition of truth must not only contain just logico-mathematical and physical terms; it must also express conditions that are necessary and sufficient for truth *in every possible world with the same laws of nature as the actual world.* Tarski's definition of satisfaction, and hence of truth, does not meet this criterion. There are many worlds with the same laws of nature as the actual world in which ' x_k is red' means that x_k is *square*, and in such worlds the clause, given above, defining satisfaction for the predicate 'is red' would be erroneous.

So Tarski's fundamental error, in Field's eyes, is that he choose the wrong *project* to serve his physicalist *program*. (See section 1.9.) He should have chosen the naturalistic project, not the extensional project. (See section 1.5.)

Field's next task is to support his (at this point undefended) claim that a physicalistic reduction requires definitions expressed with natural equivalence. He does so by drawing an analogy with another part of the physicalist program: the task of reducing the chemical concept of valence to logicomathematical and physical concepts.

The valence of a chemical element is an integer that is associated with that element, which represents the sort of chemical combinations that the element will enter into. What I mean by the last phrase is that it is possible—roughly, at least—to characterize which elements will combine with which others, and in what proportions they will combine, merely in terms of their valences. (Field 1972, 95)

If physicalism is correct it ought to be possible to explicate this concept in physical terms—e.g., it ought to be possible to find structural properties of atoms of each element that determine what the valence of that element will be. (p. 96)

Now Field asks us to compare two definitions of valence.[14] (The 'E' ranges over elements, and 'n' over integers.) Note the difference in the equivalence symbols in the two definitions.

$(E)(n)(E$ has valence n
$\equiv E$ is potassium and n is 1,
  or E is tungsten and n is 6,
  or [and so on for all the elements found in the actual world]). (D1)

To make the second definition simple, we must pretend that there are only two atomic properties relevant to the valence of an element, that each comes in degrees measurable in integers, and that the valence of an element is the total of the degrees of the two properties.

$(E)(n)(E$ has valence n
  $\leftrightarrow$ the degree of E's atomic property P plus the degree of E's atomic
    property Q equals n) (D2)

Field's argument from analogy proceeds like this: (D1) is true, because the left-hand side *is* extensionally equivalent to the right-hand side,[15] and no chemical terms appear on the right-hand side (apparently 'potassium' and 'tungsten' are physical terms, not chemical terms, for Field). But (D1) is not an acceptable definition of valence from the standpoint of the reductionist program of physicalism. This can be most clearly seen by comparing (D1) with (D2). The latter *is* acceptable. But Tarski's definition of satisfaction, or at least those clauses of it that define satisfaction for atomic open sentences, is just like (D1). It too is extensionally correct, and it has no semantic terms on the right-hand side. And just as (D1) simply lists each element and assigns each a valence, so too the basis clauses of Tarski's definition of satisfaction simply assign satisfaction conditions one by one to each predicate of the language. But if (D1) is unacceptable, then Tarski's definition must be unacceptable as well.[16]

The argument comes down to Field's claim that (D1) is unacceptable. He never quite says explicitly what is wrong with it (p. 96), but it is clear enough from the context and certain remarks he makes in later papers (e.g., Field 1986, 55) that his objection to (D1) is that it does not *explain* or *explicate* what valence is, whereas (D2) does. By analogy, then, Tarski's definition of satisfaction is unacceptable because it explains nothing about satisfaction.[17] (Strictly, Field *does* think that the recursive clauses in the definition explain the concept of satisfaction for complex sentences in terms of satisfaction for atomic open sentences, so it is the concept satisfaction for atomic open sentences that does not get explained by Tarski's definition [pp. 94-96].) As Field writes, "Tarski succeeded in reducing the notion of truth to certain other semantic notions; but ... he did not in any way *explicate* these other notions, so ... his results ought to make the word 'true' acceptable only to someone who already regarded these other semantic notions as acceptable" (p. 83; emphasis mine). So as Field conceives it, the program of reducing semantic concepts to logico-mathematical and physical concepts is not a purely philosophical program; rather, it is just a portion of the explanatory enterprise of theoretical physics itself:[18] "physicalism: the doctrine that chemical facts, biological facts, psychological facts and semantical facts are all *explicable* (in principle) in terms of physical facts" (p. 93, emphasis mine).

It may help to contrast the physicalist program, as Field views it, with another sort of semantic reduction program, advocated by Robert Cummins. Referring to any of the basis clauses of Tarski's definition of satisfaction (e.g., '$\theta = $ "x_k is red" for some k, and the kth object in S is red') as "a statement of satisfaction conditions," Cummins, like Field, complains that "Tarski tells us what satisfies what, but leaves us without a clue as to how the fact expressed in a statement of satisfaction conditions should or could be *explained*" (Cummins 1979, 355; emphasis mine). But unlike the physicalists, Cummins does not propose to reduce semantic concepts to physical concepts. Instead, he argues that semantic concepts can be reduced, via a four-step process, to *psychological* concepts. First, truth is reduced to satisfaction. Second, the satisfaction conditions for a given utterance are explained as being what they are because of the *conventional meaning* of the words in the utterance. Third, conventional meaning is explained in terms of *speaker's meaning*. (Roughly, a word W comes to have the conventional meaning M in a linguistic community if speakers in the community repeatedly use W to mean M and they succeed in communicating.) Fourth, speaker's meaning is explained in terms of the psychological notions of the *beliefs* and *intentions* of speakers and auditors (or readers). (Roughly, a speaker "uses W to mean M" if he utters W *intending* it to convey the idea of M to his auditors and they *believe* that he has just this intention.)

It is important to keep in mind that Field's sole concern is with the adequacy, or lack thereof, of Tarski's theory as a contribution to physicalism. Field does not offer a theory of truth of his own. Accordingly, he does not belong on the chart of truth theorists in section 1.8. He does, however, suggest a strategy for constructing a physicalistically acceptable definition of truth. First, we should define truth in terms of satisfaction, just as Tarski does, and the recursive clauses of Tarski's definition of satisfaction should remain unchanged. But we should define satisfaction for atomic open sentences in terms of the semantic concept of a predicate *applying to* an object (p. 86) by combining all the basis clauses of Tarski's definition into a single clause reading something like this:

$(\theta = \text{'}Px_k\text{'}$ for some k and some predicate P,
    and P applies to the kth object in S)

We then reduce the semantic concept of *application* by means of a Kripke-like causal theory of reference (p. 99). Field does not believe that the latter theory is sufficiently well worked out to make this possible at the moment, but he thinks that there is good reason to think it could be worked out, and so he is optimistic for the prospects of a physicalist reduction of semantics.[19]

The question whether Field's version of physicalism is an important and viable project will be taken up in section 6.8. In the next section I consider the more immediate question whether, *as a criticism of Tarski*, Field's remarks are well taken.

6.7 Neurath, Carnap, and the Origins of Modern Physicalism

If Tarski did think that physicalism as applied to semantics is a branch of theoretical physics and that it is an *explanatory* program, then I think we can join Field in saying that Tarski failed to answer his own physicalist ambitions. (Indeed, on this assumption it will turn out that Field was excessively lenient with Tarski. See the last paragraph of this section.) So we can agree that, whether he intended it to or not, Tarski's theory of truth does not satisfy the physicalist program as Field describes it, and that is the most important issue. There is, however, at least some historical interest in the question of whether Tarski really did conceive of the physicalist program in the same way that Field thinks of it, and hence of whether Field's argument *qua* criticism of Tarski is cogent.

So how did Tarski think of physicalism? Our knowledge that he was a physicalist derives entirely from the brief remark he once made that he wanted to bring semantics "into harmony with the postulates of the unity of science and of physicalism" (Tarski 1936, 406). In his other writings he never mentions physicalism. Although he does speak repeatedly of his desire to define semantic terms with nonsemantic terms, nowhere outside of Tarski 1936 does he specify physical terms as the target vocabulary.[20] So, discovering the nature of Tarski's conception of the physicalist program requires that we identify what writings of others he was alluding to in the preceding quotation. Fortunately, that is not difficult. Both the terms 'physicalism' and 'the unity of science' were coined by Otto Neurath and championed by Rudolf Carnap in the early 1930s. It could hardly be a coincidence that Tarski, who first made this paper public in a lecture in 1935, used just these words. Nor is it plausible to think that Tarski would mislead his audience by making this allusion, with these terms, if he meant something different by 'physicalism' and 'the unity of science' than was meant by Neurath and Carnap at the time. Hence, if we are going to be able to attribute any conception of physicalism to Tarski at all, we must identify his conception with that of Neurath and/or Carnap as it stood at the time Tarski was writing Tarski 1936. (The only intellectually respectable alternative would be to refrain from attributing any *particular* physicalist program to Tarski, in which case Field's argument, *qua critique of Tarski*, would be rendered groundless.)

The key to understanding Neurath's idea of physicalism is to recognize that he promulgated it primarily for *epistemological* reasons:

'Making predictions' is what all of science is about. At the beginning of the process are observation statements ....

With the help of observation statements we formulate laws; according to Schlick these laws are not to be seen as proper statements but as directives for finding predictions of individual courses of events; these predictions can then be tested by more observation statements. (Neurath 1931a, 53)

A prediction can be checked (controlled) by observation statements only ....What matters is that all statements contain references to the spatio-temporal order, the order we know from physics. Therefore this view is to be called "physicalism." Unified science contains only physicalist formulations. (p. 54)

But Neurath's use of the word 'physics' is apt to mislead, since we naturally take it as the name of the academic discipline of physics in parallel with 'chemistry', 'biology', 'philosophy', 'classical languages', and 'semantics'. This in turn creates the impression that Neurath, like Field, thinks of physicalism as the program of reducing all concepts, including all concepts from other academic disciplines, to concepts deemed acceptable in contemporary theoretical physics, that is, the concepts used by practicing professional physicists—concepts like electron, charge, ion, and momentum. But this is not, indeed could not possibly be, what Neurath has in mind, for the concepts of academic physics, many of them anyway, are as unobservable, and hence as useless in formulating testable predictions, as are the sorts of concepts (like empathy, God, and moral rectitude) that he and his Logical Positivist brethren ridiculed as the legacy of primitive thinking (e.g., Neurath 1930). Thus the statements of theoretical physics are as in need of reduction to statements referring to observable objects and properties as are the statements of any other subject. This seems to be the import of the rest of the preceding quotation, which continues thus: "The fate of *physics in the narrower sense* thus becomes the fate of all the sciences, as far as statements about the smallest particles are concerned. For 'physicalism' it is essential that one kind of order is the foundation of all laws, whichever science is concerned, geology, chemistry or sociology" (emphasis mine). Thus, the target vocabulary of physicalist reduction is the vocabulary of everyday observables—the language of the ordinary person when stripped of "metaphysical" terms like 'empathy', 'God', and 'moral rectitude'. He confirms this in (1931b): "In a certain sense the view advocated here starts from a given state of everyday language, which in the beginning is essentially physicalist and only gradually becomes intermixed with metaphysics.... The language of physicalism is nothing new as it were; it is the language familiar to certain 'naive' children and peoples" (p. 66).

Since Neurath did not think of physicalism as aiming at the reduction of all concepts to the concepts of theoretical physics, the reader should not be surprised that there is not a hint anywhere in Neurath's writings that physicalism has any sort of *explanatory* goals. On the contrary, the idea for Neurath is to get statements referring to nonobservables translated into equivalent statements referring only to observables, so that the truth values of the latter (and, by the equivalence, of the former too) can be tested by direct observation. But it would be preposterous to think that the latter *explains* the former: facts about the redness of John's face and his blood pressure do not *explain why* John is angry. Note too that for Neurath's epistemological program, it is only necessary that the observation statements be extensionally equivalent to the statements they translate and test, for extensional equivalence is enough to ensure identity of truth value.

Further examination of the relevant Neurath and Carnap papers available to Tarski when he wrote Tarski 1936 (Neurath 1930, 1931a, 1931b, 1932–1933; and Carnap 1932, 1932–1933) confirms that this epistemological program is what they meant by 'physicalism' and the 'unity of science'. Carnap also endorses a program that is substantially the same as what Field calls physicalism, but Carnap thinks of it as a different project from what he means by 'physicalism'. (Readers who do not want to take my word for the last two sentences should consult Kirkham, in progress.) The argument for those sentences is long and requires quite a number of long quotations from the aforementioned papers, so I think it inappropriate to include in this work. At any rate, for the reasons given above, Field's program is not what Tarski was referring to when he endorsed "the postulates of the unity of science and of physicalism," and we ought consequently, to reject Field's criticism of Tarski.[21]

What Tarski *was* endorsing with his remark was the program of reducing all statements with references to nonobservables to statements containing only references to everyday observable entities and properties. And as we saw, this program requires only extensional equivalence between the former statements and their translations, and it does not require the latter to explain the former. It would seem, then, that whatever other problems they may have, Tarski's definitions do succeed in advancing this more modest program. Field briefly considers what is substantially this interpretation of Tarski, and he dismisses it only because for some kinds of languages, such as those with ambiguous names, it is not possible to create Tarski-like definitions that even so much as *extensionally* define all semantic concepts (Field 1972, 100–101). But even if this claim is true, it does not pass muster as a reason for rejecting my interpretation of Tarski's physicalism, because Tarski made it quite clear, as we saw in section 5.5, that he had no interest in the sorts of languages Field is talking about. (See section 8.3 for why ambiguous terms cause problems.)

On the other hand, if Tarski had embraced the version of physicalism that Field attributes to him, then Field could be faulted for being *too generous* to Tarski. This is the complaint that Scott Soames (1984, 419–420) and Robert C. Stalnaker (1987, 30–31) aim at Field. If, as Field contends, the basis clauses of Tarski's definition fail to be explanatory, then the recursive clauses of that same definition must be faulted for exactly the same reason. Field contends that Tarski's recursive clauses *do* explain the satisfaction of truth-functionally compounded or quantified sentences in terms of the satisfaction of the parts of such sentences. But Soames and Stalnaker point out that the recursive clauses are just as much a "list account" of satisfaction as are the basis clauses. Whereas the basis clauses in effect define satisfaction separately for each predicate of language, the recursive clauses in effect list each truth function and quantifier in the language and define satisfaction for each one by one:

$(\theta = ` \neg \phi$' and S does not satisfy ϕ)
or $(\theta = `\psi$ or ϕ', and either S satisfies ψ or S satisfies ϕ)
or $(\theta = `(x_k) \phi$' and *every* sequence that differs from S in at most the kth place satisfies ϕ)
or $(\theta = `(\exists x_k) \phi$' and *some* sequence that differs from S in at most the kth place satisfies ϕ)].

Clauses like these no more explain satisfaction than do the basis clauses. As evidence of that, notice that if I added '#' as a truth-functional sentence connector and '@' as a quantifier to the language for which satisfaction is being defined, and asked you to add the appropriate recursive clauses for these new terms to the definition satisfaction, you would not have the foggiest idea how to do it. (Compare section 6.3.)

6.8   Objections to Physicalism

Beyond the issue of whether Field's criticism of Tarski is well taken, there is the more interesting question of whether physicalism as Field conceives it is a viable and valuable program. The literature on physicalism is immense. Just the issue of whether psychological concepts are reducible to physical concepts fills many volumes of debate. Accordingly, I limit myself here to a couple of objections to Field's paper.

Field claims that physicalism is an intrinsic and "extremely fruitful" part of scientific methodology (Field 1972, 96). Science has made progress by trying to reduce social concepts to biological ones (and dismissing as mythical any that cannot be so reduced), biological concepts to chemical concepts (and dismissing, etc.), and chemical concepts to physical concepts (and dismissing, etc.). The discovery of how to reduce valence to the physical concepts of atomic structure is only one example of this progress. But this is at best an oversimplified picture of scientific history and methodology. At worst, it is wildly false. For one thing, what counts as a physical concept in the eyes of theoretical physicists changes from era to era. Aristotle's concept of bare substratum once counted as a physical concept in just the required sense, but it does no longer. *Not* because modern physicists do not believe that it exists, for they are quite neutral on that question. Rather, neither the assertion nor the denial that there is such a thing as bare substratum would count as a statement of physics at all. What should be even more disconcerting to physicalists (in Field's sense) is that entities that once did not count as physical now do. Newton was excoriated for his postulation of gravity on the grounds that such a mysterious "force" was metaphysical and "occult," in other words, not scientifically respectable. By the nineteenth century it had become respectable. So it appears that if a concept has sufficient explanatory value, physicists are as willing to reclassify it as physical as they are to reduce it to some preexisting stock of physical concepts. Field claims that if valence, which has great explanatory value in chemistry, had not been successfully reduced, scientists would have had to abandon it or else abandon physicalism (1972, 96). In light of the history of the concept of gravity, it seems more likely that they would have reclassified valence as a physical concept.

Beyond merely reclassifying nonphysical concepts, physicist have proven themselves perfectly willing to postulate new physical entities whenever explanation seems to require it. Before Einstein, the concepts of charge, mass, and energy had become acceptable and commonplace to physicists. Since then, Einstein has made concept of space-time, indeed, space-time that "*bends*" acceptable. But even Einstein did not accept the concept of quarks. Quarks are not only accepted today; they are thought to have certain odd properties, among which are those physicists have labeled 'charm', 'spin', 'beauty', and (ironically for this context) 'truth'. But if this sort of ontological exotica is tolerable to a physicalist, then one really does begin to wonder what beef he could have with nonphysical concepts. If quanta (moving entities that have a location or a speed, but not both) are acceptable, how could empathy, God, moral rectitude, belief, truth, and denotation not be? Karl Popper has made essentially the same point in criticizing Carnap 1932–1933: "Most of the concepts with which physics works, such as forces, fields, and even electrons and other particles are what Berkeley (for example) called '*qualitiates occultae*'. . . . The fact is that we cannot explain the strength of the post by its structure alone (as Carnap suggested) but only by its structure together with laws which make ample use of 'hidden forces' which Carnap, like Berkeley, condemned as occult" (Popper 1965, 266).

Reductionist programs involve the claim that events, entities, and properties of type *A* (e.g., biological), if they are not mythical, can be completely described as events, entities, and properties of type *B* (e.g., physical), and that the latter descriptions *explain* everything that could be explained with type *A* vocabulary. An increasingly common response to such programs is to accept the first claim and reject the second. John McDowell makes just this sort of response to Field's version of physicalism. He wants to concede to Field that "(i) all events are physical events, that is, have physical descriptions; [and] (ii) under their physical descriptions, all events are susceptible of total explanations, of the kind paradigmatically afforded by physics, in terms of physical laws and other physically described events" (McDowell 1978, 128). But physical explanations are only one kind of explanation. In any scientific explanation, be it physical, chemical, biological, etc., an event or action is shown to be unsurprising because it is the inevitable outcome of natural laws. In particular, a physical explanation makes it clear that the event is an outcome of physical laws. So in a physical explanation of a semantic phenomenon—an act of linguistic behavior, the event/action is shown to be unsurprising because it is shown to be an instance of "the way the world works," an outcome of physical laws (p. 125).

But there is another kind of explanation: "Intentional explanation makes an action unsurprising not as an instance of the way the world works (though of course it does not follow that an action is *not* that), but as something which the agent can be understood to have seen some point in going for. An intentional explanation of an event does not ... offer, so to speak, to fill the same explanatory space" (p. 126). The point of this for McDowell is that the fact that a semantic phenomenon can be given a physical description under which it is "susceptible of a total [physical] explanation" is not incompatible with the claim that it can be given an intentional description in terms that are irreducible to physical terms, and that under its intentional description it can be given an intentional explanation that provides a different *kind* of understanding of the phenomenon than is provided by the physical explanation. "If intentional concepts [of which semantic concepts are a subset] are largely constituted by their role in a special kind of explanation, which does not compete with the kind physics yields but offers a different species of comprehension, then we need not expect to be able, even approximately, to reduce those concepts to physical terms. The distinctive point of the intentional concepts makes it intelligible that there should be a kind of incommensurability between them and physical concepts" (p. 126).

Physicalists will respond by claiming that the sorts of questions that intentional explanations answer only arise in the first place when, in our primitive and unenlightened way, we persist in thinking of semantic phenomena as nonphysical phenomena. If we would only stop doing that, the puzzles that intentional explanations assuage would never bother us to begin with. Thus physicalism, they would insist, does not involve *losing* intentional explanations and hence a "species of comprehension." Instead, it involves *ridding ourselves* of certain pseudopuzzles and the illusory "comprehension" that comes from explaining those puzzles. It would take us too far from the main themes of this book to pursue the debate further. It must suffice here to say that if McDowell is right, then Field has made the illicit assumption that if all events, entities, and properties are at bottom physical events, entities, and properties, then all nonsemantic concepts (if they are not entirely mythical) are reducible to, and explainable by, theoretical physics.

6.9 Chapter Summary

The survey in this chapter of objections to Tarski's theory began with a quick look at two objections to the MAC offered by Haack. The more interesting of them was her claim that the MAC presupposes the principle of bivalence. We saw, however, that this objection itself presupposes something: that there is no such thing as a vague state of affairs. Even if the latter claim is true, the MAC only presupposes the principle of bivalence when the latter is taken to be a claim about the truth values of (meaningful, declarative) sentences in the actual world, and when so interpreted, the principle is by no means obviously false. We then saw in section 6.2 how a failure to see that Tarski's theory is not intended to answer the justification project leads to foolish objections.

More potent than these is the relativity objection, which holds that by defining truth separately for each language, Tarski has failed to capture our translinguistic notion of truth. We saw that, while it is easy to delude oneself that Tarski has implicitly captured translinguistic truth if one deals only with Tarski-like truth definitions for languages one understands, the objection is essentially correct. Whether it is relevant or not depends, however, on one's goals. Tarski was not trying to capture the essence of translinguistic truth. He wanted only to capture the *extension* of truth for particular languages (each such extension being part of the extension of translinguistic truth), and this he did accomplish.

There also turned out to be a legitimate line of reasoning for a moderate version of the vacuity objection. Unfortunately, too many of those who have made this objection have supplemented, or just conflated, the legitimate argument with other, illegitimate arguments. Moreover, the rather grandiose conclusion of vacuity objectors that Tarski's theory is utterly vacuous because it is compatible with all other theories of truth is not supported by the legitimate argument for the objection. The most we can say is that an ontologically neutral Tarski-like theory is compatible with all quasi-realist theories of truth, a class that includes a great many Nonrealist theories. I argued that even this is not much of an objection, since one could perfectly well create a Tarski-like theory that is *not* ontologically neutral. Indeed, I argued in section 6.5 that someone has created just such a theory: Tarski.

The next three sections were taken up with an extended discussion of Field's claim that Tarski failed to provide a physicalistically acceptable reduction of semantic concepts to physical concepts. I concluded that *if* Tarski conceived of the physicalist program in the same way in which Field does, then he did fail in his physicalist ambitions. (Indeed, it turned out that Field was too easy on Tarski.) But since Tarski only alludes to physicalism and does not ever say what he thinks it is, we are forced to assume that he thought of it in the same way as did Neurath, its modern founder, and Carnap in those of their writings available at the time he endorsed it. An examination of those writings indicated that, while a Field-like program can be found in Carnap, in the end he and Neurath did not seem to equate physicalism with such a program. On the contrary, they thought of physicalism in such a way that Tarski's purely extensional definitions of truth do provide an adequate physicalist reduction. Attention then turned to an unfortunately but necessarily brief, and therefore indecisive, discussion of the importance and viability of Field's version of physicalism.

Let us turn now to the justification project and see some examples of how answers to the metaphysical project are put to use in evaluating answers to the former project.

7 The Justification Project

In this chapter we shall see how theories of truth play a regulatory role vis-à-vis theories of justification. I shall also examine some theories of justification that have been misleadingly labeled theories of truth. First, a few words of warning, especially to those who already have some familiarity with the topic of justification. This chapter may be irritating for what it leaves out. Although one, and usually only one, example from every major type of theory of justification theory is discussed here (briefly), many of the most renowned theories are not mentioned. Moreover, the theories discussed are not necessarily the highest-quality examples of their types. Given the purposes of the chapter, I thought it wise to include only theories that have been mislabeled theories of truth and/or theories that are simple and easy to present. Hence this chapter is in no sense a comprehensive survey of all theories of justification. That would be neither feasible nor desirable in view of the purposes of this book. Moreover, in discussing these theories, I shall not muster all of the arguments a tough-minded skeptic would marshal against one or another of them. Instead, I shall be content to examine of only the prima facie plausibility of each theory. There is simply no space or need for anything more ambitious. This is why many obvious objections that could be made to one or another of these theories go unmentioned here. Accordingly, no one ought to be under the impression that I take any of the brief arguments in this chapter as decisive. Finally, I do not endorse any of these theories. If you see flaws in them, that is all to the good. I do too.

7.1 The Relation of Theories of Justification to Theories of Truth

Theories of justification, as noted in section 1.7, try to fill the blank in the following

Truth correlates positively with ____, and it is relatively easy to determine when a proposition (sentence, or belief, etc.) has the latter characteristic.

So again, a theory of justification tries to identify some characteristic C, possibly quite complex, that correlates positively, if not perfectly, with truth and whose possession by a truth bearer is relatively easy to determine.

Some theories of justification have the same names as certain theories of truth. There is, for example, a coherence theory of justification as well as a coherence theory of truth, an instrumental theory of justification as well as an instrumental theory of truth. The coherence theory of justification identifies characteristic C as precisely the same thing that the coherence theory of truth identifies as the characteristic necessary and sufficient for truth, and the instrumental theory of justification identifies characteristic C as precisely the same thing that the instrumental theory of truth identifies as the characteristic necessary and sufficient for truth. For example, an instrumental theory of *truth* says that

$(t)(t$ is true iff t is useful to believe).

The instrumental theory of *justification* says this:

Truth correlates positively with usefulness and it is relatively easy to determine when a proposition (sentence, or belief, etc.) has this characteristic.

It is not necessary for a philosopher to endorse the theory of justification that is correlative to his theory of truth in this way, but there is an advantage, or *seeming* advantage, to doing so. For *relative* to a given theory of truth, the first conjunct of the correlative theory of justification is guaranteed to be "correct." The first conjunct of the instrumental theory of *justification* above is *entailed* by the instrumental theory of *truth* just above it. For if 'true sentence' is *defined* as one that is useful to believe, then *of course* a sentence that is useful to believe is probably true. This is a general rule: when a theory of justification of a given type (e.g., instrumental, coherence, etc.) is evaluated from the perspective of a theory of truth of that same type, then the first conjunct of the theory of justification is true.

One common response to skepticism takes advantage of the fact that theories of truth guarantee the first conjunct of their correlative theories of justification. The move begins by skipping over the metaphysical project without giving it an answer. A philosopher *first* finds a characteristic C that is apprehensible and declares that C correlates with truth, thereby creating a theory of justification. *Then* the philosopher turns back to the metaphysical project and declares that possessing characteristic C just *is* the necessary and sufficient condition for a truth bearer's being true. This insures that the first conjunct of her theory of justification is true, and the fact that she picked characteristic C precisely because it is apprehensible insures that the other conjunct of her theory is true. Thus skepticism is *apparently* refuted. As was pointed out in section 3.6 and has been noted by others, this move, or something very much like it, is (implicitly, if not explicitly) made by most philosophers who endorse Nonrealist theories of truth. In making this move, one is trying to build a refutation of skepticism into one's theory of truth. But we saw in section 3.6 that the move does not work. No really satisfying refutation of skepticism results, and one usually ends up with a theory of truth that is significantly less plausible than Realist theories in general.

7.2 Foundationalism

Foundationalism is historically associated with two doctrines:

1. Some propositions (and/or beliefs, sentences, etc.) are *basic* in that they are absolutely certain and self-evident. They are certain because they are indisputably true. They are self-evident because they need no evidence. Their truth is obvious: one only needs to think about such basic propositions and their truth will be apparent. (The most famous example of a self-evident proposition is 'I am thinking.' Merely by thinking about this proposition, however briefly, one *makes* it true. It has also been claimed that propositions describing one's own physical sensations are true whenever they are sincerely believed. For example, 'I have a pain in my knee.')
2. Other propositions are not basic. They do need justification. Specifically, they must be *inferred* from basic propositions.

Thus the standard metaphor used by foundationalists to describe the structure of a set of justified beliefs is the structure of a pyramid: just as the direction of support in a pyramid proceeds upward through successive layers of stones, so too the direction of justification is upward through successive layers of propositions. Since the middle of this century, foundationalists have been much less enthusiastic about doctrine 1. They are more likely nowadays to say (with widely varying terminology) that while basic propositions have an intrinsic *probability* (plausibility, or positive epistemic status), this probability may not be 100 percent. Basic propositions are not certain. They are innocent until proven guilty, but they *can* be proven guilty. That is, for any given basic proposition, one could, under the right circumstances, come to regard its intrinsic probability as misleading and to conclude that it is false. (See, e.g., Reichenbach 1952.) Specifically, if a basic proposition is grossly incompatible with many nonbasic propositions that are well justified (via their relations with *other* basic propositions), then it is unjustified. Hence on most contemporary foundational theories, justification proceeds to some extent downward from nonbasic to basic propositions. This, of course, weakens the appropriateness of the pyramid metaphor.

With respect to doctrine 2, contemporary foundationalists are also more likely to allow that the inference from basic propositions to nonbasic propositions can be inductive instead of deductive. (Deduction was required by Aristotle, at least in the *Posterior Analytics*, and was arguably required by Descartes [Cornman 1979, 131].)

The following would be a simplistic kind of foundational theory of justification:

Truth correlates positively with being either self-evident or inferred from propositions that are self-evident, and it is relatively easy to determine when a proposition (sentence, or belief, etc.) has one of these characteristics.

Of course, a good foundational theory would have to fill in some details, and most do. There are three parts to a more complete foundational theory. First, it identifies the set of propositions we are to take as foundational or basic. Historically, the most prominent candidates have been sensation reports (e.g., 'I am in pain'), reports of sensory experience (e.g., 'I *seem* to see a blue typewriter here'), analytic assertions, and/or the Cartesian claim 'I think'. Second, it also defines what sort of self-evidence (intrinsic-probability, noninferential justification, or whatever) is possessed by the foundational propositions. Third, it describes how nonbasic propositions are justified relative to basic propositions. Since this process is usually thought to be inferential, the second part of a foundational theory is usually, in effect, a theory of deduction or induction or both.[1]

Foundational theories generally have a good deal of initial plausibility on a Realist theory of truth, since they seem to require that we directly apprehend states of affairs in a world external to our minds. They also have some plausibility on other theories of truth. It does seem that self-evident propositions, and propositions thence inferred, are likely to cohere with one another.[2] And since such propositions seem to reveal what the facts are, they also seem somewhat more likely to be useful and to be eventually agreed to by everyone with sufficient relevant experiences.

7.3   Instrumentalism as a Theory of Justification

I noted above that when thought of as a theory of justification, instrumentalism can be formulated like this:

Truth correlates positively with usefulness and it is relatively easy to determine when a proposition (sentence, or belief, etc.) has this characteristic.

This theory has considerable plausibility, on a Realist answer to the metaphysical project; for a good explanation of why some beliefs are useful and the others are not is that the useful ones probably embrace facts independent of mind and the useless ones probably do not.[3] For example, if my belief that a life vest will keep me from drowning proves useful, this is probably because it is a fact that life vests prevent drowning. But note that the correlation is not perfect. A man may find it useful to believe that his spouse is faithful, because the belief forestalls emotional disruption in his life. But it may not be a fact that his spouse is faithful, and thus, on a Realist theory of truth, it may not be true.

If instrumentalism itself is the correct theory of truth, then, the first clause of the instrumentalist theory of justification must, of course, be correct. And since it is at least initially plausible to think that the usefulness of a belief is relatively easy to determine, the instrumentalist theory of justification is plausible relative to an instrumentalist theory of truth. But the instrumentalist theory of justification has little or no plausibility on a coherence or Peircean answer to the metaphysical project, because a useful belief per se does not seem much more likely to cohere with other beliefs or to be eventually agreed to by everyone with sufficient relevant experiences than a useless belief. But this is a matter on which intuitions are likely to differ considerably, so it is worth reminding the reader that I do not take any of the arguments, let alone *ex cathedra* claims of implausibility like this one, to be decisive.

7.4   F. H. Bradley's Coherence Theory of Justification

Brand Blanshard regarded his coherence theory to be the correct answer
to both the metaphysical and justification projects. Rather than reexamine
his theory, however, let us look at the coherence theory of F. H. Bradley,
which is intended to fulfill only the justification project.[4] His theory is not,
however, a *pure* coherence theory of justification. Such a theory, in a very
simple form, would be formulated like this:

Truth correlates positively with being a member of a coherent set of
propositions, and it is relatively easy to determine when a proposition
(sentence, or belief, etc.) has this characteristic.

Bradley was wise to avoid a pure coherence theory, for such a theory has
very little plausibility on *any* answer to the metaphysical project, save the
coherence theory of truth itself. I do not see any obvious reasons why a
coherent set of consistent beliefs is be more likely to contain conclusions
that will eventually be agreed on by competent investigators, or to contain
useful beliefs. On the other hand, a pure coherence theory of justification
does have *some* surface plausibility on a Realist theory of truth. The
reasoning would be that since the world itself is consistent, two or more
inconsistent beliefs cannot *all* be true on a Realist theory of truth, whereas
it is at least possible that every member of a consistent set is true.
Therefore, it is thought, any given member of a consistent set is more likely
to express a fact than any given member of an inconsistent set.

But it is also possible that every member of a consistent set is false, even
if the members of the set are mutually entailing. Consistency raises the
possibility of epistemic nirvana, but it also raises the possibility of
epistemic damnation. So coherence per se does not correlate with truth.
We need somehow to narrow down the number of coherent sets that count
as justified, and this can only be done by introducing elements from
noncoherence theories, Yet this suggests that whatever plausibility the
resulting impure coherence theory possesses comes largely from its
noncoherence elements.

Indeed, as Richard Foley has pointed out, consistency is not even a
necessary condition for the justification of a set of beliefs:

Many of us have evidence sufficient to justify believing that (*q*) it is not the case
6561 is greater than 6562. But, somewhere among us there might be a person who
in addition has evidence sufficient to justify that (*p*) 3^8 is greater than 6562. This

person, for example, might have a normally reliable calculator that computes that $3^8 = 6567$ and he might have as a trusted friend a mathematician who confirms this result for him, and so on. Thus, it looks as if the person here might have sufficient evidence to justify believing q and sufficient evidence to justify believing p. And yet, p implies not-q. (1979, 249)

And as Foley says, the claim that consistency is a necessary condition for justification is the very heart of the coherence theory.

The coherence theory is not improved by specifying that the members of a coherent set are tied by a network of inferential relations. Take this set:

$$p \& q \tag{1}$$

$$q \supset p \tag{2}$$

$$q \tag{3}$$

$$p \tag{4}$$

Here, (1) entails (2), (3), and (4); (2) and (3) entail (4); and (3) and (4) entail (1). But this system of circular entailments does not justify any of its members. (Suppose, e.g., p = the proposition that snow is green, and q = the proposition that snow is warm. Are these justified when plugged, identical for identical, into the above set?)

But suppose (2) and (3) are observationally justified. Now (4) and (1) are also justified, because they can be deduced from (2) and (3). But (2), (3), and (4) are not *more* justified because they are (circularly) entailed by (1). This additional fact about the set does not make its members any more justified. The justified status of any member comes *entirely* from observation or a *linear* justification from foundational premises that are themselves observationally justified. Not only does coherence not justify on its own, it does not seem to *add* any justification to propositions (beliefs, or whatever) that are foundationally justified.

Let us now consider the impure coherence theory of Bradley to see if the coherence elements in it contribute to its plausibility. Coherence theories of justification are associated with three doctrines:

1. A belief is justified to the extent that it coheres with a believer's other beliefs.
2. No subset of the beliefs is any more basic than any other.
3. No belief is certain: for any belief, even those thought by many

noncoherentists to be self-evidently certain, one could in principle have enough evidence to reject the belief.

Those coherence theorists who take (1) as the essence of a coherence theory usually use a net metaphor to describe the structure of a set of justified beliefs. Just as every knot in a net is connected to every other, so too every proposition in the set justifies, and is justified by, every other proposition in the set. The direction of justification is a series of closed circles. Those who, like Bradley, take (3) to express the essence of a coherence theory prefer the raft metaphor: repairing a raft at sea would require that we replace rotting boards one by one with passing pieces of driftwood. No more than a few boards could be removed simultaneously, but over time every board could be replaced. So too we make our set of beliefs progressively more coherent by replacing them one by one. In principle, we could eventually end up replacing all of those with which we started. As we shall see below, it is not clear that Bradley would even accept (2).

For Bradley, the characteristic of justification is membership in a coherent system of beliefs, which he defines as a set of beliefs that is both consistent and comprehensive (1914, 202). A belief is justified if it is a member of the best such system, and a system is best if every other system would be either inconsistent or less comprehensive. The formula for Bradley's theory is thus the following:

Truth correlates positively with being a member of the most consistent and most comprehensive set of beliefs, and it is relatively easy to determine when a belief has this characteristic.

Unfortunately, Bradley does not give any positive account of what 'comprehensive' means in this context. It cannot mean that for every pair of *possible* beliefs, one member of the pair being the negation of the other, one or the other must be included in the system. No set of human beliefs is *this* comprehensive. Since there is an infinite set of such pairs, it is impossible for any human to have one member of every such pair in his system of beliefs. (Think, for example, of all the pairs following the pattern 'There are n grains of sand on the beach at Waikiki' and 'There are not n grains of sand on the beach at Waikiki', where n is replaced by the same randomly chosen natural number in both members of the pair.) Perhaps what Bradley means by 'comprehensive' is that for every proposition a given person has ever encountered, the person must believe either the proposition or its negation. But this would make indecision improper, and sometimes indecision is proper, as when evidence is balanced on both sides of a question.

Bradley's failure to characterize the concept of comprehensiveness is particularly surprising in light of the importance the concept has in his response to objections against coherence theory. To the objection that a well-organized piece of fiction would be justified as true on the coherence theory of justification, Bradley says that principles governing the acceptance of propositions are themselves part of one's system of beliefs, and that no comprehensive system could include the principle that one should accept fancy as fact (1914, 213). But Bradley has misunderstood the objection. The claim being made against coherence theory is not that it would absurdly entitle us to regard as probably true those propositions that we know to be fictional (to be fancy). On the contrary, the objection is that we *cannot determine*, on coherence theory, what is fictional and what is nonfictional. The fact that a story is labeled 'fiction' or that we are aware of having made it up is irrelevant and of no use. All that is relevant, on Bradley's theory, is the consistency and comprehensiveness of the story, not its provenance. Indeed, the objector would go on, perhaps that is what scientists and other thinkers have unintentionally done: made up a fictional story of the world. On Bradley's coherence theory, how would we know whether they have or have not?

It is possible, however, to extract from Bradley a better answer to the fiction example: Bradley wants to concede that in some sense observational beliefs are more basic than other beliefs. Moreover, he does not think that we can reject all of our observations at the same time, although he does insist that any given observation can in principle be rejected (Bradley, 1914, 203–206, 209–210, 212). Let us incorporate this concession to foundationalism into the formula for Bradley's theory of justification in place of his concept of comprehensiveness:

Truth correlates positively with being a member of the most consistent set of beliefs that includes most of the epistemic agent's observational beliefs, and it is relatively easy to determine when a belief has this characteristic.

This theory does have *some* plausibility, on a Realist theory of truth, but the arguments above strongly suggest that its plausibility derives entirely

from the reference to observations. Laurence BonJour makes an adjustment to his coherence theory of justification similar to Bradley's. He
requires, in effect, that the set of beliefs must contain within it some belief
to the effect that spontaneous perceptual beliefs are probably true. A set of
beliefs that does not contain such a belief is not justified, however coherent
it might otherwise be (BonJour 1985, 141). Note that both Bradley and
BonJour are granting some sort of intrinsic epistemic status to observational beliefs, so they seem to be rejecting the second principle commonly
associated with coherence theories. Note too how similar their theories are
to contemporary foundational theories that allow that to some extent
basic propositions are justified in reference to nonbasic propositions (see
section 7.2). The boundary between these two kinds of theories is fuzzy at best.

Before ending this discussion of coherence theories of justification, I
want to rebut the unfortunate tendency in recent epistemological literature
to equate coherence theories of justification with holistic theories of
justification. In point of fact, the holistic/nonholistic distinction divides
theories of justification along a different axis than does the foundational/
instrumental/coherence distinction. A holist about justification believes
that only a whole set of propositions (beliefs, or sentences, etc.), taken as a
unit, can properly be said to possess or fail to possess the property of being
justified. An individual proposition can properly be called justified (or
unjustified) only in a trivial and parasitic sense: it is justified if and only if
the set of which it is a member is justified. A nonholist reverses this,
insisting that it is individual propositions that are justified or unjustified. If
a set of propositions can be said to be justified at all, it can be so only in a
trivial and parasitic sense: a set is justified if all or most of its members are.
Epistemic holism began with W. V. O. Quine's famous paper "Two
Dogmas of Empiricism" (1963a), originally published in 1951, and I know
of no coherence theorist before that date, except P. Duhem, who gave any
indication that he was a holist. A nonholist coherence theorist claims that
individual propositions are the primary bearers of the property of justification, and if a belief has that property, it has it by virtue of being a part of a
web of inferential relations with certain other propositions. There is no
reason why a coherence theorist need say that the set of all of those
propositions, *qua* set, also possesses the property of being justified.
Similarly, it is possible to be a holist foundationalist. This would be the
view that a whole set of propositions is justified if and only if its members
are structured by nonsymmetrical, nonreflexive inference relations from a

base of, say, sensory reports. There is no reason why such a foundationalist need say that each member of that set, *qua* individual, also possesses the property of being justified.

7.5 Chapter Summary

This chapter has been a sampler, not a survey. Its purpose has been to see how answers to the justification project are evaluated in light of answers to the metaphysical project. At least one example from every major type of theory of justification has been briefly examined. But I do not pretend that any of my examples is *the* archetypical representative of its theoretical type or even the best of its type. Many internal criticisms that I have not mentioned can be made against all of these theories. And many counter-objections could be made to the objections I *do* make. I ignore all these because it is not necessary, for the limited purposes of this chapter, to extend the dialectic about justification any further. I have dealt only with the prima facie plausibility of each theory relative to various answers to the metaphysical project. I have not tried to trace the pro and con dialogue about any of these theories beyond a very shallow level, and I have been strictly careful not to endorse or reject any of them. Accordingly, readers should not take any of the brief arguments of this chapter as decisive.

It turns out that every theory of justification is plausible relative to the theory of truth of the same name. The coherence theory of justification, for example, is plausible relative to the coherence theory of truth. This phenomenon has proved all too tempting to some philosophers. They have sought to take the easy way out regarding the problem of skepticism by first choosing a theory of justification and then declaring that its correlative theory of truth is the correct theory of truth. By doing so, they guarantee themselves the appearance of a completely successful refutation of skepticism, but only the appearance.

We have so far seen three programs in service to which an answer to the metaphysical project may be put: the epistemological enterprise, the physicalist program, and the model-theoretic program. I turn now to the examination of a fourth purpose to which answers to the metaphysical project have been put. A hope has been abroad that a theory of truth may be the key to constructing a theory of meaning for natural languages. Whether this hope has any prospects for fulfillment or whether it is just wishful thinking is the topic of the next chapter.

8 Davidson and Dummett

Tarski, as we have seen, believed that truth can only be defined for certain artificial languages. Donald Davidson, however, has claimed not only that it is possible to apply Tarski's techniques to natural languages but, furthermore, that doing so pays a startling benefit: *a theory of truth for a natural language is a theory of meaning for the language.* If Davidson is right (and that's a big 'if'), it would be hard to exaggerate the importance of his insight. Meaning—like sense, connotation, translation, and other intensional notions—has been a frustratingly obscure concept. But if Davidson is right, if a theory of meaning for a language can be constructed as a Tarski-like theory of truth, then the science of semantics has turned a historic corner. We still do not have a complete theory of meaning, but at least we know how to construct one. We know how to *do* semantics. *If* Davidson is right.

8.1 Davidson's Program

Before we can understand why Davidson thinks a Tarski-like theory of truth is a theory of meaning, we must get straight about what he conceived the task of a theory of meaning to be. For Davidson, the term 'theory of meaning' could well be replaced with the term 'theory of understanding'. The mystery of language is that we càn produce and understand an infinite number of sentences, including many that we have never heard or seen before, even though we have only a finite number of words and rules. At one level, the explanation for this phenomenon of linguistic competence is obvious: our finite pool of words can be combined in an infinite number of ways (Davidson 1965, 9). But this means that the meanings of sentences depend on their structures and the words within them, so the purpose of a theory of meaning is to show how this can be (Davidson 1967, 17; Davidson 1970, 56). But note that the fact that the meanings of sentences *depend* on the meanings of the words within them does not entail that the meanings of sentences are *built up* out of the meanings of words. Indeed, says Davidson, we need not assume that words even have meanings beyond simply affecting the meanings of the sentences in which they appear. We could, for example, explain the meaning of 'the father of' perfectly well by stating that when appended to the front of a name, the whole expression refers to the father of the person named. This implies a holistic view of language meaning. Sentences depend on their structures for their meanings, but we cannot know the meaning of any bit of structure unless we understand the meaning of every sentence in which that bit appears (Davidson 1967, 18, 20, 22). Thus at first blush it would appear that an adequate theory of meaning for a language will entail as theorems all sentences of the form

S means that p,

where S is a structural description of a sentence in the language whose meaning is under study (called the object language) and p is a sentence of the language in which the theory is expressed (called the metalanguage) giving the meaning of S. (A longer introduction to the object-language/metalanguage distinction is in section 9.3.) For example, a theory of meaning for French, expressed in English plus the concatenation symbol '^', would entail

L^a^ ^n^e^i^g^e^ ^e^s^t^ ^b^l^a^n^c^h^e means that snow is white.

The left side of the 'means that' should be read as a definite description: 'the sentence consisting of the letter "L" concatenated to the letter "a" concatenated to a space concatenated to, etc.'. Note that in this case the sentence on the right of the 'means that' is just the metalanguage translation of the object-language sentence described on the left. It will not always be this simple, as we shall see below. The metalanguage can contain all the vocabulary of the object language. When it does, then, in simple cases, the sentence used on the right of the 'means that' just is the sentence described on the left. For example, if the object language is English and the metalanguage is English plus the concatenation symbol, then one theorem will be

S^n^o^w^ ^i^s^ ^w^h^i^t^e means that snow is white.

If the theory of meaning has a finite number of axioms and yet for any arbitrary sentence of the object language, we can derive a theorem, on the above pattern, giving its meaning, then the theory can be said to explain how an infinite variety of object-language sentences can be generated from a finite vocabulary and a finite number of rules for combining words into grammatically correct and meaningful sentences. Beyond this, the theory can be said to express the knowledge possessed by a competent speaker of the object language, since such a speaker has the ability to understand an infinite variety of sentences, including some she has never encountered previously. This is not to say that every (or even a) competent speaker of the object language has *explicit* knowledge of such a theory, nor is it to say that learning a language is a matter of learning one by one the axioms of some theory of meaning for the language. The point is rather that the theory contains all of the information about the object language that a competent speaker possesses, although she may possess it in a different form and only implicitly. If someone *were* to learn the object language by memorizing the axioms of such a theory (expressed in a metalanguage she already understands) and if that someone were able to make very fast inferences, *would* she be a competent speaker of that language? Davidson says she would be. In this sense, a theory of meaning is a theory of understanding (Davidson 1990, 311–312). (Section 8.4 contains a longer discussion of implicit knowledge.) Of course, no human could know, explicitly or implicitly, an infinitely long theory. Hence Davidson's insistence that the theory have a finite number of axioms (1970, 56). Since every one-word predicate gets its own axiom, this is only possible for languages with a finite number of such predicates. However, the language could have an infinite number of compound predicates, so long as there are only a finite number of rules for compounding predicates.

Davidson has another way of putting the same point. We could *interpret* the utterances of a native speaker of an object language, call it OL, provided we are in possession of a theory of meaning (expressed in a metalanguage we already understand) for OL that meets the above constraints (Davidson 1970, 56; Davidson 1973b). Those constraints are, once again, that the theory contains a finite number of axioms, and that the theory will entail for every sentence of OL (and thus every potential sentential utterance of the native speaker) a theorem that, like those above, gives the meaning of the OL sentence (Davidson 1967, 20).

However, deriving theorems containing the phrase 'means that' would require us to first know the logic of the intensional concept of meaning, and that is one of the things theories of meaning are supposed to explain (Davidson 1967, 22). Using any other intensional concept (e.g., 'says that', 'has the sense of', in place of 'means that') poses the same problem: these are the very concepts the theory is supposed to explicate. The solution, Davidson suggests, is to revise the idea of what sort of theorems an adequate theory of meaning should entail. Let us give the structural description S its own semantic predicate and change the equivalence connection from semantic to extensional by means of the extensional equivalence symbol. Thus, '...means that...' is replaced with '...is $T \equiv ...$'. So now the theory of meaning must entail all sentences of the form

S is $T \equiv p$.

The semantic content has thus been pulled out of 'means that' and put into the predicate 'is T', which thereby allows p to be an extensional *definiens* of the semantic property T. But any theory that entails all instances of the latter schema meets Tarski's material adequacy condition for theories of truth. "[So] it is clear that the sentences to which the predicate 'is T' applies will be just the true sentences of L." (Davidson 1967, 22–23; compare Platts 1979, 45, 54). Thus the heretofore mysterious semantic property named by 'T' turns out to be truth, and a theory of meaning for a language is just a theory of truth for that language. For Tarski, S could be simply the name of a sentence. But this will not do for Davidson, because such a theory will not explain how the structure and elements of a sentence contribute to its meaning. So S must be a structural description of the sentence (Davidson 1970, 56; Platts 1979, 44). Of course, Tarski's model-theoretic program required his definition of truth to reveal, for a simple language of set theory, how the parts of a sentence affect its truth value. These thoughts lead us to the relation between Davidson's program and the model-theoretic program. The former is in some sense just an extension of the latter to natural languages. Where model theory was interested only in how the limited grammatical features of a logical language—variables, quantifiers, and truth-functional operators—affect the meaning, i.e., the truth conditions, of sentences, the Davidson Program wants to capture how all grammatical features of a natural language (e.g., adverbs, adjectives, prepositions, subordinate clauses, etc.) affect the meaning (truth conditions) of the sentences in which they appear.

As before, Davidson contends that any finite theory that meets the revised adequacy condition (which entails, for each sentence of the object language, a T-sentence giving the truth conditions for the sentence) contains the knowledge possessed by a competent speaker of the object language. Thus Davidson's idea can be seen as a fulfillment of the old adage that the meaning of a sentence consists in its truth conditions (Davidson 1965, 8; Davidson 1967, 24).

What would such a theory look like? In Tarski's hands, it consisted of a definition of truth and a definition of satisfaction; but Davidson envisions an axiomatic theory (Davidson 1970, 56). He gives no concrete examples of such axioms, so the following picture is somewhat speculative, but it is consistent with his other remarks and is accepted by his other interpreters (e.g., Martin 1987, 210; Field 1972). (For clarity, I assume in what follows that the object language is English and that the metalanguage is English enhanced with some formal symbols and enough set theory to derive the T-sentences.) In the first place, there will be axioms giving "outright the semantic properties of certain of the basic expressions" (Davidson 1973a, 70). There will be, for example, an axiom for each simple (i.e., one-word) predicate of the language giving the satisfaction conditions for an open sentence consisting of a variable concatenated to the predicate. Here are two examples:

For all integers i and sequences S, x_i^ ^i^s^ ^r^e^d is satisfied by sequence S ≡ the ith member of S is red

For all integers i and sequences S, x_i^ ^l^o^v^e^s^ ^x_k is satisfied by sequence S ≡ the ith member of S loves the kth member of S

(I shall explain in section 8.2 why these two axioms seem to imply that English contains symbols like 'x_i'.) Since natural languages include names, there will have to be an axiom giving "outright" the relevant semantic property for each one-word name as well. (See section 5.5.) Two examples are the following:

R^a^l^p^h refers to Ralph.

E^a^r^t^h refers to the earth.

Similarly, there will be an axiom for each functor in the language. For our purposes we can define a functor as a word or phrase that, when appended to a name, creates another name. In English, 'the father of' is a functor. Its axiom is,

For all N, t^h^e^ ^f^a^t^h^e^r^ ^o^f^ ^N refers to the father of whatever N refers to.

Here 'N' is a metalanguage variable ranging over names and variables in the object language. Each atomic adjective, preposition, article, adverb, etc. will have its own axiom as well, but I cannot give examples of such axioms for reasons that I give in the last paragraph of section 8.2. The presence of names in the language, whether or not compounded with functors, means that we will need, for each one-word predicate of the language, an axiom giving an account of the satisfaction conditions of a closed sentence produced by concatenating a name to the predicate. One of many axioms that would do the job for the predicate 'red' is,

For all N and S, $N^\smallfrown$ $^\smallfrown i^\smallfrown s^\smallfrown$ $^\smallfrown r^\smallfrown e^\smallfrown d$ satisfies $S \equiv x_1^\smallfrown$ $^\smallfrown i^\smallfrown s^\smallfrown$ $^\smallfrown r^\smallfrown e^\smallfrown d$ is satisfied by all sequences having the object referred to by N as their first member.

Quantifiers and truth-functional sentential operators will each have an axiom giving its effect on the satisfaction (and hence truth conditions) of the sentences in which it appears (Davidson 1973a, 70):

For all S, ψ, and ϕ, $\psi^\smallfrown$ $^\smallfrown o^\smallfrown r^\smallfrown$ $^\smallfrown \phi$ is satisfied by $S \equiv$ either S satisfies ψ or S satisfies ϕ

For all S and ϕ, $(^\smallfrown \exists^\smallfrown x_k{}^\smallfrown)^\smallfrown \phi$ is satisfied by $S \equiv$ *some* sequence that differs from S in at most the kth place satisfies ϕ

Here ψ and ϕ are metalanguage variables both ranging over object-language closed and open sentences). (Section 8.2 will make clear why the last of these seems to imply that English contains symbols like '$\exists$' and 'x_k'.) Finally, the theory will have as a last axiom Tarski's definition of truth:

$(s)(s$ is true $\equiv s$ is satisfied by all [or some] sequences)

From the axioms of the theory, it will be possible to prove T-sentences like

$R^\smallfrown a^\smallfrown l^\smallfrown p^\smallfrown h^\smallfrown$ $^\smallfrown l^\smallfrown o^\smallfrown v^\smallfrown e^\smallfrown s^\smallfrown$ $^\smallfrown t^\smallfrown h^\smallfrown e^\smallfrown$ $^\smallfrown e^\smallfrown a^\smallfrown r^\smallfrown t^\smallfrown h$ is true $\equiv$ Ralph loves the earth.

It is the theory and these proofs together that tell us how the meaning (or truth conditions) of a sentence is determined by its parts and its structure. The T-sentences per se do not tell us this (Davidson 1970, 61; Davidson 1973b, 138–139).

The fact that meaning is to be cashed in terms of truth conditions makes it possible for a Davidsonian theory of meaning to be tested empirically. Imagine that we constructed such a theory for a tribal language. The 'p' in the schema will be an English translation of the native sentence structurally described in S. So one theorem of the theory might be,

$B^\smallfrown o^\smallfrown o^\smallfrown l^\smallfrown a^\smallfrown$ $^\smallfrown k^\smallfrown r^\smallfrown a^\smallfrown n^\smallfrown g$ is true $\equiv$ the water is cold.

Now armed with a thermometer, we observe the linguistic behavior of bathing tribesmen when the water is cold and compare that with their linguistic behavior when it is warm. If they *do* tend to utter 'Boola krang' when and only when the water is cold, then we have an item of evidence in favor of the proposed theory of meaning for their language. If they do not tend to utter 'Boola krang' when the water is in fact cold, then we have empirical evidence against the theory. In that case we shall have to revise the theory. Perhaps the axiom giving the reference of 'Boola' is wrong, or perhaps the axiom for 'krang' misidentifies its satisfaction conditions, or perhaps we were wrong in thinking that 'boola' is a subject term or in thinking 'krang' is any kind of predicate. Indeed, our error may even be in thinking that 'boola' is one word instead of two words 'bo' and 'ola', each with its own meaning. Whatever we eventually decide, it is apparent that the axioms of the theory are *hypotheses*. The claim of the theory that 'boola' is one word and its claim that this word is a subject term are also hypotheses. But we do not test these hypotheses individually. Rather, the theory as a whole is tested by looking to see if the T-sentences it generates match with the linguistic behavior of the native speakers. In general, the theory is probably correct if the meanings (= truth conditions) it attributes to the utterances of a speaker of the language are intelligible in the situations in which we observe him to be (Davidson 1967, 27; Davidson 1973b, 135).

Notice that the procedure described above presupposes that the natives can tell accurately when the water is cold and when it is not. Or at the very least, it presupposes that they believe the water is cold when we do and they believe it is not when we believe it is not. There is a general principle at work here, which Davidson calls the principle of charity: when interpreting the utterances of the speakers of another language, we should assume that they believe most of the things we believe. This does not mean, however, that we assume they agree with us about everything. Suppose that the native's linguistic behavior does not seem to conform very well with the above T-sentence for 'Boola krang', and suppose further that the totality of T-sentences generated by the theory makes better sense of the native's *overall* linguistic behavior than do the T-sentences of any alternative theory of meaning for their language. In such a case it would be permissible for us to conclude that our theory (including the T-sentence for 'Boola krang') is correct after all but the natives have beliefs about when the water is cold and when it is not that are oddly different from our own. This points up another aspect of Davidson's ideas about empirically verifying theories of meaning: when we are attempting to interpret the speakers of another language, we are making hypotheses about what they believe as well as hypotheses about the meanings of their utterances. We are, in effect, simultaneously testing both a theory of meaning for their language and a theory about what they believe (Davidson 1967, 27). The unexpected behavior of the natives regarding when they assent to and dissent from 'Boola krang' told us that one or the other of our two theories was wrong, but in and of itself, their behavior did not tell us *which* was wrong.

8.2 Complications and Cautions

So much, then, for my summary of the Davidson Program. Now for some complications. The first of these is that there is something very misleading in Davidson's oft made assertion that a theory of meaning as he understands it is a theory of *truth*. For Davidson believes that when a Tarski-like answer to the metaphysical project is used as a theory of meaning it undergoes a subtle but dramatic change: the Tarski-like theory can no longer be seen as giving an informative account of the concept of truth. Although he is not *entirely* consistent on this,[1] he usually insists that it is not possible to give a theory of meaning for a language without taking at least one linguistic notion as an undefined primitive. Tarski, as he usually puts it (e.g., Davidson 1973b, 134), took the concept of translation as primitive and used it to analyze the concept of truth, while he, Davidson, wants to take truth as primitive in order to analyze, among other linguistic concepts, translation. Both of these claims require explanation. Of course, the concept of translation does *not* appear in the *definiens* of either Tarski's definition of truth or his definition of satisfaction, so it is not in that sense that he presupposes the concept. Tarski assumes translation in stating his MAC: an adequate definition of truth for a given object language must entail all metalanguage sentences on the pattern of

x is true iff p,

where x is the name of some object language sentence and p is either that same sentence, when the metalanguage contains the vocabulary of the object language, or a *translation* of that sentence into the metalanguage, when the latter does not contain the vocabulary of the object language.

Thus, if the metalanguage does not contain the vocabulary of the object language, we cannot tell if the theory of truth for the object language meets the MAC unless we have a concept of translation (Davidson 1990, 295–296, 300). But translation is one of the concepts that Davidson wants a theory of meaning to explicate, so he takes *truth* as an undefined primitive (Davidson 1977a, 218; Davidson 1990, 314).[2] This change in *how we view* a Tarski-like theory of truth does not in itself impel any changes in the theory. For a simple mathematical language, such as those with which Tarski was concerned, a Davidsonian theory of meaning for the language (save for its transformation from a many-claused definition into a series of axioms) *would look exactly the same as a Tarskian theory of truth for that language.* Similarly, a Davidsonian theory of meaning for a natural language would differ from a Tarskian theory of truth, aside from the switch from definitional to axiomatic treatment, only in that it would *add* axioms (for names, adverbs, functors, etc.) to those already present. The logical machinery of Tarski's definition and the T-sentences generated thereby (putting aside a further complication to be discussed below) remain unchanged, but we now view them as fulfilling a different task. They are no longer seen as a theory *of truth*; rather, we see them as using an antecedently understood notion of truth to explain how the truth conditions of sentences are a function of the meanings of the parts of the sentences and the structure of the sentences: "The theory reveals nothing new about the conditions under which an individual sentence is true; it does not make these conditions any clearer than the sentence itself does. The work of the theory is in relating the known truth conditions of each sentence to those aspects ('words') of the sentence that recur in other sentences, and can be assigned identical roles in other sentences."[3]

Since Davidson cannot make use of the concept of translation, he must replace Tarski's MAC with a new criterion of adequacy: a theory of meaning is best when the T-sentences it generates more accurately match the linguistic behavior of competent speakers of the object language than do the T-sentences generated by any other theory of meaning for that language. Actually, to follow up on a point made in the previous section, the new criterion applies to *pairs* of theories, one member of the pair being a theory of meaning for the language and the other a theory of what the speakers of the language believe. Hence the criterion should read something like this: a conjunction of a theory of meaning for a language and a theory of what the speakers of the language believe is best when the conjunction makes better sense of the overall linguistic behavior of the speakers of the language than does any other such pair.[4]

The second complication revolves around the linguistic concept of *deep structure*. Linguists have long known that the grammatical categories and structures we learn in schoolbooks (nouns, verbs, adverbs, moods, passive and active voices, etc.) are much too simple to account for the variety and complexity of the ways that words can interact to produce the meaning of a whole sentence. Or to put the same point another way, the surface structure of a natural-language sentence often hides its real, deep structure. Consider the sentence 'Bardot is a French actress'. It would *appear* that, in addition to axioms giving the reference of 'Bardot', the satisfaction conditions of 'is an actress', the satisfaction conditions of simple closed sentences, and the meaning (or "semantic property," whatever it turns out to be) of the adjective 'French', all we need is a single axiom telling how the presence of an adjective in the predicate changes the satisfaction conditions of the original predicate.

But a theory of meaning that pursued such a strategy would fail utterly, because surface grammar is misleading here. For Bardot to satisfy 'is a French actress', it is only necessary that she satisfy 'is French' and 'is an actress'; that is, she must be in the intersection of the set of French things and the set of actresses. The surface grammar of 'Bardot is a French actress' hides the fact that 'is a French actress' is really a conjunctive predicate: 'is French and is an actress'. And in turn, 'Bardot is French and an actress' is, at a still deeper level of structure, a simple conjunction of two atomic clauses: 'Bardot is French, and Bardot is an actress'. Hence a proper story of how the meanings of the words in 'Bardot is a French actress' affect the meaning (truth conditions) of the whole will pass through (1) the axiom for the operator 'and', (2) the axiom for atomic closed sentences having 'is an actress' as their predicate and the parallel axiom for 'is French', (3) the axiom for 'Bardot', and finally, (4) the axiom for the predicate 'is an actress' and the parallel axiom for 'is French'. At no point will the story make any reference to an axiom governing the affects that adjectives have on the satisfaction conditions of predicates. (And it is now evident that the "semantic properties" given in the axiom for 'French' will just be satisfaction conditions, for it is really functioning as just another one-word predicate.)

On the other hand, consider the sentence 'Bardot is a good actress'. The surface grammar of this sentence is identical to 'Bardot is a French actress', which would seem to suggest that the account of how the parts of one of these affects the truth conditions of the whole will precisely parallel the account for the other. But 'Bardot is a good actress' does *not* say that Bardot is a member of the set of good things and also a member of the set of actresses. Bardot could be very bad and still be a good actress (Davidson 1967, 32). So 'good' does not function the way 'French' does in the earlier sentence. These two sentences have different deep structures, and linguistics will have to recognize that 'good' and 'French' are really different parts of speech, in a more refined sense of 'part of speech' than one finds in schoolbook grammar (Davidson 1967, 32). Let 'Adjective$_1$' be the name of the part of speech of which 'French' is an example, and let 'Adjective$_2$' be name of the part of speech of which 'good' is an example. It is likely (though still uncertain in the current undeveloped state of Davidsonian semantics—see the last paragraph of this section) that we shall need an axiom governing the affects that an Adjective$_2$ has on the satisfaction conditions of predicates in order to analyze sentences in which such terms appear. The left-hand side of such an axiom would be something like this:

For all A_2, integers i, and sequences S, x_i^ ^i^s^ ^ A_2^ ^r^e^d is satisfied by sequence $S \equiv$

Here A_2 is a metalanguage variable ranging over object-language Adjective$_2$s. No one can yet say what would be on the right-hand side, since one of the unsolved problems of Davidsonian semantics is the affect Adjective$_2$s have on the truth conditions of sentences (Davidson 1967, 32).

What all this implies for the Davidson Program is just this: the sorts of axioms we have been discussing so far are directly applicable only to sentences whose surface grammar is not misleading. For sentences that do have a misleading surface grammar, we will need new axioms that pair up each such sentence with another sentence that has the same truth conditions as the misleadingly structured sentence and whose surface structure is not misleading. For example, for sentences, like 'Bardot is a French actress' we will need an axiom something like this:

For all N and A_1, N^ ^i^s^ ^ A_1^ ^a^c^t^r^e^s^s is true
$\equiv N$^ ^i^s^ ^a^n^ ^a^c^t^r^e^s^s is true and N^ ^i^s^ ^ A_1 is true,

where A_1 is a variable ranging over Adjective$_1$-type adjectives. As Davidson puts it:

The work of applying a theory of truth in detail to a natural language will in practice almost certainly divide into two stages. In the first stage, truth will be characterized, not for the whole language, but for a carefully gerrymandered part of the language. This part, though no doubt clumsy grammatically, will contain an infinity of sentences which exhaust the expressive power of the whole language. The second part will match each of the remaining sentences to one or (in the case of ambiguity) more than one of the sentences for which truth has been characterized. We may think of the sentences to which the first stage of the theory applies as giving the logical form, or deep structure, of all sentences. (1973b, 133)

By way of example, he suggests that passive-voice sentences can be handled in this way: "Suppose success in giving the truth conditions for some significant range of sentences in the active voice. Then with a formal procedure for transforming each such sentence into a corresponding sentence in the passive voice, the theory of truth could be extended in an obvious way to this new set of sentence" (1967, 30).

Although Davidson does not mention it, there will probably be cases of misleadingly structured sentences in a natural language, say English, for which there simply is no English equivalent that is *not* misleadingly structured in some way or other. In such cases we will need to invent new object-language symbols to express nonmisleadingly the deep structure of the misleading sentences and then again to use axioms to match up the misleadingly structured sentences with the nonmisleadingly structured sentences. For example, the sentence 'Something is red' is misleadingly structured inasmuch as it appears that 'something' is the name of some thing, whereas it is really just an existential quantifier. But suppose it should turn out that all English sentences with the same meaning as this one are misleadingly structured in some way or other? Then we shall have to add to English a symbol like '∃' and variables like 'x_k' to express the deep structure of the misleading sentences. This will enable us to express the truth conditions of the misleading sentences by equating them with the truth conditions of nonmisleading equivalents. In the present case this would be,

S^o^m^e^t^h^i^n^g^ ^i^s^ ^r^e^d is true
$\equiv$ (^∃^x_k^)^ (^x_k^ ^i^s^ ^r^e^d^) is true.

A third complication is forced on Davidson by the presence in natural languages of words called demonstratives or indexicals, which are, roughly, words whose reference varies from context to context. 'I', 'now', 'here', 'this', and 'that' are some of the demonstratives in English. If unmodified, a Davidsonian theory of meaning will entail false T-sentences for object-language sentences containing such terms. For example, if we substitute names of object-language sentences for structural descriptions for simplicity, the T-sentence '"I am tired" is true ≡ I am tired' will be false whenever the 'I' on the left refers to someone other than the person speaking the entire T-sentence. So Davidson modifies his idea of what sort of T-sentences an adequate theory of meaning must entail:

> It is simplest to view truth as a relation between a sentence, a person, and a time.... Corresponding to each expression with a demonstrative element there must in the theory be a phrase that relates the truth conditions of sentences in which the expression occurs to changing times and speakers. Thus the theory will entail sentences like the following:
>
> 'I am tired' is true as (potentially) spoken by p at t if and only if p is tired at t.
>
> 'That book was stolen' is true as (potentially) spoken by p at t if and only if the book demonstrated by p at t is stolen prior to t. (1967, 33–34)

And in general, the sort of theorems the theory will have to entail (when the object language is English) will be those instantiating the following schema:

> Sentence s is true (as English) for speaker u at time t if and only if p. (Davidson 1969, 45)

The p in the schema is not simply a translation of s into the metalanguage; it is a metalanguage sentence explicitly referring to t and u (Davidson 1973a, 75). Specifically, what does not get translated are demonstratives like 'I' and 'that'. Instead, the right-hand side simply tells us how to figure out what the reference of these terms is in any given context. In effect, it tells us what 'part of speech,' in the refined sense of modern linguistics, each of these terms is, what kind of affect they have on the truth conditions of a sentence. Davidson notes that this modification represents a "far-reaching revision" (1967, 34) and "a radical conceptual change" (1970, 58) in his idea of a theory of meaning. There are two reasons why the change is significant. The first, which Davidson does not explicitly acknowledge, is that the right-hand side of a T-sentence is now much more "self-conscious" in the way that it gives the truth conditions for sentence s.[5] Instead of being about the same chunk of the world that s itself is about and saying nothing more or less than what s says, the right-hand side now indirectly refers to s itself as a potential utterance made by a particular speaker at a particular time. To see the potential significance of this change, imagine for a moment that Davidson has been forced, in answer to other objections perhaps, to make T-sentences *completely* "self-conscious," so that the right-hand side does not translate *any* part of the sentence *s*. Instead, the right-hand side tells us only how each word in *s* affects the truth value of *s*. If we again replace structural descriptions with names of sentences for clarity, examples of such T-sentences are,

'Snow is white' is true as (potentially) spoken by p at $t \equiv$ any sequence S having in the kth place the object referred to at t by 'snow' satisfies, at t, 'x_k is white'.

'That book was stolen' is true as (potentially) spoken by p at $t \equiv$ any sequence S having in the kth place the object demonstrated by p at t satisfies, at t, 'x_k is a book' and satisfied, prior to t, 'x_k is stolen'.

The first of these effectively tells us that 'snow' is a noun referring to some object and that 'is white' is a predicate, but it neither tells us what object is referred to by 'snow' nor identifies the extension of 'is white'. Similarly, the second does not tell us the extension of 'is a book' or 'is stolen'. Hence one could know T-sentences like these (and thus a theory that entailed only such radically "self-conscious" T-sentences) without having the foggiest idea of what 'snow', 'white', 'book', or 'stolen' mean. Such a theory would not, therefore, contain all of the information possessed by a competent speaker of the object language. However, Davidson can fairly say that his much more modest movement in the direction of "self-conscious" T-sentences, to handle demonstratives, does not have such devastating effects for his program. Although the T-sentences for object-language sentences containing demonstratives do not give the meaning of the demonstratives, as distinct from telling us what part of speech they are and what affect they have on the truth conditions of the whole sentence in which they appear, it would be plausible for Davidson to insist that demonstratives really do not have any meaning in the way that 'snow', 'white', 'book', and 'stolen' do. Unlike the latter words, demonstratives do not have any context-independent reference or extension. Hence Davidson's modestly "self-conscious" T-sentences do give everything a competent speaker of the object language knows about the meaning of the demonstratives of that language.

The second reason why Davidson's handling of demonstratives is significant is that it forces him to use the concept of demonstration on the right-hand side of some T-sentences. Thus it would appear that he must give up any hope he might have had of producing a theory of meaning for a natural language without presupposing any semantic concept other than the concept of truth (Davidson 1970, 56–57). He tries to avoid this implication by alluding to the standard division of linguistic concepts into (1) those of syntax, which are about the relations of words to one another, (2) those of semantics, which are about the relations of words to the world, and (3) those of pragmatics, which are about the relations of words to their users, i.e., speakers. Demonstration, he insists, is a *pragmatic* concept, and thus "we may hope" to be able to explain this concept without using *semantic* concepts like truth, meaning, synonymy, or translation (Davidson 1973a, 75). This is unconvincing: demonstration by means of a *word* like 'that' or 'I', as distinct from demonstration by means of a silent gesture of pointing, certainly involves a relation between a speaker and a word; but it also involves a (context-relative) relation between the word and an object in the world. So it is as much a semantic concept as a pragmatic concept.

The last point to be made in this section is more a caution than a complication: it should not be thought that Davidson believes that anything remotely close to a complete theory of meaning can now be produced for any natural language. Quite the contrary, he is the first to admit that there are many 'parts of speech' in his sense whose affects on the truth conditions of sentences is too poorly understood to permit the construction of axioms embodying those affects. We have already seen one example of such a part of speech: the sort of word I called an Adjective$_2$ type of adjective (Davidson 1967, 32). Other types of sentences whose truth conditions are not yet well understood, or are the subject of much dispute, are those containing epistemic or doxastic operators like 'knows that' and 'believes that', those containing modal operators like 'necessarily' and 'possibly', those that assert causal relations, and those that express counterfactual conditions (i.e., 'If... then ...' sentences whose antecedents, the 'if' clauses, express states of affairs that do not obtain in the actual world). (See Davidson 1973b, 132.) Still others are sentences asserting probability relations; sentences containing mass terms like 'fire', 'water', and 'snow' (which is ironic in view of Tarski's favorite example of a T-sentence); sentences containing adverbs; sentences expressing intentional action (Davidson 1967, 37); and sentences asserting the creation and destruction of objects (McDermott 1986, 169).

8.3   Some Objections to the Davidson Program

As the reader might guess from the preceding paragraph, a common objection to the Davidson Program is simply that it is not viable: the potential constructions of natural languages are far too complex to be embodied in a finite set of axioms. Davidson remains optimistic. We can make progress, he insists, through a series of small steps. We begin by constructing a theory of meaning for a small fragment of the language that contains none of the problematic terms or structures. We can expand from there to progressively larger and larger fragments as one by one each of the above cited difficulties is solved (Davidson 1967, 28–30). But his only argument for such optimism, indeed, the only one he *could* make in view of the intimidating list of unsolved problems listed in the previous paragraph, is to note cases of apparent progress in bringing various constructions to heel. He cites his own work on sentences with doxastic operators and sentences containing quoted expressions. He also cites the work of other philosophers on mass terms, 'ought' sentences, and the way that proper names refer (Davidson 1973b, 132). But doubts are raised by the fact that Davidson does not provide any theory of meaning into which the results of such instances of progress have been integrated. Consider, for example, the simple language of set theory for which Tarski defined truth. If Davidson is right about the alleged cases of progress, it ought to be possible to produce a Davidsonian theory of meaning for a language just like that language of set theory, save that names and doxastic operators are present in the language. But he does not produce one. The problem is not simply that the work Davidson cites makes only one step in the way of progress but fails to take the second step of actually integrating the results into a theory of meaning. Rather, the problem is that if we cannot take the second step, then we really do not know if we have taken the first step. Until we can integrate the results of a semantic research project into a Davidsonian theory of meaning for some language, we have no good reason for thinking that the results of the project really represent progress, as distinct from a blind alley, from the point of view of the Davidson Program. Consider the fact that many natural languages have tensed verbs. There are at least *two* suggestions on the table for how to analyze the deep structure of sentences containing such verbs. W. V. Quine proposes that such sentences contain hidden quantification over moments or periods of time. The deep structure of 'Bill went to the store' is '$(\exists t)(t$ is before now and Bill at t is going to the store)' (Quine 1960, 170–174). But A. N. Prior proposes instead that the deep structure of such sentences contains hidden sentential operators like 'it will be the case that' and 'it used to be the case that'. Hence, on his view, the deep structure of 'Bill went to the store' is something like 'It used to be the case that Bill is going to the store' (Prior 1967). Now which of these represents progress from the standpoint of Davidson's program, if either? I contend that we cannot tell until *after* we have produced an empirically well-verified theory of meaning for the whole, or at least the vast majority of expressions, of some natural language containing tensed verbs. The right analysis of tense will show up in that theory. In the meantime, citing supposed instances of progress is more an act of faith than argument.

The presence of ambiguous terms in language also creates problems for Davidson, although he did not think so at first. Consider two T-sentences:

'That side of the Monongahela is a bank' is true ≡ that side of the Monongahela is a bank

'Merchant's Trust is a bank' is true ≡ Merchant's Trust is a bank

One of these is false unless the metalanguage term 'bank' includes both river sides and financial institutions in its extension. But therein lies just the solution, Davidson says. We should always use a metalanguage such that we can translate the ambiguous terms of the object language with metalanguage terms that are systematically ambiguous in just the same way: "As long as ambiguity does not affect grammatical form, and can be translated, ambiguity for ambiguity, into the metalanguage, a truth definition will not tell us any lies" (Davidson 1967, 30). But K. P. Parsons, among others has shown that the problem cannot be evaded so easily. Consider now the T-sentence

'George was never at a bank on Tuesday' is true as potentially spoken by p at t ≡ George was never at a bank on the Tuesday before t.

If the extension of the metalanguage 'bank' includes both financial institutions and river sides, this T-sentence implies that p will have spoken falsely if she utters the object-language sentence when in fact George was at a river-side picnic on Tuesday. Yet if the utterance is made during a bank robbery trial and George was not at a financial institution on Tuesday, it seems intuitively that the utterance is true (Parsons 1973, 383). What Parsons is getting at is that context and shared background knowledge between speakers and listeners can disambiguate ambiguous terms. We could put the point in terms of the two object-language sentences 'That side of the Monongahela is a bank' and 'Merchant's Trust is a bank'. The *object*-language predicate 'bank' is not really ambiguous in either of these. Our background knowledge that the Monongahela is a river and the Merchant's Trust a financial institution enables us to recognize that 'bank' in the first sentence has only river sides as its extension and 'bank' in the second has only financial institutions in its. So if the metalanguage predicate 'bank' *is* ambiguous, *both* of the T-sentences above are telling lies (since the right-to-left implication of each of them is false). The correct T-sentences would be these:

'That side of the Monongahela is a bank' is true ≡ that side of the Monongahela is a river side

'Merchant's Trust is a bank' is true ≡ Merchant's Trust is a financial institution

But a theory of meaning as Davidson has described it will not entail these T-sentences, since it does not take into account the context and background knowledge needed to pinpoint 'river side' as the proper translation of 'bank' in the first and 'financial institution' as proper for the second. In response to this, Davidson concedes the point: "The context of utterance might easily resolve the ambiguity for any normal speaker of English, and yet the resolution could depend on general knowledge in a way that could not (practically, at least) be captured by a formal theory. By granting this, as I think we must, we accept a limitation on what a theory of truth can be expected to do. Within the limitation it may still be possible to give a theory that captures an important concept of meaning" (1970, 59).

It is hard to see exactly what Davidson is conceding here. If he means to say that a theory of truth (= theory of meaning = theory of understanding), as he conceives it, is not possible for languages with ambiguous terms, then he is abandoning the idea that such a theory is possible for natural languages. But applying Tarski to natural languages is the raison d'être of his program, so presumably he does not mean this. My best guess is that he still regards his program as viable for natural languages *exclusive of any expressions that contain ambiguous terms*, but this is only a guess.

The next objection is relatively minor in itself, but it is interesting because Davidson's answer to it raises more profound difficulties. The

objection is that a Davidsonian theory of meaning gives little help at all in
analyzing words whose meaning has proved highly controversial, such as
moral terms like 'good' and 'right'. The theory will tell us that 'Bardot is
good' is true if and only if Bardot is good, but that does not clear up any
mysteries about the meaning of 'good' (Davidson 1967, 31). Davidson
ought to have answered that the philosophical mysteries referred to in the
objection plague even competent speakers of the language, which is to say
that a theory of meaning can claim to contain the information known by a
competent speaker even if it does not resolve such mysteries. Instead,
Davidson surprises by saying that the theory is not supposed to tell us
what individual words mean (1967, 32-33). "The task," he says, "was to
give the meaning of expressions in a certain infinite set on the basis of the
meanings of the parts; it was not in the bargain also to give the meanings
of the atomic parts" (1967, 18). Indeed, he adds that a satisfactory theory
of meaning need not suppose "that individual words must have meanings
at all, in any sense that transcends the fact that they have a systematic
effect on the meanings of the sentences in which they occur" (1967, 18).
And he accuses those who would make this objection of a "failure to
observe a fundamental distinction between tasks: uncovering the logical
grammar or form of sentences (which is in the province of a theory of
meaning as I construe it), and the analysis of individual words or
expressions (which are treated as primitive by the theory)" (1967, 30-31).
And on the next page he gives an alternate description of the former task
as that of discovering "what (logical, semantical) parts of speech we have
to deal with." And in Davidson 1970, 55, 60, he also seems to say that a
theory of meaning only gives the meaning of "independently meaningful
expressions," which include sentences but not individual words.

But these remarks cannot be taken literally. At the very least, they make
a mystery of Davidson's claim that some of the axioms of the theory will
give "outright" the basic semantic properties of the primitive terms of the
object language. Beyond this, these remarks, taken literally, would pro-
voke an even more profound problem. If a Davidsonian theory of meaning
does not tell us the meanings of individual words, then all it can do is to tell
us the deep *structure* of sentences (Harman 1974). It tells us what part of
speech (in Davidson's sense) each word is, but nothing more about any
word. In *some* cases, to know what part of speech a word is, is to know all
there is about the meaning of the word anyway. As suggested in the
previous section, demonstratives like 'that' and 'I' are like this, and so too

are logical constants like 'and' and 'or'. But most words are not like this. So if a theory does not tell us any more than what part of speech each word of the language is, it does not tell us everything a competent speaker of the language knows. Or to put it another way, the only kind of T-sentences such a theory would entail would be those called radically "self-conscious" in the previous section.

Davidson's actual view about what a theory of meaning in his style provides with respect to the meanings of individual words involves a delicately tense balance of semantic holism and semantic compositionality. The latter view holds, roughly, that the meaning of any sentence is a function of the meanings of its parts. Semantic holism, usually thought to be in opposition to semantic compositionality, holds, very roughly, that only whole sentences have meanings. Although Davidson explicitly embraces semantic holism, his view is really an attempt to reconcile the two positions. Sentences, but not words, are *independently* meaningful (Davidson 1970, 55, 60).

So in some sense, at least, the really fundamental parts of a theory of meaning are not its axioms but its theorems, the T-sentences giving the truth conditions (meanings) of whole sentences. Nevertheless, from the totality (or at least a representative sampling) of sentences in which a given (unambiguous) word appears, we can abstract a dependent meaning, a common denominator in the way in which the word affects the truth conditions of sentences: "If sentences depend for their meaning on their structure, and we understand the meaning of each item in the structure only as an abstraction from the totality of sentences in which it features, then we can give the meaning of any sentence (or word) only by giving the meaning of every sentence (and word) in the language" (Davidson 1967, 22). The common denominator is what gets expressed in the axiom for the word in question. Thus a theory of meaning as Davidson envisages it does give the meanings of individual words after all. (So Davidson's many contrary remarks, some quoted above, must be interpreted as misleadingly exaggerated expressions of his holism.) But the meaning of a given word is not given by its axiom; it is given by the T-sentences in which the word appears. The axioms are only explanatory hypotheses: we explain why the object-language sentences have the truth conditions they do by postulating that 'Ralph' refers to Ralph and that such and such a predicate has thus and so satisfaction conditions, etc. for all the primitive words of the object language (Davidson 1977a, 221–222).

Davidson's attempt to balance holism and compositionality also serves him in responding to what might be called the problem of verbal context. Return to the two sentences 'That side of the Monongahela is a bank' and 'Merchant's Trust is a bank'. The kind of context that disambiguates 'bank' in these two sentences is *verbal* context: it is the presence of the name of a river side and the name of a financial institution in the subject positions of these sentences that disambiguates them. Another example is the sentence 'John's bank is eroding'. Here the meanings of 'bank' and 'eroding' are *mutually* dependent.[6] We can take the sentence as envisaging imminent financial disaster or as a comment on the physical condition of John's estate. But either way, 'bank' and 'eroding' can be assigned meanings only as a married couple. These examples show that it is not possible to assign meanings to individual words one by one and build up the meanings of sentences therefrom, and the capacity of a theory to do just that was what was supposed to keep it to a finite size.

Davidson's self-imposed demand that a theory of meaning contain everything a competent speaker knows, and thus avoid radically "self-conscious" T-sentences, effectively requires that it provide the meanings of individual words; but the verbal-context objection seems to indicate that this just cannot be done by any finite theory. He tries to meet the self-imposed demand by emphasizing the compositional aspects of his view, but he emphasizes his holism in response to the verbal-context objection. His answer to the latter is, in effect, to deny that his view of a theory of meaning (understanding) implies that sentence meanings are "built up" out of independent word meanings. On the contrary, the latter must be abstracted out of the former. Of course, this does not completely answer the particular examples of verbal context given above, because one of the implications of those examples is that there is not any *common* denominator in the way 'bank' (or 'eroding') affects the truth value of *all* the sentences in which it appears. But this implication of the examples arises from the ambiguity of the terms 'bank' and 'eroding', and Davidson has already conceded that ambiguity puts a limit on what a theory of meaning can do.

The reader may feel at this point that Davidson wants to have his cake and eat it too. He wants to explain how we can understand natural-language sentences never before encountered by implying that our understanding is compositional, but he wants to evade certain objections by saying that understanding is holistic. To reconcile these contrary tendencies, I think we must attribute to Davidson a view of language learning that goes something like this: We first grasp the meanings (truth conditions) of a sampling of simple sentences without having any antecedent grasp of the meanings of any of the words therein. From this we abstract the meanings of the words in the sampling, and then we can grasp, in a compositional manner, the meaning of a previously unseen sentence, provided it contains no new vocabulary. Learning a new word would require that we first understand, holistically, a sampling of sentences in which it appears, after which we can abstract the meaning of the new word.

Jaakko Hintikka has argued that Davidson cannot completely evade the problems of verbal context merely by acknowledging that no semantic unit smaller than a sentence is independently meaningful. Davidson, he says, is committed to a rock solid compositionality in at least this sense: when a sentence is compounded with truth-functional operators like 'or', 'and', and 'if ... then' and all the component clauses of the compound sentence are themselves *closed* sentences, the truth conditions (meaning) of the whole is a function of the truth conditions of the component clauses. But Hintikka has found a verbal context counterexample to this claim. Consider the sentence

Any corporal can become a general.

The 'any' here is a universal quantifier, so the sentence is true if *every* corporal can become a general. But now consider the compound sentence

If any corporal can become a general, then I'll be a monkey's uncle.

When 'any' follows 'if', it is an *existential* quantifier, so the antecedent of this sentence says 'If *even a single* corporal can become a general'. (Compare 'If any member contributes, I shall be surprised'.) Hence, the truth conditions of a compound sentence are not always a function of the truth conditions of its component clauses (Hintikka 1975). I see no obvious way for Davidson to escape this objection. He cannot simply extend his holism to a higher level by saying that only compound sentences are independently meaningful and the meanings of atomic sentences are just abstractions from the totality of compound sentences in which they appear. He cannot do this because any compound sentence can itself be a component of a larger compound sentence, so there would be no level at which we finally get independently meaningful sentences from which we can abstract the meanings of smaller sentences.

Davidson appeals to his holism to answer another objection, which is implicit in Hartry Field's attack on Tarski (see section 6.6) and explicit in Harman 1974. A Davidsonian theory of meaning explains the truth conditions of sentences in terms of the semantic properties—references, satisfaction conditions, etc.—of its parts, but it provides no explanation of the nature of these semantic properties. The axiom giving the reference of 'Ralph', for example, '"Ralph" refers to Ralph', does not tell us what the reference relation is:

When the theory comes to characterize satisfaction for the predicate 'x flies', for example, it merely tells us that an entity satisfies 'x flies' if and only if that entity flies. If we ask for a further explanation or analysis of the relation, we will be disappointed. ...

Analogous remarks go for constant singular terms. Indeed if there are complex singular terms, it will be necessary to characterize a relation like reference, using recursive clauses such as: 'the father of' concatenated with a name α refers to the father of what α refers to. But for the underlying proper names, there will again be simply a list. What it is for a proper name to refer to an object will not be analyzed. (Davidson 1977a, 217–218)

Davidson concedes the point but insists that we really do not need any substantive explanation of what reference or satisfaction is. We postulate that 'Ralph' refers to Ralph only to help explain why 'Ralph is red' is true if and only if Ralph is red and why 'Ralph is round' is true if and only if Ralph is round, and so on. But if asked what the reference relation of 'Ralph' to Ralph amounts to, it is acceptable for our answer to circle back on the T-sentences themselves: what it means for 'Ralph' to refer to Ralph is simply that 'Ralph is red' is true just when *Ralph* is red, and 'Ralph is round' is true just when *Ralph* is round, etc. There is not anything more to the reference relation than this (Davidson 1977a, 220–223). Davidson thinks that in this respect his theory of meaning is precisely parallel to empirical theories in physics (1977a, 222). He gives no concrete examples, but perhaps he would accept Newton's postulation of gravity as one: we explain why unsupported objects fall to the ground and why the planets stay in orbit round the sun and why comets follow the path that they do and why light bends when it passes near the sun by postulating that there is an attractive force between objects having mass. We can describe with mathematical precision the effects gravity has on objects, but if we are asked to peer into gravity itself and say what it is, there can be no noncircular answer. All that it means to say that objects with mass have gravitational attraction to one another is that objects fall to the ground, planets stay in their orbits, comets follow such and such a path, light bends near the sun, etc.

Quine in 1960 advocated what has become known as the indeterminacy-of-translation thesis, which for our purposes we can take as the claim that for a given object language there can be more than one Davidsonian theory of meaning that equally well account for the utterances of the native speakers of the language. We may well find, for example, that the object-language word 'gavagai' can be taken as referring to rabbits or to undetached rabbit parts. That is, a theory with

G^a^v^a^g^a^i refers to rabbits

as an axiom and

'Gavagai noonoo' is true ≡ roasted rabbit is good

as a T-sentence may match the utterances of the speakers of the language just as well as, but no better than, a theory having the axiom

G^a^v^a^g^a^i refers to undetached rabbit parts

and the T-sentence

'Gavagai noonoo' is true ≡ roasted undetached rabbit parts are good.

Davidson agrees that the available evidence may not enable us to narrow down our candidate theories to just one, but he contends, plausibly, that it does not matter. Both theories capture what a competent speaker of the language knows (Davidson 1970, 62; Davidson 1977a, 224–225). Since there are rabbits where and only where there are undetached rabbit parts, then, regardless of which theory we use, we will be able to interpret any native's utterance containing 'gavagai', and we will be able to make our own object-language utterances containing 'gavagai' without fear of being told by a native that we are misusing the language. Suppose that they conceive of gavagai as collections of undetached rabbit parts and we conceive of gavagai as rabbits, how would either party detect the difference?

Finally, Scott Soames has argued that a Tarski-like theory of truth is incompatible with any semantic program. Indeed, Soames claims that Davidson's attempt to combine the two is "absurd" (Soames 1984, 222–224, esp. the footnotes). The objection is sufficiently devastating, if well-taken, that it deserves at least a brief discussion, even though the issues involved are sufficiently complex that we cannot hope to reach any final judgment on the matter here.

The problems begin with the fact that certain sentences that contain the predicate 'is true' and that it seems any Davidsonian would want to endorse come out false when the *definiens* of a Tarski-like definition of truth is substituted for the 'is true'. Soames offers this example: "If *x* knows that which is expressed by the relevant instance of

'*S*' is true in *L* iff *p*

for each sentence of *L*; then *x* is a competent speaker of *L*" (1984, 224 n. 23). If we substitute 'is satisfied by all sequences' for the 'is true' in this sentence and then substitute the *definiens* of Tarski's definition of satisfaction for 'is satisfied by all sequences in L', the displayed line will end up reading '*p* iff *p*'. Yet you can know that *p* iff *p* about every sentence *p* of a language and not be a competent speaker of it. (Indeed, you already do know this about every sentence of every language.)

To see how a Davidsonian would likely react to this, we must make use of a broader sense of the word 'intension' than the sense discussed in section 1.4. Notice that '9' is extensionally equivalent to 'the number of planets', but if you substitute the latter phrase for the first appearance of the numeral in

Necessarily, $9 = 9$,

which is true, you get

Necessarily, the number of planets $= 9$,

which is false because there are possible worlds where earth's solar system has 10 planets. This phenomenon—the fact that one can substitute, within the scope of the intensional operator 'necessarily', one expression for an extensionally equivalent expression and end up changing the truth value of the sentence—is called failure of substitutivity. Substitutivity also fails within the scope of certain other operators, e.g., 'knows that':

Everyone knows that Cicero is the same person as Cicero

is true, but although 'Cicero' is extensionally equivalent to 'Tully' (they are different names for the same person),

Everyone knows that Cicero is the same person as Tully

is false. Substitutivity also fails within the scope of a subjunctive-mood verb. Philosophers have come to call all grammatical forms within which substitutivity fails "intensional contexts." Whether this practice does not purchase more confusion than clarity is a matter about which I have grave doubts, but for better or worse, the practice is now institutionalized in philosophy.

I think that at one time Davidson's answer to Soame's problem would have been to point out that a Tarski-like definition of truth is extensional and that in Soames's problematic sentence the truth predicate is within an intensional context, 'to know'. Hence it is neither surprising nor alarming that substitutivity will fail. Soames anticipates this answer and responds that a "natural demand growing out of" the view that "the meaning of a sentence is closely related to its truth conditions" is "that all legitimate theoretical purposes served by the explicandum (truth), be equally well served by the explicatum [that is, by the *definiens* of a definition of truth].... Thus, substitution of explicatum for explicandum in intensional contexts contained in one's total explanatory theory must be countenanced, even if such substitution is not always countenanced in ordinary discourse" (1984, 222–223 and n. 21). Since Soames's sentence is part of a Davidsonian total explanatory theory, Soames concludes that the *definiens* of whatever definition of truth the Davidsonian endorses ought to be substitutable into the sentence.

The obvious reply for Davidson is to simply reject this "natural demand." A Tarski-like definition of truth, in Davidson's hands, is not meant to be an informative definition of the concept of truth anyway. At most, it tells us the extension, for a particular language, of a primitive, indefinable concept of truth. So there just is not any *explicatum* for the concept of truth.[7]

8.4   Dummett's Theory of Meaning

If the Davidson Program can succeed, it would constitute a very detailed and impressive filling out of the slogan that the meaning of a sentence consists in its truth conditions. But is that slogan even true anyway? Michael Dummett has suggested that it is not. On the contrary, he claims, the meaning of a sentence consists in its *justification* conditions. That is, if a, b, and c are the conditions that would justify anyone in asserting sentence s, then

Sentence s *means that* items a, b, and c obtain.

One of the most striking characteristics of Dummett's method is his apparent desire to equate ontological disputes and disputes about the meanings of sentences. Indeed, Dummett can be interpreted as making a four-way conflation. He sometimes seems to take the ontological doctrine of realism *and* the doctrine that meaning is truth conditions *and* Realist theories of truth *and* the doctrine of bivalence as all being, in effect, different names for the same doctrine. But there are also passages in which he is much more circumspect, claiming only that one or another of these doctrines in combination with other premises would lead one to infer the others.[8] But on any interpretation, Dummett's arguments against truth-conditional semantics are the foundation of his philosophy. It is from here that he argues, either directly by making the equivalences just noted or indirectly, to the denial of ontological realism, bivalence, and Realist theories of truth.[9] Hence, it is to these arguments contra truth-conditional semantics that I attend in the sequel.

Some of the confusion arises from Dummett's habit of shifting between two versions of his theory of meaning. Dummett's words would naturally lead one to think that he sometimes endorses one and sometimes the other of the following logically incompatible theses:

A. Truth is correctly analyzed with a Realist theory of truth.[10] But meaning does not consist in truth conditions. Truth should be *replaced* as the "central notion" in the theory of meaning with the concept of justification. (A Realist theory of truth, for Dummett, is any theory that allows that if a statement is true, then it is so regardless of whether or not we have, or can have, any justification for it.[11])

B. Truth *is* the key concept in a theory of meaning because meaning *does* consist in truth conditions. But truth is *not* correctly analyzed with a Realist theory of truth. Rather, a correct analysis of truth would equate truth with justification or verification, e.g., sentence s is true if, and only if, s is justified. Or it would analyze truth partly in terms of justification.

It is one thing to say that a Realist answer to the metaphysical project is irrelevant to this or that philosophical program, which is all that (A) says. It is quite another thing to say, as (B) does, that a Realist theory is an incorrect analysis of truth. Here are some examples of Dummett's mode (A) remarks:

> We must, therefore, replace the notion of truth, as the central notion of the theory of meaning for mathematical statements, by the notion of *proof*. ... The appropriate generalization of this, for statements of an arbitrary kind, would be the replacement of the notion of truth ... by that of verification. (1975a, 225–227)

> ... dethroning truth and falsity from their central place ... in the theory of meaning. (1959, 19)

> ... If we accept the redundancy theory of 'true' and 'false' ..., we must abandon the idea which we naturally have that the notions of truth and falsity play an essential role in any account ... of the meaning of statements.[12]

Here are some examples of his mode (B) remarks, beginning with one from the next page after the last quoted mode (A) remark:

> The sense of a statement is determined by knowing in what circumstances it is true and in what false. (1959, 8)

> The dispute [between realists and antirealists] thus concerns the notion of truth appropriate for statements of the disputed class.[13]

Dummett is not unaware of the difference and there *is* a point about which he has never made up his mind, but the distinction between the two versions is not so great as (A) and (B) make it appear. Dummett has never meant to deviate from any of these:

1. Realist theories of truth are incorrect.
2. Truth should be analyzed at least partly in terms of justification.
3. Truth should be replaced as the "central notion" in the theory of meaning with the concept of justification.
4. The "central notion" for a given theory of meaning is whatever concept gets recursively defined when the theory is applied to nonatomic statements (Dummett 1959, 17–18). (Thus, for Dummett, the key concept for a theory of meaning, M, is *not*, contrary to what one would naturally assume, always whatever concept would correctly fill the blank in 'Theory M analyses meaning immediately in terms of ____ conditions.')

What he is unsure of is whether the concept of truth, even with a nonrealist flavoring, need play any role at all in the theory of meaning. Hence the two versions of his thesis are really the following:

A'. All of (1) through (4) plus the claim that truth plays no role whatever in the theory of meaning.

B'. All of (1) through (4) plus the claim that truth plays an essential but subsidiary role, inasmuch as meaning is immediately cashed in terms of truth conditions, but they in turn are cashed in terms of recursively defined justification conditions.

Most writers, if they see the difference between (A') and (B') at all, take the latter to be his thesis.[14] However, Richard Rorty and Anthony Appiah have spotted the difference between (A') and (B') and seem to agree that the former is Dummett's actual thesis. Crispin Wright also sees the difference and he endorses (B') as *his* own view, but he detects Dummett's inconsistent language, and he avoids finally identifying either one as Dummett's view.[15] Interestingly enough, all of Dummett's *arguments* on the question (see below) directly support (A'), not (B'), so I shall write in the (A') mode hereafter. At any rate, one can see how remarks like the last two quotations above, separated as they usually are in Dummett from the other clauses of (B'), could lead G. P. Baker and P. M. S. Hacker, and Alexander George, to lump Dummett confusingly in with Donald Davidson as an advocate of truth-conditional semantics.[16]

It is unfortunate that Dummett did not simply take (A), distinct from (A') as well as (B) and (B'), as his thesis, because, as we saw in section 2.2, the doctrine that truth can be analyzed even partly in terms of justification is of dubious intelligibility. (This issue is taken up again in section 8.7.) Mode (A) also captures the essence of Dummett's view least misleadingly (which seems to be Field's point; see Field 1986, 63–64).

When speaking in the (A') mode, Dummett's primary dispute with Donald Davidson is about whether it is the metaphysical project or justification project that is most relevant to the philosophy of language: In terms of what sort of conditions should we analyze the meaning of a sentence? Davidson is claiming that truth conditions are the relevant sort, while Dummett is claiming that the meaning of a sentence should be analyzed by its justification conditions. When speaking in the (B') mode, Dummett is saying that, although Davidson is right to think that a correct answer to the metaphysical project is relevant to the analysis of meaning, he, Davidson, is working with an incorrect answer to that project, an incorrect theory of truth. In either mode, Dummett is saying, along with William James, John Dewey, and Brand Blanshard, that (at least part of) the correct answer to the question 'What is truth?' is the same as the correct answer to the question 'What is justification?' I shall return to theses (A') and (B') below. In the meantime, let me set the stage for our examination of Dummett's arguments with a quick summary of his views on meaning.

The first thing to note is Dummett's modesty. He admits that we have a much better idea of what a Davidsonian theory of meaning looks like than any of its rivals, and that these rivals face difficulties every bit as fearsome as those that face Davidson's. For these reasons he admits that he is not *sure* that it is wrong to explicate meaning in terms of truth conditions (Dummett 1976, 67–68). Hence Dummett's negative thesis regarding meaning as truth conditions is much more developed than his positive doctrine. But let us examine that positive doctrine, such as it is.

Dummett has been accused by Devitt and Sterelny, by George, and by Baker and Hacker of contending that knowledge of a language is propositional knowledge.[17] Dummett holds, they suppose, that a competent speaker of English knows a series of propositions that constitute a theory of meaning for the language. (See below for details.) And 'accuse' is just the word, for the "propositional assumption" as Devitt calls it, is certainly false. Obviously, many competent speakers of English do not have any propositional knowledge of its semantic structure.[18] But in fact, Dummett holds that linguistic competence is a practical ability, so a theory of meaning must *model* (or *represent*; Dummett uses the two words interchangeably) this practical ability (1975a, 217). The model is a set of propositions that *represent* what a competent speaker of the language knows. This does not mean that a competent speaker of the language has propositional knowledge of these propositions. Knowing a language is a knowing-how not a knowing-that. It is ability knowledge not propositional knowledge. (Or as the artificial intelligence scientists would put it, it is algorithmic knowledge not declarative knowledge.) But ability knowledge can be *represented* by propositions (Dummett 1976, 70–71). Since the distinction may not be familiar to everyone, an example is in order. I know how to touch-type, that is, type accurately without looking at the keyboard, but like most touch-typists, when confronted with a blank sheet of paper and asked to draw a map of the keyboard labeling all the keys and to do so without looking at the keyboard, I cannot do it accurately. Nor can I accurately write down a series of propositions describing the relative positions of the letters (e.g., 'The "B" is to the left of the "N"') unless I look at the keyboard. To put it in a colorful way, it seems as if my fingers know how to type, but my mind does not. I have algorithmic knowledge of the relative positions of the keys, but I do not have propositional knowledge of it. But notice that it would be possible for one to *represent*, or model, my knowledge as a series of propositions describing the relative positions of the keys. I do not actually have such propositional knowledge, but my digital behavior at the keyboard makes it seem *as though* I did have such knowledge and *as though* I inferred from such propositions where to move my fingers. Someone else could memorize these propositions, and if he could make very fast inferences, he would exhibit the same typing ability I do. Dummett would label the sort of epistemic relationship I have with these propositions as "implicit knowledge," meaning that I do not really know the propositions at all, but it is as though I did.

So for Dummett, as for Davidson, linguistic competence is *implicit* knowledge of a set of axioms and theorems in a theory of meaning for the language. (See Dummett 1976, 69–70, and compare Platts 1979, 231–237.) But here again he explains that he means only that one could *represent* a competent speaker's linguistic behavior with a list of such propositions. He does *not* mean that the speaker *really* knows these propositions. Yet someone who is not now competent in English *could* memorize the propositions of such a theory for English, and if he could make inferences fast enough, his linguistic behavior in English would match that of a native speaker (assuming the theory is accurate).[19] Precisely because of this we can say of the native speaker that it is *as though* he has propositional knowledge of the theory.[20] We can now see the error in using the phrase 'implicit propositional knowledge', as Devitt and George do, to label Dummett's idea of what a competent speaker knows. For Dummett would regard the phrase, when taken literally as Devitt and George take it, as a contradiction in terms. 'Implicit knowledge' for Dummett just *means*, among other things, *nonpropositional* knowledge.

The reader ought beware, therefore, of passages like this in the literature:

The attribution of the propositional assumption ... to Dummett is well based but not certain. Philosophers who make the assumption usually hedge their bets. Dummett is no exception. It is clear that he thinks of competence as "a practical ability," but ... he mostly writes as if the ability consisted in propositional knowledge of truth conditions. However, rather than straight-forwardly identifying the ability with the knowledge, he seems to prefer to say that it can be "represented" as that knowledge. ... Further he thinks that part of this knowledge is only "implicit" or "tacit." ... This use of weasel words in stating the propositional assumption casts doubt on Dummett's commitment to it. (Devitt 1984, 205–206)

"Casts doubt" is putting it mildly. Dummett does not use such words "in stating the propositional assumption." He uses them to deny it. Nor are these "weasel words." To have *implicit* knowledge of the proposition that *p* is to have a bit of nonpropositional knowledge, an ability, which can be *represented* with the proposition that *p*. In his use of 'represented' Dummett is not trying to hedge any bets or find a nonstraightforward way of "identifying the ability with the knowledge." The word 'represent' can be ambiguous, but it is never used in *this* way. Were Dummett to say that he has a representation of his wife on his wall, would he be accused of weaseling and hedging his way out of a straightforward admission that he has hung his wife from the wall? Dummett's use of 'represent' is not at all mysterious. Think again of the man who can touch-type by virtue of having memorized propositions describing the keyboard. Since I have the same ability, these propositions represent my ability as well as his, even though I do not know them. Finally, Dummett does not "mostly" write as if linguistic competence "consisted in propositional knowledge." He never writes this way. He always writes as if it consisted in abilities that can be *represented* with propositions. So far from being "well based," the attribution of the propositional assumption to Dummett has no basis at all.

On this much Davidson and Dummett can agree. They agree also that a complete theory of meaning must include axioms that specify the reference of terms and application of predicates. For example,

'The earth' denotes the earth.
It is true to say of something 'It moves' iff that thing moves.

From these axioms are deduced theorems in the form of T-sentences:

'The earth moves' is true iff the earth moves.[21]

And from these we deduce further theorems in the form M-sentences:

'The earth moves' means that the earth moves.[22]

These axioms and theorems model what a speaker knows when he knows a language. (Recall from my discussion of Davidson that when I speak of a hypothetical non-English speaker learning English by virtue of memorizing these propositions, the theory of meaning for English that this imaginary person uses to learn English is itself written in *his* native language, so all parts of the axioms and theorems that are not within quotation marks appear in his language.)

8.5   Dummett's Argument against Construing Meaning as Truth Conditions

The notion of an undecidable sentence plays a key role in Dummett's arguments. An undecidable sentence is one where we have no foolproof procedure applicable in every circumstance by which we can ascertain its truth value. A sentence will still count as undecidable even if there are *some* circumstances in which we *can* determine its truth value. Subjunctive conditionals (e.g., 'If Chicago were to win the championship, its citizens would celebrate') are one kind of undecidable. So long as the antecedent remains a mere possibility we have no foolproof way of determining the truth value of the conditional. But should the antecedent be actualized, we can determine the truth value of the consequent (in this case by observing the behavior of the good burghers of Chicago) and hence the truth value of the conditional (Dummett 1973, 467, 514; Dummett 1976, 80–81). Some other kinds of undecidables are sentences quantifying over infinite domains and those referring to regions of space or time inaccessible even in principle. We now have sufficient clarification to return to the central issue about whether truth or justification ought to be the key concept in a theory of meaning.

The essence of Dummett's arguments can be explained with an analogy. Suppose someone not previously able to ride a bicycle (but who can make very fast inferences) were to memorize a certain set of propositions. If he still cannot ride a bicycle, then, of course, the set of propositions would be an inadequate model of bicycle-riding ability. But there is another way in which the propositions might fail to be an adequate model. Suppose our subject can ride a bicycle after memorizing the propositions, but suppose he can do more than this. Suppose that his knowledge of the propositions gives him the remarkable psychokinetic ability to *sit perfectly still* on the bicycle and still make it go. In this case we would suspect that his bicycle-riding ability is very different from ours and that the propositions in question do not really model *our* ability. They model some psychokinetic ability *we* do not have. In other words, the model predicts behavior that we never display. It models abilities we do not possess. There is no explanatory power in attributing to us an implicit knowledge of the model, because our behavior does not match the abilities of one who had explicit knowledge of the model. In Dummett's terms, the model is without content or meaning. He also argues that a truth-conditional theory of meaning is vacuous. He means by this not that it explains too little but that it "explains" too much. It models an ability that no one in fact possesses: the ability to determine in every circumstance the truth value of undecidables. It predicts behavior that we do not, indeed, cannot, ever display. Thus, Dummett says, a truth-conditional "theory of meaning is left unconnected with the practical ability of which it was supposed to be a theoretical representation" (1976, 71; compare Dummett 1973, 467). On the other hand, a theory of meaning, a model, in terms of justification conditions can perfectly well account for any and all behavior actually displayed by competent speakers.

So the central questions in evaluating Dummett's arguments are:

1. Is it the case that one who knows the truth conditions for an undecidable would be able in every circumstance to ascertain its truth value?

2. Would any other behavior manifest knowledge of the truth conditions of undecidables, as distinct from mere knowledge of the justification conditions?

3. If the answer to (2) is 'yes', then do speakers ever display the behavior in question?

If the answer to (3) is yes, it is not vacuous to attribute to those speakers implicit knowledge of truth conditions. For their behavior needs explaining and cannot be explained merely by attributing to them implicit knowledge of justification conditions. Since it is true by definition that no one can ascertain the truth value of an undecidable in every circumstance, a 'yes' answer to (2) and (3) entails a 'no' answer to (1). So the task of one who would refute Dummett's arguments is to pinpoint some piece of behavior actually displayed by speakers that cannot be explained save by attributing to them implicit knowledge of truth conditions (as distinct from justification conditions).

Dummett has at least four arguments to his conclusion that truth-conditional theories of meaning are without content or meaning. They are found at Dummett 1976, 70-72, 81-83, and Dummett 1975a, 216-217,

224–225. The last of these comes closest to capturing the essence of his thinking and I provide a literal-minded paraphrase here:

1. When a statement is decidable, there is a decision procedure that in any circumstance will tell us its truth value, and we can always get ourselves into a position where we know its truth value.

2. Anyone who knows a statement's truth value can manifest this knowledge with his linguistic behavior.

3. Therefore, if someone knows the decision procedure for a statement, then in *every* circumstance, he could, by using the procedure, manifest knowledge of the statement's truth value. (From 1, 2.)

4. The *only* way to manifest *fully* a knowledge of a statement's truth conditions is to show that one could, no matter what the circumstances, get oneself into a position in which one could manifest in linguistic behavior a knowledge of the statement's truth value.

5. Therefore, demonstrating a mastery of a statement's decision procedure fully manifests a knowledge of that statement's truth conditions. (From 3, 4.)

6. Undecidable statements are those for which we do not have a decision procedure that works in every circumstance.

7. Therefore, for undecidable statements there are circumstances in which we cannot determine the truth value of the statement. (From 6.)

8. Therefore, there are circumstances in which we cannot linguistically manifest a knowledge of an undecidable statement's truth value. (From 7.)

9. Therefore, one cannot show that in every circumstance one could get oneself into a position where one could linguistically manifest a knowledge of an undecidable statement's truth conditions. (From 8.)

10. Therefore, one cannot *fully* manifest a knowledge of an undecidable statement's truth conditions. (From 4, 9.)

11. An ascription of implicit knowledge to a person is meaningful only if the person is capable of *fully* manifesting that knowledge.

12. Therefore, one cannot meaningfully ascribe to anyone implicit knowledge of the truth conditions of undecidable statements. (From 10, 11.)

13. Theories of meaning that assert that meaning consists in truth conditions ascribe implicit knowledge of truth conditions to speakers.

14. Therefore, theories of meaning that assert that meaning consists in truth conditions are not meaningful for languages with undecidable statements. (From 12, 13.)

Note that the argument supports thesis (A') and is quite irrelevant to (B'). It has this in common with Dummett's other arguments.

8.6   A Critique of Dummett's Argument

Premises (4) and (11) are the key ones and there are parallels to both in all four of Dummett's arguments. The import of (4) is that there is no behavior, other than behavior that demonstrates the speaker's mastery of a decision procedure for a statement, that can be taken as fully manifesting a speaker's implicit knowledge of the truth conditions for the statement. The import of the word 'fully' is that the speaker must do more than display behavior that *can* be interpreted as implicit knowledge of truth conditions. He must display behavior that cannot be explained otherwise. In particular, he must do more than display behavior that can equally well be explained by attributing to him implicit knowledge of mere justification conditions. That this is what Dummett means by 'fully' here is brought out by comparing this argument with his argument at 1975a, 216–217.

The import of (11) is that there is no explanatory power to an attribution of implicit knowledge to a person unless that person actually displays some behavior that the attribution would explain.

Dummett offers no defense of (11), but it has a surface plausibility, and one must beware of the overly facile counterexamples that may come to mind. Consider a man who has implicit knowledge of x and who can manifest this knowledge. Then a terrible accident makes it physiologically impossible for him to manifest this knowledge, not even by speaking or blinking his eyes. Even so, it seems meaningful to claim that he *still* has knowledge of x. And in the absence of evidence that the accident harmed his memory, would we not endorse just such a claim? Think of x, for example, as the set of propositions, that, though he has no *explicit* knowledge of them, model his ability to ride a bicycle. (For example, 'One ought push down with the right foot while letting up with the left.') Surely the accident, which has not affected his brain, has not caused him to forget how to ride a bicycle. Note that with a miraculous recovery he would once again be able to manifest his knowledge. Would it not be silly to say that during the time of his paralysis he did not know how to ride a bicycle and that he has now reacquired that knowledge? Of course, bike riding is not a linguistic ability, but the counterexample is not directed to (12) or (14) but to (11), the premise on which they rest, and (11) is a general claim about all kinds of implicit knowledge, even nonlinguistic.

But the failure of this counterexample becomes apparent when we remember what 'meaningful' means for Dummett when applied to an attribution of implicit knowledge. There is, I think Dummett would concede, *some* sense of 'meaningful' in which the attribution of implicit knowledge of bicycle riding to this unfortunate man, even while he is laid up, is quite meaningful and, indeed, justified. But notice that his preaccident and postrecovery behavior can be explained by saying that he had such knowledge before the accident and had it again after his recovery. There is no further explanatory power gained by the additional postulation that he had the knowledge in question even while he was laid up. He did not demonstrate any behavior during his incapacity the explanation of which would require this additional postulation. It is in this special sense of explanatory pointlessness that the additional attribution is "meaningless." (Obviously, many issues relevant to the evaluation of explanations, e.g., issues of simplicity in explanation, are being overlooked here. But it would take us too far from the issues of this book to pursue them. Let it suffice to say that a good case could be made that the realist explanation described here is not at all pointless.)

Much more could be said about (11), but I shall concede it to Dummett hereafter so that we may move on to (4). The 'only' in the premise is necessary to the validity of the argument, but it is also a point of vulnerability. However, we cannot refute it by saying that the fact that we use undecidable statements correctly manifests our knowledge of their truth conditions, for this would beg the question against Dummett. It is agreed on all sides that we understand undecidables. The question is which model, truth-conditional or justification-conditional, best explains this ability. Neither side can point to the very ability whose analysis is at issue as evidence for their analysis. Dummett's point is that the fact that we do understand undecidables, combined with his argument that we do not know their truth conditions, shows that our understanding of them cannot be explained as implicit knowledge of their truth conditions. Both Colin McGinn (1980, 28–30) and Anthony Appiah have made arguments against (4) that look suspiciously like this question-begging argument. I shall deal only with Appiah's argument here:

> Suppose the sentence is: "It rained on the Earth a million years ago." Why is it not evidence that someone assigns this sentence the correct truth conditions, that they use 'rain' properly in sentences about present rain, that they can count to a million, know how long a year is, and display a grasp of the past tense in relation to the recent past?... To suppose that it [is] not is like supposing that you can only discover that something is fragile by breaking it.... The centrality of assent to sentences in explication of meaning does not require that evidence about the meaning of sentences should be about assent to them: assent to other sentences, with syntactically related properties, can suffice. (Appiah 1986, 80)

The problem with this argument can be brought out if we ask whether the evidence Appiah adduces is really evidence for the specific claim that the individual assigns the correct truth conditions to the undecidable sentence or whether it is only evidence for the vaguer, undisputed claim that the individual understands its meaning. It seems obvious to me that Appiah's evidence supports only the latter claim. We can leap to the more specific claim only by assuming that meaning consists in truth conditions, which, of course, begs the question at issue. A speaker with the abilities Appiah describes would almost certainly know (at least implicitly) either the justification conditions for 'It rained on the Earth a million years ago' or the truth conditions for it or both. But Appiah's argument gives us no reason for preferring one of these options over another.

There may be a non-question-begging way of trying to show that (4) is false. Consider the pair of statements 'Dummett's only great-grandson will marry' and 'Dummett's only great-grandson will always be a bachelor'. Both of these are undecidable because there are circumstances, the present one for example, in which we cannot determine the truth value of either. But one who knows their truth conditions can manifest that knowledge, for he can answer 'no' to the question 'Can these both be true?' On the other hand, it seems that one who did not know the truth conditions for this pair would have to answer 'I do not know', because he would not recognize that it is impossible for the truth conditions for both statements to obtain. One could come up with a pair of inconsistent statements for any corner of space or time. And there are, of course, logically inconsistent pairs of statements that quantify over infinite domains, and logically inconsistent pairs of subjunctive conditionals (e.g., 'If Chicago had won, then New York would have lost' and 'if Chicago had won, then New York would have won also').

But is it really the case that the ability to discern the logical incompatibility of these two sentences can *only* be explained by attributing implicit knowledge of the truth conditions of the sentences to those who have the ability? Wright contends that a competent speaker's ability to recognize relations of logical consequence can be explained by attributing to her merely an implicit knowledge of justification conditions (1987, 17, 242). (I presume Dummett would agree, since this ability does seem to be an essential ingredient in linguistic competence.) If this is correct, a model in terms of justification conditions would be sufficient to represent the same ability as displayed by native speakers. There would be no further explanatory power in a model in terms of truth conditions. More to the immediate point, the above counterexample to (4) would collapse.

By way of example, Wright imagines a situation in which a competent speaker is facing several bowls each containing some substance or other. With regard to such propositions as 'This is salty', 'This is sweet', 'This is bitter', and the like, the speaker has a number of abilities. One is that she can recognize relations of logical consequence holding among them (e.g., she can recognize that 'This is salty or sweet' and 'This is not salty' entail 'This is sweet'.) She can also directly, as it were, recognize whether or not the state of affairs that constitutes the truth of one of these propositions obtains by simply tasting the substance in question. This last fact makes these statements decidable. But suppose the speaker suffers from a congenital absence of a sense of taste. For her, these are undecidables. She can know the justification conditions for the propositions. She knows, for example, that if others tend to sprinkle one of the substances on their oatmeal and to spit out oatmeal with another substance sprinkled on it, then she is justified in asserting that the first is sweet and that the second is not. Moreover, according to Wright (1987, 17), she still has the ability to discern relations of logical consequence that hold between these various propositions.

To determine whether or not this is true, we must imagine someone who knows the justification conditions for the propositions in question but who does not know the truth conditions. Would such a person display the sort of behavior we take to manifest an ability to discern relations of logical consequence? One way in which speakers manifest such an ability is by making explicit utterances containing the words 'logical consequence' (e.g., as when a speaker utters 'p is a logical consequence of q'). Another way in which a speaker might manifest an ability to recognize that p is a logical consequence of q is by displaying a tendency to assert p and/or behave as if it were true whenever she is justified in asserting q. Suppose the speaker is justified in asserting 'This is either sweet or salty' and in asserting 'This is not salty'. Now if she knows the justification conditions but not the truth conditions for 'This is sweet', would she in these circumstances assert 'This is sweet' or behave as though it were true? Well, since she knows the justification conditions for this statement, she knows that 'This is sweet or salty' and 'This is not salty' are together a conclusive justification for 'This is sweet', so she would tend to assert the latter and to behave as though it were true. So far, so good for Wright's contention. But would she *assert* '"This is sweet" is a logical consequence of "This is sweet or salty" and "This is not salty"'? Given her ignorance of truth conditions, would she, could she, possess the ability to recognize logical consequence as distinct from conclusive justification?

The answer is no. If this is right, here is an ability and a piece of behavior that is possessed and manifested by competent speakers but that cannot be manifested by anyone who does not have knowledge of truth conditions. The problem, as I see it, is that 'logical consequence' is defined in terms of truth conditions, not justification conditions: p is a logical consequence of q if and only if p cannot possibly be *false* if q *true*. Thus our speaker, for whom we are supposing that p and q are undecidables, cannot infer from her knowledge that q conclusively justifies p the fact that p is a logical consequence of q, for in hypothesizing that she knows nothing of the truth conditions for the relevant statements, one of the things we are in effect hypothesizing is that she does not know that the truth of q is a sufficient condition for the truth of p whenever q is conclusive justification for p. To put it another way, the justification conditions for 'p is a logical consequence of q' (which conditions the speaker does know) are themselves cashed in terms of the *truth* conditions for p, *not* the justification conditions for p (or even the "conclusive justification" conditions for p). And the speaker does not know the truth conditions for p. Thus, while she knows that a sufficient justification condition for 'p is a logical consequence of q' is that p cannot possibly be false when q is true, this, for her, is a useless piece of information because, lacking any knowledge of the truth conditions for q and p, she has no way of ever knowing when this justification condition for 'p is a logical consequence of q' obtains.

All of the above follows on the classical definition of 'logical consequence', but intuitionists and constructivists are not shy about redefining logical terminology, so perhaps Wright (and/or Dummett) can escape the counterexample to (4) by proposing an alternate definition of 'logical consequence'. If we attribute such a move to Wright (and Dummett), we can no longer see him as intending to include on the list of abilities one can have even without knowledge of truth conditions the ability to recognize relations of logical consequence (classically defined) among undecidables. On the contrary, he means to deny that any competent speaker can have this ability. What we can do is recognize relations of conclusive justification, and for this, even in the case of undecidables, we need only have knowledge of the justification conditions. So the revised definition of 'logical consequence' would be that p is a logical consequence of q if and only if it is impossible for p not to be justified if q is. Now on this view, there is no question that our tasteless person can recognize that 'This is sweet' is a 'logical consequence' (in the new sense) of 'This is sweet or salty' and 'This is not salty', and she would even tend to assert this explicitly. (This is provided she defines, at least implicitly, 'logical consequence' in the revised sense. If she does not, then Wright still has no explanation of how she can correctly make explicit assertions of the form 'p is a logical consequence of q'.)[23]

It should not be assumed that one with broad sympathy for the program of creating a Davidsonian-Dummettian style theory of linguistic competence is limited to the choice of analyzing meaning in terms of either justification conditions or (Realistically construed) truth conditions. David Wiggins (1980) has suggested we approach the program by *first* asking what sort of property P could be such that a theory that entailed all sentences of the form

$$(S \text{ is } P) \equiv p$$

(where S and p are as in the Davidson Program) could be properly said to give the meaning of all the sentences in the object language. It might turn out that P cannot be *either* truth or justification (Wiggins 1980, 192–194). Indeed, Wiggins argues that P will turn out to be roughly the sort of property that Peirce calls truth. (Wiggins does not mention Peirce, however.) For example, P would have to be such that sentences that possess it would tend over the long run to be agreed to by investigators. And whether or not a sentence possessed P would be independent of any one person's beliefs about whether the sentence possessed it but not independent of the whole community's beliefs. Hence P would be not an objective property of sentences but an intersubjective property (Wiggins, 1980, 205–211). (At the end of his paper [pp. 217–219] Wiggins declares that *P* is just truth, but a key premise in his argument for this claim is that the sort of Davidsonian-Dummettian program of linguistic competence is the *only* one for which we need a concept of truth.)

Finally, it should be clear that Dummett does not belong on the chart of truth theorists in section 1.8. He is offering a theory of linguistic competence, not a theory of truth. Indeed, except in the narrow context of mathematics, where he endorses intuitionistic logic as the standard of justification, he does not even offer an answer to the justification project.

8.7   Truth-as-Justification and Skepticism Again

In this section I return to the truth-as-justification thesis first discussed in section 2.2. This is the thesis that truth should be equated with, or analyzed partly in terms of, justification, or some near synonym thereof, such as warranted assertibility. I argued there that the thesis produces hopelessly circular or unintelligible analyses of truth, but I also pointed out that most of those who seem to embrace the thesis or have had it attributed to them do not really mean it literally. Rather, the thesis is most often just a muddled, misleading, and ill-advised metaphor for some other thesis. Some of the theses for which the truth-as-justification thesis has served as stalking horse are the following:

1. There really is no legitimate philosophical program in which a theory of truth could play an important role. Hence we really do not need a theory of truth, as distinct from a theory of justification.
2. Truth is relative to a conceptual scheme.
3. Truth is a vacuous concept while justification is not.
4. Truth is not the value our justificatory procedures are aiming at, and/or it is not the value those procedures succeed in obtaining for us.
5. Such and such Nonrealist theory (e.g., coherence, instrumental, etc.) is the correct answer to the metaphysical project.
6. The only correct answer to the metaphysical project is a generic quasi realism that remains neutral on ontological questions.

As noted in section 2.2, Ellis 1988 is a clear case in which thesis 5 is being expressed with the truth-as-justification thesis. Specifically, Ellis is using the latter to assert an instrumental theory of truth. We are now in a position to see other specific cases of the phenomenon. As was hinted at in section 8.4, Dummett is most charitably interpreted as using the truth-as-justification thesis to express a mild version of thesis 1. Specifically, he is saying that the concept of truth has either no role or at least no important role in a Davidsonian program of creating an axiomatic theory of understanding for a given object language. In chapter 10, we shall see examples of those who would embrace thesis 1 just as it is. A close reading of Putnam 1981 reveals that Putnam's endorsement of the truth-as-justification thesis is just a way of expressing theses 3, 6, and possibly 2. Rorty is usually careful to reject the truth-as-justification thesis, but not always, and he often does not distinguish among theses 1 through 6, but I think that in the end theses 1, 2, 4, and 6 are all that he wants to endorse (Rorty 1982, the introduction).

Let us turn our attention to an importantly different thesis: the claim that, while our actual, present concept of truth is not correctly analyzed in terms of justification, probability, assertibility, or some near synonym thereof, we ought nonetheless to *revise* our concept of truth so that it is so analyzable. As a case study, let us examine an earlier paper of Ellis's (1969), in which he argued that we ought to throw away the old notion of truth and replace it with what he calls an "epistemological" concept of truth. All we need, he says, is a theory of justification that will justify statements to varying degrees of probability. Truth should be thought of as the limiting case of probability value. A true statement is one with a probability of 1. A false statement is one with a probability of 0. But Ellis recognizes that this proposal is incompatible with a correct analysis of our actual, present notion of truth, and that it requires a "radical linguistic revision" (1969, 71). We will look at Ellis's arguments for the supposed uselessness of our actual present notion of truth in a moment, but first I must point out that there is something puzzling about the revisionist strategy. Why go to the trouble of a radical linguistic revision? We do not gain anything by doing so. The revisionists want us to throw out the concept presently designated 'truth', but, for reasons they leave mysterious, they want to retain the *word* 'truth'. Moreover, they want to have it designate a concept that already has a perfectly good name. In Ellis's case the concept is that of probability to a degree of 1. What is wrong with continuing to use this phrase to designate this property?

Ellis has two arguments in support of his claim that the actual, present notion of truth is unneeded. First, we can communicate perfectly well by taking 'It is true that' to mean 'It is certain or almost certain that'. Second, "the purpose of arguing is to adjust our system of beliefs, and this clearly is an epistemological function" (Ellis 1969, 71).

In answer to the first argument, there are many useful locutions in which 'true' figures that would become impossible on Ellis's proposed revision, particularly in situations in which we believe that the only evidence available is misleading: 'There is overwhelming evidence for the proposition that p, but I am convinced it is not true.' 'I take it on faith that God exists, even though it is almost certain that he does not.' 'Human beings are so constructed psychologically that we find many things certain that are not in fact true.' 'There is no evidence for the proposition that p, but it is true.' But if 'true' is made interchangeable with 'certain or almost certain' or with 'has a probability of 1', then all of these locutions become paradoxical. As to Ellis's second argument, the purpose of argument is *not* to "adjust our beliefs." The purpose of *advertising* is to adjust our beliefs. Adjustment of belief is a psychological function, not an epistemological one, as Ellis claims. The purpose of *argument* is to discover the *truth*, or to point out the truth to those who believe (we think) falsehood. If a person is intellectually honest and of sound mind, he will adjust his beliefs in light of the truth. But it is *he* who does the adjusting, not the argument. It can only point out the truth to him. Perhaps we can say that arguments help indirectly in the adjustment of belief, but it is misleading to say this and not also say how arguments do this differently than the way advertising does: by (trying to) reveal what is *true*.

Even if an "epistemological concept of truth" would serve perfectly well for the two purposes Ellis mentions, it would not follow that a metaphysical concept is useless. For there are purposes that a metaphysical concept can serve but that an epistemological concept cannot. A metaphysical concept can be used to evaluate competing theories of justification *and competing theories of probability logic*. No revised concept of truth along the lines suggested by Ellis can do this noncircularly.

There are other problems with Ellis's proposal. First, it would count every statement with a probability between 0 and 1 as neither true nor false, whereas in fact all such statements are either true or false. (Any argument showing that a statement lacks a truth value would serve equally well to show that it lacks a probability value, for if a statement is meaningless or simply not a piece of fact-stating discourse, then it would be as nonsensical to give it a probability value as to give it a truth value.)

Second, just as there is no such thing as justification *simpliciter*, so too there is no such thing as probability *simpliciter*. To be probable is to be probably *true*. On Ellis's revision, '*p* is probably true' would become the senseless '*p* is probably probable to a degree of 1' or '*p* is probably certain', and '*p* is probable to a degree of .7' would become '*p* is probably probable to a degree of .7' or possibly even the unintelligible '*p* is probable to a degree of 1 to a degree of .7' In answer to this Ellis says that from the fact that 'He is happy' just means 'He is a happy soul' it does not follow that the concept of happiness presupposes the concept of soul (1969, 71–72). But the first of these is interchangeable with the second either because 'soul' here is a harmless redundancy, synonymous with 'person,' 'guy,' or 'bloke', or because 'soul' is being used here as a synonym for 'sentient being', but then Ellis's argument by analogy is ruined because the concept of happiness *does* presuppose the concept of sentience.

In section 3.6, I noted that skeptical worries are the most common motivation for Nonrealist theories of truth. The same point applies to the truth-as-justification thesis (in either its descriptive or revisionary guises) and to thesis 2, the thesis that the only truth there is, is truth relative to a conceptual scheme or, as it is sometimes put, truth within a system. All three of the views in question are attempts to redefine truth so as to make it something attainable and thereby create an illusion that skepticism is refuted.

But what, it will be asked, ought we to do if it turns out that we cannot refute skepticism without pulling some such trickery? What if it turns out, that is, that our beliefs cannot be objectively justified as (at least probably) nonrelativistically true? Some would answer by saying that if skepticism cannot be refuted, then we are entitled to ignore it, or we are entitled to dismiss it with flimsy gestures toward common sense, or we are entitled to redefine truth in such a way that the *appearance* of a refutation of skepticism can be quickly assembled. There is an alternative attitude, though it is rarely expressed: if skepticism is irrefutable, then perhaps that is a point in its favor. The consequences of skepticism may yet turn out to be less traumatic than we fear. It is true that on a traditional sense of epistemic rationality, according to which a necessary condition for epistemic rationality is the possession of beliefs objectively justified as probably true, we could no longer claim to be epistemically rational. But perhaps there are other important senses of rationality on which we can still claim to be rational. Richard Foley (1987) has argued, in effect, that there is an important sense of epistemic rationality that requires subjective rather than objective justification. Alternatively, we might explore senses of rational belief according to which being justified as probably *true* is not a necessary condition for being a rational belief. Rather, a belief counts as rational if it has some *other* value, such as explanatory and/or predictive power. This is just thesis 4. (This suggestion also, in effect, gives a nontraditional answer to the question 'Justified as *what*?' See section 2.2.)

Now some would claim that a belief's possession of explanatory/predictive power just is objective evidence that it is *true*. But that claim is not compulsory; one can endorse the alternative sense of rationality being alluded to here without making that additional claim (and thereby collapsing the alternative sense of rationality into the traditional sense). Moreover, the claim is irrelevant in this context: we are considering how to respond if the skeptic should prove irrefutable. This means, among other things, that we are considering what to do if we have been unable to show in a non-question-begging way that explanatory/predictive power really does constitute objective evidence of truth. Similarly, some instrumentalists about truth would claim that it is a necessary truth that a belief with explanatory/predictive power is true. But again, instrumentalism is itself a way of responding to skepticism, and at issue here are *other* ways of responding to skepticism, ways that allow us to keep a Realist theory of truth and not indulge in any pretense of having refuted skepticism. Specifically, the suggestion under discussion is that we embrace the spirit of instrumentalism while disdaining the sleight of hand, with respect to skepticism, involved in equating truth with instrumental values.

But as I envisage it, the strategy of the nontraditional conception of rationality requires that we admit to the skeptic that we have lost something. We do not pretend that all we really wanted in the first place was subjective justification or beliefs justified as having explanatory power. We do not deny that having beliefs objectively justified as depicting (or at least corresponding to) a mind-independent world is one of the things Western civilization has been aiming at. (And once again, the context is one in which we are assuming that there is no non-question-begging way of showing that beliefs with explanatory/predictive power are even so much as isomorphic to such a world.) We mourn the loss of our friend the extramental facts of the matter. We do not prop up a mannequin in his favorite chair and pretend he is still with us. Moreover, paeans to the nobility of the *objective* search for *truth*, found chiefly in the commencement addresses of university presidents, would have to be treated hereafter as mere metaphors. My suggestion is very much in the spirit of Rorty's vision of what he calls a "post-philosophical culture" (1982, introduction). He certainly believes that skepticism is irrefutable (1982, xix–xx, xxxix) and that we should see rationality as aiming at the acquisition of beliefs that have the instrumental quality of helping us "cope with reality," instead of beliefs that depict a mind-independent world (1982, xvii, xliii). One of the ways in which I disagree with Rorty is that he seems to think that his program requires that we reject Realist theories of truth, and this leads him to embrace thesis 6 (1982 xiii, xxv). But this is unnecessary: if in the end we are going to abandon *both* truth and correspondence with extramental reality as values that we want our beliefs to have, then it matters not a whit whether we see them as different values or the same one.

All of this is just a *proposal* for how we might respond to skepticism in an intellectually honest way. But it is only a proposal. So far as this work goes, I am simply offering this as something to think about, I have not *argued* for skepticism or for my proposed way of responding to it.

Finally, nothing I have said here entails that there is no such thing as justification within a system or justification relative to a conceptual scheme. And I suppose that one could invent the concepts of true within a system or true within a conceptual scheme to name the maximal degree of justification within a system and justification within a conceptual scheme. But there is no point to doing so, and it is dangerously misleading to do so. The concept in question can just as well be named 'maximally justified within a system'. If we call it 'true within a system', we are nearly bound to forget sooner or later that truth within a system and truth are two different things. Thereafter we shall quickly fall into the delusion that if we can establish our beliefs as true within a system, then we have successfully refuted skepticism.

8.8   Chapter Summary

This chapter began with an extended look at Davidson's attempt to put an answer to the metaphysical project to use in a new way. A Tarski-like theory of truth for a language is, he claims, nothing less than a theory of meaning, or better, a theory of linguistic competence. It turned out, however, that it is misleading for Davidson to call such theories "theories of *truth*" since he does not believe such a theory analyzes truth. Rather, such a theory takes for granted an undefinable concept of truth. We looked briefly at a selection of objections to Davidson's program, and then examined rather more extensively Michael Dummett's critique of both the Davidson Program and the whole idea of cashing meaning in terms of truth conditions. Dummett's critique is of special interest because, while he agrees with Davidson on most issues, he argues, in the terminology of this book, that Davidson has identified the wrong project as the key component in a theory of linguistic understanding: it is the justification project, not the metaphysical project that should be put to use in such a theory. No definitive conclusion on the viability of the latter idea was reached. However, I suggested that if we define the concept of logical consequence in the classical way, there is some linguistic behavior actually displayed by human beings that can only be explained by postulating knowledge of truth conditions. Finally, I returned to the thesis of truth as justification again and to discussion of some of the other theses with which it is often confused. I suggested that the skeptical worries that incline some philosophers to the truth-as-justification thesis can be more respectably dealt with by reexamining what it means to be rational, rather than by embracing unintelligible analyses of truth and/or sleight-of-hand "rebuttals" of skepticism.

In the next chapter, I take up a problem that is potentially devastating to almost any quasi-realist answer to the metaphysical project: the Liar Paradox.

9 The Liar Paradox

9.1 Damnable Lies

The Paradox of the Liar, in its legendary form, stars one Epimenides of Crete, who is said to have proclaimed that all Cretans are liars. But since Epimenides himself is a Cretan, if what he says is true, then he himself is a liar, so what he says is a lie. Thus, if what he says is true, then what he says is false. But if what he says is false, then he, like any other Cretan, is not a liar. So what he says is true. Thus, if what he says is false, then what he says is true.

Actually, in its legendary form there is really no paradox here. To call someone a liar is not to say that *everything* he says is a lie. So while it is true that Epimenides is calling himself a liar, it does not follow that his declaration is itself a lie. It could well be nonparadoxically true. Unfortunately, tighter versions of the paradox have been developed that are not so easily solved. The classic modern version of the paradox centers around the following sentence (hereafter called the liar sentence):

This sentence is false.

If the liar sentence is true, then it is false, because what it says is that it is false. So if it is true, then it is false (and thus true and false). But if it is false, then it must be true, since it *is* just what it *says* it is. So if it is false, then it is true (and thus true and false). Now it has to be either true or false, and either way it is both. But it is a contradiction to say of anything that it is both true and false, so this derivation leads to a contradiction. (Note that the derivation cannot stop after the second sentence. All that has been proven to that point is that one cannot consistently assume that the liar sentence is true. But for all we know at that point, one could consistently suppose it to be false.)

One's first inclination is to dismiss the liar sentence as a piece of nonsense, in the literal sense of 'nonsense'. But if there is anything objectionable about the sentence, it is far from obvious what it is, for the sentence is grammatically correct, it is neither vague nor ambiguous, and it commits no category mistake: sentences are among the things that can bear truth values. It is self-referring, but there is nothing inherently nonsensical about that. 'This sentence has five words' is self-referring, but not nonsensical. Moreover, there are versions of the paradox that contain no self-reference:

The next sentence is false.
The previous sentence is true.

So the liar sentence, for all its oddness, seems unobjectionable. One could, of course, try to show that the liar sentence *is* objectionable, but one would have to *show* it, and that has proved to be a devilishly tricky thing to do.

Let us look again at the derivation of the contradiction. When a valid argument ends in a contradiction, one of three things is the case. Either one or more of the premises is a contradiction, or the premises are mutually inconsistent, or both. Set out in more detail, the derivation (hereafter called 'the liar derivation') is as follows:

1. The liar sentence says of itself that it is false and says nothing more.
2. If a sentence s is true and it says that p is the case and says nothing more, then p is the case.
3. If p is the case and a sentence s says that p is the case and says nothing more, then s is true.
4. Every sentence is true or false. (Principle of bivalence.)
5. The liar sentence is true. (Conditional premise.)
6. Ergo, the liar sentence is false. (By 1, 2, 5.)
7. Ergo, the liar sentence is true and false. (By 5, 6.)
8. Ergo, if the liar sentence is true, then it is true and false. (By conditional proof.)
9. The liar sentence is false. (Conditional premise.)
10. Ergo, the liar sentence is true. (By 1, 3, 9.)
11. Ergo, the liar sentence is true and false. (By 9, 10.)
12. Ergo, if the liar sentence is false, then it is true and false. (By conditional proof.)
13. Ergo, the liar sentence is true and false. (By 4, 8, 12.)

Now the first premise seems undeniable. So the problem would appear to be with premises (2), (3), or (4). One or more of them is self-contradictory, or they are mutually inconsistent, or one or more of them is inconsistent with the seemingly undeniable (1). So at least one of (2), (3), or (4) is false.

Therein lies the importance of the paradox. For (2) and (3) are theorems of all quasi-realist theories of truth, a class that would include all Realist theories of truth and most Nonrealist theories. And (4) is a theorem of any theory that entails bivalence, which would include virtually all quasi-realist theories, the exceptions being those that allow such things as vague states of affairs (see section 6.1). (And even the latter theories would not escape the paradox unless one maintains that the liar sentence expresses just such a vague state of affairs.)

So the liar sentence is a counterexample to all theories that have (2), (3), and (4) as theorems. To disarm the counterexample, we must either find a reason to reject the first premise after all or abandon theories that entail (2), (3), and (4) or find some inferential step in the liar derivation that is invalid. (There is a fourth, very exotic way out of the paradox, which I shall discuss in section 9.7.)

There are five criteria of adequacy commonly imposed on solutions to the paradox:

Specificity. A solution must actually show that the liar derivation is unsound or fallacious by pointing out which seemingly acceptable premise or inferential step is really unacceptable.

No ad hoc postulations. A solution must provide independent reasons for rejecting the premise or step, independent, that is, from the fact that such a rejection will solve the paradox. In other words, we ought not reject some premise *simply* on the grounds that if we do not, paradox results. (There is the old vaudeville joke about the man who goes to the doctor and, raising his arm above his head, says, 'Doctor, it hurts whenever I do this.' To this the doctor replies, 'Then don't do that.' The ban against ad hoc postulations is meant to rule out solutions to the paradox that treat it as this doctor treats his patient's ailments.)

Avoid overkill. A solution must be minimal in the sense that it must not require us to abandon perfectly reasonable inferential patterns or types of sentences that are quite unobjectionable.

Completeness. A solution ought to apply to all versions of the paradox. It is of little use if it dissolves one version and leaves the others unscathed.

Conserve intuitions. A solution ought to be compatible with our semantic intuitions about the meaning of 'true' and our intuitions about the validity or invalidity of arguments.

A simple ban on self-referring sentences would violate the completeness criterion because, as noted above, there are some versions of the paradox that involve no self-reference. It would also violate the criterion of avoiding overkill because, again as noted, many self-referring statements are not paradoxical. Similarly, a *simple* rejection of the principle of bivalence with respect to the liar sentence alone violates the criterion of no ad hoc postulations. We ought to be given an independent reason for thinking that the liar sentence is different from other declarative sentences.

These criteria seem plausible on the face of them, but I have doubts about three of them. The completeness criterion ought to admit of degrees. A solution that does not handle all versions of the paradox is not *perfectly* adequate to be sure. But what if it dissolves all but one version? Surely it ought not be dismissed as utterly useless. Some progress has been made. Also, the criterion seems to presuppose that in the end all versions of the paradox share some common essence, and hence there must be just one solution to all them. This seems to be a reckless assumption. If two solutions *between them* dissolve every version of the paradox and they are logically compatible with each other, then it seems we should not dismiss them both as inadequate.[1]

The ban against ad hoc postulations seems overly demanding as well, at least if one interprets it, as Susan Haack does (1978, 138-139), in an absolute way. Of course, one ought to be suspicious of ad hoc solutions: a solution ought not to say merely, as the doctor does, 'Don't do that.'[2] But we ought not presuppose that it will be possible to resolve the paradox without *some* ad hoc element. Quine, for example, asserts that for some paradoxes (including the liar) there is simply *nothing* wrong with the derivation that leads to the contradiction. Such paradoxes Quine calls "antinomies," and he notes that since, by all traditional standards of reasoning, there is nothing wrong with the derivation, we have no choice but to postulate ad hoc and counterintuitive revisions of the traditional standards of reasoning. Hence the principle of conserving intuitions is also unsatisfiable when interpreted absolutely (Quine 1962, 4-9). By way of making such ad hoc revisions more plausible, he offers the following historical argument.

Each resort is desperate; each is an artificial departure from natural and established usage. Such is the way of antinomies.

... An antinomy, however, packs a surprise that can be accommodated by nothing less than a repudiation of part of our conceptual heritage.

Revision of a conceptual scheme is not unprecedented. It happens in a small way with each advance in science, and it happens in a big way with the big advances, such as the Copernican revolution. ... We can hope in time even to get used to the biggest such changes and to find the new schemes natural. There was a time when the doctrine that the earth revolves around the sun was called the Copernican paradox, even by men who accepted it.

Conversely, the falsidical paradoxes of Zeno must have been, in his day, genuine antinomies. We in our latter-day smugness point to a fallacy: the notion that an infinite succession of intervals must add up to an infinite interval. But surely this was part and parcel of the conceptual scheme of Zeno's day. (Quine 1962, 4–9)

But if Haack has gone too far in one direction, I think that Quine goes too far in the other. If we take the preceding remarks literally, he is saying that any solution, however ad hoc, is acceptable. If the solution seems counterintuitive, this is only because it represents a radical revision of our conceptual scheme, which takes some getting used to. Therein lies the problem. We can get used to anything, given enough time, so Quine leaves no room for any further adjudication between proposed revisions. They are all equally good in that they can all eventually be gotten used to. Yet some revisions are more elegant and less ad hoc than others, and some are just plain wrong. Copernicus might have postulated that the sun is just an illusion. We would have gotten used to this too in time. A middling course between Haack and Quine is the best steer: the no ad hoc postulations and the conserve intuitions criteria should be interpreted as matters of degree. All things being equal, a solution is better to the extent that it minimizes ad hoc elements and minimizes damage to our existing intuitions.[3]

An examination of all of the different solutions that have been proposed to the Liar Paradox is not possible in the space available, but there is room to introduce a few of the best known.

9.2   Russell's Theory of Types

Russell believed that all of the semantic and set-theoretic paradoxes rest on a violation of what he calls the vicious-circle principle (VCP): "Whatever involves *all* of a collection must not be one of the collection" (Russell 1908b, 63). The word 'involves' here is highly ambiguous, but it has to be if the principle is to cover all the different semantic and set-theoretic paradoxes, and it is important to Russell that the principle be seen as encompassing the essence of the problem in all the paradoxes, for as we shall see, the ad hoc quality of his solution to the Liar Paradox is partly mitigated by his claim that the very same solution resolves all of the semantic and set-theoretic paradoxes. An example of a violation of the VCP would be a proposition about all propositions (including itself). Propositions that violate the VCP are meaningless, according to Russell.

The Liar Paradox, like all paradoxes, can be seen as a violation of the VCP. 'I am lying' is equivalent to 'There is a proposition that I am affirming and that is false', and this in turn is equivalent to 'It is not true of all propositions that either I am not affirming them or they are true.' It is clear in this last formulation that the liar proposition is talking about all propositions but is itself a proposition. So the liar proposition is a member of the very collection that it "involves." Hence it violates the VCP and is meaningless (Russell 1908b, 61).

So far Russell's solution appears to consist in an ad hoc declaration that anything that violates the VCP is meaningless. He pushes back the ad hoc element to a deeper level by postulating a theory of types (see below), which *entails* that such propositions are meaningless. But it must be remembered that the theory itself is ad hoc. Russell has no reason to create this theory save that by doing so he can resolve the paradoxes. He says as much himself: "The division of objects into types is necessitated by the reflexive fallacies which otherwise arise" (1908b, 61).

But note that in one sense this postulation is not ad hoc; he does have an independent reason for it. The theory of types will not only help solve the Liar Paradox; it helps solve all of the semantic and set-theoretic para-doxes, or so Russell claims. Suppose Russell is right about this. He could then claim with *some* justification that his solution is not at all ad hoc. That is, he could say, 'My solution to paradox *A* is not ad hoc because I have an independent reason for postulating what I do, namely, the same postulations help solve paradox *B*. And my solution to paradox *B* is not ad hoc because these very same postulations help solve *A*.' In other words, the principle is that any *one* solution of two or more paradoxes is not ad hoc. This seems a bit extreme, but there is some truth in it. A solution tends to lose its ad hoc quality the wider the variety of paradoxes it resolves.

"A type is defined as the range of significance of a propositional function (open sentence), i.e. as the collection of arguments for which the said function has values" (Russell 1908b, 75). So we can think of a type as a collection of things, to put it very broadly. But the things within each type have something in common. That *something* determines to which type each belongs. For example, one type of thing is the collection of individuals. An individual is the sort of thing named by the subject term of an elementary proposition having no variables. The types form a hierarchy, with individuals being the lowest type. The next highest type, the second type, is the collection of all first-order propositions. (The numbers get confusing here. The rule is that the *type* of a proposition is always one greater than the *order* of the proposition.) First-order propositions include elementary propositions and also propositions that have variables ranging over individuals. In other words, the domain of the variable in a given proposition is always the collection of things that form the next *lower* type. An example of a first-order proposition would be 'All x are blue or not blue', where x ranges over individuals. The third type is the collection of all second-order propositions. The variables in second-order propositions range over the next lower type. That is, they range over first-order propositions (Russell 1908b, 75–76). The hierarchy of types continues upward infinitely.

So what 'I am lying' really says is 'There is a proposition of order n which I affirm and that is false'. This is equivalent to 'There is some x such that x is a proposition of order n that I affirm and that is false'. The variable x ranges over propositions of order n, so given the theory of types, *this* proposition must itself be of order $n + 1$. But the speaker is *claiming* to be affirming a proposition of order n, so what he says is false. Not both true and false, but merely false.[4] Similarly, 'This proposition is false' is, on a Russellian analysis, equivalent to 'This is a proposition of order n that is false'. But the proposition is itself of order $n + 1$, not n, so it is false. To put Russell's point in terms of the liar derivation, he is denying premise (1): the liar sentence says more than just that it is false; it also misidentifies its own order.

There is a tension between Russell's claim here that the liar sentence (for him, the liar *proposition*) is plain false and his earlier desire to call it meaningless. What Russell means is that any proposition about a proposition (whether itself or some other) must attempt to specify (accurately or not) the order of the proposition it is talking about. If the liar sentence does this, it is meaningful but false. If it does not attempt to specify, it is meaningless.

Various criticisms have been made of Russell's theory of types (see Copi 1978, 229–238), but the only ones I shall consider apply also to Alfred Tarski's response to the liar, so I shall postpone discussion of them.

9.3   The Object-Language/Metalanguage Distinction

Tarski diagnoses the paradox as a problem resulting from the fact that
natural languages are what he calls "semantically closed." A semantically
closed language is one with semantic predicates, like 'true', 'false', and
'satisfies', that can be applied to the language's own sentences. All other
languages are semantically open. No sentence of a semantically open
language can predicate a semantic property of any sentence in the
language. So, of course, no sentence of a semantically open language can
predicate a semantic property of itself. Thus the liar sentence cannot be
expressed in a semantically open language, and there is hence no Liar
Paradox for such languages. So Tarski's solution, in a nutshell, is to ignore
semantically closed languages. These, he says, are hopelessly inconsistent,
and we do not need them for any scientific or mathematical purpose. We
simply create artificial languages none of which contains semantic predicates applicable to its own words and sentences (Tarski 1944, 19–20).

   But whatever happened to the program of establishing the foundations
for a science of semantics? Tarski's plan was to define satisfaction in
nonsemantic terms, truth in terms of satisfaction, and all other semantic
concepts in terms of truth. But how are we going to do all this if our
artificial languages do not have any semantic predicates like 'true' and
'satisfies'? The answer is that we define truth for a particular language by
means of *another* language. This second language will contain predicates
that refer to the semantic properties of the first language. But the second
language, like the first, will be semantically open. It will not have
predicates that name its *own* semantic properties. So the Liar Paradox
cannot arise in the second language either:

Since we have agreed not to employ semantically closed languages, we have to use
two different languages in discussing the problem of truth. ... The first ... is the
language which is "talked about." ... The definition of truth which we are seeking
applies to the sentences of this language. The second is the language in which we
"talk about" the first language, and in terms of which we wish ... to construct the
definition of truth for the first language. We shall refer to the first language as "*the
object-language*" and to the second as "*the meta-language*." (Tarski 1944, 21–22)

So the metalanguage will have predicates like 'true' and 'false' and
'satisfies', but these are just abbreviations for 'true-in-the-object-language', 'false-in-the-object-language', and 'satisfies-in-the-object-lan-

guage'. So while these are words of the metalanguage, they do not refer to semantic properties of the metalanguage.

So Tarski's definitions of satisfaction and truth, given in section 5.4, are not expressed in the language for which these terms are being defined. Even the T-sentences are sentences of the metalanguage, although they are *about* sentences of the object language. For example,

'Snow is white' is true ≡ snow is white

is *entirely* an expression of the metalanguage. The string of symbols

'Snow is white'

(including the quotation marks) is a metalanguage name for an object-language sentence. 'Is true' is an abbreviation for 'is-true-in-the-object-language'. The 'snow is white' (not including the quotation marks) on the right-hand side is a metalanguage clause that *translates* the object-language sentence named by the string 'Snow is white' on the left-hand side. Calling it a translation may seem funny, since it looks like exactly the same sentence, but it is technically a translation. It just so happens that in this case the metalanguage has nearly the same vocabulary as the object language. In particular, they both use the same words to name snow and whiteness and to express the third-person singular of the verb 'to be'. So they both use exactly the same expression to say that snow is white. But the vocabularies are not exactly the same: the object language has no semantic expressions at all, while the metalanguage has names for the semantic properties of the object language, but it has no names for its own semantic features. (This is what makes them both slightly different from English.)

It is not necessary that the metalanguage and object language share the same nonsemantic vocabulary. The metalanguage could be French or, rather, a French-like language that contained no words for its own semantic properties:

≪ Snow is white ≫ est vrai ≡ la neige est blanche

Or we could use an English-like metalanguage to define truth for a French-like object language:

'La neige est blanche' is true ≡ snow is white.

How would one define truth for sentences of the metalanguage, that is, how would one define 'true-in-the-metalanguage'? By means of a meta-metalanguage. 'True-in-the-metalanguage' is an expression of the meta-metalanguage.

To see how the distinction between object language and metalanguage solves the Liar Paradox, recall that 'is false' is a metalanguage abbreviation for 'is false-in-the-object-language'. So

This sentence is false

is an abbreviation for

This sentence is false-in-the-object-language.

But this last sentence is a metalanguage expression. It must be, because it contains a predicate naming a semantic property and the object language has no such predicates. So this is a metalanguage expression declaring itself to be false in the object language. But metalanguage sentences are not false or true in the object language, because they are not in the object language at all. So the liar sentence does not have the property it claims for itself. Thus, it is plain false. More precisely, it is plain false-in-the-metalanguage, it is not both true and false (in any language). Nor does the fact that it is false-in-the-metalanguage entail that it is true-in-the-metalanguage, so no contradiction can be derived. Hence Tarski, like Russell, is rejecting the first premise of the liar derivation: the liar sentence does not merely predicate falsehood of itself; it predicates falsehood-in-the-object language of itself.

It should not be surprising that Tarski and Russell should be seen as attacking the same point in the liar derivation, since their solutions are so much alike. Both are what might be called language-level solutions. Russell postulates a hierarchy of orders of propositions, none of which can talk about propositions of its own or a higher level. Tarski postulates a hierarchy of languages, none of which can talk about the semantic features of its own or a higher level of language.

It might be wondered why Tarski does not believe that the paradox can be solved for natural languages. Why can we not simply regard a natural language like English to be really *two* languages, one of which, meta-English contains names of the semantic properties of the other, object English? The reasons why this move is not viable become clear in the next section.

9.4   Criticisms of the Language-Levels Approach

Tarski's solution violates the criterion of no ad hoc postulations (interpreted absolutely) because Tarski has no independent reason for postulating the distinction between object language and metalanguage other than
to solve the Liar Paradox. But Tarski has managed to postpone the
entrance of the ad hoc element a bit (Fox 1989, 177). He has not simply
declared that no sentence can predicate a semantic property of itself. The
dissolution of the paradox comes as an implication of a theoretical
construct, just as it does for Russell.

A stronger criticism of both Tarski's and Russell's language-level
approach has been made by Saul Kripke. Tarski's defeatism with regard to
natural languages is not very satisfying, and Russell thought his own
language-levels approach could solve the paradox for natural languages.
Kripke argues otherwise: We cannot assume that a speaker implicitly
indexes his truth-value predicates (or propositions) to the appropriate
level of metalanguage (or, in Russell's terminology, to the appropriate
type). This is because in many cases the speaker does not know at what
level he is speaking. Suppose that Jones says, 'All Nixon's utterances
about Watergate are false.' Now if none of Nixon's utterances about
Watergate ascribe truth or falsity to any sentences, then the speaker's
remark is at the metalevel. But the speaker cannot be sure that Nixon's
utterances do not include 'Dean is a liar'. If they do, Jones's sentence is at
the meta-metalevel. And if Dean himself said, 'Haldeman speaks the
truth', then Jones's utterance is at the meta-meta-metalevel (Kripke 1975,
58–60).

But the problem goes deeper than this. Sometimes it is *logically*
impossible to assign levels to all the relevant sentences. Suppose again that
Jones says, 'All Nixon's utterances about Watergate are false', but
suppose that one of Nixon's utterances about Watergate is 'Everything
Jones says about me is false'. Now Jones's and Nixon's remarks are meta
to each other, which destroys the possibility of the object-language/
metalanguage distinction as a solution to the paradox (Kripke, 1975,
58–60). Treating the object language and metalanguage as meta to each
other simply produces a new version of the paradox:

(1) The next sentence is false-in-the-object-language.

(2) The preceding sentence is true-in-the-metalanguage.

The first of these is a metalanguage sentence, the second an object language sentence. So if (1) is true-in-ML, then (2) is false-in-OL, since that is what (1) says about it. But if (2) is false-in-OL, then (1) must be false-in-ML. So if (1) is true-in-ML, then it is false-in-ML and thus both true-in-ML and false-in-ML. On the other hand, if (1) is false-in-ML, then (2) is true-in-OL, but if (2) is true-in-OL, then (1) is true-in-ML. So if (1) is false-in-ML, then it is true-in-ML, and thus both true-in-ML and false-in-ML.

9.5   Saul Kripke's Theory of Truth-Value Gaps

In this section (and section 9.8) I assume more knowledge on the part of the reader than I do in the rest of the book. The Kripke solution to the Liar Paradox is simply too advanced to be summarized accurately and fairly without making use of advanced logical and set-theoretic terminology. On the other hand, it seems unreasonable to deprive those who do have the requisite background knowledge of a discussion of Kripke's theory. Those without this knowledge are urged to read this section anyway. Much of it *is* understandable to persons whose logical background is more limited, and later sections contain some retrospective references to these simpler passages.

In one of the most valuable insights in to the Liar Paradox, Kripke points out that the paradox is not just a piece of philosophical exotica. It can arise in real life situations. Indeed, almost any ascription of truth or falsity can turn out to be paradoxical. It depends on what the empirical facts of the situation are. Suppose Smith and Jones are opposing candidates in an election and the *only* thing Smith says about Jones is

(3) A majority of what Jones says about me is false.

Now suppose that Jones says *only* the following three things about Smith:

(4) Smith is a big spender.

(5) Smith is soft on crime.

(6) Everything Smith says about me is true.

If the empirical facts are that (4) is true and (5) is false, then both (3) and (6) are paradoxical. Each is true if and only if it is false. This shows that there need be nothing *intrinsic* to a paradoxical sentence that makes it paradoxical. It depends on contingent, empirical facts (Kripke, 54–55).

What we need is a solution to the paradox that, unlike the language-levels approach, can dissolve the paradox for natural languages as well as artificial ones and that is sensitive to the empirical facts that can produce paradox. So we must have (1) *one* truth predicate, not levels of them, and (2) a justifiable reason for saying that certain sentences in certain circumstances have no truth value but those very same sentences in certain other circumstances do have a truth value. Specifically, we want a *nonarbitrary* way of saying that 'A majority of what Jones says about me is false' has no truth value in just those circumstances in which paradox would arise if it had a truth value; and that it does have a truth value in just those circumstances in which no paradox would arise. To put it another way, we need a theory of truth in which the very contingent facts that would otherwise make a sentence paradoxical will show, in conjunction with the theory, that in fact the sentence has no truth value (Kripke 1975, 62).

Since this theory is going to say that some sentences in some circumstances do not have a truth value, it must, of course, deny bivalence. Metaphorically, it says that there is a gap between the extension and antiextension of 'true'. But it must do more than that. It must tell us what sentences in what circumstances are neither true nor false. In favor of theories that deny bivalence, Kripke notes that even some nonparadoxical sentences, like 'This sentence is *true*' have obscure truth conditions (Kripke 1975, 57). One can consistently assume that it is true, but one can also consistently assume that it is false (though not, of course, at the same time). Thus it is already clear what the essence of Kripke's solution is. He is denying premise (4) of the liar derivation, the principle of bivalence.

The trick, as it were, is to build a language that contains its own truth predicate, that is, that can ascribe truth (or falsity) to its own sentences. If we build in the right way, paradoxical sentences will turn out not to have any truth value in the completed language. They will fall into the gap between truth and falsity. Moreover, the construction process will be such that, for any natural language, we can imagine it having been built in the same way.[5] Hence, paradoxical sentences will not have a truth value in any natural language.

I begin with a very simple interpreted language, LI_0, whose domain of discourse contains only fifteen items. The first two are nonlinguistic items, snow and grass. The other thirteen are sentences of LI_0 itself, which I number for later reference:[6]

D = {snow, grass,

'Snow is white',	(7)
'Grass is green',	(8)
'Snow is green',	(9)
'"Snow is white" is printed in the N.Y. *Daily News*',	(10)
'"Snow is white" is true',	(11)
'"Snow is white" is false',	(12)
'"Snow is green" is true',	(13)
'"Snow is green" is false',	(14)
'"Snow is white" is printed in the N.Y. *Daily News* and is true',	(15)
'Something printed in the N.Y. *Daily News* is true',	(16)
'"Something printed in the N.Y. *Daily News* is true" is true',	(17)
'This sentence is false',	(18)
'This sentence is true'}	(19)

The interpretation of LI_0, call it I_0, assigns sets of objects from the domain to each predicate of the language. Each such set is called the extension of the predicate. It also assigns objects from the domain to the antiextension of each predicate.[7] For convenience, I mention only two of the antiextensions, 'not green' and 'false'.

I_0(is white) = {snow}

I_0(is green) = {grass}

I_0(is not green) = {snow}

I_0(is printed in the N.Y. *Daily News*) = {'Snow is white'}

I_0(is true) = the empty set

I_0(is false) = the empty set

None of the extensions or antiextensions has more than one member. This is just a function of the simplicity of LI_0 and the small size of its domain. The important characteristic of LI_0 is that *none* of its sentences is true or false. This is clearly not the language we want, but it is a foundation on which we can build a language in which paradoxical sentences have no truth value (Kripke 1975, 67).

The first step in building the sort of language we want is to construct a language LI_1 that is just like LI_0 except that its interpretation, I_1, assigns a little bit more to 'is true' and 'is false' than does I_0 (Kripke 1975, 67–69). Specifically, it will turn out that I_1(is true) is the union of two sets. The first is just I_0(is true), and the second is the set of all atomic sentences in the domain such that the object named by the subject of the sentence is a member of the set of things assigned to its predicate by I_0.

There are several rules that determine what I_1 does and does not assign to 'is true' and 'is false', but I need mention only four of them for the moment. First, I_1 assigns to 'is true' everything that I_0 assigns to it. Second, I_1 assigns to 'is false' everything that I_0 assigns to it. (As it happens, I_0 assigns nothing to either 'is true' or 'is false', so these first two rules seem pointless, but we shall see below why it is important to mention them.) Third, for every atomic sentence in the domain, if the object named by the subject of the sentence is a member of the set of things that I_0 (*not* I_1!) assigns to the predicate of the sentence, then I_1 assigns the sentence to 'is true'. So sentences (7), (8), and (10) are assigned to 'is true' by I_1. Fourth, for every atomic sentence in the domain, if the object named by the subject of the sentence is a member of the set of things that I_0 (*not* I_1!) assigns to the antiextension of the predicate of the sentence, then I_1 assigns the sentence to 'is false'. So I_1 assigns sentence (9) to 'is false'. Thus again, I_1(is true) is the union of two sets one of which is I_0(is true) and the other of which is the set of all atomic sentences in the domain such that the object named by the subject of the sentence is a member of the set of things assigned to its predicate by I_0. So that I can keep using this result to build higher interpretations, I make it formal and generalize it as follows:

$$I_{i+1}(T) = I_i(T) \cup \{a \in A : (a = \ulcorner Pc \urcorner) \text{ and } (c \text{ denotes } d) \text{ and } (d \in I_i(P))\}$$

$$I_{i+1}(F) = I_i(F) \cup \{a \in A : (a = \ulcorner Pc \urcorner) \text{ and } (c \text{ denotes } d) \text{ and } (d \in I_i(\neg P))\}$$

Here 'A' ranges over the set of atomic sentences in the domain, 'T' is 'is true', and 'F' is 'is false'.

Notice that if d is not in either $I_0(P)$ or $I_0(\neg P)$ then Pc is not in either I_1(is true) or I_1(is false). So there is a gap between truth and falsity on I_1. In other words, there are some atomic sentences in the domain that I_1 does not assign to either 'is true' or 'is false'. Sentences (11) and (18), for example. Although the object named by the subject of (11), (which is, of course, just sentence (7), is assigned to 'is true' by I_1, it is not so assigned by I_0, and what I_0 does with the subject of (11), is what matters in determining what I_1 does with (11) as a whole. Similarly, the subject of sentence (18), which is just (18) itself, is *not* assigned by I_0 to either its predicate ('false') or the antiextension of its predicate ('true'). Therefore, I_1 does not assign (18) as a whole to either 'true' or 'false'. The key insight in Kripke's resolution of the paradox is now becoming clear, at least insofar as it applies to atomic, self-referring sentences that predicate truth or falsity of themselves: if we continue building new interpretations from old ones according to the above two rules, then a given interpretation I_1 will assign a truth value to such a pathological sentence only if the preceding interpretation, I_{i-1}, already assigned the same sentence to the same truth value, and I_{i-1} will do so only if *its* predecessor, I_{i-2} did so, and so forth. But since the original interpretation, I_0, did not assign any sentences to either truth value, *a pathological sentence of this sort will not be assigned a truth value by any interpretation.*

A second point to note is that while we continue to build new languages from old ones, the hierarchy thereby produced is different from Tarski's in crucial ways. The truth predicate of each language in Tarski's hierarchy refers only to sentences of the lower languages in the hierarchy, and the hierarchy goes up infinitely. But as will become clear below, with Kripke's hierarchy we eventually reach a highest language in the sense that every sentence that will ever have a truth value has already received one at a lower level. Moreover, this highest language can predicate truth values of its own sentences (Kripke 1975, 69). The sole relevance of the hierarchy in Kripke's theory is that the highest language is defined in terms of the lower languages. But our real interest is only in the highest language (Kripke 1975, 70 n. 23).

Following our two previous definitions, LI_2 will be just like LI_1 except that it will add sentences (11) and (14) to the extension of 'is true' and (12) and (13) to the extension of 'is false'. To construct LI_3 and LI_4, we must make explicit two more clauses each in the definitions of $I_{i+1}(T)$ and $I_{i+1}(F)$ left unmentioned before simply because they would not have applied.

$$I_{i+1}(T) = I_i(T) \cup \{a \in A:(a = \ulcorner Pc \urcorner) \text{ and } (c \text{ denotes } d) \text{ and } (d \in I_i(P))\}$$

$$\cup \{\phi \in S:(\exists \alpha, \beta \in S)((\phi = \ulcorner \alpha \& \beta \urcorner)$$
$$\text{and } [(\alpha \in I_i(T) \text{ and } (\beta \in I_i(T))])\}$$

$$\cup \{\phi \in S:(\exists \alpha \in S)[(\phi = \ulcorner (\exists x)\alpha \urcorner) \text{ and } (\exists c)(\alpha c/x \in I_i(T))]\}$$

$$I_{i+1}(F) = I_i(F) \cup \{a \in A : (a = \ulcorner Pc \urcorner)$$
$$\text{and } (c \text{ denotes } d) \text{ and } (d \in I_i(\neg P))\}$$

$$\cup \{\phi \in S : (\exists \alpha, \beta \in S)((\phi = \ulcorner \alpha \ \& \ \beta \urcorner)$$
$$\text{and } [(\alpha \in I_i(F)) \text{ or } (\beta \in I_i(F))])\}$$

$$\cup \{\phi \in S : (\exists \alpha \in S)[(\phi = \ulcorner (\exists x)\alpha \urcorner) \text{ and } (\forall c)(\alpha c/x \in I_i(F))]\}$$

(Here 'S' ranges over the set of all sentences and open sentences in the domain, and '$\alpha c/x$' means 'the sentence just like α save with c replacing x wherever the latter appears in α'.) The first addition to the definition of $I_{i+1}(T)$ simply tells us that if both halves of a conjunction are assigned to truth by I_i, then the conjunction as a whole is assigned to truth by I_{i+1}. On the other hand, the first addition to the definition of $I_{i+1}(F)$ tells us that if even one conjunct is assigned to falsehood by I_i, then the conjunction as a whole is assigned to falsehood by I_{i+1}. Even a conjunction, however, can fall into the gap. If neither conjunct is in $I_i(F)$ and at least one conjunct is also not in $I_i(T)$, then the conjunction as a whole will not be in either $I_{i+1}(T)$ or $I_{i+1}(F)$.[8] This, however, is not the case with sentence (15). Since both its conjuncts are in $I_2(T)$, (15) as a whole is added to the extension of 'is true' by I_3. This in turn means that sentence (16) will be added to the extension of 'is true' by I_4, because the second new clause added to the definition of $I_{i+1}(T)$ simply tells us the conditions under which an existential claim will be assigned to 'is true' by I_{i+1}. Suppose the claim is '$(\exists x)\alpha$'. Then we are to imagine first dropping the '$(\exists x)$' from the beginning, which leaves us with only α. Next we look for a constant that, when substituted for the variable in α, would create a new sentence β such that β is in $I_i(T)$. If there is such a constant, then the original existential claim as a whole is a member of $I_{i+1}(T)$.[9] Sentence (16) is of the form 'There is an x such that x is printed in the N.Y. *Daily News* and x is true'. Now if we drop the quantifying phrase and replace x with '"Snow is white"', then the resulting sentence is just (15). Thus, since (15) is in $I_3(T)$, (16) is in $I_4(T)$. Note that by the last clause in the definition of $I_{i+1}(F)$ an existential claim will be false on I_{i+1} only if for *every* constant, substituting that constant for the variable (and dropping the quantifying phrase) would produce a sentence that is false on I_i. Thus there is a big gap into which an existential claim could fall. If there is no substitution that would produce a sentence true on I_i and there is at least one substitution that would produce a sentence that is also not in $I_i(F)$, then the existential claim as a whole will be neither true nor false on I_{i+1} (Kripke 1975, 64).

It should be easy to see that sentence (17) will be put into the extension of 'is true' by I_5. So

$I_5(T) = \{(7), (8), (10), (11), (14), (15), (16), (17)\}$

$I_5(F) = \{(9), (12), (13)\}$

The only sentences that do not have a truth value in LI_5 are (18) and (19). But notice that because these sentences are in neither $I_5(T)$ nor $I_5(F)$ and because they are themselves the very objects their subjects name, they will not be given a truth value in LI_6 either. Nor, by parallel reasoning, in LI_7, nor hence in LI_8, etc. Therefore, since every other sentence in the domain already has a truth value in LI_5, the extensions of 'is true' and 'is false' are not going to change any further. But the extensions of these two terms are the only things that ever change in the construction process. In every other respect each language is identical to its predecessor. So LI_6, LI_7, LI_8, etc. are all identical to LI_5. They are just different names for the same language. Hence L_5 is a "fixed point"; it is the highest language in the hierarchy (Kripke 1975, 66–67). So sentences (18) and (19) are *never* going to get a truth value (Kripke 1975, 71). Kripke next defines a true (false) sentence as one that is in the interpretation of 'is true' ('is false') on the fixed-point language. Therefore, (18) and (19) are neither true nor false. Hence premise (4) of the liar derivation is false. So the existence of the liar sentence, (18), in LI_5 does not entail a contradiction. The basic paradox is resolved.

Now what of the Smith and Jones case? First of all, we make our language rich enough for the problem to arise by adding Smith and the following sentences to the domain:

D' = D ∪ {Smith,

'Smith is a big spender'	(20)
'Smith is soft on crime'	(21)
'Everything Smith says about me (Jones) is true'	(22)
'A majority of what Jones says about me (Smith) is false'}	(23)

There are four more predicates and two more antiextensions that must be interpreted:

I_0(is a big spender) = ?

I_0(is soft on crime) = ?

I_0(is said by Jones about Smith) = {(20), (21), (22)}

I_0(is said by Smith about Jones) = {(23)}

I_0(is *not* a big spender) = ?

I_0(is *not* soft on crime) = ?

Which sentences get truth values will depend on how we replace the question marks.

Indeed, how we replace the question marks will determine whether or not we have a potentially paradoxical situation here in the first place. It will turn out that in every potentially paradoxical situation the sentences that would have been paradoxical had they received truth values will not get truth values on Kripke's theory. But those same sentences will get truth values in precisely the situations in which they would not be paradoxical. To see why this is so, note first that sentence (22) has a universal quantifier and (23) has a 'majority of' quantifier. To handle such sentences we must add two more clauses each to our definitions of $I_{i+1}(T)$ and $I_{i+1}(F)$. So each of these turns out to be a union of six sets. Let $M_P x$ be the majority quantifier. So '$(M_P x)\alpha$' means roughly 'For a majority of the objects d that are in the interpretation of predicate P, $\alpha c/x$ is true, where c denotes d'. Somewhat closer to English would be 'A majority of P are such that α'. Let $\#P$ be the total number of objects d in $I_i(P)$. Let '$\#P\alpha T$' mean 'the number of d in $I(P)$ such that $\alpha c/x \in I_i(T)$, where c denotes d'. Then the completed definition for $I_{i+1}(T)$ is as follows:

$$I_{i+1}(T) = I_i(T) \cup \{a \in A : (a = \ulcorner Pc \urcorner) \text{ and } (c \text{ denotes } d) \text{ and } (d \in I_i(P))\}$$

$$\cup \{\phi \in S : (\exists \alpha, \beta \in S)((\phi = \ulcorner \alpha \& \beta \urcorner)$$
$$\text{and } [(\alpha \in I_i(T) \text{ and } (\beta \in I_i(T))])\}$$

$$\cup \{\phi \in S : (\exists \alpha \in S)[(\phi = \ulcorner (\exists x)\alpha \urcorner) \text{ and } (\exists c)(\alpha c/x \in I_i(T))]\}$$

$$\cup \{\phi \in S : (\exists \alpha \in S)[(\phi = \ulcorner (\forall x)\alpha \urcorner) \text{ and } (\forall c)(\alpha c/x \in I_i(T))]\}$$

$$\cup \{\phi \in S : (\exists \alpha \in S)[(\phi = \ulcorner (M_P x)\alpha \urcorner) \text{ and } (\# P\alpha T > (\# P)/2)]\}$$

Let '$\# P\alpha F$' be defined in a way precisely parallel to the definition of

'$\#P\alpha T$' above. So the complete definition of $I_i + 1(F)$ is this:

$$I_{i+1}(F) = I_i(F) \cup \{a \in A : (a = \ulcorner Pc \urcorner) \text{ and } (c \text{ denotes } d)$$
$$\text{and } (d \in I_i(\neg P))\}$$

$$\cup \{\phi \in S : (\exists \alpha, \beta \in S)((\phi = \ulcorner \alpha \ \& \ \beta \urcorner)$$
$$\text{and } [(\alpha \in I_i(F)) \text{ or } (\beta \in I_i(F))])\}$$

$$\cup \{\phi \in S : (\exists \alpha \in S)[(\phi = \ulcorner (\exists x)\alpha \urcorner) \text{ and } (\forall c)(\alpha c/x \in I_i(F))]\}$$

$$\cup \{\phi \in S : (\exists \alpha \in S)[(\phi = \ulcorner (\forall x)\alpha \urcorner) \text{ and } (\exists c)(\alpha c/x \in I_i(F))]\}$$

$$\cup \{\phi \in S : (\exists \alpha \in S)[(\phi = \ulcorner (M_P x)\alpha \urcorner) \text{ and } (\#P\alpha F \geq (\#P)/2)]\}$$

The fourth line of the definition of $I_{i+1}(T)$ simply tells us that if some sentence of the domain is a universal generalization it will be counted as true by I_{i+1} if and only if the open sentence α following the quantifier is such that for *all c*, $\alpha c/x$ is counted true by I_i. And the corresponding clause of the definition of $I_{i+1}(F)$ tells us that I_{i+1} will count the universal generalization false if there is even one c such that $\alpha c/x$ is in $I_i(F)$. Here again room has been left for a gap between truth and falsity. If there is no c such that $\alpha c/x$ is in $I_i(F)$ but there is at least one c such that $\alpha c/x$ is also not in $I_i(T)$, then '$(\forall x)\alpha$' will be neither true nor false on I_{i+1} (Kripke 1975, 57 n. 7, 64).

The last line of the definition of $I_{i+1}(T)$ tells us that a 'majority of' sentence is true if and only if more than half the objects in $I_i(P)$ are such that for the c's that denote these objects $\alpha c/x$ is in $I_i(T)$. The last line of the definition of $I_{i+1}(F)$ tells us that a 'majority of' sentence is false if and only if at least half the objects in $I_i(P)$ are such that for the c's that denote these objects $\alpha c/x$ is in $I_i(F)$. Here too there is a gap. If, for no more than half the objects in $I_i(P)$, $\alpha c/x$ is counted true by I_i and, for fewer than half the objects in $I_i(P)$, $\alpha c/x$ is counted false by I_i, then the 'majority of' sentence will be neither true nor false on I_{i+1}.[10]

Now suppose that Smith is a big spender and soft on crime. Then Smith will be in I_0(is a big spender) and I_0(is soft on crime). So both (20) and (21) are in $I_i(T)$, (23) is in $I_2(F)$, and (22) is in $I_3(F)$. In these circumstances both (22) and (23) get truth values, but they get only one truth value each, so they are not paradoxical. They are potentially paradoxical if Smith is in I_0(is a big spender) and also in I_0(is *not* soft on crime). But in these circumstances, (20) is in $I_1(T)$, and (21) is in $I_1(F)$. So fewer than half the objects in I_1 (is said by Jones about Smith) are in $I_i(T)$, and fewer than half are in $I_1(F)$. Therefore, (23) falls into the gap, and thus so does (22). In these circumstances, neither of them will get a truth value in the fixed point (Kripke 1975, 72).

Extending Kripke's theory to natural languages involves a couple of small wrinkles. For every sentence s in a natural language, there is an infinite sequence of additional sentences each of which predicates truth of the preceding sentence. So if s is in the language, so too are

's' is true,

'"s" is true' is true,

'"'s' is true" is true' is true,

etc.

Each of these can be put into the extension of 'is true' or 'is false' only after its predecessor has been put into one of these extensions at an earlier level of interpretation. It might appear, then, that there is no fixed point for a natural language, because there will always be sentences that have not yet been put in the extension of either 'is true' or 'is false'. But as Kripke points out, for every natural language, there will be a *transfinite n* such that I_n is a fixed point for that language (Kripke 1975, 68–69). As they presently stand, the definitions of $I_{i+1}(T)$ and $I_{i+1}(F)$ do not have clauses for all the different logical operators in natural languages. The definitions will have to be expanded to take account of 'or', 'if … then', etc. Also the clauses for atomic sentences, as they presently stand, pretend that all predicates are one-place predicates. This, of course, will also have to be changed before the theory can apply to natural languages. Kripke says, correctly, that all these reformations can be won with standard model-theoretic techniques (Kripke 1975, 64). He also claims, but does not show, that one can easily adjust the definition to take account of all of the different kinds of quantifiers in natural language (e.g., 'a few', 'several', 'many') (Kripke 1975, 71). Finally, he suggests that the theory can be adjusted to handle modal operators (Kripke 1975, 78).

Kripke's solution is no more and no less ad hoc than is Russell's or Tarski's. He has no independent reasons, other than to solve the paradox, for placing the restrictions he does on what can and cannot have a truth value. But Kripke's solution, like Russell's and Tarski's, is an implication of a theoretical construct. He does not simply *declare* that sentences lack truth value in those circumstances in which they would entail contradictions if they had a truth value. The ad hoc element has been pushed to a deeper level.

At one point, however, Kripke makes an adjustment to his theory that, if allowed to stand, would vitiate his otherwise successful attempt to postpone the entrance of an ad hoc element. As noted above, the truth-teller sentence ('This sentence is true'), while sharing some of the peculiarities of the liar sentence, is not itself paradoxical. One can consistently assume that it is true, or one can consistently assume that it is false. As it stands, Kripke's theory does not allow the truth-teller to have any truth value. In a misguided attempt to accommodate those whose intuitions tell them that the truth-teller should have a truth value, Kripke suggests the following emendation of his theory. Instead of taking $I_0(T)$ and $I_0(F)$ to be empty, one puts 'This sentence is true' in one or the other of them, according to one's intuitions about its truth value. Thus it will have a truth value at I_1 and keep it through all succeeding interpretations including the fixed point.

But if the truth-teller sentence can be thrown into $I_0(T)$ or $I_0(F)$, what nonarbitrary reason is there for insisting that the liar sentence cannot be thrown into one or the other of these? Kripke's only reply is to say that the liar derivation "easily yields a proof" that this cannot be done (Kripke 1975, 73). He must have in mind something like this: Assume that the liar sentence is in $I_0(T)$. Then by the definition of $I_{i+1}(T)$, it is also in $I_1(T)$. But then, since the liar sentence is atomic, the object named by the subject of the sentence must be in the set of things I_0 assigns to the predicate. But the object named by the subject of the liar sentence is just the liar sentence itself, and its predicate is 'is false', so the liar sentence must also be a member of $I_0(F)$. But this is a contradiction, since nothing can be in both the extension and antiextension of a predicate. Therefore, the liar sentence is not in $I_0(T)$. By similar reasoning, we show that the liar sentence cannot be in $I_0(F)$. Notice, however, that all this "proof" really amounts to is the claim that the liar sentence cannot be in $I_0(T)$ or $I_0(F)$, because paradox would result if it were. The whole of Kripke's theoretical construct has been rendered pointless. He might just as well throw it out and simply *declare* that the liar sentence has no truth value, since paradox would result if it did. Such is what he ends up doing anyway. At least that is what he ends up doing when he adjusts his theory to allow the truth-teller sentence to have a truth value. Therefore, this adjustment should not be made. We should continue to insist that $I_0(T)$ and $I_0(F)$ are empty and hence that the truth-teller sentence has no truth value.

A serious objection to Kripke's theory is that it does not solve a paradox known as the Strengthened Liar. There are several ways of expressing the Strengthened Liar sentence:

This sentence is false or neither true nor false.

This sentence is false or has no truth value.

This sentence is false or undefined.

This sentence is not true.

Regardless of how the Strengthened Liar is expressed, it leads to a contradiction:[11]

1. If the Strengthened Liar sentence is true, then it is just the opposite of what it claims to be, so it is false (and thus not true).
2. So if it is true, it is both true and not true.
3. If it is false (and thus not true), then it is precisely what it claims to be, so it is true.
4. If it is neither true nor false (and thus not true), then it is precisely what it claims to be, so it is true.
5. If it is not true, then it has to be either false or neither true nor false, and either way it is true (from (3) and (4)). So if it is not true, then it is true.
6. So if it is not true, then it is both true and not true.
7. But it has to be either true or not true, and either way it is both true and not true (from (2) and (6)),

Theories that deny bivalence, like Kripke's, do not necessarily solve the Strengthened Liar because the derivation of a contradiction from the Strengthened Liar sentence does not assume bivalence. Bivalence is the principle that any sentence must be either true or false, but the derivation from the Strengthened Liar assumes trivalence: every sentence is either true, or false, or neither true nor false. To put it another way, it assumes strengthened bivalence: every sentence is either true or not true. Moreover, it would be quite pointless to evade the Strengthened Liar by denying trivalence or strengthened bivalence. To do so would require postulating some fourth thing that a sentence could be besides true, false, or neither true nor false. But then one could formulate a superstrong liar:

This sentence is false, or neither true nor false, or the fourth thing.

But this sentence plus the principle of *quadvalence* will lead to a contradiction. Clearly we are off on an infinite regress.[12]

Tarski's (and Russell's) theories *do* solve the Strengthened Liar. 'This sentence is not true' is a metalanguage abbreviation of 'This sentence is not true-in-the-object-language'. The latter is merely true, not both true and not true. (Alternatively, we could follow Robert Rogers in adding another hyphen between the 'not' and the 'true' and taking the Strengthened Liar to be an abbreviation for 'This sentence is not-true-in-the-object-language'. *This* sentence, as Rogers points out, is merely false, not both true and false, because it claims to be in the object language and it is not (Rogers 1963, 57). Kripke seems to acknowledge that his solution does not apply to the Strengthened Liar, and ironically, he suggests that a Tarskian language-levels approach is, at the moment, the only way to solve it (Kripke 1975, 80; compare Hellman 1975). Note that for any theory that entails bivalence, 'false' and 'not true' are synonymous terms, so for such theories there is no distinction between the Liar and the Strengthened Liar paradoxes.

9.6 A. N. Prior's Solution

Tarski (and Russell) can solve both the Liar and the Strengthened Liar paradoxes for artificial languages but they can solve neither for natural languages. Kripke can potentially solve the Liar Paradox for both natural and artificial languages, but he cannot solve the Strengthened Liar for either kind of language. The highest remaining priority is to find a solution to the Strengthened Liar for natural languages (or to solve the Liar Paradox for natural languages with a theory of truth that entails bivalence and hence has no Strengthened Liar paradox.)

A. N. Prior has pointed out that the liar derivation can be derailed if the liar sentence is, despite its unobjectionable appearance, a self-contradictory statement. Before we see why that is, let us find out just what is involved in taking the liar sentence to be a self-contradiction in and of itself. All it explicitly says is that it is false. So if it is self-contradictory, it must *implicitly* say something incompatible with this, that is, it must implicitly say that it is true. But we must not *simply* postulate that the liar sentence implicitly predicates truth of itself, for that would be too ad hoc. But we can push the ad hoc element to a deeper level if the fact that the liar sentence predicates truth of itself can be seen as an implication of another, broader postulation. So I shall have to postulate that *all* sentences, whatever else they say, also implicitly predicate truth of themselves; that is, all sentences are hidden conjunctions. This approach, like Russell's and Tarski's, involves the denial of premise (1) of the liar derivation: on Prior's analysis the liar sentence does not say only that it is false. It says that it is true and false, so if it is false, then what follows is that it is *not* both true and false. It does not follow that it is true. So we can without contradiction assume that it is false (Prior 1958, 70–75; Prior 1962, 136–141).

If this solution works at all, it works for the Strengthened Liar as well as the Liar. Prior died before he could develop the idea, which he attributed to C. S. Peirce and John Buridan (Prior 1958, 70–71). Indeed, even the suggestion that *all* sentences implicitly predicate truth of themselves is my emendation. I suspect that Prior's approach will force certain changes in propositional logic; among them, we shall have to say that the special implicit conjunct in a proposition cannot be detached by the rule called simplification or conjunction elimination. I suspect that his solution can be extended to a wide variety of versions of the paradox, but, until further investigation, it is not clear that it would dissolve the paradox in the Smith and Jones case nor hence whether it would work for natural languages.

9.7 Truth-Value Gluts

Graham Priest and Bradley Dowden have independently arrived at the same bizarre, but impressive, approach to the Liar Paradox. They suggest that the failure to secure a satisfying solution to the Liar Paradox indicates that there is no solution and that we really ought to learn to live with the paradox. That is, we ought to accept that some sentences are both true and false (Priest 1979; Priest 1984; Dowden 1979; Dowden 1984). In other words, there is nothing at all wrong with the liar derivation; it is a sound argument to a contradiction. What is wrong is our fear of contradictions. Metaphorically, the suggestion is that there is an oversupply, a glut, of truth values. So some sentences have to get more than one.

It is, of course, not for nothing that philosophers have a phobia about contradiction. For by standard logic, anything can be derived from a contradiction, even some crazy claim we know to be false. Let q be any such crazy claim, say 'Santa Claus is the prime minister'. Then,

1. p and $\neg p$.
2. Ergo, $\neg p$ (From 1.)
3. Ergo, if p, then q. (From 2.)
4. Ergo, p. (From 1.)
5. Ergo, q. (From 3 and 4 by *modus ponens.*)

So a theory of truth that entailed a contradiction would, via that contradiction, entail anything at all. But as Priest points out, we can avoid this consequence by rejecting standard logic just as well as we can avoid it by refusing to countenance contradictions. What we need is a nonstandard logic that will allow some contradictions but that nevertheless will not allow us to deduce anything and everything (Priest 1979, 224). Priest and Dowden each produce just such a logic. I describe only Priest's logic here. It has three truth values: only true, only false, and true-and-false.[13] The most salient characteristic of this logic is that certain deductive rules of standard logic, including *modus ponens*, are no longer valid. (There are ways to derive any random proposition from a contradiction without using *modus ponens*, but each of them uses at least one rule of inference that Priest's logic would rule invalid.) It is precisely this characteristic that ensures that the logic will not entail anything and everything (Priest 1979, 231–234).

However, a problem arises here. The resulting logic is so impoverished in deductive rules that it will not allow us to prove many entirely unparadoxical conclusions that we know darn well we ought to be able to conclude. For example, from 'If Bob is stupid, then Mary is smart' and 'Bob is stupid' we ought to be able to conclude 'Mary is smart'. Yet we cannot do this on Priest's logic as it now stands. But he points out that the deductive rules his system has proscribed are "quasi-valid" even if they are not valid, which simply means that they *do* preserve truth values through a chain of inference *if none of the ultimate premises of the inference have the value true-and-false.* Consequently, he proposes that we allow ourselves to continue to use the (otherwise proscribed) deductive rules of standard logic whenever we have no specific reason for thinking one or more of the premises is true-and-false. Of course, some of the rules of standard logic are valid (not merely quasi valid) even on Priest's system. These can be used no matter what the truth values of the ultimate premises. The result, he claims, is that almost any desirable deduction allowed by standard logic will be allowed by his logic as well (Priest 1979, 234–237).

Priest's suggestion that we learn to live with certain contradictions is not motivated simply by philosophical defeatism: the belief that the Liar Paradox cannot be solved. There are, he claims, theoretical advantages to allowing sentences that are both true and false: Kurt Gödel's proof that there are some arithmetic sentences that can neither be proven nor disproven in any *consistent* formal system of mathematical reasoning becomes itself a kind of paradox when we notice that some of these same sentences *can* be proven true in the intuitive, informal sense of 'proof'. Yet the very formal systems Gödel's theorem is about are *supposed* to be formal representations of the intuitive, informal pattern of mathematical reasoning. The explanation for this is that in our informal system of reasoning, we allow ourselves to refer to the properties of the system itself. So in Tarski's terminology, we reason informally in a semantically closed language, and thus in a language in which paradox can result. So our informal system is not consistent and that is why Gödel's proof does not work for it.[14] If we decide to accept contradictory sentences as a fact of life, then in formalizing mathematical reasoning, there is no reason to restrict ourselves to consistent (and thus semantically open) languages. Hence we can produce formal systems that *accurately* represent our informal reasoning. (See Priest 1979, 221–224; compare Priest 1984, 164–173.)

But, it will be asked, doesn't all this just show that our informal system of reasoning is uselessly inconsistent and ought to be abandoned? Priest's answer is that being inconsistent and being useless are not always the same thing. If we suppose that our informal system embodies a more or less standard logic, then the fact that it entails some contradictions means that it will entail anything at all and would thus be useless. But why make this supposition? Let us conclude instead that our informal system does not embody a standard logic (Priest 1979, 224). It is germane here to recall Foley's argument (from section 7.4) that one can be justified in holding inconsistent beliefs.

The flavor of Priest's idea is summed up in his attitude toward the Strengthened Liar paradox. It turns out that, in Priest's system, 'This sentence is not only true' is both only true and not only true. But the fact that he cannot avoid this paradox is not a problem for his theory, because the theory does not *avoid* the Liar Paradox itself. The point of his theory is not to avoid paradoxes but to learn to live with them (Priest 1979, 239). Dowden, however, is not willing to go this far. The notion that a sentence can be true and not true at the same time would require too drastic a revision in the meaning of the word 'not' (Dowden 1979, 142). On the other hand, since anything that is false is also not true, it may seem that Dowden has already, in effect, gone this far. To avoid this implication, he suggests that we revise our notion of falsity so that some false things, presumably those that are false and true, no longer count as *not true* things (Dowden 1979, 52–57).

The disagreement between Dowden and Priest on the treatment of the Strengthened Liar touches on an important issue for the truth glut approach. Any theory that countenances contradictions skirts the borderline of unintelligibility. Both Dowden and Priest do an admirable job of staying on the good side of the border when treating the ordinary Liar Paradox. But extending the approach to the Strengthened Liar, as Priest wants to do, is at least arguably incoherent. Indeed, he is willing to allow sentences that are simultaneously x and not x even when the x does not stand for true, for he claims at one point that some sentences are both paradoxical and nonparadoxical (Priest 1984, 160).

9.8   Situational Semantics and the Liar Paradox

In this section, as in section 9.5, the complexity of the material forces me to make use of set-theoretic terminology. But again, I urge readers without the requisite background to read the section anyway.

Jon Barwise and John Etchemendy have recently proposed a solution to the Liar Paradox from the standpoint of situational semantics (Barwise and Etchemendy 1987). In brief, their claim is that situational semantics shows that the liar sentence is ambiguous. Interpreted in one way, it is merely false; interpreted in another way, it is merely true; but there is no consistent interpretation on which it is paradoxically both true and false. The liar derivation trades on the ambiguity.

Before we can see their argument for this conclusion, 1 must set up a few tools of the trade. A *state of affairs* is represented by an ordered $(n + 2)$-tuple $\langle R, a_1, \ldots, a_n; i \rangle$, where R is some n-place relation, $a_1, \ldots, a_n$ is a sequence of n objects, and i is one or the other member of the polarity $\{0, 1\}$ (Barwise and Etchemendy 1987, 30). For example, if $H =$ having,

j = John, and b = a blue Chevy, then the state of affairs of John's having a blue Chevy is represented by $\langle H, j, b; 1 \rangle$. On the other hand, the state of affairs of John's not having a blue Chevy is represented by $\langle H, j, b; 0 \rangle$. Two states of affairs like these, identical except for the polar member, are called *duals* of one another. Propositions, which is Barwise and Etchemendy's name for what Austin calls statements, can also be objects in states of affairs. In particular, $\langle \text{Tr}, p; 1 \rangle$ is the state of affairs of p being true, and $\langle \text{Tr}, p; 0 \rangle$ is the state of affairs of p not being true. A *situation* is simply a set of states of affairs (Barwise and Etchemendy 1987, 75–76). The following is an example:

$$\{ \langle H, j, b; 1 \rangle, \langle \text{Tr}, p, 0 \rangle, \langle G, m, t; 0 \rangle \}$$

Propositions, according to Barwise and Etchemendy, are about situations; they mean *all* propositions, not just the ones, like 'It is raining', that are obviously about situations. For example, 'John has a blue Chevy' is about a situation s (determined more or less precisely by the context), and the proposition says that situation s is of the type where John has a blue Chevy. We can represent this proposition by $\{s: [H, j, b; 1]\}$, where s is the name of the situation that the proposition is about and $[H, j, b; 1]$ is a description of the *type of situation* that s is alleged by the proposition to be a member of. In fact, every proposition says of some situation that it is of this or that type. For example, $\{s; [H, j, b; 0]\}$ says that situation s is of the type in which John does *not* have a blue Chevy. In ordinary English, this is the proposition 'John does not have a blue Chevy'. Similarly, 'Proposition p is true' is $\{s; [\text{Tr}, p; 1]\}$ that is, 'Situation s is of the type where p is true'. And 'Proposition p is false' is $\{s; [\text{Tr}, p; 0]\}$ (Barwise and Etchemeny 1987, 124–125).

Representing propositions in this way makes it possible to distinguish between a *denial* and a *negation*. A denial of $\{s; [H, j, b; 1]\}$ is simply $\neg \{s; [H, j, b; 1]\}$, which says that situation s is *not* of the type in which John has a blue Chevy. But the negation of $\{s; [H, j, b; 1]\}$ is the proposition $\{s; [H, j, b; 0]\}$, which says that situation s *is* of the type in which John does *not* have a blue Chevy. So a negation simply reverses the polarity of the type of situation, while a denial leaves the polarity alone but adds a '$\neg$' to the front of the proposition being denied (Barwise and Etchemendy 1987, 166). Of course, this symbol is normally called the negation sign, but this is just a symptom of the fact that logic usually conflates negation and denial.

The liar proposition is ambiguous on just this point. It might be the negation of itself, or it might be the denial of itself. Barwise and Etchemendy call the first of these the assertive liar and name it 'f'. The second is called the denial liar, 'd'. Hence,

$f = \{s; [\text{Tr}, f; 0]\}$ = situation s is of the type where this proposition is false;

$d = \neg\{s; [\text{Tr}, d; 1]\}$ = situation s is *not* of the type where this proposition is true.

It turns out that the Liar Paradox can be solved on either interpretation.

Let us begin with the assertive liar. We first need a definition of truth. Following J. L. Austin, Barwise and Etchemendy suggest that a proposition is true if and only if the particular situation that the proposition is about is of the type that the proposition alleges it to be. Thus, where T ranges over types of situations,

$\{s; [T]\}$ is true $\equiv \langle T \rangle \in$ s.

So

$\{s; [H, j, b; 1]\}$ is true $\equiv \langle H, j, b; 1 \rangle \in s$,

$\{s; [H, j, b; 0]\}$ is true $\equiv \langle H, j, b; 0 \rangle \in s$,

$\{s; [\text{Tr}, p; 1]\}$ is true $\equiv \langle \text{Tr}, p, 1 \rangle \in s$,

$\{s; [\text{Tr}, p; 0]\}$ is true $\equiv \langle \text{Tr}, p, 0 \rangle \in s$,

and for the assertive liar,

$\{s; [\text{Tr}, f; 0]\}$ is true $\equiv \langle \text{Tr}, f, 0 \rangle \in s$.[15]

Next we need the notion of a model of the world. Here in particular I must simplify Barwise and Etchemendy's story. I shall say that a model of the world, W, is a collection of states of affairs that meets certain coherence requirements. These requirements, listed below, are meant to capture our pretheoretical ideas about the relations holding between states of affairs, truth values, and the world. Situations were defined above as sets of states of affairs. I add here that every nonempty subset of W is a situation. (But as we shall see below, one of these subsets, W itself, cannot be talked about.) The coherence conditions on W are the following:

(1a) No state of affairs and its dual are both in W.

(1b) For every state of affairs and its dual, one of them is in W.

(2a) $\langle \text{Tr}, p; 1 \rangle \in W \equiv p$ is true.

(2b) $\langle \text{Tr}, p; 0 \rangle \in W \equiv p$ is false.[16]

Now suppose that the assertive liar is true. Then by the definition of truth, $\langle \text{Tr}, f, 0 \rangle \in s$. But s is a subset of W, so $\langle \text{Tr}, f, 0 \rangle \in W$. But then by condition (2b), the assertive liar is false. So we cannot consistently suppose that the assertive liar is true (Barwise and Etchemendy 1987, 132).

However, we *can* consistently take it to be false. Now this might not seem to be the case. It might seem that we can make an argument, parallel to the preceding one, that shows that the assumption that the assertive liar is false also leads to a contradiction: Suppose that the assertive liar is false. Then $\langle \text{Tr}, f, 1 \rangle \in s$. But since s is a subset of W, $\langle \text{Tr}, f, 1 \rangle \in W$. But then by condition (2a), the assertive liar is true. But this argument goes astray in the very first step, for the supposition that the assertive liar is false does not entail that $\langle \text{Tr}, f, 1 \rangle \in s$. Rather, it entails, by the definition of truth, that $\langle \text{Tr}, f, 0 \rangle \notin s$, and no contradiction follows from this. On the other hand, it might seem that we can reverse the direction of the argument at the top of this paragraph and argue thus: Suppose that the assertive liar is false. Then, by condition (2b), $\langle \text{Tr}, f, 0 \rangle \in W$. So $\langle \text{Tr}, f, 0 \rangle \in s$ for some subset s of W. Then by the definition of truth, the assertive liar is true. But this argument is also faulty. It is correct only to the point of concluding that $\langle \text{Tr}, f, 0 \rangle \in s$ for some subset s of W. But the emphasis here should be on the word 'some'. Although the fact that the assertive liar is false is a member of *some* situation, it does not follow that it is a member of the very situation that the assertive-liar proposition is about. And if it is not a member of this very situation, the paradoxical conclusion that the assertive liar is true if it is false does not follow. Thus, conclude Barwise and Etchemendy, we can consistently hold that the assertive liar is merely false if we acknowledge that the fact of its falsity cannot be a fact in the very situation that the assertive liar is about (Barwise and Etchemendy 1987, 135). But the fact of its falsity *is* a fact in the world. So which situation (that is, which subset of W) is this fact in? It is in $s^{\sim}$, the complement of s relative to W.

Now there is another proposition, call it f', such that

$$f' = \{s^{\sim}; [\text{Tr}, f'; 0]\}.$$

This too is an assertive liar, and it is about $s^{\sim}$, not s. But here also we need not assume that the fact of its falsity is a member of $s^{\sim}$. We can take it that the fact that f' is false is a member of $s^{\sim\sim}$, that is, s. By so taking it, we can consistently assume that f' is merely false. Indeed, there is a different assertive liar for every situation. Each of them is merely false. For each of them, the fact of its falsity is not in the very situation it is about. But for each of them, the fact of its falsity *is* in the world.

Suppose that we define s' as

$$s' = (s \cup \{\langle \text{Tr}, f, 0 \rangle\}).$$

Here, of course, *by definition* $\langle \text{Tr}, f, 0 \rangle \in s'$, but we still have no paradox, because f is about s, not s'.

Suppose, then, that we define s'' and f'' as follows:

$$s'' = \{\langle \text{Tr}, f'', 0 \rangle\}$$

$$f'' = \{s''; [\text{Tr}, f''; 0]\}$$

Barwise and Etchemendy judge f'' to be true, because $\langle \text{Tr}, f'', 0 \rangle$ is a member of s''. However, s'' is a nonactual situation. That is, it is a set with no real-world situation as a counterpart (Barwise and Etchemendy 1987, 129–131).

Finally, suppose that we define f'' as

$$f''' = \{W; [\text{Tr}, f'''; 0]\}.$$

Since W includes every fact, it certainly includes the fact of f''' being false. To avoid paradox in this case, Barwise and Etchemendy simply stipulate that no proposition can be about the whole world (1987, 154 ff.). It is at this point especially that an ad hoc element enters into their account. More will be said about this below.

One of the nice features of this analysis of the paradox is that it allows us to keep the intuitions that every proposition is true or false, and none is both. This entails

$$\langle H, j, b; 1 \rangle \in s \text{ or } \langle H, j, b; 1 \rangle \notin s, \text{ but not both},$$

and

$\langle H, j, b; 0 \rangle \in s$ or $\langle H, j, b; 0 \rangle \notin s$, but not both.

But Barwise and Etchemendy would deny that

$\langle H, j, b; 1 \rangle \notin s \equiv \langle H, j, b; 0 \rangle \in s$.

This means that their analysis would allow that for some s, both $\{s; \{H, j, b; 1\}\}$ and $\{s; \{H, j, b; 0\}\}$ are false. This situation is not one of the type in which John has a blue Chevy, but it is also not of the type in which John does not have a blue Chevy (Barwise and Etchemendy 1987, 126–128). However, this does not mean that the world as a whole is somehow incoherent for by condition (1b),

$\langle H, j, b; 1 \rangle \notin W \equiv \langle H, j, b; 0 \rangle \in W;$

that is,

$(\forall s)(\langle H, j, b; 1 \rangle \notin s) \equiv (\exists s')(\langle H, j, b; 0 \rangle \in s').$

Does the denial liar, the proposition that denies itself, lead to a contradiction? First we expand the definition of truth to handle the '$\neg$' symbol:

$\neg \{s[T]\}$ is true $\equiv \langle T \rangle \notin s$.

So

$\neg \{s; [H, j, b; 1]\}$ is true $\equiv \langle H, j, b; 1 \rangle \notin s,$

$\neg \{s; [H, j, b; 0]\}$ is true $\equiv \langle H, j, b; 0 \rangle \notin s.$

The denial liar, once again, is defined so:

$d = \neg \{s; [\text{Tr}, d; 1]\}$

Hence the T-sentence for the denial liar is:

$\neg \{s; [\text{Tr}, d; 1]\}$ is true $\equiv \langle \text{Tr}, d; 1 \rangle \notin s.$[17]

Now assume that d is false. Then by the expanded definition of truth, $\langle T, d; 1 \rangle \in s$. But then $\langle \text{Tr}, d; 1 \rangle \in W$. So by condition (2a), d is true. So we cannot consistently assume that d is false (Barwise and Etchemendy 1987, 167). But we *can* consistently take it to be true. The arguments for this point follow, *mutatus mutandus*, the arguments for the claim that we can consistently take the assertive liar sentence to be false. There is a parallel implication too: the fact of d's truth cannot itself be a member of the situation that d is about.

So the assertive liar sentence is merely false, and the denial liar sentence is merely true. Neither is paradoxically both true and false. The liar derivation commits the fallacy of equivocation. The reasoning from premise (5) to (6) of that derivation works only if the liar sentence is interpreted as the assertive liar sentence, but the inference from (9) to (10) works only if the liar sentence is interpreted as the denial liar sentence. Hence, the derivation equivocates on the term 'the liar sentence'. Another way of putting the same point is that premise (1) of the liar derivation is hopelessly ambiguous. It does not specify whether the liar sentence negates itself or denies itself.

Like the other solutions I have surveyed, the situational-semantics approach is not completely free of an ad hoc element. As we have seen, the fact that the assertive liar is false cannot be a part of the very situation that the assertive liar is about, and the fact that the denial liar is true cannot be a part of the very situation that the denial liar is about. This has the implication that neither the assertive liar nor the denial liar can be about the whole world; otherwise we would be faced with the absurdity of saying that the assertive liar is false, but the fact of its falsity is not a part of the world, and the fact of the denial liar's truth is not a part of the world. Barwise and Etchemendy reduce the ad hoc flavor of this somewhat by saying that *no* proposition can be about the whole world (1987, 154). Nevertheless, if the only reason in the first place for saying that the liar sentence cannot be about the whole world is that otherwise paradox would result, then there is an ad hoc element here.

Moreover, there is something counterintuitive about Barwise and Etchemendy's suggestion, for it does seem that we *can* talk about the whole world. They defend their solution with an argument from analogy. Russell showed there can be no universal set U, because, on pain of paradox, no set U can contain the set $\{x \in U : x \notin x\}$. So too the Liar shows that no situation that we can talk about can contain all the facts in the world, because on pain of paradox no situation s can contain the fact $\langle \text{Tr}, f, 0 \rangle$, where $f = \{s; [\text{Tr}, f, 0]\}$ (Barwise and Etchemendy 1987, 154–155). The analogy seems weak to me. The set of all sets is an unfamiliar postulation we meet only in set theory, so we do not bring to set theory any pretheoretical intuitions that there is any such thing in the first place. But we do bring to the study of semantics strong intuitions that some propositions *can* be about the whole world. Hence Russell's solution to the set-theoretic paradox does not ask us to give up any intuitions we already have, but Barwise and Etchemendy's solution to the Liar Paradox does.

They ease the pain somewhat by pointing out that we need not think of their conclusion (or Russell's) as representing a restriction on our logico-linguistic abilities. We can think of it rather as a demonstration of just how powerful our abilities really are. We should not think of Russell's argument as showing that there is no universal set so much as we should think of it as showing the great power of our set-making abilities. We attempt to gather all sets into one set, but no sooner have we done this then we discover, via his argument, that there is still one more set not gathered. So too Barwise and Etchemendy want their argument to be taken as demonstrating the great power of our proposition-making abilities. Collect all the states of affairs you believe to exist into one gigantic 'situation.' No sooner have you done this than Barwise and Etchemendy will show you that either there is a proposition that is not about that situation or there is a state of affairs that is not in the situation. Thus for however many nonsemantic facts (and nearly all semantic facts) you previously thought of as constituting the whole world, you can still talk about that set of facts. In that sense, nothing has been lost. You simply cannot continue to call that set of facts the whole world.

But still, *something* of importance has been lost. For in some of our utterances about the whole world, the connotation of 'the whole world' is important, as in a theists's assertion of 'The whole world was created *ex nihilo*.' It is some comfort, but not a lot, to be told that we can still talk about the set of all states of affairs that we used to think constituted the whole of the world. For, to continue the example, no matter how big that set is, the theist wants to claim that something bigger than just that set was created.

Moreover, Barwise and Etchemendy's argument, like Russell's is a diagonal argument, and like all such arguments, what it really shows is that we can accept the negation of its conclusion only on pain of paradox (Barwise and Etchemendy 1987, 154–155). That is, it does not *directly* show that q is the case; it does so only via the intermediate conclusion 'q or $(p \& \neg p)$'. This is normally enough to establish that q is the case beyond dispute, but we are not in a normal situation here. Where the Liar Paradox is concerned, our most fundamental semantic and logical intuitions are under attack. Indeed, the liar derivation shows that we cannot salvage *all* of these intuitions. Something has got to go, so we ought to give up the intuition to which we are least wedded. In a normal philosophical context, '*p* & ¬*p*' is more absurd than anything that '*q*' could possibly stand for, so there is no question about what we should give up. But where the Liar Paradox is the issue, there is room for intelligent minds to disagree. Priest would prefer that we keep the possibility of talking about the whole world and accept '*p* & ¬*p*' along with changes in our logic sufficient to ensure that not just anything can be derived therefrom. Barwise and Etchemendy would rather keep classical logic and avoid contradiction, even at the price of never being able to talk about the whole world. But even those who agree must recognize the limited power of diagonal arguments in contexts of this sort. For diagonal arguments are in the end just appeals to intuition, and thus they are convincing only to those who share the arguer's intuitions.

If we do accept such counterintuitive aspects as it has, the situational-semantics approach solves the Liar Paradox for both natural and artificial languages. And again, there is no difference between the Liar and the Strengthened Liar paradoxes for theories that, like Barwise and Etchemendy's theory, entail bivalence. So they also solve the latter paradox.

9.9   Chapter Summary

In this chapter I have surveyed some responses to the Liar Paradox, which, until solved, stands as a counterexample to all quasi-realist theories of truth. We have seen that the language-levels response can solve both the Liar and the Strengthened Liar paradoxes for artificial languages, but it can solve neither for natural languages. The approach of truth-value gaps can solve the Liar Paradox for both artificial and natural languages, but it cannot solve the Strengthened Liar for either. Neither can the approach truth-value gluts, save at risk of unintelligibility. The situational-semantics approach solves both paradoxes for both kinds of languages, but only if we accept the impossibility of talking about the whole world. We also looked at a relatively unexplored area of research: the view that all sentences implicitly predicate truth of themselves, and so the liar sentence is self-contradictory.

This is the last falsehood in this chapter.

10 The Speech-Act Project and the Deflationary Thesis

What are we *doing* when we ascribe truth? Or not to beg the question, what are we doing when we make utterances whose surface grammar makes them *appear* to predicate the property of truth to some truth bearer? (Hereafter I shall use the phrase 'apparent truth ascriptions' and variations thereof to label these utterances.) Are we actually ascribing such a property to such an entity, are we saying something else, or are we perhaps not *saying* anything at all? These are the questions that the various projects I have grouped under the generic title of the speech-act project are trying to answer. The assertion project works from the point of view, either assumed or concluded from prior reasoning, that we are *saying* something when we make such utterances. The illocutionary-act project, on the other hand, does not assume that we are *saying* anything at all when we make such utterances. A discussion of some of the theories intended, or at least most charitably interpreted as intended, to fulfill one or another division of the speech-act project is the first of three major tasks that will occupy us in this chapter. Most of these theories are among those that are traditionally grouped under the generic title 'deflationary theories of truth'. But this is a misleading practice, since the deflationary thesis, as I will call it, is not built into these theories. Indeed, it does not even follow from any of them without the help of other premises. The deflationary thesis holds that there is no property of truth. And hence the metaphysical project in all its subdivisions is wrongheaded right from the start: since there is no such property as truth, there cannot be a theory of what truth is. Thus my second task is to evaluate this deflationary thesis. Finally, I end the chapter with a discussion of Paul Horwich's metaphysical-project theory. It was not included in the chapters on the metaphysical project simply because it can be better understood in light of the aforementioned speech-act-project theories.

10.1 Strawson, Price, and the Illocutionary-Act Project

P. F. Strawson's performative theory was briefly introduced in section 1.7. He contends that apparent truth ascriptions are performative utterances, much like 'I promise to ...', and 'I do' (when uttered at the appropriate moment in a marriage ceremony). In brief, the theory is that to utter the sentences '"Snow is white" is true' or 'What Percy says is true' is not to *say* anything at all. (A claim from which he retreated in the 1960s.[1]) It is to *do* something. What, then, are we doing when we utter ascriptions of truth? According to Strawson, we are *agreeing to*, or *confirming*, the proposition to which truth is apparently being ascribed. The two utterances are equivalent to 'I agree that snow is white' and 'I agree with what Percy says'. So 'is true' functions like 'I agree that'. They both signal the performance of an action, namely, the act of agreeing. But neither 'is true' nor 'I agree that' *describe* the speaker's action (Strawson 1950, 45–53). What Strawson is suggesting is that ascriptions of truth are really *gestures*. Just as nodding one's head up and down is to gesture one's agreement without saying or asserting anything (not, at any rate, in any familiar sense of 'say' or 'assert'), so too, to apparently ascribe truth is to signal one's agreement without saying or asserting anything. So when we utter '"Snow is white" is true', we are not saying anything at all about the sentence 'Snow is white'.

Strawson is aware, of course, that 'is true' figures in a wider variety of locutions than just simple ascriptions. There are, for example, such locutions as 'Is it true that ... ?' and 'If it is true that ... then ... '. In these cases, according to Strawson, 'is true' functions, like the adverb 'really', as an expression of surprise, doubt, or disbelief. Just as 'Did the dam *really* collapse?' expresses the speaker's doubt that the dam collapsed, so too 'Is it true that the dam collapsed?' is a way for the speaker to express his doubt (Strawson 1964, 78). And sometimes 'is true' can be used to concede a point, as it does in the following exchange:

Jones: Furthermore, the Democrats have produced a long list of corrupt mayors.

Smith: It is true that there have been a lot of corrupt Democrats, but the Republicans have had their share as well.

Two problems must be noted here. First, it appears that Strawson does not have *one* theory about 'is true'; he has several. Peter Geach has pointed out one dubious consequence of this: on Strawson's theory, the following argument is invalid by virtue of committing the fallacy of equivocation, for the first 'is true' is an expression of doubt or some such, while the second 'is true' is the performance of an action.

If x is true, then p.

x is true.

Ergo, p.

(Indeed, since 'x is true' is an *action*, it is not really a premise at all.) But we know that the argument *is* valid, so there must be something wrong with Strawson's theory (Geach 1960, 223). A closely related objection comes from Horwich (1990, 40): if apparent truth predications are illocutionary acts, there is no way to make sense of the inference from 'Oscar's claim is true' and 'Oscar's claim is that snow is white' to the conclusion 'Snow is white'.

A second problem is that Strawson's explanation of 'is true' when it appears in conditionals and questions is oversimplified. Sometimes 'Is it true that . . . ?' is an expression of simple ignorance about what the facts of the matter are, not an expression of surprise, doubt, or disbelief. Surely, 'Is it true that it is raining?' is sometimes asked by a speaker who is wondering whether or not he should take his umbrella. Note that to express surprise, doubt, or disbelief about x, one must first be inclined to believe that x is *not* the case. Being undecided or having no opinion is not enough. If I have not the foggiest idea whether or not it is raining out, I would not be surprised, doubtful, or disbelieving were someone to tell me that it is. The point is that one who asks 'Is it true that it is raining?' may be completely unsure as to whether or not it is raining, so his asking the question cannot be an expression of surprise, doubt, or disbelief. Similarly, the conditional 'If it is true that the plane has been hijacked, that would explain why it is off course' (uttered by one radar operator to another) may be simply a statement of grim fact, not an expression of surprise, doubt, or disbelief. Indeed, the speaker here may believe that it is all too likely the plane has been hijacked.

Third, Strawson concedes that certain conditions in the nonlinguistic world must obtain before one may properly signal one's agreement. Here the force of 'properly' is not 'appropriate from the standpoint of honesty or accuracy' but 'appropriate from the standpoint of correct usage'. For example, one ought not utter the words '"The dam has collapsed" is true' unless *it is a fact that the dam has collapsed*: "Certainly, we use the word 'true' when the semantic conditions described by [J. L.] Austin [see section 4.3] are fulfilled; but we do not, in using the word, *state* that they are fulfilled" (Strawson 1950, 44). But this creates a puzzle. If uttering an apparent truth ascription is just to signal one's agreement, why do the facts of the matter have any relevance? If 'is true' in no way asserts that these conditions are fulfilled, how and why are these conditions conditions for uttering 'x is true'? One can, after all, *signal* agreement, dishonestly, even when one does not in fact agree. Gertrude Ezorsky tries to defend Strawson on this point by suggesting that while 'I agree' signals bare agreement, 'is true' signals *justified* agreement (Ezorsky 1967, 88–90). But this is more a surrender than a defense, for the difference between merely agreeing and claiming justifiable agreement is that in the latter case one is claiming that evidence shows that the facts of the matter accord with one's belief. In other words, to express justifiable agreement is not only to gesture one's agreement but also to *say* something about the facts of the matter. (It is just this point that Strawson was later to concede: while he continued to insist that to utter 'is true' is to perform an action, he acknowledged that to utter 'is true' is *also* to *say* something.[2])

Fourth, Strawson's account of the purposes to which we put utterances of 'true' is incomplete. Sometimes it is used to emphasize the inescapability of some fact, a way of saying 'Face facts!' or 'Stop kidding yourself!'. Jones has just heard that his worst enemy has become his new boss:

Jones: I just heard about Johnson's promotion. Tell me it isn't true. I can't believe it. I just can't believe it!

Smith: It is true he got the promotion, and it is true he hates you. Now get a hold of yourself and figure out what you are going to do.

And sometimes, as Kincade notes (1957, 44), we might say 'True' to prod an interlocutor to go on to his next sentence.

Finally, Huw Price (1988, 131) points out that Strawson's theory makes it a mystery why 'is true' is only applicable to indicative sentences. Why can't we use it to endorse the appropriateness of some question (e.g., "'Is snow white?' is true") just as we can use it to endorse someone's assertion? And why can't we say "'Shut the door!' is true" to express our endorsement of the importance of obeying this command? It would miss Price's point to say that we have other predicates that can do these jobs, e.g., 'is a good question' and 'ought to be obeyed'. At most, this simply forces a rewording of Price's question. Why do we have *different* predicates to signal approval of indicatives, interrogatives, and imperatives? Why not just have "'s" is good', where s can be a sentence in any mood? If the answer to these questions is either that our three separate predicates each signal a distinctly different kind of approval, that each is more precise, or that each is appropriate to sentences in a distinctly different mood, then the field belongs to Price, for any account of why the three predicates are different would have to concede that they *mean* different things, and this would imply that each of them *says* something.

Strawson is the first of several theorists we shall examine in this chapter who endorses the deflationary thesis: there is no property of truth, and hence nothing is a truth bearer. Thus the metaphysical project is moot. We do not need an analysis of truth, because there is no property of truth; there is nothing here to analyze.

We need to modify this description of the deflationary thesis because, as it stands, it is not sufficiently sensitive to the distinction between nominalism and platonism. Nominalism holds that there are *no* properties in the world. *No* predicate, nominalists would say, really ascribes a *property* to anything. But even nominalists believe that there is a distinction between genuine and nongenuine predicates. A genuine predicate, they would say, has an extension, a set of objects to which it applies. But nongenuine predicates do not have an extension, and hence utterances with nongenuine predicates have some purpose in language other than to assert that some object is a member of the extension of the predicate. Thus, disputes over the deflationary thesis transcend nominalist versus platonist disputes. So we need to state the thesis in a way that is neutral with respect to the latter dispute: so expressed, the thesis says that 'is true' is not a genuine predicate. Again, nominalists and platonists will disagree on what a genuine predicate is, the former thinking it refers to an extension, the latter that it refers to a property, but that dispute should be suppressed when deflationism is at issue. (Nevertheless, there will be times when brevity and clarity are enhanced if I refer to the deflationary thesis in ways that presuppose platonism. All such passages could be rewritten in a neutral, albeit wordy, way.)

Not untypically for a deflationist, Strawson gives no explicit argument for the deflationary thesis. He seems to be presupposing the following principle of philosophical method: one ought postulate only such entities as one needs to postulate in order to explain the various syntactic and semantic features of our language. Put another way, the principle is that we ought believe in the existence of a given entity if and only if not so believing would leave us unable to make sense of one or another of the many kinds of utterances we make. Since the performative theory, we can imagine Strawson saying, provides an account of our use of 'is true' that does not require us to think that the predicate names some property (or has an extension), it is not a genuine predicate. (Evaluation of this argument, and for the most part, evaluation of deflationism, will be postponed until section 10.7. See also section 2.7 for a discussion of Strawson's implied principle of philosophical method.)

Huw Price has recently offered what might be called a Darwinian answer to the illocutionary-act project. The purpose of apparent truth (and falsity) ascriptions, he says, is to reward (or punish) other speakers when they say things we agree (or disagree) with, and thereby provide "speakers with an incentive to justify their utterances to others" (Price 1988, 134). But, of course, this cannot be all there is to it. You will not be flattered that I call you noble if you believe that 'noble' is not a genuine predicate and is *only* used to flatter. Similarly, no one would be rewarded by hearing their utterances labeled 'true' if they did not believe that 'is true' is a genuine predicate. If word spreads that 'true' is *only* an honorific, it will effectively cease to be one. To his credit, Price realizes that the system works only because most people do not realize that 'is true' is not a genuine predicate: "Truth [is] a 'mythical' goal of enquiry, whose popularity is to be accounted for in terms of the benefits of subscribing to such a myth" (Price 1988, 150). So what are the benefits of the myth? What is the larger purpose served by the practice of encouraging people to justify their utterances?

The development of such a system of linguistic incentives suggests an underlying behavioural advantage.... This advantage presumably turns on the behavioural consequences of the mental states exposed to criticism in such linguistic disputes. In particular it might lie in the survival advantages of basing one's mental attitudes on as wide a body of experience as possible. (Price 1988, 150)

Our behaviourial dispositions can thus be tested against those of other speakers, before they are put to use in the world. (P. 145)

Thus, according to Price, there is survival value in having the predicates 'is true' and 'is false' in our language. We use them to alert each other to points on which we agree and disagree. When two of us discover that we disagree about something, then, often enough anyway, we both look at the matter more closely and try to resolve the disagreement. But why would there be any advantage to having mental states supported by those around us—mental states based "on as wide a body of experience as possible"? The most obvious answer is that such mental states are more likely *true* than mental states that tilt against conventional wisdom. But this answer is not available to Price, since it presupposes that 'is true' is a genuine predicate after all. Instead, he answers the question by invoking what he calls "the Same Boat Property."[3] A type of mental state has this property when the behavioral advantages/disadvantages of any mental state of the type are approximately the same for anyone. If we grant Price that most types of mental states have this property and that, of any two incompatible mental states, usually one has a greater net advantage than the other, then disagreement tends to indicate that one party or the other is behaviorally disadvantaged (Price 1988, 152).

While this answer does explain, without invoking the concept of truth, why disagreement signals that one party is in a disadvantageous state, it does not tell us why *agreement* is advantageous. To get to the latter conclusion, we would have to presuppose that our methods for resolving disagreement tend to move us to the more advantageous mental state rather than to the less advantageous one. It is not easy to see how are we going to account for such a tendency without saying, more or less, that our methods of resolving disagreement tend to reveal the *truth*.

A second objection to Price's theory is that the process he describes requires us to be able to recognize when we disagree with others. And this means that we must be able to spot incompatibilities, able to spot, in other words, that certain sets of mental states cannot all be *true*. Price anticipates this objection and denies that our recognition that two beliefs cannot both be true is logically prior to our recognition that they are incompatible: "It is a nice question just how we notice such incompatibilities. But it is hard to see why anyone should think that perceiving that *P* and *Q* could not both be true is any more easy, or primitive, than perceiving that *P* implies not-*Q*, or than utilizing one's belief that *P* in 'perceiving' that not-*Q*" (1988, 148). But this will not do, for two reasons. First, the concept of *implication* is akin to the concepts of justification, proof, warrant, and their other near synonyms: it cannot be made sense of save in terms of the concept of truth (see section 2.2). Second, if there were such a thing as perceiving that *p* implies not *q* (or perceiving that not *q* on the basis of one's belief that *p*) independently of perceiving that they cannot both be true, *then the former perception would not alert us to their incompatibility*.

10.2   The Assertion Project

We have arrived at the other main division of the speech-act project: the assertion project. As noted in section 1.4, we formulate assertion-project theories by means of the intensional-equivalence symbol, ' $=_{syn}$ '. On the left side of the symbol is an (apparent) ascription of truth. On the right is a statement or description of what the theory in question takes to be a synonymous utterance. So the general form of an assertion-project theory is as follows:

$(t)(t$ is true $=_{syn}$ _____$)$

Here 't' ranges over whatever the theory takes to be the bearers of apparent truth ascriptions, and filling the blank would be a statement or description of what the theory in question takes to be a synonymous utterance. This is translated into English, or something close thereto, by inserting the phrase 'To say that' immediately after the quantifier and reading the symbol ' $=_{syn}$ ' as 'is to say that'. Hence the preceding formula reads 'For all t, to say that t is true is to say that ...'.

Of course, one possible answer to the assertion project is that when making apparent truth-ascribing utterances, we are saying exactly what it appears that we are saying. We are predicating a certain property, truth, of some truth bearer or other. This presumably would be the preanalytic answer that a nonphilosopher and nonlinguist would immediately give to the assertion project, and hence to the speech-act project, if he had any reason to ask himself the question in the first place. For one who subscribes to this view, the assertion project becomes the ascription project. But this view is regarded by deflationists as a naive and slavish devotion to the surface grammar of the utterances in question. (Note, however, that this view is not in itself in conflict with Strawson's or Price's theories per se. They are both deflationists, but the latter is an extra doctrine they held in addition to their theories of the illocutionary act performed with apparent truth ascriptions. The deflationary thesis does not even follow from their theories without the help of the principle of philosophical method described in the last section and discussed at greater length in sections 2.7 and 10.7.) Nevertheless, it bears emphasizing, especially since it is often forgotten in the literature on deflationism, that most predicates are genuine predicates, and thus the burden of proof falls squarely on the deflationists. To think otherwise, as some deflationists gives signs of doing (see section 10.7), is to assume as a principle of linguistic method that for any predicate, we ought to assume that it is not a genuine predicate until it is proven to be so. But in view of the current undeveloped state of semantics, this principle would imply that it is presently rational for us to believe the self-contradictory claim that most predicates are not genuine predicates.

If, however, we do reject the surface grammar of these utterances (but do not reject the assertion project in favor of the illocutionary-act project), then we are saying that they have a deep, hidden semantic/syntactic structure that expresses accurately what the utterances say. If we take this view, the assertion project becomes *eo ipso* the deep-structure project. So I turn now to the latter.

10.3   The Theory of Truth-as-Appraisal

Alan R. White notes that we use the word 'true' in a lot of contexts other than those in which we (apparently) ascribe truth to one or another of the various traditional bearers of truth. We often say things like 'He is a true Englishman' or 'He is a true socialist' or 'That is a true likeness'. Other philosophers have tended to ignore these usages, apparently in the belief that 'true' is used in these cases in a metaphorical or derivative manner. In these idioms 'true' is being used to grade or appraise something relative to an appropriate scale or relative to a conceptual paradigmatic type.[4] When we say that so and so is a 'true Englishman', we are saying that so and so fits the profile of the archetypical Englishman, a hypothetical person who has all the characteristics we take to be peculiarly English. White's suggestion is that when we call sentences, propositions, beliefs, and so forth 'true', we are appraising them relative to some scale or some conceptual paradigm. So at bottom, calling a sentence true is the same sort of assertion as calling a man a true Englishman (White 1957). This has become known as the truth-as-appraisal theory.

Now the scale or paradigmatic type by reference to which Englishman are appraised for their Englishness is different from the standard for being a true Socialist. Likewise, neither of these standards is at all the same as the standard for a true statement. Indeed, White insists that there is not even one common standard for all types of statements. The standard for everyday empirical statements is correspondence, for analytic statements it is coherence, and for scientific hypotheses it is instrumentalism (White

1957, 323). So White does see a point to the metaphysical project (although he thinks it has different correct answers according to the kind of statement at issue). Hence he does not subscribe to the deflationary thesis.

When one appraises a statement, or an Englishman for that matter, as true, the particular scale or paradigmatic type relevant to the case is not itself included, according to White, in the content of what we are saying: to say 'Smith is a true Englishman' is *not* the same thing as saying 'Smith wears a bowler and carries an umbrella and weeps at the loss of India [etc., for all the characteristics the speaker regards as defining the true Englishman]'. On the contrary, to say 'Smith is a true Englishman' is to say something vaguer: it is to say 'Smith ranks high on the appropriate scale' or 'Smith meets the paradigm of the appropriate type'. This would have to be so because, as White points out, one could know that 'true' is a term of appraisal and not know what the criteria of its application are for some type of object, in this case Englishmen. On the other hand, one could know the criteria of a 'true Englishman' and not know that 'true' is an appraising word (White 1957, 319). Hence, to say that a statement is true is to say only that there is *some* standard for true statements, and that whatever that standard might be, it has been met for *this* statement. So, putting truth as appraisal into the basic formula for assertion (and hence deep-structure) theories would yield something like this:

$(t)(t$ is true $=_{syn} t$ meets the appropriate standard, whatever it is, for statements of its type)

Recall from section 1.7 that Strawson's theory would be utterly inexplicable if I had not made the kind of project distinctions I made there, in particular, if I had not distinguished the speech-act project from the metaphysical project. A similar point can be made about White's theory, for it would be utterly vacuous as an answer to the metaphysical project: it would say, in effect, the single necessary and sufficient condition for truth is that the necessary and sufficient conditions for truth be met. This gives us further evidence that we must make the kinds of project distinctions I made in chapter 1 if we are to unravel the four-dimensional confusion described there.

Note also that one could plausibly see White's theory as an answer to the illocutionary-act project instead of interpreting it, as I have, as a response to the deep-structure branch of the assertion project. That is, one could see White as claiming that to make one of the utterances in question is not to *say* anything; rather, it is to perform the *act* of appraising some statement. However, such an interpretation is arguably insufficiently charitable, since it is hard to see how one could appraise a statement *publicly* (for these are utterances, not internal thoughts) without saying something about it. Perhaps the best interpretation of all is to see White as claiming that these utterances have both a locutionary and illocutionary purpose.

10.4   F. P. Ramsey's Redundancy Theory

Invention of the redundancy theory, sometimes called the disquotational theory, is usually credited to F. P. Ramsey, although it may have its origins in remarks by Frege (1892, 64) and Hawtry (1908, 201). The claim of the redundancy theory is *not* that the predicate 'is true' *repeats* what has already been said in the sentence in which it appears. (Ramsey does not mean that 'is true' is redundant in the sense that '"Caesar was murdered" is true' says 'Caesar was murdered' *twice*.) Rather, the claim is that 'is true' is vacuous, that it says nothing at all. 'It is true that Caesar was murdered' says nothing more than 'Caesar was murdered' (Ramsey 1927, 16–17). Similarly, '"Caesar was murdered" is true' also says nothing more than 'Caesar was murdered' (1927, 16–17). So 'is true' is redundant ('gratuitous' would be a better word) relative to the resources of English as a whole because anything that can be said with it can also be said without it. Thus Ramsey seems to agree with Strawson that we are not saying something about a truth bearer when we make apparent truth ascriptions. However, unlike Strawson, he insists that when we seem to ascribe truth, we are saying *something*, not merely performing an act. We are saying precisely what we would be saying if we simply uttered the proposition itself. So if the proposition is 'Caesar was murdered', then '"Caesar was murdered" is true' does not say anything about the proposition 'Caesar was murdered'. Instead, it says something about Caesar: that he was murdered.[5] So Ramsey accepts all instances of the schema

The proposition that p is true $=_{\text{syn}} p$.

And Ramsey endorses all of what we might call *strong* T-sentences, which include

That snow is white is true $=_{\text{syn}}$ snow is white,
That grass is green is true $=_{\text{syn}}$ grass is green.

The key difference between Ramsey's strong T-sentences and Tarski's T-sentences is that the latter are about sentences and thus are only true if the equivalence sign is the extensional ' ≡ '. This again is because there are worlds where snow is white and grass is ugly but where the token 'Snow is white' is *false* because in that world it means grass is lovely. But the strong T-sentences are about *propositions*, and propositions are abstract, trans-linguistic entities that cannot possibly mean something different than they do, because they do not *mean* at all. On the contrary, a proposition is usually said, by those who believe in propositions, to *be* the meaning of the sentence that expresses it. Hence strong T-sentences can be true even with the ' =$_{syn}$ ' connector.[6]

Thus on Ramsey's view, the deep structure of an apparent truth-ascribing utterance is actually *simpler* than the surface grammar: the quotation marks and the 'is true' cancel each other out, which is why the redundancy theory is often called the disquotational theory. Even a redundancy theorist ought agree that the truth predicate is not always literally *disquotational*, because sometimes we (apparently) ascribe truth 'blindly,' that is, without actually quoting the proposition in question (Davidson 1990, 284–285). Examples of blind ascriptions are 'What Percy says is true', 'That's true', 'Everything he says is true', 'What he has *just* said is true', and 'What the Pope says is true'. (Note that the last example is ambiguous. Depending on the context, it might be synonymous with either of the two examples that immediately precede it.)

Suppose that Percy has just said that the dam collapsed, but suppose that Ralph does not know that the dam has collapsed and that Percy has just remarked on the fact. Now Ralph might very well say 'What Percy says is true'. (Exactly *why* Ralph would say it is not important. Perhaps Jim has challenged Percy's veracity and Ralph, with a depthless faith in the accuracy of Percy's pronouncements, has risen to the latter's defense.) Now what exactly would Ralph be saying? Ramsey's theory so far seems to suggest that Ralph is saying exactly the same thing Percy has said; that is, Ralph is saying 'The dam has collapsed'. But this is dubious in view of the fact that Ralph does not know what Percy has said or even that the dam has collapsed.

Ramsey is aware of the problem, and he reacts in a surprising way. For blind ascriptions he offers an entirely new theory in which 'is true' is not vacuous: to say 'Everything he says is true' is to say 'For all *a*, *R*, *b*, if he asserts *aRb*, then *aRb*'. Presumably, Ramsey would add that to say 'What

Percy just said is true' is to say 'For all a, R, b, if Percy just asserted aRb, then aRb', and to say 'That's true' is to say 'For all a, R, b, if you just asserted aRb, then aRb'.[7]

In offering this second theory, Ramsey is suggesting that 'is true' has a purpose entirely different in blind ascriptions from what it has in explicit ascriptions. The latter just say the same thing as the proposition to which they ascribe truth, but the former make a quantified, *conditional* statement about what is implied by Percy's (or whomever's) saying something. Thus, 'is true' is not vacuous (Davidson 1990, 282–283). Nevertheless, Ramsey's theory of blind truth ascriptions is a redundancy theory, since it holds that anything we can say with such an ascription can also be said without the use of 'is true'.

What would be the point of having a redundant predicate in our language? Ramsey thought its purpose was to provide us with variety in the styles we use to make assertions, but W. V. O. Quine has seen a more important use, which has been embraced by post-Ramsey redundancy theorists: the truth predicate makes it possible for us to talk about reality indirectly by talking about sentences that themselves talk about reality. Quine calls this phenomenon "semantic ascent," and he contends that it is particularly helpful in making certain kinds of generalizations:

> We can generalize on 'Tom is mortal', 'Dick is mortal', and so on, without talking of truth or of sentences; we can say 'All men are mortal'.... When on the other hand we want to generalize on 'Tom is mortal or Tom is not mortal', 'Snow is white or snow is not white', and so on, we ascend to talk of truth and of sentences, saying 'Every sentence of the form "p or not p" is true'....
>
> If we want to affirm some infinite lot of sentences that we can demarcate *only* by talking about sentences, then the truth predicate has its use. We *need* it to restore the effect of objective reference when for the sake of some generalization we have resorted to semantic ascent. (Quine 1970, 11–12; emphasis mine)

This passage is often taken as evidence that Quine endorsed the redundancy theory (e.g., Fox 1989, 176; Price 1988, 26; Grover, Camp, and Belnap 1975, 114; and Horwich 1990), and Quine 1960, 24, may be a confirmation of this attribution; but in fact Quine does not mention either Ramsey or the redundancy theory, and it is important to realize that his endorsement of Tarski's theory of truth does not per se commit him to the redundancy thesis that anything we can say with 'is true' we can say without it.[8] (The words I have italicized in the quotation suggest that Quine would deny this thesis.) Indeed, Quine's account of the usefulness of the truth predicate can be endorsed by one who believes 'is true' *also* refers to a property and, for that matter, one who has a quasi-realist or even Realist theory of that property. Indeed, a quasi realist could claim that his view gives something a redundancy theory does not give. It gives an *explanation* for why we can talk about reality indirectly by talking about the truth values of sentences. (See section 10.7 for a further discussion.)

One common objection to the redundancy theory is that there is no obvious way to generalize it; that is, there is no obvious way to turn the schema

The proposition that p is true $=_{\text{syn}} p$

into a quantified formula without quantifying over propositional variables; and quantification over propositional variables is, objectors insist, unintelligible. This is one of the technical disputes described briefly in section 4.4, and I shall not pursue it here. However, the difficulty that redundancy theorists have in generalizing their theory is just an instance of a broader problem facing the deflationary thesis, so I shall take up the issue again in section 10.7.

Referring to the distinction between syntax, semantics, and pragmatics (see section 8.2), Grover, Camp, and Belnap (1975, 79, 101) object that the redundancy theory gets the pragmatics of blind apparent truth ascriptions all wrong. There is a difference in the pragmatic force of Mary's utterances in the following two conversations:

John: Bob loves Sally.
Mary: That's true.

John: Bob loves Sally.
Mary: Bob loves Sally.

'That's true' does not simply repeat something that has just been said. It also *acknowledges* that the proposition has already been uttered. (Compare Srzednicki 1966, 388.) This does not seem to be a telling objection, however, since Ramsey's analysis of blind ascriptions such as 'That's true' is not that they simply repeat what another has said. Rather, such ascriptions say something about the implications of another's assertion: for all a, R, b, if you just asserted aRb, then aRb. So, Ramsey's analysis does at least acknowledge the possibility of an earlier utterance of the proposition in question, and it is not clear anyway that an analysis of the deep structure of the *semantics* of an utterance is required to capture its *pragmatic* force as well.

Price believes that the redundancy theory is vulnerable to the same sort of objection he made to Strawson's theory: the redundancy theory makes it a mystery why we cannot apply the truth predicate to questions and commands as well as to indicative sentences. In effect, he is suggesting that stylistic variation and semantic ascent are just as valuable with respect to interrogatives and imperatives as they are with indicatives.

10.5   C. J. F. Williams's Redundancy Theory

The earliest really detailed working out of a deflationary view was done by C. J. F. Williams. His theory can be classified as a redundancy theory, since it implies that anything we can say with the help of 'is true' can be said without it. Before I address Williams's theory, however, one problem of interpretation should be acknowledged at the outset. Although Williams is more conscientious than most in providing symbolic or partially symbolic formulas to express his theory, he clearly provides only that portion of his theory corresponding to the right-hand side of the formulas I have been using throughout this chapter, the side to the right of ' $=_{syn}$'. The left side and the connector between the two sides is embedded in the preceding text, and it is not always expressed with the same language. However, he seems to favor the construction 'To say that ... is to say that ...', which, of course, is exactly what I have been using to translate ' $=_{syn}$'.[9]

Williams recognizes that a good answer to the deep-structure project must take account of blind as well as explicit ascriptions of truth. Indeed, Williams tends to go to the other extreme in that he deals exclusively with blind ascriptions, leaving it to the reader to figure out exactly how his theory applies to explicit ascriptions (1976, xiv–xv). Williams's first, simplified version of his theory is in fact nearly identical to Ramsey's theory for blind ascriptions:

What Percy says is true $=_{syn} (\exists p)$(Percy says that p and p)[10]

He seems to suggest (pp. xii, 28) that this is equivalent to

What Percy says is true
$=_{syn} (\exists p)$(Percy's statement states that p and p).

This in turn would seem to suggest the following quantified formula, with x ranging over statements:

$(x)[x$ is true $=_{syn} (\exists p)(x$ states that p and $p)]$

On the other hand, Williams wants to deny that there really is anything that the x could be thought to range over. I shall return to this issue later. In the meantime I follow Williams in speaking only of the right side of the formula. Now it certainly *appears* that the formula

$(\exists p)(x$ states that p and $p)$

consists of a subject term, x, and a complex predicate, namely,

$(\exists p)(\underline{\quad}$ states that p and $p)$.

And this in turn would naturally lead one to conclude that 'is true' in 'x is true' is also a genuine predicate. But according to Williams, appearances are misleading in this case. If we are going to analyze ascriptions of truth, we ought to go all the way; that is, we ought to analyze them into as small a number of logical/linguistic concepts as we can. Williams believes that he can analyze these ascriptions into just three concepts: quantification, identity, and conjunction. To put it another way, Williams claims he can analyze truth ascriptions in terms of 'some', 'the same', and 'and'. Moreover, he claims that when such an analysis is made, it becomes clear that 'is true' is not a predicate and does not name a property (1976, xii, 28, 84–85).

As we saw in section 2.7, Williams's first argument to the conclusion that 'is true' is not a predicate centers on his claim that the sort of expression that can fill the blank in the last formula above cannot be a name. He points out first that 'what Percy says' in 'What Percy says is true' is like 'what the postman brought' in 'What the postman brought is on the mantel': 'What the postman brought' is not a name, because no word or string of symbols can replace it in every sentence in which it appears. Rather, it is an "incomplete symbol," like the word 'something', in that it will make a grammatically correct sentence when a predicate is appended to the end of it, but it does not name anything anymore than 'something' does. He notes also that while 'something' and 'what the postman brought' can be negated, a name (e.g., Joseph) cannot be. Hence 'what Percy says' is also an incomplete symbol, not a name (Williams 1976, xii, 33). And since it does not name anything, there is not any *thing* to which truth is being ascribed in 'What Percy says is true'. To put it another way, there is no such thing as a truth bearer. Nothing *has* the property truth, so there is no such property as truth. Thus 'is true' does not name a property. (In nominalist terms, it does not have an extension.)

I find a number of problems with this argument. First of all, note that here more than anywhere Williams's overemphasis on blind ascriptions to the exclusion of explicit ascriptions raises doubts. For surely "'The dam has collapsed'" in

'The dam has collapsed' is true

is a name. After all, this is precisely what putting quotation marks around an expression does: the quotation becomes the *name* of the expression.

Williams does not deny that apparent ascriptions of truth *do* say something more than would be said by just repeating the statement in question. They say not only that there is some p but also that somebody stated that p. What they do not do is ascribe truth to anything.

Williams has a second argument, which begins with the claim that 'What Percy says is true' says, among other things, that Percy says just one thing. Accordingly, he modifies his analysis of 'What Percy says is true' to read as follows.

$$(\exists p)(q)\{[(p = q) \equiv Jq] \text{ and } p\}$$

(I have transformed his Polish notation into the standard notation used in this book.) The 'Jq' means 'Percy says that q.' The formula reads, 'There is some p such that, for all q, q is identical to p if and only if Percy says that q, and p.' Now Williams asks us to compare this with an analysis of 'What Percy says is believed by Pauline':

$$(\exists p)(q)\{[(p = q) \equiv Jq] \text{ and } Dp\}.$$

The 'Dp' here means 'p is believed by Pauline.' In this case the 'D' corresponds to the predicate 'believed by Pauline', so the rest of the formula,

$$(\exists p)(q)\{[(p = q) \equiv Jq] \text{ and } \underline{\quad} p\},$$

must correspond to 'what Percy says'. But note that the entire symbolized analysis of 'What Percy says is true',

$$(\exists p)(q)\{[(p = q) \equiv Jq] \text{ and } p\},$$

is identical to what stands for 'what Percy says' in the analysis of 'What Percy says is believed by Pauline' except that the gap has been closed up. So while 'D' is present in the one case to correspond to the predicate 'believed by Pauline', there is *nothing* in the analysis of 'What Percy says is true' to correspond to the phrase 'is true'. Therefore, he concludes, 'is true' is not a predicate.[11]

Williams recognizes that anyone claiming that 'is true' is not a genuine predicate owes us an explanation of why we have such a phrase in our language in the first place. Williams's own explanation is that the phrase 'is true' has the form of a predicate, but not the substance. It is used to make a complete sentence out of 'what Percy says', and this is all it does. The rules of English require a predicate, or at least something with the *form* of a predicate, in every sentence. So 'is true' allows us to reaffirm "blindly" what someone else has said without violating the requirement that one speak in complete sentences. Thus 'is true' gives 'What Percy says is true' the *structure* of a complete sentence without giving it the *content* of a complete sentence. It has the form of a predicate, but it is not any *particular* predicate (Williams 1976, 47). Thus, on Williams's view, 'What Percy says is true' is the linguistic equivalent of an optical illusion: it appears to be a name concatenated to a predicate; but in reality *it contains neither a name nor a predicate*. It is an incomplete symbol concatenated to a sort of generic predicate form. (But Williams does not think the utterance is just an illocutionary act. It does *say*, among other things, that there is some p such that Percy says that p.)

Let me note that Williams makes one last revision in his formula (1976, 61–73), motivated by his belief that 'What Percy says is true' asserts two things: first, 'Percy says just one thing' and, second, 'For all r, if Percy says that r, then r'. So the final version of Williams's theory is

What Percy says is true $=_{\text{syn}} \{(\exists p)(q)[(p = q) \equiv Jq] \, \& \, (r)(Jr \supset r)\}$,

where the predicate symbol 'J' means 'Percy says that'.

But the above formula is only an analysis of one particular (apparent) truth ascription, namely, 'What Percy says is true.' If there is no way for Williams to give a *general* account of apparent truth ascriptions, then he is saying, in effect, that there is a different account for each of the infinite number of potential apparent truth ascriptions. So can there be a Williams-like general theory for all (apparent) truth ascriptions? Suppose we tried this:

$$(x)(x \text{ is true} =_{syn} \{(\exists p)(q)[(p = q) \equiv xJq] \& (r)(xJr \supset r)\}),$$

where 'J' is now a two-place predicate meaning 'states that'. But this use of the x is incompatible with Williams's theory, for the x must range over *something*, whether it be statements or sentences or whatever. Yet according to Williams, *nothing* bears truth. *Nothing* is the object of truth ascriptions. Suppose, then, we try use a variable ranging over whole truth ascriptions:

$$(a)(a =_{syn} \{(\exists p)(q)[(p = q) \equiv Jq] \& (r)(Jr \supset r)\}).$$

This would translate as 'For all truth ascriptions a, to say that a is to say that, etc.' But what could 'J' mean in this formula? Surely not 'the statement to which a ascribes truth states that', for again, this implies that truth ascriptions ascribe the property of truth to statements, and Williams's claim is that they do not. It seems, then, that Williams's insistence that there is just nothing that bears truth insures that he cannot have a *general* theory of what truth ascriptions say. Each blind ascription will have to have its own analysis, with 'J' meaning something slightly different in each. For 'What Percy says is true' the 'J' will mean 'Percy says that', while for 'What the Pope says is true' the 'J' will mean 'the Pope says that'.

It is also not clear how a Williams-like analysis could be formulated for explicit truth ascriptions. In the formula

$$\text{'Snow is white' is true} =_{syn} \{(\exists p)(q)[(p = q) \equiv Jq] \& (r)(Jr \supset r)\},$$

'J' presumably means '"Snow is white" says that'. But there is a curious lack of parallelism here. In the other formulas it was *people* who said things. Here it is a sentence or statement that says something.

10.6 The Prosentential Theory of Truth

When a pronoun picks up the reference of an antecedent, as 'she' does in 'Mary loved Dad, but she hated Mom', it is said to be anaphoric to its antecedent, in this case 'Mary'. English also contains proverbs, such as the 'did' in 'Mary ran quickly, Bill did too' and the 'do' in 'Dance as we do'. There are also proadjectives, like 'such' in 'The happy man was no longer such', and proadverbs, like 'so' in 'she twitched violently, and while so twitching, expired'.

Following up on an idea from Brentano 1904, Grover, Camp, and Belnap suggest that there is such a thing as a prosentence. 'So' is sometimes used this way. It is so used, for example, in 'I think so' and 'I do not believe Rachel is sick, but if so, she should stay home' (Grover, Camp, and Belnap 1975, 88, 91). More to the immediate point, they contend that the phrases 'it is true' and 'that is true', despite their subject-predicate structure, are really prosentences (p. 82). They explain the use of 'it is true' and 'that is true' on analogy with a language just like English, save that it contains the atomic prosentence 'thatt' (they do not claim that English itself has this term even in its deep structure). 'Thatt' is always an anaphor for some antecedent (pp. 88–89). Just as the pronoun 'she' can simply take the place of its antecedent, as it does in 'Mary loved Dad, but she hated Mom', so too 'thatt' can simply take the place of its antecedent, as it does in the following conversations:

John: Snow is white.
Mary: Thatt

Bill: There are people on Mars.
Susan: If thatt, then we should see signs of life soon.

But the relation of anaphora is often more complicated than mere substitution. Consider, for example, the quantificational use of 'its' in 'Every dog has its day'. Obviously we cannot substitute 'every dog' for 'its'. By the same token, there are quantificational uses of 'thatt' in our imaginary language:

For every proposition, either thatt or not thatt.
For every proposition, if John says that thatt, then thatt.

Grover, Camp, and Belnap contend that 'it is true' and 'that is true' function in English exactly in the way that 'thatt' functions in the imaginary language. Each of these phrases should be holistically thought of as a prosentence. The 'it' and 'that' in such phrases has no independent meaning. Neither does 'is true', so it is not a genuine predicate in its prosentential use.

All well and good, but we use 'is true' outside of the phrases 'it is true' and 'that is true'. So, even granted for the sake of argument that the latter phrases are prosentences, what about uses of 'is true' other than the prosentential use? Actually, Grover, Camp, and Belnap answer, there are no such other uses. All expressions in which 'is true' appears outside of one of the two prosentences have a misleading surface grammar. In the deep structure of any sentence with the seemingly separable predicate 'is true', that predicate appears only in one or the other of the two prosentences (p. 83). For example, the deep structure of 'Everything John says is true' is 'For every proposition, if John says that *it is true*, then *it is true*', where the 'it is true' should be thought of as a unit, on analogy with 'thatt' in the imaginary language. Similarly, the deep structure of 'Goldbach's conjecture is true' is 'There is a unique proposition such that Goldbach conjectured that it is true and it is true'.[12] The deep structure of the explicit apparent ascription '"Snow is white" is true' is 'Consider: snow is white. That is true' (p. 103).

Thus Grover, Camp, and Belnap believe that *as a separable predicate* 'is true' can be eliminated from English. But they do not believe that 'it is true' or 'that is true' can be eliminated, so they do not believe that we can say without 'is true' anything we can say with it. Thus, theirs is not a redundancy theory (p. 101). They do, however, subscribe to the deflationary thesis, since they contend that 'is true' is not a genuine predicate (pp. 107, 119). On the contrary, they say, it is always a fragment of a prosentence (p. 83).

Why, then, is the anaphoric nature of 'is true' not reflected in our surface grammar? Why, that is, do we seem to have the separable predicate 'is true' in our surface grammar, and why are our prosentences broken up into three words instead expressed with just 'thatt', as in the imaginary language? Because, they answer, we express so many things in English with the subject-predicate form, it is convenient to put other things in this form as well. Thus the complex 'For every proposition, if John says that it is true, then it is true' gets squeezed down to 'Everything John says is true'. Moreover, having nonatomic prosentences makes them easier to modify. We can modify the tense, as in 'That will be true', the mood, as is 'That might be true', or we can negate, as in 'That is not true' (pp. 96, 99–100).

This raises the question of how modified uses of 'is true' are to be analyzed on the prosentential theory. Grover, Camp, and Belnap postulate that the deep structure of English contains a number of sentential operators including 'It-was-true-that', 'It-will-be-true-that', 'It-might-be-true-that', and 'It-is-not-true-that'. Armed with these, they can analyze all modified uses of 'is true' as having a deep structure involving one or the other of the two prosentences within the scope of one of these operators. Thus the deep structure of 'Everything John says will be true' is 'For all propositions, if John says that it is true, then it-will-be-true-that it is true', where, again, the 'it is true' is a prosentence. To analyze apparent predications of falsehood, they postulate the operator 'It-is-false-that'. Thus the deep structure of 'That's false' is 'It-is-false-that that is true', where 'that is true' is a prosentence (p. 95).

As the reader might have guessed, the prosentential account of modified uses of 'is true' (and of uses of 'is false') raises what is perhaps the most serious objection to the prosentential theory. Specifically, 'true' appears in the sentential operators that the theory postulates, and it is not easy to see how it is going to be analyzed so that it does not turn out to refer to a property of truth. If a prosentential analysis of these operators were possible, there would have been no need to postulate them in the first place. Nor can Grover, Camp, and Belnap declare that the operators are vacuous, as Ramsey declares that the operator 'It is true that' is vacuous, because that move would make 'It-is-false-that that is true' say no more than 'It is true', and thus 'That's false' would be synonymous with 'That's true'! It does no good to point out that these operators are deep-structure entities (p. 97), for that in no sense either explains the meaning of the word 'true' where it appears in them or moots the need for such an explanation. Grover, Camp, and Belnap's use of hyphens to connect the words of the operators suggests that they want these operators to be thought of holistically, as though each were a single word. That is, they want to insist that the 'true' in these operators has no more independent meaning than the 'ti' in 'holistically'. But this suggestion does not look promising, for it is not at all clear how we could explain the meanings of these one-word operators without using a substantive notion of truth, and even if we could, our explanations of such one-word operators would miss out entirely on the common element in the meanings of, say, 'It-will-be-true-that' and 'It-was-true-that'.

Another objection to the prosentential theory is that other predicates applied to propositions, such as 'is surprising', 'is profound', and 'is exaggerated', seem to be genuine predicates, so the prosentential theory makes 'is true' implausibly unparallel with these other predicates. Grover, Camp, and Belnap respond that while these predicates are genuine, they are *not* applicable to propositions, or statements, or sentences. They are applicable to *acts of stating* (pp. 104 ff.). Thus, on their view, what is surprising when John tells me I've won a million dollars in the lottery is not *what he said* but rather *that he said it*. This is not a very plausible answer, however, especially with regard to the predicate 'is profound': Einstein's act of writing down the theory of relativity is not profound. What is profound is the theory itself, the propositions that make it up. Also, Forbes (1986, 35–37) notes genuine predicates that simply make no sense if applied to acts instead of propositions. e.g., 'is inconsistent with Goldbach's Conjecture'.

10.7 The Deflationary Thesis

We have encountered the deflationary thesis only briefly so far. It is time now to give it a more complete treatment, beginning with some clarifications, elaborations, and methodological recommendations.

1. Of the various theories intended to fulfill one or another subdivision of the speech-act project that we have surveyed, all but White's has been married by its author to the deflationary thesis.[13] It should not be surprising that this is so. While *linguistics* eventually wants an analysis of the locutionary and illocutionary purposes of every expression in every language, the analysis of particular expressions is of interest to *philosophers* only where there is hope that such an analysis either will reveal the answer to some metaphysical, epistemological, moral, or other philosophical question or will reveal that the question itself is based on a confusion about language and hence that there really is no issue concerning it. If a philosopher did not think either that an analysis of 'is true' would show that it is not a genuine predicate (and thus that the whole of the metaphysical project is based on a confusion about language) or that such analysis would reveal the answer to the metaphysical project, then he or she would see little point in offering such an analysis in the first place.

2. As Michael Williams has pointed out (1986, 224, 240), it is a mistake to identify the deflationary thesis with the truth-as-justification thesis.[14] Indeed, it is self-contradictory to do so: if truth is not a property at all, then it certainly is not an epistemic property.

3. It is also inadvisable simply to equate, inadvertently or by stipulation, the deflationary thesis with some particular theory fulfilling the speech-

act project, as Forbes (1986, 29) and Vision (1988, 40, 114) do in equating it with the redundancy theory. One can consistently endorse almost any of these accounts of the *use* of 'is true' and still insist that 'is true' is a genuine predicate (which, for a nominalist would mean insisting that it has an extension and, for an platonist, insisting that it names a property). One could hold, for example, that 'is true' is sometimes used to name a property and othertimes used merely to signal agreement, assert something in a stylish way, generalize over sentences via semantic ascent, and/or anaphorically pick up the meaning of an antecedent. Alternatively, one could hold that 'is true' always, or at least sometimes, *simultaneously* names a property and signals agreement (asserts something in a stylish way, etc.). For that matter, one could hold that truth is a property but the human predicament is such that we never need to refer to that property with a predicate and thus 'is true' is *only* used to signal agreement (assert in a stylish way, etc.). The latter position would be implausible but not logically inconsistent. What all this, especially the last example, shows is that one can reject the claim that 'is true' is *used* to name a property (or refer to an extension) and still believe that there *is* a property of truth (or that it has an extension). One needs an additional premise to get from one of these illocutionary or deep-structure theories to the deflationary thesis.

4. The extra premise needed, as noted in sections 2.7 and 10.1, is a principle of philosophical method: one ought postulate all and only such entities as one needs to postulate in order to explain the various syntactic and semantic features of our language. As Vision points out (1988, 121–123 & 117), this principle is never made explicit by deflationists. But if we do not attribute it to them, there simply is not anywhere in the literature anything that can be called an argument for the deflationary thesis (as distinct from attempts to rebut antideflationist arguments). It is not surprising that this key principle is left implicit in deflationist accounts, for two reasons. First, the principle is so ubiquitous in twentieth-century philosophy that it has come to be taken for granted. Second, when it is made explicit like this, it is plain that the principle is false. We want to explain a lot more than just *linguistic* phenomena: the syntax and semantics of our language. We want to explain all manner of natural and philosophical phenomena as well. That's why we have other disciplines besides linguistics. (See section 2.7 for an example of an ontological issue that *can* be dissolved via

linguistic analysis alone.) Some recent deflationists have come to see that a more reasonable principle would be that one ought to postulate all and only such entities as one needs to postulate to create the most general and elegant explanatory view of the world. But, of course, in conjunction with this principle we would need more than just a showing that our use of 'is true' does not require that we postulate a property of truth. We would need to show that there is *nothing* we cannot explain without postulating such a property.

5. M. Williams indicates (1986, 228, 240) that the burden is on those who oppose the deflationary thesis to give us a reason why we should think that 'is true' is a genuine predicate, but whether or not Williams meant it, this is a view that cannot be taken seriously, for the reason given in section 10.2: it presupposes as the relevant dialectical principle that we should assume that a predicate is not genuine until given a reason to think it is. And that principle in turn implies, given the present undeveloped state of semantics, that right now it is rational for us to believe the contradiction that *most* predicates are not genuine predicates. Since, by definition, most predicates are genuine, the proper principle is that we ought to assume a predicate is genuine unless given good reason to think otherwise.

Having laid out the course and specified the rules with (1) to (5), I turn now to the contest proper. We know from (5) how the game *ought* to be played: the antideflationist ought to sit back and wait for deflationists to make an argument for the deflationary thesis and then attempt to refute it. Specifically, from (4), antideflationists should wait for an argument to the effect that (in platonist terms) there is nothing whose explanation requires the postulation of a property of truth. That is pretty much the way things have gone with regard to linguistic phenomena, specifically, our use of 'is true': deflationists have offered theories that show 'is true' to be eliminable (at *least* as a separable predicate), and antideflationists have tried to find flaws in those accounts. Strangely, with regard to nonlinguistic, especially epistemic, phenomena, deflationists have behaved as though the burden were on the antideflationists to show that this or that cannot be explained without the concept of truth, and antideflationists have let them get away with it. I shall look at a couple of antideflationist proposals along these lines and at how deflationists have responded, but it should be remembered throughout what follows that even if antideflationists cannot identify a phenomenon whose explanation requires that we take 'is true' as a genuine predicate, the most we can conclude is that *so far* no one has yet identified such a phenomenon. (And even that conclusion will not follow unless there is some answer to the speech-act project that holds that apparent truth ascriptions are not really truth ascriptions, and that can resolve the objections made to it.) What would *not* follow is that 'is true' is not a genuine predicate. Again, for that conclusion, the deflationists must make a positive argument of their own.

The most common antideflationist proposal is that we need the concept of truth to explain the success of our theories and beliefs. For example, the theory that nothing goes faster than light works because it is true, and my belief that I should turn left out of my driveway instead of right helps me succeed in getting to work because it is true. Unfortunately, this way of putting the proposal invites easy responses from deflationists. Instead of explanations like 'The theory that nothing goes faster than light works because it is true', we could have explanations like 'The theory that nothing goes faster than light works because nothing goes faster than light'.[15] Of course, this is no answer to the antideflationist's demand for a *general* explanation of the success of our beliefs. Presumably, the deflationist explanation of this would be along the lines suggested by Huw Price (1988, 139-141): we are successful because for most p, if we believe that p, then p. But this raises again the controversy about quantification over propositional variables. It is worth a digression to take a look at that controversy more closely.

In the literature, the issue is usually narrowly described as a problem confronting the redundancy theory: the latter endorses all sentences instantiating the schema

The proposition that p is true $=_{syn} p$.

So even if we put blind ascriptions to one side, it appears that the redundancy theory will be an infinitely long conjunction unless we can find a way to generalize it, and as we saw in section 10.4, that would appear to require quantifying over the 'p'. (Recall from section 10.5 that C. J. F. Williams's account, which deals exclusively with blind ascriptions, also uses quantification over propositional variables.[16]) But now we can see that the problem of generalizing the redundancy theory is just one more instance of a broader problem confronting deflationism. The deflationist has a lot to explain without using 'is true' as a genuine predicate. One of those things is the success of our beliefs, another is how we use the phrase 'is true'. In either case, if he follows Ramsey's or C. J. F. Williams's strategy, he sooner or later must confront the problem of making certain kinds of generalizations, precisely the kind for which Quine thought we *need* the predicate 'is true'. (See section 10.4.) But the deflationist must make these generalizations without using 'is true'. (More accurately, he must do it without using 'is true' as a separable predicate, as Grover, Camp, and Belnap would remind us.) There are other places where the deflationist will confront the same problem. For example, at some point he'll need to explain our use of the noun 'truth' as it figures in such generalizations as 'Truth is sometimes stranger than fiction' and 'The search for the truth is always a noble venture'.

Before we see why quantification over propositional variables is controversial, let us take a quick look at five ways in which a deflationist might try to make the generalizations needed without quantifying over propositional variables in a controversial way.[17] First, suppose we just use ordinary object variables to range over propositions. In that case, 'Truth is sometimes stranger than fiction' (on one interpretation of its meaning) would come out as

$(\exists x)(\exists y)[(x$ is true and y is false) and x is stranger than $y]$.

But this, of course, doesn't eliminate the concept of truth, since 'is true' is present. Suppose, then (a second strategy), we invent a language just like English except that it has the prosentence 'thatt' in it. Then we can express Price's explanation of successful beliefs with the following:

Our beliefs are successful because, for most propositions, if the organism believes that thatt, then thatt.

But as Grover, Camp, and Belnap would be the first to insist, expressing the problematic generalizations in another language is of little help unless we can understand all the expressions of that other language without the use of the concept of truth, and it is not clear that we can understand 'thatt' without thinking of it as a translation of 'that is true', where 'is true' is a separable, genuine predicate (Forbes 1986, 37).

A third strategy by which a deflationist might seek to evade quantification over propositional variables, recommended by Grover, Camp, and Belnap, would require that deflationism abandon the attempt to entirely get rid of 'is true'. Instead, they would say, the deflationist can do something that is every bit as good. He can explain all he needs to explain, and make the generalizations he needs to make, without ever using 'is true' as a separately meaningful predicate. If we postulate that 'that is true' and 'it is true' are prosentences, then we can make these generalizations so that 'is true' turns out to be, in and of itself, a meaningless fragment of a prosentence. On this strategy, Price's explanation of the success of our beliefs would be expressed just as above, except that the non-English 'thatt' is replaced with the English prosentence 'that is true'. But we already saw in section 10.6 that this third strategy cannot account for generalizations requiring tensed or otherwise modified uses of 'is true' without postulating such propositional operators as 'it-was-true-that', and it is not clear how we can understand such operators without a substantial notion of truth. Also, the prosentential account makes 'is true' implausibly imparallel with predicates like 'is profound'.

The fourth and fifth strategies to which the deflationist might resort both involve what is called the substitutional interpretation of quantification. We saw in section 2.1 that, on the ordinary interpretation of quantifiers (called the objectual interpretation when it is being contrasted with the substitutional interpretation), the variables in a sentence such as

$(x)(x$ howls at night)

range over objects and the sentence says that every one of those objects howls at night. On the substitutional interpretation, however, the variables do not really range over anything, or, in an extended and loose sense of 'range', they range over *names* of objects. And what the sentence says is 'For every name in the language, if we substitute the name for the "x" in "x howls at night," we produce a true sentence'. The difference between the two interpretations can be important. Suppose that our universe of discourse includes five objects and, of these, only four have names and only these four howl at night. Then the sentence above will be false on the objectual interpretation but true on the substitutional interpretation (since what unnamed objects do or do not do is irrelevant on the substitutional interpretation).

Both the fourth and fifth strategies suggest that the deflationist can express the problematic generalizations by quantifying over propositional variables and yet avoid the usual problems of such quantification (see below) by interpreting the quantifiers substitutionally. So if we use the little subscript 'sub' on our quantifiers to indicate that they are to be substitutionally interpreted, then we can generalize, say, Ramsey's schema as

$(p)_{sub}$(the proposition that p is true $=_{syn} p$).

What exactly does this say? On the usual reading of substitutional quantifiers, which is what the fourth strategy recommends, it reads, 'For each sentence in the language, if we substitute the sentence for the "p" in "the proposition that p is true $=_{syn} p$", then we produce a *true* sentence'. But this is of no help to the deflationist, because it does not eliminate 'true'. The fifth strategy attempts to remedy this by offering an alternate reading of the preceding quantified statement. We should take the statement as just shorthand for an infinitely long conjunction:

The proposition that snow is white is true $=_{syn}$ snow is white,
and the proposition that snow is green is true $=_{syn}$ snow is green,
and the proposition that grass is green is true $=_{syn}$ grass is green,
and the proposition that John loves Mary is true $=_{syn}$ John loves Mary,
etc.

But this strategy at least arguably misses the whole point of generalization and quantification. We need to express in a finite number of symbols ideas that would otherwise be inexpressible, and we need our finite expression of such an idea to be graspable by our finite minds. The fifth strategy does give us a finite expression of Ramsey's theory, but it cannot give an explanation of what that expression means in a way that is graspable by finite minds. The 'etc.' merely gestures toward something graspable only by an infinite mind (Forbes 1986, 34–35).

It seems, then, that the deflationist will have to use objectually interpreted quantification over propositional variables to make the generalizations in question. For example, 'Truth is sometimes stranger than fiction' will have to be expressed as:

$(\exists p)(\exists q)[(p \ \& \ \text{not} \ q) \ \& \ p \ \text{is stranger than} \ q]$.

We noted some of the problems with this sort of quantification in section 4.4. The most important is that it appears that 'p' is being used as two distinctly different kinds of variables in the formula. Where it appears as a complete conjunct by itself, it seems to have the character of a grammatically complete clause, but where it appears concatenated to the predicate 'is stranger than', it seems to have the character of a name needing completion by a predicate.[18]

Let me end the digression on the problems of deflationism with these generalizations and return to the question of whether there is any kind of phenomena whose explanation requires the use of 'is true' as a genuine predicate.

We were considering how a deflationist would explain the success of our beliefs. A more aggressive and very common deflationist response would be to deny that there is anything here that needs explaining: I have the belief that I should turn left out of my driveway because that belief has worked in the past. And in general, we have the beliefs we do because they work. One doesn't need to explain why s got x when s intended to get x (e.g., M. Williams 1986, 228).

But this is not an adequate response to the question. After all, s fails all too often to get what she sets out after, so when success is attained, we need to say more to explain how she did it than just 'She intended to'. A partial explanation for why my car functions well is that I intend that it work well and take steps to ensure that it does. But notice that this does not preclude the need for a further explanation in terms of internal combustion, forces, gases, etc. By analogy, then, we need to say something about the *properties* of s's beliefs to complete our explanation of why they work.

Leeds (1978, 117) has a better deflationist response. We can explain the success of our beliefs in terms of properties *other than truth*. Specifically, Leeds says that our beliefs are successful because they have a great deal of predictive power; they help us to know what to expect in given situations and what sort of outcome we'll get in response to a given manipulation of a chunk of the world. Why our beliefs have predictive power could presumably be explained in Darwinian terms: the evolutionary process favors organisms capable of forming beliefs (mental states) that entail other beliefs of the form 'If I manipulate such and such objects in such and such a manner, then such and such will occur'. This is not quite right, because organisms with *false* beliefs of this sort are not favored. So perhaps we must specify that organisms with true beliefs of the form in question are the favored ones, in which case we must rely on truth in our explanation after all. But we can reform the Darwinian explanation without mentioning truth, by specifying that the favored organisms are those caused to *abandon* a belief of the sort at issue whenever, having brought about the antecedent, they do not get the kind of sensory input that would be caused by the state of affairs described by the consequent.

In section 2.1, I argued that epistemologists need an answer to the metaphysical project in order to evaluate answers to the justification project; that is, they need a substantial concept of truth to evaluate theoriès of justification. Thus section 2.1 provides, in effect, another antideflationist suggestion of a program for which we need a substantial notion of truth. (And section 2.2 can be seen as an argument that it is not possible to use the concept of justification in place of the concept of truth in this program.) It would be possible to rewrite section 2.1 in such a way that the traditional epistemological program is seen to be an *explanatory* program, but let me not waste time doing that. Under either description, the deflationist must deal with the suggestion that a substantial notion of truth is needed in the epistemological program.[19]

Stephen Leeds and M. Williams are the only deflationists who consider this second programmatic need for a substantial concept of truth. In a paper entitled "Do We (Epistemologists) Need a Theory of Truth?" Williams responds to the suggestion that we need truth in the traditional epistemological enterprise by in effect declaring that we ought to just assume that skepticism is wrong and thus assume that the epistemological enterprise of *showing* it is wrong (described in section 2.1) is unneeded. Hence, skepticism cannot be a source of any *need* for a notion of truth as a property (or, in nominalist terms, any *need* for 'is true' as a genuine predicate) (M. Williams 1986, 234–236). Now the view that we ought to abandon the traditional epistemological enterprise described in section 2.1 is not without its adherents, but it is not a view we ought to accept without good reason. Specifically, we ought to insist on a non-question-begging argument to the conclusion that it is permissible to beg the question against skepticism. Chisholm (1973) has unsuccessfully tried to provide such an argument. No one else has even tried. In the meantime, those who still adhere to the traditional picture of epistemology's task are entitled to believe that Williams has shown that epistemologists do not need a theory of truth only by assuming that there is no need for epistemology, or for epistemologists!

Unlike Williams, Leeds takes the traditional epistemological program seriously, and he concurs, for essentially the reasons I gave in section 2.2, that we cannot define truth in terms of justification (1978, 126). Yet he remains a deflationist, apparently because he thinks that the need òf the epistemological program for a substantial notion of truth depends on the false assumption that either our methods of justification do not change at all in light of our changing beliefs about the rest of the world or they change in a way that is *completely* determined by the changes in our beliefs about the rest of the world (1978, 126–127). But antideflationism needs no such assumption. A given individual's current theory of justification will depend on

1. his current, substantial notion of truth,
2. his current beliefs about what properties of beliefs correlate with the property of truth,
3. his current beliefs about how easy or difficult it is for a human to apprehend, for each property referred to in (2), whether or not a given belief has the property (see section 1.7),
4. how efficient he is at making inferences from (1), (2), and (3) to a theory of justification.

An antideflationist is quite at home with the claim that the individual's theory of justification may change in response to changes in (2) or (3). And the antideflationist is equally comfortable with the idea that an individual's theory of justification will sometimes change even when (2) and (3) and for that matter (4) remain unchanged, because the antideflationist has no reason to deny that (1) can change. His view is that we need *some* substantial notion of truth in the epistemological program, but he is not, *qua* antideflationist, committed to any particular answer to the metaphysical project. There are places where Leeds seems to assume that his antagonists are committed to at least the generic class of correspondence-as-congruence theories (e.g., 1978, 122), but in fact, antideflationists are not even committed to quasi-realist theories.

Although I have contended that the burden of proof is on deflationism, let me end this section on the deflationary thesis with an argument by S. Korner (1955) to the conclusion that 'is true' must be a genuine predicate. The argument rests on a principle that Korner believes is implicit in the work of Immanuel Kant: X is a genuine predicate if and only if X is incompatible with some Y that Y is indisputably a genuine predicate. Kant argues that 'exists' is not a genuine predicate because there is no indisputably genuine predicate such that it would be contradictory to apply both 'exists' and that other predicate to the same object. None of the following, for example, would be contradictory when applied to the same object, 'is a lion and exists', 'is a lion and does not exist', 'is a unicorn and exists', and 'is a unicorn and does not exist'. (Note that it is not part of the meaning of 'lion' that lions exist or part of the meaning of 'unicorn' that unicorns don't.) But Korner claims that there is an indisputably genuine predicate that cannot be consistently conjoined with 'is true'. If 'X' is the name of some sentence, then, he says, the following is self-contradictory:

X is true but not theoretically appropriate,

where 'theoretically appropriate' means roughly 'grammatical'. Apparently, Korner is appealing to the intuition that a meaningless sentence doesn't say anything true (or false) because it doesn't *say* anything at all. But it seems that a sentence could be mildly ungrammatical and still be meaningful and true. To skip over a lot of steps, I think a search for the kind of predicate Korner is looking for would eventually lead us to

X is true and unintelligible even to an omniscient and maximally intelligent being.

Even if it is possible for a sentence to be true but unintelligible to any human being, it does seem impossible that it could be true (or false) if it is unintelligible to a being that can make sense of anything that can be made sense of. And unlike such predicates as 'meaningless', 'senseless', or 'contradictory', whose genuineness *might* be disputed by some, I do not believe anyone would dispute the genuineness of 'intelligible' or any modified version of it (although there would be a great deal of dispute over just what sort of property intelligibility is, e.g., physical or nonphysical).

10.8   Paul Horwich's Minimalist Answer to the Metaphysical Project

I end the book with a return to the metaphysical project. Paul Horwich's minimalist theory, as he calls it, has been called a redundancy theory, but while he has been strongly influenced by deflationism, he is neither a redundancy theorist nor a deflationist himself.[20] On the contrary, Horwich makes it quite clear that he thinks truth is a property and that the minimalist theory is a theory of what truth is (1990, 38). Specifically, it is, in the terminology of this book, an answer to the essence project.[21] I have postponed discussion of his theory till now only because, for reasons that will become clear, it is easier to understand in light of my discussion of the speech-act project.

The minimal theory (MT) cannot be stated, according to Horwich (1990, 12), because it is infinitely long. It can, however, be described as the conjunction of all sentences instantiating the following schema:

The proposition that $p \Leftrightarrow p$

(See section 1.4 for an explanation of the symbol '$\Leftrightarrow$'.) Thus, a portion of MT is:

The proposition that quarks exist is true $\Leftrightarrow$ quarks exist
and the proposition that lying is bad is true $\Leftrightarrow$ lying is bad
and etc.

Three points about MT: First, these conjuncts are true even with the relatively strong connector '$\Leftrightarrow$' because propositions are the truth bearers, not sentences. (See section 10.4.) Second, to highlight his belief that we do not need separate answers to the essence project for different kinds of discourse (see section 3.8), Horwich deliberately used as examples a sentence about a theoretical entity and a moral sentence (1990, 5). Third, MT is meant to apply to more than just the propositions expressible in English or even just the propositions expressible in any actual language. It is meant to apply to every proposition expressible in *some* language in *some* possible world (Horwich 1990, 19 n. 4). So some of the conjuncts in MT are not actually expressible, which is another reason why the theory cannot be completely expressed (Horwich 1990, 21).

Why does Horwich insist that MT must be an infinite conjunction? For essentially the same reasons that deflationists have difficulty making generalizations: there seems to be no way to generalize MT with a finite statement without quantifying over propositional variables. Specifically, Horwich thinks, there is no way to do it without using substitutional quantification over propositional variables. But for Horwich, the whole point of having a truth predicate is that it enables us to do without substitutional quantification.

The truth predicate exists solely for the sake of a certain logical need. On occasion we wish to adopt some attitude towards a proposition—for example, believing it, assuming it for the sake of argument, or desiring that it be the case—but find ourselves thwarted by ignorance of what exactly the proposition is. We might know it only as 'what Oscar thinks' or 'Einstein's principle'; ... or ... we may wish to cover infinitely many propositions (in the course of generalizing) and simply cannot have all of them in mind. In such situations the concept of truth is invaluable. For it enables the construction of another proposition, intimately related to the one we cannot identify, which is perfectly appropriate as the alternative object of our attitude. (Horwich 1990, 2–3)

The alternate propositions are blind ascriptions, such as 'What Oscar thinks is true' and 'Einstein's principle is true'. If our language allowed substitutional quantification with propositional variables, then we could use them to express these alternate propositions. For example, 'What Oscar thinks is true' could be expressed as

$(p)_{sub}$(if Oscar thinks that p, then p).[22]

Thus the usefulness of 'is true' is precisely that it allows us to have a language that is simpler than it would otherwise be. It allows us to have a language without the complications of substitutional quantification over propositional variables (Horwich 1990, 4 n. 1, 32–33). (Recall from section 10.7 that a substitutionally quantified statement cannot be understood without reference to the concept of truth. This was a problem for deflationists because they claimed that substitutional quantification allows us to do without 'is true'. But this is not a problem for Horwich, because he is claiming the opposite: 'is true' allows us to do without substitutional quantification.)

Herein lies the reason that Horwich thinks an infinite conjunction is all the theory we need: A speaker does not need a finite, general theory of truth to use the truth predicate in the manner described. Simply knowing that, *whatever* proposition p Oscar is thinking about, there is a conjunct in the theory saying 'The proposition that p is true if and only if p' is enough to allow the speaker to use 'What Oscar thinks is true' as an alternate proposition to p. It is not necessary that the speaker know what p is. It is not even necessary that p be expressible in any actual language.

But, as we saw in the previous section, there do *seem* to be other purposes for which we need a theory of truth in addition to its use in identifying appropriate alternative propositions. There is the task of explaining the success of our beliefs, and there is the epistemological program. Then too there are the programs mentioned earlier in this book. The program of constructing a semantics, or model theory, for quantified logic, the physicalist program of reducing semantic terminology to scientifically respectable terminology, the Davidson Program of constructing a theory of meaning for a natural language in terms of truth conditions. It becomes necessary, therefore, for Horwich to argue for each of these programs either that it is a bogus program to begin with, or that it can be successfully carried out with an infinite and not completely expressible theory of truth. He takes what is essentially the bogus program strategy for the physicalist and Davidson programs. I shall not review his arguments thereto, since the viability of those programs has already been discussed in this book. With regard to the others, Horwich's task becomes parallel, but not identical with, the task of deflationists. Whereas they needed to show that the programs in question can be carried out without any answer at all to the metaphysical project in any of its branches, Horwich has the somewhat easier task of showing that they can be carried out with no more of an answer at our disposal than MT.

Before we see Horwich's general strategy for arguing that MT is all we need, let me give a quick example of MT in action. Field has argued (contra deflationists) that we need to postulate a property of truth to explain the success of our beliefs and theories. Moreover, he argues that the explanations in question require something as substantial as a correspondence theory of truth. A theory as minimal as Horwich's would not do. His argument comes down to this: If we want to explain why one batsman is more successful than another and we know a great deal about cricket, then we do not need truth in our explanation. For example, since we know that a batsman should do action A in circumstances C and A' in C', etc., then we can explain the batsman's success by saying "Because he believes he ought to do A in C and A' in C' and, etc." There is no need to mention truth. But what if we do not know much about cricket? Then we do not know what it is that the batsman believes that leads to his success. We only know that there's *something* he believes that leads to his success. So we must use the concept of truth in our explanation. We must say, that is, something like "Because he has *true* beliefs about what to do in C and C' and, etc." (Field 1986, 93–99). Why can't the concept of truth used in the preceding explanation be minimal truth? Because, according to Field, minimal truth is only defined for sentences of the languages the speaker understands. I can give no sense to 'is (minimally) true' when predicated of a sentence I do not understand or when predicated of a thought state of a person whose language I do not understand. According to Field, '"p" is true iff p' is no more understandable than 'p' is (1986, 58, 79 ff.). Horwich would admit that minimal truth is not defined for languages we do not understand in the sense that we cannot express the clauses of MT for sentences (thought states) in such languages. But that, he would insist, is not necessary. We can *describe* the theory so that we know for any thought state p, even one we do not understand and can refer to only as 'what Smithson thinks about cricket', there is a clause somewhere in the theory saying 'p is true iff p'. So the 'true' in the explanation "Because what Smithson believes about cricket is true" can so be minimal truth. More generally, Horwich's strategy is to begin by admitting that some theories that (try to) capture the essence of truth in a finite formula *seem* to be able to explain, all by themselves, phenomena that MT cannot explain *all by itself*. But this is an illusion, he claims. These other theories are not really just theories of truth. Each of them is a combination of a theory of truth integrated with a theory of something else, such as a theory of reference, a logic, a theory of meaning, a theory of justification, and/or a theory of human psychology (Horwich 1990, 22, 25–26). MT, with the help of one or more of these theories of something else, can explain anything that any competing answer to any branch of the metaphysical project can explain. Indeed, he claims that it is preferable to have one's theory of truth separate from these other theories:

When distinct theories of X and Y *can* be given, then they *should* be given, otherwise, a misleading illusion of interdependence is conveyed and the cause of simplicity and explanatory insight is poorly served.

For this reason it seems to me not merely legitimate but important to separate, if we can, what we say about truth from our theories of reference, logic, meaning, verification, and so on.

... Therefore, it is quite proper to explain the properties of truth by conjoining the minimal theory with assumptions from elsewhere. (1990, 25–26)

Of course, simplicity is not the only desideratum of theories. We also want our theories to have what is often called *scope*. This means roughly that we want to explain as many phenomena as we can with as few theories as we can. (For example, one of the virtues of Newton's theory of gravity is that it explains *both* the movement of heavenly bodies *and* why this book will fall if you let go of it.) But what Horwich is getting at in the first paragraph of this quotation is that if a combined theory of truth and theory of something else is really just a *conjunction* of the two, i.e., if its deep structure is simply '[theory of truth] and [theory of something else]', then it is just an illusion to think that its really *one* theory, and this is surely right.

Let's look at one of his examples of how MT with the help of two theories of something else, in this case, a classical logic and a theory of meaning, explains a phenomenon. The phenomenon to be explained is that if one proposition materially implies another and the first is true, then so is the second. In the following quotation (from 1990, 23), Horwich uses the angle brackets as a shorthand for the phrase 'the proposition that'. For example, '$\langle p \rangle$' reads 'the proposition that p' and '$\langle\langle p\rangle$ is true$\rangle$' reads 'the proposition that the proposition that p is true'. (I make the notation conform to that of this book.)

(1) We can account for each individual proposition of the form,
$([p \ \& \ (p \supset q)] \supset q)$ [logic]

(2) Therefore we can explain every proposition of the form,
$\langle[\langle p\rangle \text{ is true} \ \& \ (p \supset q)] \supset \langle q\rangle \text{ is true}\rangle$ [from 1 and MT]

(3) Given the meaning of 'implies', we have every proposition of the form,
$\langle\langle p\rangle \text{ implies } \langle q\rangle \supset (p \supset q)\rangle$ [premise]

(4) Therefore we have every instance of
$\langle[\langle p\rangle \text{ is true} \ \& \ (p \text{ implies } q)] \supset \langle q\rangle \text{ is true}\rangle$ [from 2, 3]

(5) Therefore every proposition of the form,
$\langle[\langle p\rangle \text{ is true} \ \& \ (p \text{ implies } q)] \supset \langle q\rangle \text{ is true}\rangle \text{ is true}$ [from 4 and MT]

Notice how, in addition to citing MT twice, he cites in (3) the axiom from a theory of meaning that gives the meaning of 'implies', and in (1) he cites an axiom of classical logic. Like Dummett, Horwich believes that meaning can be explained in terms of assertibility conditions. But assertibility and the axioms of classical logic are among the things that others have thought the concept of truth could explain. Thus his claim that MT (with help) can explain everything any of its competitors can explain depends partly on the claim that a lot of things those competitors *claim* to explain cannot be explained by *any* theory of truth. This book has said enough already about truth and assertibility, but let me pursue Horwich's argument that classical logic cannot be explained by the concept of truth. In the following quotation, where Horwich uses 'rules of inference' or 'rules', read respectively 'rules of inference and axioms' and 'rules and axioms'. And where he refers to the 'logical constants' of a logic, he is referring to the connectors and operators of the logic, e.g., 'and', 'or', 'if ... then'.

The concept of truth plays no substantial role in the justification of logic. To see this consider how a system of rules of inference, L, could conceivably be justified. One strategy, it might be thought, is to specify the meanings of the logical constants by principles in which truth is the primary semantic notion—by means of truth tables—and then to show on the basis of these principles that the rules of L preserve truth. The trouble with this strategy is that it is blatantly circular; for the principles specifying the meanings of the constants are just trivial reformulations of the very rules we want to justify. (1990, 77)

And Horwich ends up concluding that the rules and axioms of classical logic neither need nor can be given any justification by reference to truth or any other value (1990, 79). But this argument is at best misleading. The semantics of a logic ("the principles specifying the meanings of the constants") is *not* just a trivial reformulation of the proof theory of the logic (the rules and axioms). If it were, there would be no need for *proofs* of completeness and soundness (proofs, that is, of being truth-preserving). But there is a need for such proofs, as every weary student of metalogic will attest: it is all to easy to inadvertently create a system of rules and axioms that is not sound, not complete, or neither. (Indeed, Gödel's incompleteness theorem shows that the standard logic of mathematics is incomplete.) To put the point another way, in reasoning about the proof theory of logic *L*, we can arrive at theorems of the form '*p* is provable from *q*', while in reasoning about the semantics of *L*, we can reach theorems of the form '*p* is a logical consequence of *q*'. If Horwich were right, then 'is provable from' and 'is a logical consequence of' would be *synonymous*. But they are not, even when the logic is complete and sound. (And when it is not both complete and sound, they are not even extensionally equivalent.) The first sort of theorem says something about the rules and axioms of the logic and *nothing* about the meanings of the connectors and operators (i.e., the logical constants) of the logic. The second sort of theorem says something about the meanings of the constants and *nothing* at all about its rules and axioms. (In response to this, some might say that the semantics at least *implies* something about the rules and axioms. *Exactly.* That's why soundness and completeness proofs, or disproofs, as the case may be, are possible.)

The *real* problem with depending on proofs of completeness and soundness to justify the rules and axioms of a logic, as John Etchemendy (1990, 4–6) points out, is that such proofs take the semantics of the logic for granted. That is, such proofs assume that we have got the meanings of the constants right. We need a justification of the semantics before we can be said to have justified the rules and axioms. At first glance this would seem to require an empirical study of how competent speakers use the constants 'and', 'or', etc. But since even competent speakers sometimes use these terms in ways we regard as fallacious (e.g., they utter things like 'If John is late, I'll go hungry. He's not late, so I will not go hungry'), what we really want is a kind of idealized picture of how the constants would be used if they were always used properly. But to figure out what 'properly' means here, we need to decide what it is that users of the language are *trying* to do when they make utterances containing these constants. Are they trying to say and infer *true* things, things with explanatory power, things with predictive power, or what? If 'True things' is not the answer to this question, then classical logic will turn out to be unjustified. But the context here is that we are asking, with Horwich, how classical logic is justified. So we are assuming that classical logic does have the semantics of 'and', 'or', etc., right. The question here is only how we would noncircularly *show* that it is right. *Here* is where the notion of truth plays its justificatory role: the classical semantics of the constants is shown to be correct relative to our idea of what truth is; that is, the truth-tables are correct because they conform to our pretheoretical idea of *truth*.

The very simple logical languages for which Tarski wanted to define truth do not consist of anything more than a few logical constants, predicates, and variables. So for Tarski, a theory of truth is simply *constituted* and exhausted by the semantics of the constants. But, as we saw in section 6.3, we cannot even recognize that a Tarski-like definition of truth for a language is correct unless we presuppose some other, more fundamental, translinguistic notion of truth. Davidson thinks that that other notion is indefinable, but I still have hopes that it can be captured by some series of instantiations of schema (C) (see section 4.5), one each for each kind of entity that can possess truth value. At any rate, I think that the account of the constants given by classical logic, and thus the truth-preservingness of the rules and axioms, could and would be justified relative to such a theory of truth. (Again, MT, as Horwich concedes, will not justify logic.)

To say that, however, is not quite to say that the rules and axioms of classical logic are justified absolutely. One could accept all of the previous two paragraphs and yet also insist that we ought to cease seeing truth, as distinct from, say, explanatory power, as the value we want our beliefs to have. In that case, the truth-preservingness of the rules and axioms of classical logic will no longer be of much interest. *If* there were no other program for which a theory of truth more substantial than MT were needed, we might end up agreeing with Horwich after all, though not for the same reasons. Note, however, that one who rejects truth as a value (see the last four paragraphs of section 8.7) would not necessarily be committed either to the claim that there is no property of truth or to the claim that there is no program for which we need a more substantial *notion* of truth than just MT. One can reject truth and still recognize that others have not done so. Thus there would still be a need to convince others that skepticism is irrefutable, that we simply cannot justify our beliefs *as true*. But the program of determining whether or not skepticism can be refuted is just the epistemological program (see section 2.1), and it requires a notion of truth at least as substantial as an instantiation of schema (C).[23]

Closely related to the question of whether MT can (with help) explain all that any other answer to the metaphysical project can explain is the fact that, as Horwich realizes, MT produces a new 'why' question of its own: if the infinite series of conjuncts constituting MT are all there is to say about truth, then one can fairly ask why these conjuncts are true. Horwich acknowledges that MT cannot explain why its own conjuncts are true, but he has three arguments to the effect that these conjuncts either cannot be explained by any theory or need no explanation.[24]

First, "if our thesis about the *function* of truth is correct, then the minimal theory constitutes our *definition* of 'true', and consequently is simply *not open* to explanation. ... Stipulated facts are not susceptible of explanation" (Horwich 1990, 52). But a reader can be forgiven for feeling astonished at Horwich's declaration, 52 pages into the book (and never repeated later), that his theory is just a stipulation. At any rate, if it is a stipulation, it can neither answer the metaphysical project nor do anything one might want to do with an answer to that project.

Second, according to Horwich, leaving the conjuncts of MT unexplained is objectionable only if there are some true lawlike statements about truth that MT cannot explain, but there are no such statements (1990, 51). To this one can respond that Horwich himself has, in effect, made statements of this sort in describing the function of the truth predicate. Suppose again that I want to affirm some proposition that Oscar is thinking, but since I do not know what that predicate is, I am forced to affirm an alternate proposition created with the help of the truth predicate: 'What Oscar is thinking is true.' Now MT can, in a sense, explain this particular instance of how I was able to use 'is true' to affirm an alternate proposition. It can do this by noting that whatever proposition p Oscar was thinking, there is a conjunct somewhere in MT asserting that p is true if and only if p. But now consider the *law* that people can *always* create expressions of perfectly appropriate alternate propositions by concatenating 'is true' to a name or description of the proposition they are really interested in. MT cannot explain this law.

Third, the conjuncts of MT are known a priori (known without need for experience or observation), says Horwich. This means that they cannot possibly be explained by a theory known only a posteriori (known with the help of experience or observation) and asserting the coextensiveness of the property of truth with some other, possibly complex, property, such as the property of corresponding to reality, cohering with other propositions one believes, or expressing some state of affairs that obtains (Horwich 1990, 50–52).[25] To this we can reply in two ways: (1) Whether or not our knowledge of the conjuncts of MT counts as a priori knowledge, it certainly depends on our already having a more substantive notion of truth. That was the thrust of the argument in section 6.3. (2) In the sort of explanation whose possibility Horwich is denying, the conjuncts of MT are playing the role of data, and the claim that truth is coextensive with this or that property is a theoretical postulation made to explain that data, so the theory is known via argument to the best explanation. I can see nothing wrong with such a procedure. So, if knowledge by argument to the best explanation is always a posteriori knowledge, then this just means we *can too* explain a priori data with a posteriori theories. If one wants to argue that such just cannot happen, then one should take such an argument as showing that theories known via argument to the best explanation are known a priori whenever the data they explain are so known.

Since MT is a quasi-realist theory and Horwich accepts the principle of bivalence (1990, 80), he is committed to all the premises crucial to generating the Liar Paradox (see section 9.1). Horwich acknowledges this and also admits that he has no solution to the paradox (1990, 42), but he seems to think this is a relatively minor flaw. However, Morton (forthcoming) notices that the absence of a solution to the paradox goes right to the heart of Horwich's claim that MT says all that needs to be said about truth: "If a non-minimal theory could motivate a plausible line on semantical paradoxes it might claim to have uncovered an essential feature of truth about which the [MT] is silent." Indeed, as Horwich says, he needs a way to exclude certain conjuncts from MT, specifically the conjuncts for paradoxical propositions (and sentence tokens) like 'This proposition [or sentence token] is false.' But it is very difficult to see how this could be done, especially when we recall the lesson of Kripke in section 9.5: whether or not a given proposition or sentence token is paradoxical will depend on contingent, nonsemantic facts, such as whether or not Smith is soft on crime.

I end my examination of Horwich's theory with another suggestion from Morton. MT may not work as an answer to the essence project, but it is not implausible if we see it as answering a certain psychological question: What is it for a human to have the concept of truth? The Horwichian answer: To have the concept of truth is to have a disposition to accept, without evidence, the conjuncts of MT.

10.9 Chapter Summary

The chapter began with a look at the last of the three major project types, the speech-act project. Like the term 'metaphysical project', the term 'speech-act project' is really a generic title for three different sorts of projects. These projects have in common only that they all involve trying to get straight on what we are *doing* when we make what appear to be ascriptions of truth, as distinct from trying to get straight on what truth is. The illocutionary-act project asks what sort of nonsemantic act, if any, is performed when we make apparent truth-ascribing utterances. We saw two proposed theories about this, from Strawson and Price, and found reason to quarrel with both. The assertion project assumes that at least one of the things we are doing when we make apparent truth-ascribing utterances is *saying* something. If the surface grammar of the utterances in question can be taken as a reliable guide, then apparent truth-ascribing utterances are not just apparent. But anyone who thought this would see little interest in pursuing the speech-act project in the first place, so it is not surprising that none of those who seem to be pursuing the project think that the surface grammar of the utterances in question is reliable. Hence, for all of them, the assertion project reduces to the deep-structure project, not the ascription project.

We examined four answers to the deep-structure project: White's truth-as-appraisal theory, Ramsey's rather simple redundancy theory, C. J. F. Williams's more ingenious redundancy theory, and the equally clever prosentential theory of Grover, Camp, and Belnap. Ramsey, Williams, and Grover, Camp, and Belnap have in common with Strawson and Price the belief that 'is true' is not a genuine predicate. This claim is the deflationary thesis. Some have thought that all that is needed to show the thesis is true is to show that we can give a complete account of what we are doing with truth-ascribing utterances without having to suppose that 'is true' is a genuine predicate. We saw, however, that that is not so. Even if we never use 'is true' to ascribe truth, there might still be a property of truth, and it might still be a property we need to refer to in order to explain certain phenomena, especially epistemic phenomena. Indeed, we saw reason to doubt that we can explain all epistemic phenomena without postulating a property of truth. At any rate, in examining the two deflationary answers to the illocutionary act project and the three deflationary answers to the deep-structure project, we saw reason to doubt that any of them can really account for our apparent truth-ascribing utterances without postulating that at least sometimes such utterances do more than merely *apparently* ascribe truth.

Finally, I returned to the metaphysical project, specifically, the essence project, long enough to critically examine Horwich's minimalist theory of truth. Horwich claims that his describable but inexpressible theory is all we need in the way of a concept of truth to explain all the things that any theory of truth could hope to explain. I argued, however, that a more substantial concept of truth can explain the rules and axioms of classical logic, while MT, as Horwich acknowledges, cannot. He also acknowledges that MT cannot explain its own conjuncts and he has three arguments that try to show that no other theory can explain them either. However, questions were raised about all three of those arguments. Finally, I pointed out that Horwich's concession that MT contains no solution to the Liar Paradox may be a more profound admission than he thinks.

Notes

Chapter 1

1. Arguably, D. J. O'Connor and Brian Carr make this mistake when criticizing the coherence theory of truth in their (1982, 168). Also, Max Black's (1948, 60-61) and Wilfred Sellars's (1963a, 197-198) attacks on the semantic theory of truth make the same mistake.

2. Other brief remarks on the purpose of a theory of truth can be found in Blackburn 1984, 232; Williams 1976, xiv-xv; Mackie 1973, 30-2, 40, 42; Rescher 1973, 4.

3. Williams 1976, the title. Compare "The wrong question to ask about truth is 'what is truth?'... The task... is made easier by asking 'what is it for a proposition... to be true?'" (Grayling 1982, 125).

4. O'Connor and Carr 1982, 165. Compare Austin's remark, "For 'truth' itself is an abstract noun, a camel, that is, of a logical construction, which cannot get past the eye even of a grammarian... But philosophers should take something more nearly their own size to strain at. What needs discussing rather is the use, or certain uses, of the word 'true'. *In vino*, possibly, *'veritas'*, but in a sober symposium *'verum'*" (1950, 117).

5. I use 'vague' in its ordinary, dictionary sense as meaning unclear, not in its technical sense as referring to terms whose applicability to a given object is a matter of degree.

6. Davidson (1967, 24) has found the situation so confused as to be "futile."

7. In calling this distinction a "commonplace," I do not mean to imply that it is uncontroversial. Also, I ignore, on grounds of irrelevance to my purposes, such questions as whether all or only some expressions have both a sense and a reference. I am also being rather bold in equating reference, denotation, and extension. Some philosophers and linguists, for example, take the reference of a predicate to be not a *set* but a property, universal, or platonic form. The extension of the predicate, they would say, is the set of things instantiating the property, universal, or form. Here too my ultimate purpose, to distinguish the various projects, is not harmed by ignoring the disputes.

8. To some extent the phrase 'necessary and sufficient condition' shares the ambiguity of the phrase 'if and only if' (see below). Occasionally philosophers use the former phrase to refer to a condition that is necessary and sufficient in *any* possible world. For reasons I give below, this ambiguity will prove advantageous.

9. The intension of 'the morning star' is *not* 'the *planet* visible around dawn'. 'The morning star' does not convey the information that the object in question is really a planet. The latter was an empirical discovery made after the morning star got its name.

10. There is no characterization of the notion of intensional equivalence that can be considered the standard view. And notoriously, there are those, like Quine, who deny that the notion of intension and hence the extension/intension distinction have ever been made completely clear. This book is not the place to take on the relevant issues vis-à-vis the analysis of intensionality. My point is to clarify what the various projects are about. For this I need only a recognition that there is a distinction (however ill defined and however fuzzy the boundary) between extension and intension, and even Quine will allow this much. He must, since he frequently gives examples of what he calls "opaque" (intensional) contexts and contrasts them with nonopaque (extensional) contexts. If there were no distinction here, he would be unable to do this.

11. What I say in this paragraph does not contradict the facts about the failure of substitutivity in intensional contexts. Terms that fail to substitute *salve veritate* in such contexts are not themselves intensionally equivalent; they have some weaker equivalence.

For example, 'Necessarily, $9 = 9$' is true while 'Necessarily, the number of planets $= 9$' is false precisely because '9' and 'the number of planets' are only extensionally equivalent, not intensionally equivalent.

12. Some philosophers, e.g., David Lewis (1973, 84–91), believe that all possible worlds are just as real as the actual world. The phrase 'actual world' is just a name for the possible world we happen to inhabit. It carries no ontological weight. I shall ignore these ontological disputes.

13. There are, of course, some possible worlds where the set of things with a heart is the empty set. But in these worlds the set of things possessing a blood-pumping organ is also the empty set.

14. Gerald Vision (1988, 115) notes also that these are not logical truths, yet he claims that they are both necessary truths. Even the latter claim is disputable. Think, e.g., of *abstract* objects.

15. If it helps, the reader may simply read the ' $=_{syn}$' as 'is synonymous with', but this is not strictly correct, since the latter phrase expresses a relation between two *expressions* and would only make sense with quotation names on both sides of it.

16. The more obvious names one might choose for these projects are all misleading for one reason or another. For example, 'semantic project' cannot replace 'assertion project', because it will turn out that the theories historically called "semantic theories of truth" are attempts to fulfill the metaphysical project. Similarly, the theories called in recent decades "epistemological theories of truth" also turn out to be attempts to fulfill the metaphysical project.

17. Note that the naturalistic project is *not* an attempt to analyze natural necessity or the concept of naturally necessary truth. Those who do not find this obvious are invited to insert 'at least contingently' between 'being' and 'true' in the project description.

18. Again, the essence project is *not* an attempt to analyze necessity or the concept of necessary truth. If you do not find this obvious, insert 'at least contingently' between 'being' and 'true' in the project description.

19. See note 17.

20. See note 18.

21. Occasionally 'if and only if' is even used to express a relation of synonomy, the relation expressed in this book with ' $=_{syn}$'.

22. Not even those who equate truth with justification could think that a theory of justification provides a *definition* of truth. See below and section 2.2.

23. I have not yet explained what coherence and foundationalism are, but the logic of my point about Rescher's twistings and turnings can be understood without knowing this information.

24. Rescher 1973, 10. The view Rescher calls "Intuitionistic" should not be confused with the very different doctrine of mathematical intuitionism.

25. None of the persons Rescher cites are defenders of such a theory, although some *are* foundationalists with respect to justification.

26. Rescher 1973, 207. For another example of what at least appears to be a case of a philosopher mislabeling his theory of justification as a theory of truth, see Davidson 1986. Davidson uses the phrase 'test of truth' to describe his project here. In fact, as we shall see in section 8.1, the only genuine theory of *truth* Davidson endorses, if he can be properly said to endorse any, is that of Alfred Tarski. For an earlier example, see Reichenbach 1931 and Ratner 1935. Almeder (1986) also arguably seems not to see the distinction between the two

projects. As Geyer noted as far back as 1917, it is not as common for the distinction to be completely missed as it is for a philosopher alternately to see and then not to see it. Ducasse (1968) and C. I. Lewis are good examples of this phenomenon. See Milmed (1956) for a study of Lewis with respect to this matter. Roy W. Sellars (1959) has the metaphysical, justification, and speech-act projects hopelessly mixed together.

27. I am by no means the first one to suspect that philosophers of truth have often failed to distinguish different kinds of projects. Several philosophers, including Chisholm (1982, 189) and Haack (1978, 88-89), have said that there are *two* types of theories of truth. But both of them conflate the metaphysical project with one of the other two major project types. Mark Platts labels three truth projects, but his labels are so vague and terse that even he admits to being unsure that they are really distinct from one another (Platts 1979, 9). Mackie (1976, 22, 30, 40, 42) implicitly makes a tripartite division of truth projects, and D. W. Hamlyn (1970, 116) may be implicitly doing so. Ralph C. S. Walker also seems to see a further distinction among truth projects beyond just the distinction between theories of truth and theories of justification. The further distinction is between theories that tell us "what truth consists in" and theories that tell us merely how to fill the blank in 'It is true if and only if ___ ' (Walker 1989, 2). Leslie Armour (1969, 3, 6) implicitly detects the difference between what I call the speech-act and metaphysical projects. Finally, Gerald Vision (1988, 25-50) distinguishes ten different questions about truth and Paul Horwich (1990, 37) spots five. Their lists match up fairly closely with my project distinctions.

28. The reason that we cannot take this as a decisive clue is that some philosophers, such as Brand Blanshard, believe quite literally that truth comes in degrees. See section 3.5.

29. We cannot take this as a decisive clue because some philosophers, such as John Dewey, literally believe that truth is something that happens to an idea.

30. Tarski 1944, 25, and Tarski 1933, 187. Compare Quine 1956, 196, Davidson 1967, 24, Davidson 1990, 294-295, and Grayling 1982, 159, all of whom concur in this interpretation.

31. The kind of guarantee provided by a metaphysical-project theory is not the same as that provided by an assertion-project theory. The latter guarantees that *by definition* a theory meeting the proposed criteria is true. The former does not. Nevertheless, from the fact that a given proposition meets the criteria proposed by a metaphysical-project theory (even an extensional or naturalistic project theory), it can be deduced by *modus ponens* that the proposition is true.

32. For examples of works that seem at times to confuse truth-theory projects with broader philosophical programs, see Harman 1973, 71, Soames 1984, and Wiggins 1980.

Chapter 2

1. Two points about general skepticism, as defined here, need to be made. First, it makes a more radical claim than does a skepticism that denies merely that we *know* anything, for the latter position is not incompatible with the claim that some, indeed most, of our beliefs are considerably better justified than their negations. A skeptic about knowledge insists only that for each of our beliefs, our justification for it is either not of sufficient degree or not of the right type to allow the belief to count as an item of knowledge. Second, in denying that we are justified in *any* way, the skeptic is, of course, denying among other things that we are *pragmatically* justified in thinking any belief is more likely true than its negation. For a more thoroughgoing discussion of the varieties of skepticism, see Pappas 1978.

2. This implication would not hold for skepticism about knowledge as distinct from skepticism about justification. See the preceding note. For more on the implications of skepticism, see Unger 1975, chaps. 4-6, and Kekes 1975, 38.

3. Readers should not be put off by my terminology. If the metaphysical project is of interest to epistemologists, it might be thought that it should be called the epistemological project. But it should now be clear why this would be a misleading name. Epistemologists are interested in *both* the justification and metaphysical projects, so neither one is *the* epistemological project. Nor can we call attempts to fulfill the metaphysical project 'epistemological theories of truth', because this term has already been appropriated by others to mean something different (e.g., Ellis 1969).

4. I claim neither that this formula is a summary of all foundational theories nor that it expresses the lowest common denominator in all foundational theories. Many foundationalists would have no use for the concept of self-evidence. The formula expresses *one* foundational theory. Even if no one would endorse it, that would not be relevant to the points I am making here.

5. The word 'obtain' is being used here in its philosophical sense, which is a variation on the intransitive sense of the word. The philosophical meaning of 'obtain' covers the ground from 'exist' to 'happen'. Philosophers usually use the word when they want to appear neutral in disputes about which ontological category (object, state, event, etc.) a certain entity belongs to. Until you have read enough philosophy to develop your own intuitions about the meaning of this term, you are advised to follow this policy: when a nonabstract *object* is said to obtain, take 'obtain' as synonymous with 'exist', and when an *event* is said to obtain, take 'obtain' as synonymous with 'happen', but in this case, where *conditions* are said to obtain, take the phrase 'do obtain' as synonymous with 'are fulfilled'.

6. The reader will note that an implication of this is that the justification project also has subdivisions paralleling those of the metaphysical project (and for that matter, of the speech-act project too). Since the focus of this book is on truth and not justification, I think it wise to simplify the account of the latter project.

7. But see section 9.5 for how to define a 'most' quantifier in a three-valued logic.

8. But an epistemologist does not necessarily assume that all other kinds of truth bearers get their truth *from* beliefs, as though there would be no truth if there were no beliefs.

9. Brian Ellis (1988), for example, defines the pragmatic theory of truth *just as* the thesis that truth is to be equated with justification.

10. Dewey 1957, 159. For other expressions of this thesis, see Dewey 1951, 109, and Dewey 1938, chap. 1, 6, 25.

11. Reading those who swallow the truth-as-justification thesis often leaves one wondering if one's leg is being pulled: Grattan-Guinness (1984, 132) equates truth and justification and then promptly postulates something he calls "ontological correctness" to play the role that truth has played for the past couple of millennia.

12. Pitcher 1964, editor's introduction, 5–7.

13. Pitcher 1964, editor's introduction, 5–7.

14. Baylis 1948, 463–464; Haack 1978, 77; Pitcher 1964, editor's introduction, 5–6.

15. For pedagogical reasons I wrote the preceding paragraph as though there could only be one "right" definition of 'sentence-type' and as though a given sentence token could be a member of only one type. Of course, the "rightness" of a definition is relative to one's purposes. Moreover, any given sentence token is a member of many types: any relation of similarity, whether it be in meaning or physical appearance or whatever, can be used to define *a* type.

16. James 1909, 3. This was not James's only candidate for truth bearers.

17. See sections 2.7, 10.1, 10.4, and 10.5 for details.

18. Mathematically, for any domain D there is some function that maps the elements of D into the set of states of affairs. We *stipulate* which mapping is a theory of truth, and thus we stipulate which domain is the domain of truth bearers.

19. On an instrumental theory, the token would change truth value if it ceased to express a useful belief. On a coherence theory, it would change truth value if it ceased to cohere with other sentence tokens.

20. Lest fans of R. Cartwright's paper "Propositions" (1962) accuse me of ignoring his position, let me point out that he makes no argument against any claim I make here. After distinguishing nine different truth-bearer candidates, including statements, assertions, sentence tokens, and sentence meanings, Cartwright declares, without argument, that *sentence meanings* cannot bear truth values. And he declares further, again without argument, that it is "surely obvious" that statements and assertions *can*. Nowhere does he even suggest that *sentence tokens* cannot bear truth value.

Chapter 3

1. Compare Chisholm's definition of 'state of affairs' (1977, 88).

2. There are important issues here concerning the ontological status of nonobtaining states of affairs, especially those that *necessarily* fail to obtain. It is not possible, however, to do justice to these issues without substantially lengthening the book.

3. Acton (1935, 178) saw this point, but others, including Forbes (1986, 37–38) and Vision (1988, 29), miss it.

4. I have not yet described the correspondence or semantic theories, but let me note for those already familiar with these terms that one implication of the foregoing is that not every theory falling under one or the other of these terms is a Realist theory. See sections 4.6 and 6.4.

5. Michael Dummett has claimed that a Realist theory of truth is just another way of expressing a doctrine of ontological realism. To endorse one is to endorse the other, and to embrace an antirealist ontology is to embrace a Nonrealist theory of truth. Thus, he claims, the ontological debate can be reduced to a dispute about a semantic concept, namely truth. (See Dummett 1978, 145–146, where Dummett uses 'correspondence theory' to label what I call Realist theories.) But this claim has been cogently refuted by others. An ontological realist can consistently reject Realist theories of truth. Compare Rorty 1979, 276; Soames 1984, 412–414; and Devitt 1984, 198. See also my discussion of Samuel Alexander's theory in section 6.4.

6. I shall hereafter refer to Peirce's collected papers (1931–1958) in the now traditional way by volume number and section number. Thus, '5.414' refers to volume 5, section 414.

7. See, for example, the title essay of Lovejoy's *Thirteen Pragmatisms and Other Essays* (1963).

8. Taken literally, this would imply that Peirce thinks 'is true' *means* 'would be agreed to, etc.', that is, that they are *intensionally* equivalent. But I can find no passages in his writings that could count as a defense of this claim, as distinct from a claim of mere essential equivalence. Hence, partly to be fair to Peirce, I interpret him as attempting to fulfill the essence project.

9. Peirce identifies propositions as the (only) truth bearers on those occasions when he is self-conscious about truth bearers (5.53, 5.569). On occasions when he is not, which is most of the time, he treats opinions, beliefs, answers, and other items as truth bearers.

10. See the end of this section for a discussion of whether the equivalence is extensional, naturalistic, or essential.

11. I use x instead of the propositional variable p to avoid controversies about quantification over the latter type of variable and because in this formula the variable is substitutable with a name of a proposition, not a proposition itself.

12. I shall use P as an abbreviation of James's *Pragmatism* (1907) and MT as an abbreviation for James's *Meaning of Truth* (1909).

13. In particular, my interpretation of James will rest heavily on MT. This was his last treatment of the subject, and unlike P, it was intended to be a scholarly, not popular book. The work is a collection of mostly previously published articles, but all save two of them were written within five years of the book's publication. Moreover, it is known that James considerably rewrote the book version of many of these papers, and his preface gives no hint that he wants to retract anything that remains. (See pp. 205 and 227 of the editor's chapter "The Text of *The Meaning of Truth*".) There are, however, as many inconsistencies within this work as between it and James's other writings.

14. James had an admirably pluralist attitude about truth bearers: "The relation called 'truth'... may obtain between an idea (opinion, belief, statement, or what not) and its object" (MT, 3).

15. James seems to endorse ontological realism at MT, 15, but since the remark is in a paper written twenty years before, and is incompatible with, the rest of the book, I feel safe in ignoring it.

16. At MT, 72, a paper written twenty years after that mentioned in the previous note, he actually denies the existence of a world independent of mind.

17. The German 'Ding an Sich' literally means thing in itself, which we may here take to mean independent of mind.

18. James is referring to Pratt 1909.

19. A partial justification for attributing the essence project to James is the following remark (which admittedly yields to alternative interpretations): "[Pragmatism] content[s] itself with the word truth's *definition*. 'No matter whether any mind extant in the universe possess truth or not,' it asks, 'what does the notion of truth signify *ideally*?' 'What kind of things would true judgments be *in case* they existed?'... It is not a theory about any sort of reality, or about what kind of knowledge is actually possible; it abstracts from particular terms altogether, and defines the nature of a possible relation between the two of them" (MT, 100–101).

20. The reference is to Russell 1908a.

21. In some places, e.g., MT, 142–143, James speaks of absolute truth and defines it in a Peircean manner as "an ideal set of formulations toward which all opinions may in the long run of experience be expected to converge" (p. 143). Perhaps there is a way of integrating such remarks with his endorsement of relativism, but I shall not attempt to do so in this book.

22. This definition of IRT leaves unanswered precisely the questions left unanswered in the literature. Do relativists mean their relativism to apply to *all* propositions or only some? If all, do they mean that *in the actual world* each proposition is true for at least one person and false for at least one, or do they mean only that for each proposition, there is some possible world where it is true for one person and false for another? The former choice seems stronger than what most relativists have had in mind, but the latter seems too weak, since it is compatible with the claim that in the actual world there is no proposition that is true for one person and false for another.

23. James himself does not always keep subjectivism and relativism distinct, e.g., at MT, 105, and at MT, 129, he actually seems to endorse IST. I ignore this passage as atypical.

24. Curiously, in the following chapter (p. 135) Putnam refers back to this argument (correctly) as an argument against subjectivism. I take this as further evidence that he is conflating subjectivism with relativism.

25. Rorty attributes this claim to James without offering any textual evidence (1980, 162).

26. For example, the title, Donald Davidson matches a correspondence theory of truth with a coherence theory of justification in "A Coherence Theory of Truth and Knowledge" (1986). Laurence BonJour (1985) makes the same marriage.

27. So Blanshard does have reasons, however ill considered they are, for thinking that the conditions for justification are also the necessary and sufficient conditions for truth. So, contrary to Chisholm's criticism (1982, 192), he is not just *supposing* they are the same.

28. I suggested in section 1.8 that a philosopher's endorsement of the notion that truth comes in degrees is a good clue that he is pursuing the justification project. And Blanshard does believe his theory is an answer to the justification project, but as we have seen, he also thinks it is an answer to the essence project.

29. Mackie (1973, 22–25) interprets Nonrealist theories as proposals to *change* the meaning of 'true' so as to make truth something attainable. Specifically, he thinks that they propose a change in connotation to preserve denotation. Davidson (1986, 313) makes the identical interpretation, as does Blackburn (1984, 248–249). Blackburn points out that on coherence theory "Descartes demon ... would put us in a world which is truly as we take it to be ..." (p. 249).

Chapter 4

1. There can be no doubt that Russell was proposing a theory of truth and not a theory of justification from these remarks of his: "We are not asking how we can know whether a belief is true or false: we are asking what is meant by the question whether a belief is true or false.... It is very important to keep these different questions entirely separate, since any confusion between them is sure to produce an answer which is not really applicable to either" (Russell 1912, 119–120).

2. This formula raises, in an acute way, the controversial issues surrounding quantification over predicate variables, for in any instantiation of this formula, the 'R' in its second appearance is replaced by a noun, such as 'loving', but in its third appearance it is replaced with a verb, such as 'loves'. See section 4.4 for a little more on such issues.

3. Of course, not every fact involves a two-term relation. Some involve relations of three terms or more ('The lamppost is between you and me'), and others involve one-term relations, that is, *properties* ('The table is purple'). Still others are so complex they are expressible only with quantifiers. For example, the relation between John and Mary when it is true that there is at least one thing that loves John more than it loves Mary is expressible not with a predicate but with the open sentence '$(\exists x)(x$ loves y more than x loves $z)$'. Presumably, Russell would want us to take account of all this. I believe that there are now formal techniques for accomplishing this. They are too complex to introduce in this book, but see Etchemendy 1990, 45–46, for a brief introduction and examples of their use. These techniques may be of use with respect to the issues mentioned in the previous note as well.

4. Compare Bencivenga 1980. George Bealer (1982, 11, 186–203) offers a correspondence-as-congruence theory that *identifies* the fundamental elements of thoughts with the fundamental elements of states of affairs, and consequently his theory faces the same problems. Laurence BonJour (1985, 166–167) suggests that the relation in question should be one of reference, not identity, but this obviously is not of much help in dealing with nonreferring terms like Santa Claus. H. B. Acton (1935, 185, 192) avoids these problems in his theory of

correspondence as congruence by taking not beliefs but sentences-under-analysis (type or token unspecified) as the primary truth bearers.

5. The theory of belief to be removed is

$(b)(x)(y)(R)[(b$ is the belief that $xRy \Leftrightarrow (\exists B)(b = \langle B, x, R, y \rangle)]$,

where the ranges of the variables is as before. In particular, the set over which b ranges is defined as the set of ordered quadruples in which the first member is a believer, the second an object, the third a two-term relation, and the last another object. Russell's combined theory of belief and truth is equivalent to the conjunction of this formula and the formula just below the text marker for this note.

6. Acton (1935, 193) tries to defend the correspondence-as-congruence theory from the problem of one-word sentences by suggesting that "men must have had private languages before they came to communicate." The symbols of these languages were mental images that had structure isomorphic to facts. Verbal sentences, including one-word sentences, are only expressions of these images. But this answer will not do, for two reasons. First, as Wittgenstein has argued, the notion of a private language is dubious. Second, Acton is implicitly taking mental images as the primary truth bearers. But as we saw in note 4, his answer to the problem of nonreferring terms depended on his taking sentences-under-analysis as the primary truth bearers.

7. The idea of a correspondence theory that does *not* postulate a structural isomorphism between truth bearer and fact was so unfamiliar at the time that some have failed to see that Austin's theory *is* a correspondence theory, despite his so calling it (Austin 1954, 154). Jon Wheatley is so trapped by the assumption that any correspondence theory must be a correspondence-as-congruence theory that he attributes to Austin, without citing any textual evidence, the view that it is the grammatical subject of a statement that does the demonstrating and the predicate that does the describing (Wheatley 1969, 229, 233-234). But this attribution is completely alien to the holistic nature of the demonstrative and descriptive conventions Austin presents.

8. A more charitable interpretation of Austin is possible, though exceedingly hard to justify by his text. He may have been simply trying to defend the importance of the metaphysical project from what will be called, in chapter 10, the deflationary thesis. The latter implies, among other things, that the metaphysical project itself is wrong-headed from the start.

9. Austin's theory of meaning that is cut away below is:

$(s)(x)[s$ means that $x \Leftrightarrow (\exists r)(\exists t)(t$ is used to make s) & (s refers to x)
& (t describes r) and (x is of type r)],

where the ranges of the variables are as before. Austin's combined theory of meaning and truth is equivalent to the conjunction of this formula and the formula just after the text marker for this note.

10. I squeeze out Russell's theory of belief and Austin's theory of meaning only to highlight a similarity between them. I do not mean to belittle or deny the importance of the theories thereby expelled.

11. C. A. Baylis's theory of truth (1948) also seems to be a correspondence-as-correlation theory, despite his apparent desire (p. 466) to be neutral on the question of whether truth bearers and facts are structurally isomorphic when they correspond: he suggests that the correspondence relation is a relation of *exemplification*. A fact, such as that this rose is red, exemplifies a proposition, in this case the proposition of a rose's being red, just as a red object exemplifies universal redness (p. 460).

12. This suggestion will, of course, bring no comfort to those extreme extensionalists, like Quine, who reject any sort of second-order quantification.

13. For a selection of views on the issues of this section, see Blackburn 1984, 258; Chisholm 1977, 138; Haack 1978, 40, 78–79; Mackie 1976, 31, 60–61; Pap 1952, 210 n. 2; Platts 1979, 14–15; Prior 1971, 22; Tarski 1944, 29–30; and Williams 1976, 6–10.

14. The notion of a schema or open sentence will be explained in section 5.4. Readers who are not familiar with this notion should have no difficulty understanding the points being made in this section if they simply take the '*R*' in schema (C) as holding the place of some relational verb.

15. Note that the '*R*' in the formula for Russell is not correlative to the '*R*' of the schema. Rather, the 'is the belief that' in former is correlative to the '*R*' of the latter.

16. Chisholm 1977, 138.

17. Hamlyn 1962, 201–202. Commenting on the same Aristotelian remark quoted at the end of section 4.1, Hamlyn says, "It is noteworthy, however, that nothing is said about correspondence in the passage. We are told only that propositions are true *by reason of* the facts" (p. 195).

18. Another reason for which Davidson abandons his lifelong fealty to the correspondence theory is that he has somehow got it into his head that the correspondence theory, *by definition*, involves a modally weak, global fallibilism to the effect that there is some possible world where all our best justified beliefs are false, and he finds the latter thesis incomprehensible (1990, 308).

19. For one version of the objection, see White 1970, 104.

Chapter 5

1. See the editor's historical note on p. 277 of Tarski 1933.

2. Tarski 1944, 22–23, and Tarski 1936, esp. 406–407. Etchemendy (1988, 51–53) says that Tarski was not interested in the semantic-foundations program, but the passages of Tarski cited here, especially the title of the second of these articles ("The Establishment of Scientific Semantics") does not leave much room for doubt.

3. The truth tables are an incomplete definition because they give no account of truth for atomic sentences.

4. Tarski 1944, 16. The modifying phrase 'to which the word "*true*" refers' does not belong in the instantiation conditions for the '*p*' of the schema. The '*p*' can in fact be replaced by *any* sentence of the language. In other presentations of schema T, Tarski did not make this mistake. See Tarski 1933, 155–156, and Tarski 1936, 404.

5. Tarski 1969, 63–64. Compare Mates 1974, 386.

6. Tarski 1944, 14, 17. In section 2.3, I made a distinction between sentence types and sentence tokens. Tarski was inconsistent about whether it is tokens or types he takes to be truth bearers. Originally he took them to be sentence types at (1933, 156 n. 1). But later in life he rejected types in favor of sentence tokens (1969, 63, 68).

7. Tarski 1969, 65; Tarski 1933, 188.

8. There is a way to transform a recursive definition into a definition that does not even give the appearance of circularity, but it involves formal techniques not likely to be familiar to much of the intended audience for this book.

9. Here and throughout the book (except in section 9.5) I make do with ordinary quotation marks where corner quotation marks are more strictly correct, because much of the audience for this book is likely to find the distinction confusing and is not likely to find anything mysterious about the use of ordinary quotation marks in this context. In other words,

persons who have not yet been introduced to the distinction just naturally and implicitly give the quotation marks in this context the meaning a logician would reserve for corner quotation marks.

10. Tarski 1933, 189; Tarski 1944, 25. Compare McDowell 1978, 112.

11. See note 9 on ordinary versus corner quotation marks.

12. This gives the form of the T-sentence, but it is not itself a T-sentence, since it has the unbound variables 'k' and 'ϕ'.

13. Tarski 1933, 193. Regarding the use of quotation marks in my version of this definition, see note 9.

14. Compare Davidson 1967, 32, and Quine 1970, 41. Quine writes, "There is such a clause for *each* one-place predicate in the lexicon. Similarly, for *each* two-place predicate" (emphasis mine).

15. It is not clear that Tarski ever explicitly acknowledges the problem, though he may be doing so at 1933, 164, or 214; 1944, 25; or 1936, 402.

16. Most logicians would share only Tarski's goal of a model theory, and for them, the move in question is unobjectionable.

17. Compare Prior: "Part of Tarski's aim was to avoid the use of 'intensional' conceptions like that of 'meaning'; but ... if we do not restrict ourselves in this way, and get our grammar straight, it *is* possible to define 'true' very straightforwardly" (1962, 138).

18. Tarski 1944, 16. For other statements of schema T and its instantiation conditions, see Tarski 1933, 155–156; Tarski 1936, 404; Platts 1979, 16; and Black 1948, 52.

19. We would also need a premise connecting the concept of meaning with the concept of saying or expressing.

20. Quine 1963b, 36; Prior 1971, 22; Lehrer 1974, 31; and Pap 1952.

21. O'Connor 1975, 23. O'Connor's remark, however, is a good example of how the various truth projects have been conflated. The question what are we *asserting* when we *assert* that *P* is true is different from the question what is "required for *P* to *be* true." Hence, O'Connor conflates the metaphysical and assertion projects.

22. And as I argued in section 2.6, 'There are six protons in the carbon atom' is never *in* any language other than English.

23. Compare Mates 1974, 396. I do not mean to assume that Etchemendy would endorse a possible-worlds semantics for modal terms, but this is incidental to the point being made here.

At one time, Hamlyn seemed to argue against the claim I am defending here: "If Smith says that the cat is on the mat, *one* necessary condition of what he says being judged true is that he means by the word 'cat' an animal of the sort which is in fact on the mat.... Another necessary condition would be that there is a cat at all ..., but the only *general* necessary condition of the statement being judged true is that the cat is in fact on the mat. Hence, the fact that the cat is on the mat is the only general sufficient and necessary condition for the assertion being judged true" (1962, 193–205). If Hamlyn means to say no more than that T-sentences are true, there can be no complaint. But he seems to deny that "'The cat is on the mat" means that the cat is on the mat' expresses a necessary condition for 'The cat is on the mat' being true (in addition to the condition that the cat be on the mat). If so, then his own argument does not support his conclusion. As he points out at the top of the quoted passage, the words in 'The cat is on the mat' must have a certain meaning if the sentence is to be true. Notice, incidentally, how Hamlyn's use of the word 'judged' conflates the justification and metaphysical projects.

24. Tarski 1933, 161-162. Compare Davidson's interpretation of this passage in Davidson 1977b, 174.

25. Mackie 1973, 28; Haack 1978, 100, 110, 112; and Keuth 1978, 424. The latter argues that Tarski's definition is incompatible with the correspondence theory, but his argument depends on treating the T-sentences as though they were Tarski's definition and assumes that the 'iff' of the T-sentences is meant to express synonymy, instead of mere extensional equivalence.

26. Davidson 1986, 309; and Davidson 1969, 37-40, 48. In his most recent pronouncement on the subject, Davidson renounces his earlier classification of Tarski as a correspondence theorist, but apparently Davidson's only reason for doing so is that he (Davidson) no longer believes in the correspondence theory. See Davidson 1990, 304.

27. Popper 1962; Popper 1974; Sellars 1963a, 197-198; and Platts 1979, 34.

28. Vision 1988, 44; Field 1974, 203 n. 3; and Ayer 1959, editor's introduction, 20-21.

29. Tarski 1944, 14-16. Tarski repeats exactly this analysis at 1969, 63.

30. Tarski did say that the word 'true' is ambiguous partly because philosophers have offered so many conceptions of truth (correspondence, utilitarian, etc.). But he did not claim that any *one* of these conceptions (e.g., the correspondence conception) is in itself, ambiguous (1944, 14).

Chapter 6

1. Tarski 1969, 65; and 1933, 188.

2. I have oversimplified here. The proper clause would read 'or (s = "Blue is the sky" and *either* snow is blue *or* snow is is *or* snow is the *or* snow is sky)'.

3. In effect, those who make mistake (1) are conflating Tarski's metalanguage T-sentences with *meta-meta*language sentences on the pattern of:

'"Snow is white" is true' has the same truth value as 'snow is white'

Since the latter provide no noncircular analysis of truth and are acceptable to almost everyone, no matter what their theory of truth, the conflation of these with the T-sentences produces the illicit conclusion that the T-sentences are also acceptable to all.

4. Donald Davidson's answer to Sellars seems to be essentially like this. See Davidson 1969, 50-51.

5. In Quine's case the conflation of Tarski and Ramsey is a little more understandable, since he denies that there is a sharp distinction between intensional and extensional equivalence and thus would deny that there is a sharp distinction between the extensional and assertion projects. But he must admit that there is *some* distinction, else he could not, as he frequently does, give examples of what he calls opaque (read 'intensional') contexts and distinguish them from extensional contexts.

6. There is some evidence that Sellars misinterpreted the semantic theory as an attempt to fulfill what I have called the essence project or possibly even the assertion project, for he misinterprets the relationship in the equivalence instances of schema T as a "logical equivalence" of mutual entailment, whereas it is, as we have seen, a relation of mutual material implication, that is, extensional equivalence. See Sellars 1963a, 206.

7. Blackburn 1984, 272-273. Putnam (1981, 129) also seems to be gesturing toward this more legitimate line of reasoning for the vacuity objection.

8. It is the preceding legitimate argument for the vacuity objection that Israel Scheffler overlooks in *assuming* that Tarski is, in my terminology, a Realist. See Scheffler 1982, 122. Herbert Hochberg (forthcoming) also overlooks the legitimate argument (and on Hochberg's presentation, so does G. E. Moore). The same complaint could once have been made about Davidson.

> What Convention T, and the trite sentences it declares to be true, like "'Grass is Green" spoken by an English speaker, is true if and only if grass is green', reveal is that the truth of an utterance depends on just two things: what the words as spoken mean, and how the world is arranged. There is no further relativism to a conceptual scheme, a way of viewing things, a perspective.
> ... I think we can draw two conclusions from these reflections.... Second, a theory of knowledge that allows that we can know the truth must be a non-relativized, non-internal form of realism. (1986, 309)

(In the last clause Davidson is referring to an ontological view Hilary Putnam calls "internal realism," which, despite its name, is a breed of antirealist ontology.) Whether Davidson still thinks of Tarski as an ontological realist, and hence a Realist about truth, is uncertain, since Davidson has recently renounced ontological realism himself and his interpretation of Tarski generally changes to conform to the latest changes in his (Davidson's) own views. See Davidson 1990, 281, 298–299.

9. Michael Devitt makes the same point (1984, 39, 94).

10. Among those who have interpreted Tarski to be expressing ontological instead of epistemological neutrality are Horwich (1990, 59 n. 2), Soames (1984, 412), Putnam (1978, 9), Romanos (1983, 157–159); and Grayling (1982, 163–164).

11. To say that Tarski's theory is not an answer to the justification project is not to say that it is neutral with regard to theories of justification. Some such theories will be more plausible on Tarski's theory of truth than others. For example, the "theory" that tells you always to accept the authority of your Aunt Minnie is implausible, on Tarski's theory of truth.

12. If the language contained the predicate 'loves', the corresponding basis clause would contain a (metalanguage expression of) this concept: ($\theta = $ 'x_k loves x_j', for some k and j, and the kth object in S loves the jth object in S). But this would mean at most that those who seek to reduce emotion terms to physical terms have so far failed; it would not count against Tarski's claim to have successfully reduced semantic terminology.

13. Field 1972, 95, 108 n. 14.

14. Field does not *explicitly* provide anything corresponding to my (D2), but it is implied at the middle of p. 97 in Field 1972.

15. But the two sides are not naturally equivalent. There are some possible worlds with the same laws of nature as ours but that contain, at the moment, no elements with atomic numbers below, say, 112, so they contain none of the elements found in the actual world. So all of the disjuncts on the right-hand side of (D1) will be false. (In another split second, some of the atoms in each of these worlds will decay into atoms with atomic numbers of 103 or lower and thus become atoms of elements found in the actual world.)

16. Field gestures to what is in effect another argument by analogy when he remarks, "By similar standards of reduction, one might prove that witchcraft is compatible with physicalism, as long as witches cast only a finite number of spells: for then 'cast a spell' can be defined without use of any of the terms of witchcraft theory, merely by listing all the witch-and-victim pairs" (Field 1972, 101).

17. Field 1972, 86. But notice also his remarks on pp. 91 and 103 that a physicalist definition of truth is not intended to explain the *meaning* of the word 'true'. In my terminology, the physicalist program should not be confused with the assertion project. Compare also this

remark by Field from a later paper: "By a correspondence theory of truth, I mean a theory that says that the notion of truth can be *explained* by appealing to the relation between words on the one hand and the objects that they are about on the other. ... The central feature of a correspondence theory is that it *explains* truth in terms of some correspondence relations between words and the extralinguistic world" (Field 1974, 200; emphasis mine).

18. This appears to be the standard interpretation of Field. Compare, e.g., Fox 1989, 173; Stalnaker 1987, 30; Leeds 1978, 121; McDowell 1978, 111; and Soames 1984, 418. On the other hand, Robert Cummins (1975, 33–37) seems to conflate Field's objection with what I called the relativity objection above.

19. Following up on some hints in Tarski's footnotes, Field (1972, 84–86) also shows how the envisaged reductionist program can be extended to truth definitions for languages with names and functions.

20. Field (1972, 88) seems not to have noticed this when, e.g., he quotes from Tarski 1933: "I shall not make use of any semantical concept if I am not able previously to reduce it to *other* concepts" (emphasis mine).

21. Fox (1989, 173) reaches the same conclusion about Field and Tarski, although he does so for reasons different than mine.

Chapter 7

1. For a survey of the wide variety of ways in which the first part of a foundational theory can be filled out, see Alston 1971. Cornman (1979) performs a similar service for the ways in which the third part can be filled out.

2. Walker (1989, 172–173) gives another argument to the effect that a foundational theory of justification can be married to a coherence theory of truth.

3. My argument here presupposes that a proposition is justified if it has explanatory power. What I should strictly say is that the instrumental theory combined with a best-explanation theory of justification is plausible on a Realist theory of truth.

4. Haack (1978, 95) gives the reasons why Bradley should be interpreted as trying to fulfill only the justification project.

Chapter 8

1. In 1990, 286 n. 20, Davidson scolds himself for having said in 1967 that "we could *both* take a Tarski truth definition as telling us all we need to know about truth *and* use the definition to describe an actual language." Actually, I do not think he did say this in Davidson 1967. What he was thinking of, perhaps, is Davidson 1970, 55, where he does seem to say that a Tarski-like definition of truth provides an informative account of the concept of truth.

2. By 1990, 281–288, Davidson realized that Tarski's theory also implicitly relies on a pretheoretical, undefined concept of translinguistic truth. His argument is substantially the one I make in section 6.3. But he also seems to think that Tarski was aware of this (Davidson 1990, 299). I can find no textual evidence for the latter claim about Tarski.

3. Davidson 1967, 25. Compare Davidson 1990, 296, and Romanos 1983, 173–175.

4. This is a good place to note that Davidson was well aware of the distinction between what I have called the metaphysical and speech act projects, and he disavowed any intention that a theory of meaning, in his sense be an answer to the latter project (Davidson 1967, 24; and 1969, 41).

5. I owe this point to Adam Morton.

6. I owe this example to Ray Elugardo.

7. A couple of recent remarks by Davidson, however, indicate that he might not answer Soames in this way. Since no merely extensional definition will meet this "natural demand" and even Soames acknowledges the inappropriateness of an intensional analysis of the truth predicate for theoretical semantics, Soames's objection effectively demands that the 'if and only if' in a theory of truth express what I called natural equivalence in section 1.5.

Thus Soames, like Field, would like a definition of truth to express a law of nature. It should be true not just in the actual world but also in all possible worlds with the same laws of nature as this one. Surprisingly, in 1982 Davidson added a footnote to Davidson 1967 in which he says that the sentences of a theory of truth in his sense are lawlike and must support appropriate counterfactuals (p. 26 n. 11). In 1990, 313, Davidson says, "T-sentences thus have the form and function of natural laws; they are universally quantified bi-conditionals, and as such are understood to apply counterfactually and to be confirmed by their instances." I find this hard to reconcile with his repeated insistence that T-sentences express only extensional equivalence (at, e.g., 1973a, 65; and 1990, 294–295). If a quantified T-sentence like '$(p)(t)$ "That book was stolen" is true as (potentially) spoken by p at t if and only if the book demonstrated by p at t is stolen prior to t' is intended to express a law of nature, then it is false. There are worlds with the same laws of nature as this one where *in English* 'stolen' means what 'burned' means in this world. (I presume that the variables p and t are what he has in mind when he calls T-sentences universally quantified. Nowhere does he present any quantified T-sentence.)

Perhaps Davidson is worried about the fact that if a theory of meaning entailing '"Snow is white" is true if and only if snow is white' is empirically well verified, then a theory differing from the first only in that it entails '"Snow is white" is true if and only if snow is white and grass is green' as its T-sentence for 'Snow is white' will be equally well verified. Insisting that T-sentences be lawlike gives him a way to eliminate the second theory as a contender. But there is another way in which he can eliminate the second theory: if two theories are otherwise equally good, the *simpler* of the two is preferable, and the first theory accounts for native utterances of 'Snow is white' in a simpler way.

8. For discussions of this issue and references to some of the relevant passages in Dummett, see Devitt 1984, 198–200; George 1984, 516–517; McDowell 1976, passim, esp. 48; Walker 1989, 32–33; and Wright 1987, 317–320. See also Dummett 1981, 434–435.

9. Wright (1987, 320) says that it is Realist theories of truth that Dummett's arguments "most directly attack." But he cites no such arguments. In fact, Dummett's arguments (see below in the text) *directly* attack the explanatory power of truth-conditional models of linguistic competence, which is not the same thing as attacking the correctness of Realist theories of truth per se.

10. Dummett uses the term 'correspondence theory of truth' to denote the set of theories I call Realist. This again is because he does not see that a correspondence theory can be merely quasi realist and thus Nonrealist.

11. Dummett 1978a; Dummett 1973, chap. 13, passim.

12. Dummett 1959, 7. Other mode (A) remarks can be found at Dummett 1976, 67, 110–111; and Dummett 1973, 467, 586, 684.

13. Dummett 1978a, 146. Other mode (B) remarks can be found at Dummett 1978a, 149, 156; and Dummett 1975a, 239. At page xxii of the preface to Dummett 1978b he seems explicitly to reject (A) and (A') (see below) in favor of (B) or (B'), but the only reason he gives for doing so is that he thinks (A) is obscure.

14. See Devitt 1984, chap. 12, passim; McGinn 1980, 19; Grayling 1982, 235; Devitt and Sterelny 1987, 194; Baker and Hacker 1984, 50; and George 1984, 517. McDowell seems not to see the difference between the two theses (see McDowell 1976, 48).

15. Rorty 1979, 280; Appiah 1986, xvi, 27; and Wright 1987, 38–40, 205 n. 4.

16. Baker and Hacker 1984, passim, and George 1984, 5–7, 519–520.

17. Devitt 1984, 209; Devitt and Sterelny 1987, 147, 194; and George 1984, 519–520. Baker and Hacker are inconsistent on this point. In 1984, 276–277, 360, they attribute to Dummett the propositional assumption. But on pages 239–240, 341, and 357 of the same work, they seem to recognize that he does not have this belief.

18. For other objections to the propositional assumption, see Devitt 1984, 209–211; Baker and Hacker 1984, 276–277; Platts 1979, 232; and Harman 1975, 285–286.

19. Platts 1980, editor's introduction, 15. Neither Platts, Dummett, nor I mean to suggest that this would be a pedagogically efficient way to learn a language. The question is purely hypothetical: *If* someone were to learn a language in this way, *would* they have the same linguistic competence as a native speaker?

20. For a fuller discussion of these issues than is possible here, see Wright 1987, essay 6.

21. In using 'is true' here instead of 'is justified', Dummett is talking in the (B′) mode.

22. Dummett 1975b, 109.

23. In Kirkham 1989, I offered what I thought was a counterexample to (4) even on the revised sense of 'logical consequence'. I have become convinced by Stern 1990 that my counterexample does not work.

Chapter 9

1. For a longer discussion of this point, see Kirkham, forthcoming.

2. Graham Priest (1979, 220) shares my belief that this criterion can never be met if it is interpreted absolutely. Because he does so interpret it, he concludes that it is not possible to solve the paradox. What we must do is learn to live with the paradox. (See section 9.7.)

3. Quine acknowledges this (Quine and Ullian 1978, 78).

4. Russell 1908b, 79. Strictly speaking, Russell's phrase 'which I affirm' does not convey the idea that the utterance in which it appears is the very one being affirmed. It should read 'which I am now affirming with this very utterance'.

5. I follow Kripke in speaking of "building" a language with its own truth predicate, but like Kripke, I mean this as only a pedagogically advantageous metaphor. The definition Kripke eventually arrives at (which he never makes completely explicit) is not a constructivist definition.

6. Kripke 1975, 66, 66 n. 20. For purposes of simplification, Kripke defines truth directly instead of via the concept of satisfaction (p. 70). In what follows, I do likewise.

7. Kripke 1975, 64. A crucial point is that the 'antiextension' of a predicate P, as Kripke uses the term, is not synonymous with the 'complement' of P relative to the domain. Although nothing can be in both the extension and antiextension, some objects from the domain can be in neither. In section 9.7 below I shall discuss a view that allows some sentences to be in both the extension and antiextension of 'true'.

8. Kripke 1975, 64. The valuation scheme allowing gaps is essentially that of S. C. Kleene's three-valued logic. See Kleene 1952, 332–340. However, Kripke is at pains to say that there is not necessarily one "correct" scheme. Further study might show that some other gap scheme might be better for certain purposes (Kripke 1975, 76).

9. Following Kripke (1975, 70), I assume for purposes of simplification that the language contains a name for every object in the domain.

10. Kripke himself does not define a 'majority of' quantifier. The definition here is my own. It is intended to have a Kleene-like flavor.

11. Nothing that I say about the Strengthened Liar presupposes that 'neither-true-nor-false' names a third truth value. Nor do I presuppose that it does not name a third truth value. The fact is that sentences that are neither true nor false are a third category of sentence. Whether such sentences have a truth value or not is irrelevant to the derivation of a contradiction.

12. There may be philosophical contexts in which the denial of bivalence leads to real progress on this or that issue, so what I say here should not be interpreted as meaning that such a denial is absolutely pointless.

13. Priest 1979, 226–231. The semantics are essentially those of S. C. Kleene's three-valued logic, except that for Kleene, the third truth value is "undefined," not "true-and-false," as it is for Priest see Kleene 1952, 332–340.

14. Priest conjectures that not only does Gödel's proof not work when we allow semantically closed languages, Gödel's incompleteness theorem itself is false (Priest 1979, 237).

15. Barwise and Etchemendy 1987, 124.

16. Barwise and Etchemendy 1987, 131–132.

17. Barwise and Etchemendy 1987, 166.

Chapter 10

1. Strawson 1964, 68.

2. Strawson 1964, 68. Warnock too seems to take this compromise position (1964, 54).

3. His initial answer to the question is to repeat that truth is a mythical goal (see the quotation above). But this is in no way relevant to the question of why conformity to consensus opinion really does have survival value.

4. World-renowned cyclist-philosopher Adam Morton points out a *verb use* of 'true': to *true* a bicycle wheel is to make the tension in the spokes uniform from spoke to spoke. This seems connected to the usage that White has focused on, since to true a wheel seems to amount to making it meet a certain standard.

5. Whatever implausibility there is in claiming that '"Caesar was murdered" is true' says nothing about the proposition 'Caesar was murdered' was hidden from Ramsey by his unfortunate decision to leave out the inner set of quotation marks and write simply 'Caesar was murdered is true'. The exact line is, "Its value 'Caesar was murdered is true' is the same as 'Caesar was murdered'" (Ramsey 1927, 17). But this, of course, is just incorrect English, for what we have here is a noun and *two* predicates (of different tenses!). Without the inner quotation marks,

Caesar was murdered

cannot serve as the subject of a sentence, for it is not a noun, gerund, noun clause, or anything else that makes sense as a subject.

6. The distinction between propositions and sentences, and hence between strong and weak T-sentences, is overlooked by Harre when he argues against the *redundancy* theory on the grounds that T-sentences can be false (Harre 1957).

7. Ramsey 1927, 17. Ramsey notes that not all assertions have two-place predicates, but he claims that a more complicated formula can easily account for n-place predicates. Davidson (1969, 40) expresses doubts, suggesting that there is no way in which Ramsey can extend his theory of blind ascriptions to propositions more complex than aRb without using Tarski's

recursion and satisfaction techniques. (And this, Davidson claims, would make Ramsey's theory a correspondence theory.) I would think, however, that Ramsey could make use of the techniques I allude to in note 3 of chapter 4.

8. The fact that the equivalence symbol in Tarski's definitions of truth and satisfaction is merely extensional is crucial. Let p be '"Snow is white" is true', and let q be the *definiens* of the Tarski-like definition of p (i.e., '"Snow is white" is satisfied by all sequences'), and let r be the *definiens* of the Tarski-like definition of q. So one who endorses the Tarski-like definition of truth for the language is committed to $p \equiv q \equiv r$. Now let K be some intensional operator, say 'John knows that' and recall from the end of section 8.3 that substitutivity of extensionally equivalent expressions fails within an intensional context. This means that an endorser of Tarski's definition is *not* committed to the claim that $Kp =_{syn} Kr$. So since 'is true' appears in p, Tarski's definition does not imply that we have some way of saying what Kp says without using 'is true'. The general claim here is that the fact that the concept of truth does not appear in the *definiens* of Tarski's definition of truth in terms of satisfaction or in the *definiens* of his definition of satisfaction does *not* mean that acceptance of these definitions commits one to the claim that 'is true' is eliminable from the object language.

9. Williams 1976, 1. Some of the other expressions he uses, or implicitly suggests be used, where I use ' $=_{syn}$' are 'means no more than', 'is verified by all propositions of the form', and 'the meaning of... is given by' (pp. xi, xiv, xv). Compare Prior 1971, 21-22.

10. Williams 1976, 1. Williams is using quantification over propositional variables, which, as we saw in section 4.4, is controversial, but I will not rehash those issues here.

11. Williams 1976, 41-42. 47. Of course, this argument can only be made if formulas quantifying over propositional variables are intelligible. Williams argues that they are at (1976, 9-10). See section 4.4.

12. This simplified version of the prosentential analysis of 'Goldbach's conjecture is true' is designed to dodge technical problems not germane to the main issues of this chapter (Grover, Camp, and Belnap 1975, 95).

13. Field (1986, 60) claims that Ramsey, considered by deflationists to be their founding father, would reject the deflationary thesis and embrace a correspondence answer to what I call the metaphysical project (while giving a redundancy answer to the speech-act project). Textual evidence one way of another is scarce, but Field's interpretation seems hard to reconcile with the spirit of Ramsey's remarks on truth.

14. Field (1986, 62) stipulates that the truth-as-justification thesis is to count as a branch of deflationism that he labels "modified disquotational." This practice drains the category of disquotational theories of truth of any common denominator save that they are all theories Field rejects.

15. See Horwich 1990, 50. Horwich is not himself a deflationist in the end.

16. We saw there that Williams's theory cannot be generalized either, but this was because of a special restriction his theory imposes: there is nothing that bears truth ascriptions, so there is no set of things over which the appropriate variable can range.

17. What follows is patterned after Graeme Forbes's excellent canonical discussion of the issue (1986).

18. A deflationist might try to contend that the 'is stranger than' is not a predicate but a propositional operator, much like 'not' or 'necessarily' in 'not p' and 'necessarily p' except that while the latter two operate on just one proposition, 'is stranger than' operates on pairs of propositions. See Forbes 1986, 31-32, for an attack on this strategy.

19. If I did present the epistemological program as an explanatory program, then on an instrumental theory of justification, this explanatory program would turn out to be identical to the one just considered, the explanation of the success of our beliefs. They would be

identical because, on an instrumental theory of justification, the phenomena to be explained —in the one case the fact that Ron's belief that he exists is justified and in the other case the fact that Ron's belief that he exists is successful—would be identical. But on any noninstrumentalist theory of justification they are not identical, so the two programs are not essentially the same program, contra what Leeds sometimes seems to say (1978, 125).

20. Dummett calls Horwich's theory a redundancy theory on the back cover of Horwich 1990.

21. Horwich 1990, 22 n. 6. Horwich *also* offers an independent answer to the speech-act project *and* claims to have a theory of how we can *understand* 'true' *and* a theory of the *concept* of truth (1990, 37–38).

22. This presentation oversimplifies. One instantiation of this formula is the nonsensical 'If Oscar thinks that la neige est blanche, then la neige est blanche.' Horwich deals with the problem adequately (1990, 19 n. 4), but it would take too many words to explain his technique to the intended audience of this book, so I simply ignore the matter here.

23. Moreover, one might see a residual use for classical logic. There may be a need to make, in a truth-preserving way, certain chunks of what is overall an explanatory-power-preserving inference. Seeing a need for such truth-preserving inferential chunks would not contradict a denial that our beliefs are ever justified as true, since one could insist that the premises on which such chunks operate are not themselves justified as true.

24. He has a fourth argument, which I combine with the third one listed below.

25. The last complex property listed would be more relevant to linguistic truth bearers than propositions, but, as we shall see below, Horwich cannot complain about my including it here, since he claims there can be an MT of sentence tokens as well as an MT of propositions.

References

Acton, H. B. 1935. "The Correspondence Theory of Truth." *Proceedings of the Aristotelian Society* 35:177-194.

Alexander, S. 1920. *Space, Time, and Deity*. Vol. 2. London: Macmillan.

Almeder, Robert. 1985. "Peirce's Thirteen Theories of Truth." *Transactions of the Peirce Society* 21:77-94.

Almeder, Robert. 1986. "Fallibilism, Coherence, and Realism." *Synthese* 68:213-223.

Alston, William P. 1971. "Varieties of Privileged Access." *American Philosophical Quarterly* 8:223-241. All page references are to the reprint in Chisholm and Swartz 1973, 376-410.

Alston, William P. 1979. "Yes, Virginia, There Is a Real World." *Proceedings of the American Philosophical Association* 52:779-808.

Appiah, Anthony. 1986. *For Truth in Semantics*. Oxford: Blackwell.

Armour, Leslie. 1969. *The Concept of Truth*. Assen, Neth.: Van Gorcum.

Armstrong, D. M. 1973. *Belief, Truth, and Knowledge*. Cambridge: Cambridge University Press.

Austin, J. L. 1950. "Truth." *Proceedings of the Aristotelian Society*, supp. vol. 24: 111-128. All page references to the reprint in Austin 1970, 117-133.

Austin, J. L. 1954. "Unfair to Facts." Read to the Oxford Philosophical Society. Published in Austin 1970, 154-174.

Austin, J. L. 1956. "Performative Utterances." BBC radio address. Published in Austin 1970, 233-252.

Austin, J. L. 1970. *Philosophical Papers*. Edited by J. O. Urmson and G. J. Warnock. Oxford: Oxford University Press.

Ayer, A. J., ed. 1959. *Logical Positivism*. New York: Free Press.

Baker, G. P., and P. M. S. Hacker. 1984. *Language, Sense, and Nonsense*. Oxford: Blackwell.

Bar-Hillel, Y., ed. 1965. *Proceedings of the International Congress for Logic, Methodology, and Philosophy of Science*. Amsterdam: North-Holland.

Barwise, Jon, and John Etchemendy. 1987. *The Liar: An Essay on Truth and Circularity*. New York: Oxford University Press.

Baylis, C. A. 1948. "Facts, Propositions, Exemplification, and Truth." *Mind* 57:463-464.

Baynes, K., J. Bohman, and T. McCarthy, eds. 1987. *After Philosophy: End or Transformation*. Cambridge: MIT Press.

Bealer, George. 1982. *Quality and Concept*. Oxford: Oxford University Press.

Bencivenga, Ermanno. 1980. "Truth, Correspondence, and Non-denoting Singular Terms." *Philosophia* 9:219-230.

Black, Max. 1948. "The Semantic Definition of Truth." *Analysis* 8:49-63.

Blackburn, Simon. 1984. *Spreading the Word*. Oxford: Oxford University Press.

Blanshard, Brand. 1941. *The Nature of Thought*. Vol. 2. New York: Macmillan.

BonJour, Laurence. 1985. *The Structure of Empirical Knowledge*. Cambridge: Harvard University Press.

Bradley, F. H. 1914. *Essays on Truth and Reality*. Oxford: Oxford University Press.

Brentano, F. C. 1904. *The True and the Evident*. Edited and translated by R. M. Chisholm. London: Routledge and Kegan Paul, 1966.

Brown, Robert, and C. D. Rollins, eds. 1969. *Contemporary Philosophy in Australia*. New York: Humanities Press.

Butler, R. J., ed. 1962. *Analytical Philosophy*. New York: Barnes and Noble.

Carnap, Rudolf. 1932. "Die physikalische Sprache als Universalsprache der Wissenshchaft." *Erkenntnis* 2:432–465. All page references are to the English translation published as Carnap 1934.

Carnap, Rudolf. 1932–1933. "Psychologie in physikalischer Sprache." *Erkenntnis* 3:107–142. All page references are to the English translation of George Shick, titled "Psychology in Physical Language," in Ayer 1959, 165–198.

Carnap, Rudolf. 1934. *The Unity of Science*. Translated by Max Black. London: Kegan Paul, Trench, Trubner, and Co.

Cartwright, R. 1962. "Propositions." In Butler 1962, 81–103.

Chisholm, Roderick M. 1973. *The Problem of the Criterion*. Milwaukee: Marquette University Press. All page references are to the reprint in Chisholm 1982, 61–75.

Chisholm, Roderick M. 1977. *Theory of Knowledge*. 2nd ed. Englewood Cliffs: Prentice-Hall.

Chisholm, Roderick M. 1982. *The Foundations of Knowing*. Minneapolis: University of Minnesota Press.

Chisholm, Roderick M., and Robert J. Swartz, eds. 1973. *Empirical Knowledge*. Englewood Cliffs: Prentice-Hall.

Copi, Irving M. 1978. "Criticisms of the Simple Theory of Types." In Copi and Gould 1978, 229–238.

Copi, Irving M., and James A. Gould, eds. 1978. *Contemporary Philosophical Logic*. New York: St. Martin's Press.

Cornman, James W. 1979. "On Justifying Non-basic Statements by Basic Reports." In Pappas 1979, 129–149.

Cummins, Robert. 1975. "Truth and Logical Form." *Journal of Philosophical Logic* 4:29–44.

Cummins, Robert. 1979. "Intention, Meaning, and Truth-Conditions." *Philosophical Studies* 35:345–360.

Dauer, Francis W. 1974. "In Defense of the Coherence Theory of Truth." *Journal of Philosophy* 71:791–811.

Davidson, Donald. 1965. "Theories of Meaning and Learnable Languages." In Bar-Hillel 1965, 383–394. All page references are to the reprint in Davidson 1984, 3–15.

Davidson, Donald. 1967. "Truth and Meaning." *Synthese* 17:304–323. All page references are to the reprint in Davidson 1984, 17–36.

Davidson, Donald. 1969. "True to the Facts." *Journal of Philosophy* 66:748–764. All page references are to the reprint in Davidson 1984, 37–54.

Davidson, Donald. 1970. "Semantics for Natural Languages." In *Linguaggi nella Società e nella Tecnica*. Milan: Edizioni di Comunità. All page references are to the reprint in Davidson 1984, 55–64.

Davidson, Donald. 1973a. "In Defence of Convention T." In LeBlanc 1973, 76–86. All page references are to the reprint in Davidson 1984, 65–75.

Davidson, Donald. 1973b. "Radical Interpretation." *Dialectica* 27:313–18. All page references are to the reprint in Davidson 1984, 125–139.

Davidson, Donald. 1977a. "Reality without Reference." *Dialectica* 31:247–253. All page references are to the reprint in Davidson 1984, 215–225.

Davidson, Donald. 1977b. "The Method of Truth in Metaphysics." In *Studies in the Philosophy of Language*, vol. 2 of Midwest Studies in Philosophy, pp. 244–254. All page references are to the reprint in Baynes, Bohman, and McCarthy 1987, 166–183.

Davidson, Donald. 1984. *Inquiries into Truth and Interpretation.* Oxford: Oxford University Press.

Davidson, Donald. 1986. "A Coherence Theory of Truth and Knowledge." In LePore 1986, 307–319.

Davidson, Donald. 1990. "The Structure and Content of Truth." *Journal of Philosophy* 87:279–328.

Devitt, Michael. 1984. *Realism and Truth.* Princeton: Princeton University Press.

Devitt, Michael, and Kim Sterelny. 1987. *Language and Reality.* Cambridge: MIT Press.

Dewey, John. 1938. *Logic: The Theory of Inquiry.* New York: Holt.

Dewey, John. 1951. *The Influence of Darwin on Philosophy.* New York: Peter Smith.

Dewey, John. 1957. *Reconstruction in Philosophy.* Boston: Beacon Press.

Dowden, Bradley. 1979. *A Theory of Truth: The Liar Paradox and Tarski's Undefinability Theorem.* Ph.D. dissertation. Stanford University.

Dowden, Bradley. 1984. "Accepting Inconsistencies from the Paradoxes." *Journal of Philosophical Logic* 13:125–130.

Ducasse, C. J. 1968. *Truth, Knowledge, and Causation.* London: Routledge and Kegan Paul.

Dummett, Michael. 1959. "Truth." *Proceedings of the Aristotelian Society*, new series, 59:141–162. All page references are to the reprint in Dummett 1978b, 1–19.

Dummett, Michael. 1973. *Frege: Philosophy of Language.* London: Duckworth.

Dummett, Michael. 1975a. "The Philosophical Basis of Intuitionistic Logic." In Rose and Shepherdson 1975, 5–40. All page references are to the reprint in Dummett 1978b, 215–247.

Dummett, Michael. 1975b. "What Is a Theory of Meaning?" In Guttenplan 1975, 97–138.

Dummett, Michael. 1976. "What Is a Theory of Meaning? (II)." In Evans and McDowell 1976, 67–137.

Dummett, Michael. 1978a. "Realism." In Dummett 1978b, 145–165.

Dummett, Michael. 1978b. *Truth and Other Enigmas.* Cambridge: Harvard University Press.

Dummett, Michael. 1981. *The Interpretation of Frege's Philosophy.* Cambridge: Harvard University Press.

Ellis, Brian. 1969. "An Epistemological Concept of Truth." In Brown and Rollins 1969, 52–72.

Ellis, Brian. 1988. "Internal Realism." *Synthese* 76:409–434.

Etchemendy, John. 1988. "Tarski on Truth and Logical Consequence." *Journal of Symbolic Logic* 53:51–79.

Etchemendy, John. 1990. *The Concept of Logical Consequence.* Cambridge: Harvard University Press.

Evans, Gareth, and John McDowell, eds. 1976. *Truth and Meaning.* Oxford: Oxford University Press.

Ezorsky, Gertrude. 1967. "The Performative Theory of Truth." In *Encyclopedia of Philosophy*, vol. 6, edited by Paul Edwards. New York: Macmillan.

Fann, K. T., ed. 1969. *Symposium on Austin*. London: Routledge and Kegan Paul.

Feigl, Herbert, W. Sellars, and K. Lehrer, eds. 1972. *New Readings in Philosophical Analysis*. New York: Appleton-Century-Crofts.

Field, Hartry. 1972. "Tarski's Theory of Truth." *Journal of Philosophy* 69:347–375. All page references are to the reprint in Platts 1980, 83–110.

Field, Hartry. 1974. "Quine and the Correspondence Theory." *Philosophical Review* 83:200–228.

Field, Hartry. 1986. "The Deflationary Conception of Truth." In MacDonald and Wright 1986, 55–117.

Findlay, J. N. 1984. *Wittgenstein: A Critique*. London: Routledge and Kegan Paul.

Foley, Richard F. 1979. "Justified Inconsistent Beliefs." *American Philosophical Quarterly* 16:247–257.

Foley, Richard F. 1987. *The Theory of Epistemic Rationality*. Cambridge: Harvard University Press.

Forbes, Graeme. 1986. "Truth, Correspondence, and Redundancy." In MacDonald and Wright 1986, 27–54.

Fox, John. 1989. "What Were Tarski's Truth-Definitions For?" *History and Philosophy of Logic* 10:165–179.

Frege, Gottlob. 1892. "On Sense and Reference." *Zeitschrift für Philosophie und philosophische Kritik* 100:25–50. All page references are to the translation in Geach and Black 1960, 56–78.

Geach, Peter. 1960. "Ascriptivism." *Philosophical Review* 69:221–225.

Geach, Peter, and Max Black, trans. and eds. 1960. *Translations from the Philosophical Writings of Gottlob Frege*. Oxford: Blackwell.

George, Alexander. 1984. "On Devitt on Dummett." *Journal of Philosophy* 81:516–517.

Geyer, Denton L. 1917. "The Relation of Truth to Tests." *Journal of Philosophy, Psychology, and Scientific Methods* 13:626–633.

Grattan-Guinness, I. 1984. "On Popper's Use of Tarski's Theory of Truth." *Philosophia* 14:129–135.

Grayling, A. C. 1982. *An Introduction to Philosophical Logic*. Totowa: Barnes and Noble.

Grosz, B., K. Sparck-Jones, and B. Webber, eds. 1986. *Readings in Natural Language Processing*. Los Altos: Kaufman.

Grover, Dorothy L., Joseph L. Camp, Jr., and Nuel D. Belnap, Jr. 1975. "A Prosentential Theory of Truth." *Philosophical Studies* 27:73–125.

Gunderson, K., ed. 1975. *Language, Mind, and Knowledge*, vol. 7 of Minnesota Studies in the Philosophy of Science. Minneapolis: University of Minnesota Press.

Gupta, Anil. 1982. "Truth and Paradox." *Journal of Philosophical Logic* 11:1–60.

Guttenplan, S. D., ed. 1975. *Mind and Language*. Oxford: Oxford University Press.

Haack, Susan. 1974. *Deviant Logics*. Cambridge: Cambridge University Press.

Haack, Susan. 1978. *Philosophy of Logics*. Cambridge: Cambridge University Press.

Hamlyn, D. W. 1962. "The Correspondence Theory of Truth." *Philosophical Quarterly* 12:193–105.

Hamlyn, D. W. 1970. *The Theory of Knowledge*. Garden City: Anchor Books.

Harman, Gilbert. 1973. *Thought*. Princeton: Princeton University Press.

Harman, Gilbert. 1974. "Meaning and Semantics." In Munitz and Unger 1974.

Harman, Gilbert. 1975. "Language, Thought, and Communication." In Gunderson 1975, 270–298.

Harre, R. 1957. "... Is True." *Australasian Journal of Philosophy* 35:119–124.

Hawtry, Ralph George. 1908. "Pragmatism." *New Quarterly* 1:197–210.

Hellman, Geoffrey. 1975. Untitled review of four articles on the Liar Paradox. *Journal of Symbolic Logic* 50:1068–1071.

Hintikka, Jaakko. 1975. "A Counterexample to Tarski-Type Truth Conditions as Applied to Natural Languages." *Philosophia* 5:207–212.

Hochberg, Herbert. Forthcoming. "Truth, Facts, and Possibilities in the Correspondence Theories of Wittgenstein, Moore, and Russell." Paper delivered at the University of Oklahoma, April 19, 1991. To be published in the proceedings of a symposium on Wittgenstein.

Horwich, Paul. 1990. *Truth*. Oxford: Blackwell.

James, William. 1907. *Pragmatism*. Cambridge: Harvard University Press, 1975.

James, William. 1909. *The Meaning of Truth*. Cambridge: Harvard University Press.

Kant, Immanuel. 1781. *The Critique of Pure Reason*. New York: St. Martins, 1965.

Kekes, John. 1975. "A Case for Skepticism." *Philosophical Quarterly* 25:28–39.

Keuth, Herbert. 1978. "Tarski's Definition of Truth and the Correspondence Theory." *Philosophy of Science* 45:420–430.

Kincade, J. 1957. "The Physicalistic and Semantic Theories of Truth." *Hermathena* 90:33–46.

Kirkham, Richard. 1989. "What Dummett Says about Truth and Linguistic Competence." *Mind* 93:207–224.

Kirkham, Richard. 1991. "On Paradoxes and a Surprise Exam." *Philosophia* 21:31–51.

Kirkham, Richard. In progress. "Tarski's Physicalism."

Kleene, S. C. 1952. *Introduction to Metamathematics*. New York: Van Nostrand.

Korner, S. 1955. "Truth as a Predicate." *Analysis* 15:106–109.

Kripke, Saul. 1975. "Outline of a Theory of Truth." *Journal of Philosophy* 72:690–716. All page references are to the reprint in Martin 1984, 53–81.

LeBlanc, Hugues, ed. 1973. *Truth, Syntax, and Modality*. Hague: North-Holland.

Leeds, Stephen. 1978. "Theories of Reference and Truth." *Erkenntnis* 13:111–127.

Lehrer, Keith. 1974. *Knowledge*. Oxford: Oxford University Press.

LePore, Ernest, ed. 1986. *Truth and Interpretation*. Oxford: Blackwell.

Lewis, David. 1973. *Counterfactuals*. Cambridge: Harvard University Press.

Linsky, Leonard, ed. 1952. *Semantics and the Philosophy of Language*. Urbana: University of Illinois Press.

Loux, Michael J., ed. 1976. *Universals and Particulars*. Rev. ed. Notre Dame: University of Notre Dame Press.

Lovejoy, A. O. 1963. *The Thirteen Pragmatisms and Other Essays*. Baltimore: Johns Hopkins University Press.

McDermott, Drew. 1986. "Tarskian Semantics, or No Notation without Denotation." In Grosz, Sparck-Jones, and Webber 1986, 166–169.

MacDonald, Graham, and Crispin Wright, eds. 1986. *Fact, Science, and Morality*. Oxford: Blackwell.

McDowell, John. 1976. "Truth Conditions, Bivalence, and Verificationism." In Evans and McDowell 1976, 42–66.

McDowell, John. 1978. "Physicalism and Primitive Denotation: Field on Tarski." *Erkenntnis* 13:137–152. All page references are to the reprint in Platts 1980, 111–130.

McGinn, Colin. 1980. "Truth and Use." In Platts 1980, 19–39.

Mackie, J. L. 1973. *Truth, Probability, and Paradox*. Oxford: Oxford University Press.

McTaggart, J. M. E. 1921. *The Nature of Existence*. Vol. 1. Cambridge: Cambridge University Press.

Martin, Robert L., ed. 1984. *Recent Essays on Truth and the Liar Paradox*. Oxford: Oxford University Press.

Martin, Robert M. 1987. *The Meaning of Language*. Cambridge: MIT Press.

Mates, Benson. 1974. "Austin, Strawson, and Tarski on Truth." In *Proceedings of the Tarski Symposium*. Providence: American Mathematical Society.

Milmed, B. K. 1956. "Lewis and the Theory of Truth." *Journal of Philosophy* 53:569–583.

Moravcsik, Julius, ed. 1974. *Logic and Philosophy for Linguists*. Atlantic Highlands: Humanities Press.

Morton, Adam. Forthcoming. Review of Horwich 1990. *Philosophical Books*.

Muirhead, J. H., ed. 1924. *Contemporary British Philosophy*. London: Allen and Unwin.

Munitz, Milton K., and Peter Unger, eds. 1974. *Semantics and Philosophy*. New York: NYU Press.

Nagel, Ernest, Patrick Suppes, and Alfred Tarski, eds. 1962. *Logic, Methodology, and Philosophy of Science*. Stanford: Stanford University Press.

Neurath, Otto. 1930. "Wege der wissenschaftlichen Weltauffassung." *Erkenntnis* 1:106–125. All page references are to the English translation in Neurath 1983, 32–47.

Neurath, Otto. 1931a. "Physikalismus." *Scientia* 50:297–303. All page references are to the English translation in Neurath 1983, 52–57.

Neurath, Otto. 1931b. "Soziologie im Physikalismus." *Erkenntnis* 2:393–431. All page references are to the English translation in Neurath 1983, 58–90.

Neurath, Otto. 1932–1933. "Protokollsätze." *Erkenntnis* 3:204–214. All page references are to the English translation in Neurath 1983, 91–99.

Neurath, Otto. 1983. *Philosophical Papers, 1913–1946*. Edited and translated by Robert S. Cohen and Marie Neurath. Dordrecht: D. Reidel.

O'Connor, D. J. 1975. *The Correspondence Theory of Truth*. London: Hutchinson.

O'Connor, D. J., and Brian Carr. 1982. *Introduction to the Theory of Knowledge*. Minneapolis: University Minnesota Press.

Pap, Arthur. 1949. *Elements of Analytic Philosophy*. New York: Hafner, 1972.

Pap, Arthur. 1952. "Note on the 'Semantic' and 'Absolute' Concept of Truth." *Philosophical Studies* 4:1–8. All page references are to the reprint in Feigl, Sellars, and Lehrer 1972, 208–213.

Pappas, G. 1978. "Some Forms of Epistemological Skepticism." In Pappas and Swain 1978, 309–316.

Pappas, G., ed. 1979. *Justification and Knowledge*. Dordrecht: D. Reidel.

Pappas, G., and M. Swain, eds. 1978. *Essays on Knowledge and Justification.* Ithaca: Cornell University Press.

Parsons, Kathryn Pyne. 1973. "Ambiguity and the Truth Definition." *Noûs* 7:379-393.

Peirce, Charles S. 1931-1958. *Collected Papers of Charles Sanders Peirce.* Vols. 1-8. Edited by Charles Hartshorne and Paul Weiss (vols. 1-6) and A. W. Burks (vols. 7-8). Cambridge: Harvard University Press.

Peirce, Charles S. 1966. "Letters to Lady Welby." In Wiener 1966, 380-432.

Pendlebury, Michael. 1986. "Facts as Truthmakers." *Monist* 69:177-188.

Pitcher, George, ed. 1964. *Truth.* Englewood Cliffs: Prentice-Hall.

Platts, Mark. 1979. *Ways of Meaning.* London: Routledge and Kegan Paul.

Platts, Mark, ed. 1980. *Reference, Truth, and Reality.* London: Routledge and Kegan Paul.

Popper, Karl R. 1962. "Some Comments on Truth and the Growth of Knowledge." In Nagel, Suppes, and Tarski 1962, 285-292.

Popper, Karl R. 1965. *Conjectures and Refutations: The Growth of Scientific Knowledge*, 2nd ed. New York: Harper and Row.

Popper, Karl R. 1974. "Some Philosophical Comments on Tarski's Theory of Truth." In *Proceedings of the Tarski Symposium*, 400-402. Providence: American Mathematical Society.

Pratt, J. B. 1909. *What Is Pragmatism?* New York: Macmillan.

Price, H. H. 1932. *Perception.* London: Methuen.

Price, Huw. 1988. *Facts and the Function of Truth.* Oxford: Blackwell.

Priest, Graham. 1979. "The Logic of Paradox." *Journal of Philosophical Logic* 8:219-248.

Priest, Graham. 1984. "The Logic of Paradox Revisited." *Journal of Philosophical Logic* 13:153-179.

Prior, A. N. 1958. "Epimenides the Cretan." *Journal of Symbolic Logic* 23:261-266. All page references to the reprint in Prior 1976, 70-77.

Prior, A. N. 1962. "Some Problems of Reference in John Buridan." *Proceedings of the British Academy* 48:281-296. All page references to the reprint in Prior 1976, 130-146.

Prior, A. N. 1967. *Past, Present, and Future.* Oxford: Oxford University Press.

Prior, A. N. 1971. *Objects of Thought.* Oxford: Oxford University Press.

Prior, A. N. 1976. *Papers in Logic and Ethics.* Edited by P. T. Geach and A. J. P. Kenny. London: Duckworth.

Putnam, Hilary. 1978. *Meaning and the Moral Sciences.* London: Routledge and Kegan Paul.

Putnam, Hilary. 1981. *Reason, Truth and History.* Cambridge: Cambridge University Press.

Putnam, Hilary. 1985. "A Comparison of Something with Something Else." *New Literary History* 17:61-79.

Quine, W. V. 1956. "Quantifiers and Propositional Attitudes." *Journal of Philosophy* 53:177-187. All page references are to the reprint in Quine 1976, 185-196.

Quine, W. V. 1960. *Word and Object.* Cambridge: MIT Press.

Quine, W. V. 1962. "Paradox." *Scientific American* 206 (April): 84-96. All page references are to the unedited version, "The Ways of Paradox," in Quine 1976, 1-18.

Quine, W. V. 1963a. "Two Dogmas of Empiricism." Revised in Quine 1963b, 20-46.

Quine, W. V. 1963b. *From a Logical Point of View.* New York: Harper and Row.

Quine, W. V. 1970. *Philosophy of Logic.* Englewood Cliffs: Prentice-Hall.

Quine, W. V. 1976. *The Ways of Paradox and Other Essays*. Rev. ed. Cambridge: Harvard University Press.

Quine, W. V., and J. S. Ullian. 1978. *The Web of Belief*. 2nd ed. New York: Random House.

Ramsey, F. P. 1927. "Facts and Propositions." *Proceedings of the Aristotelian Society*, supp. vol. 7: 153–170. All page references are to the reprint of the relevant passage in Pitcher 1964, 16–17.

Ramsey, F. P. 1931. *The Foundations of Mathematics*. London: Routledge and Kegan Paul.

Ratner, Joseph. 1935. "Correspondence Theory of Truth." *Journal of Philosophy* 32:141–52.

Reichenbach, Hans. 1931. "Der physikalische Wahrheitsbegriff." *Erkenntnis* 2:156–171. All page references are to the translation by E. Schneewind titled "The Physical Concept of Truth," in Reichenbach 1978, 1:343–355.

Reichenbach, Hans. 1952. "Are Phenomenal Reports Absolutely Certain?" *The Philosophical Review* 61:147–159.

Reichenbach, Hans. 1978. *Selected Writings, 1909–1953*. 2 vols. Translated by E. Schneewind, M. Reichenbach, and R. S. Cohen and edited by M. Reichenbach and R. S. Cohen. Dordrecht: D. Reidel.

Rescher, Nicholas. 1973. *The Coherence Theory of Truth*. Oxford: Oxford University Press.

Rogers, Robert. 1963. "A Survey of Formal Semantics." *Synthese* 15:17–56. All page references are to the reprint in Moravcsik 1974, 48–82.

Romanos, George D. 1983. *Quine and Analytic Philosophy*. Cambridge: MIT Press.

Rorty, Richard. 1979. *Philosophy and the Mirror of Nature*. Princeton: Princeton University Press.

Rorty, Richard. 1980. "Pragmatism, Relativism, and Irrationalism." *Proceedings of the American Philosophical Association* 53:719–738. All page references are to the reprint in Rorty 1982, 160–175.

Rorty, Richard. 1982. *Consequences of Pragmatism*. Minneapolis: University of Minnesota Press.

Rose, H. E., and J. C. Shepherdson, eds. 1975. *Logic Colloquium '73*. Amsterdam: North Holland.

Russell, Bertrand. 1908a. "Transatlantic 'Truth.'" *Albany Review* 2:393–410.

Russell, Bertrand. 1908b. "Mathematical Logic as Based on a Theory of Types." *American Journal of Mathematics* 30:222–262. All page references are to the reprint in Russell 1971, 59–102.

Russell, Bertrand. 1912. *The Problems of Philosophy*. Oxford: Oxford University Press.

Russell, Bertrand. 1924. "Logical Atomism." In Muirhead 1924, 357–383. All page references are to the reprint in Russell 1971, 321–344.

Russell, Bertrand. 1971. *Logic and Knowledge*. New York: Capricorn Books.

Scheffler, Israel. 1982. *Science and Subjectivity*. 2nd ed. Indianapolis: Hackett.

Sellars, Roy W. 1959. "'True' as Contextually Implying Correspondence." *Journal of Philosophy* 56:717–722.

Sellars, Wilfred. 1963a. *Science, Perception, and Reality*. New York: Humanities.

Sellars, Wilfred. 1963b. "Abstract Entities." *Review of Metaphysics* 16:627–671. All page references are to the reprint in Loux 1976, 156–205.

Soames, Scott. 1984. "What Is a Theory of Truth?" *Journal of Philosophy* 81:411–429.

Srzednicki, Jan. 1966. "It Is True." *Mind* 75:385–395.

Stalnaker, Robert C. 1987. *Inquiry*. Cambridge: MIT Press.

Stern, Cindy. 1990. "On Justification-Conditional Models of Linguistic Competence." 99: 441–445.

Strawson, P. F. 1950. "Truth." *Proceedings of the Aristotelian Society*, supp. vol. 24: 129–156. All page references are to the reprint in Pitcher 1964, 32–53.

Strawson, P. F. 1964. "A Problem about Truth—A Reply to Mr. Warnock." In Pitcher 1964, 68–84.

Stroud, Barry. 1984. *The Significance of Philosophical Skepticism*. Oxford: Oxford University Press.

Suckiel, Ellen Kappy. 1982. *The Pragmatic Philosophy of William James*. Notre Dame, Ind.: University of Notre Dame Press.

Tarski, Alfred. 1933. *Pojecie Prawdy w Jezykach nauk Dedukcyjnych*. Warsaw. All page references are to the translation "The Concept of Truth in Formalized Languages," in Tarski 1983, 152–278.

Tarski, Alfred. 1936. "O Ugruntowaniu Naukowej Semantyki." *Przeglak Filozoficzny* 39:50–57. All page references are to the translation "The Establishment of Scientific Semantics," in Tarski 1983, 401–408.

Tarski, Alfred. 1944. "The Semantic Conception of Truth." *Philosophy and Phenomenological Research* 4:341–376. All page references are to the reprint in Linsky 1952, 13–49.

Tarski, Alfred. 1969. "Truth and Proof." *Scientific American* 220 (June): 63–77.

Tarski, Alfred. 1983. *Logic, Semantics, Metamathematics*. 2nd ed. Translated. by J. H. Woodger. Indianapolis: Hackett.

Unger, Peter. 1975. *Ignorance*. Oxford: Oxford University Press.

Van Straaten, Zak, ed. 1980. *Philosophical Subjects*. Oxford: Oxford University Press.

Vision, Gerald. 1988. *Modern Anti-realism and Manufactured Truth*. London: Routledge.

Walker, Ralph C. S. 1989. *The Coherence Theory of Truth*. London: Routledge.

Warnock, G. J. 1964. "A Problem about Truth." In Pitcher 1964, 54–67.

Wheatley, Jon. 1969. "Austin on Truth." In Fann 1969, 226–239.

White, Alan R. 1957. "Truth as Appraisal." *Mind* 66:318–330.

White, Alan R. 1970. *Truth*. New York: Doubleday.

Wiener, Philip P., ed. 1966. *Charles S. Peirce: Selected Writings*. New York: Dover.

Wiggins, David. 1980. "What Would Be a Substantial Theory of Truth?" In van Straaten 1980, 189–221.

Williams, C. J. F. 1976. *What Is Truth?* Cambridge: Cambridge University Press.

Williams, M. 1986. "Do We (Epistemologists) Need a Theory of Truth?" *Philosophical Topics* 14:223–242.

Wright, Crispin. 1987. *Realism, Meaning, and Truth*. Oxford: Basil Blackwell.

Index

^. *See* Concatenation
⇔. *See* Essential equivalence, symbolically expressed
(∃x). *See* Existential quantifier
= . *See* Identity
= ₛᵧₙ. *See* Intensional equivalence, symbolically expressed
Mₚx. *See* Majority quantifier
≡ . *See* Material equivalence
⊃ . *See* Material implication
↔. *See* Natural equivalence
#P. *See* Number function
<. *See* Sequences
>. *See* Sequences
(x). *See* Universal quantifier

Absolute idealism. *See* Ontological idealism
Acton, H. B., 116, 139, 355 (n. 3), 357 (n. 4), 358 (n. 6)
Alexander, S.
confuses metaphysical and justification projects, 189
interpreted as ontological realist but as Nonrealist, 189, 191
interpreted as rejecting quasi realism, 189, 355 (n. 5)
sympathetically interpreted, 190
theory of, interpreted as incompatible with semantic theories of truth, 190
'All' quantifier. *See* Universal quantifier
Almeder, Robert, 79, 352 (n. 2)
Alston, William P., 77
Ambiguity problem for Davidson Program, 239–240
Anaphora, 325–326
Antirealism, 117
Appiah, Anthony, 251, 259, 260
Aristotle, 119
Armour, Leslie, 353 (n. 27)
Armstrong, D. M., 56, 58
Ascription project, 21, 31, 37, 314
Assertibility. *See* Justification-condition semantics; Truth-as-justification thesis
Assertion project, 18, 34, 314–315. *See also* Ascription project; Deep-structure project
attributed to Grover, Camp, and Belnap, 37
attributed to Mackie, 34
attributed to Ramsey, 30, 37
attributed to White, 37
attributed to Williams, 37
contrasted with illocutionary-act project, 28

defined, 21, 28, 314
does not make extensional project gratuitous, 9, 18, 19
extended discussion and comparison with other projects, 21, 30–31, 314–315
has ascription and deep-structure projects as subdivisions, 21, 30, 314–315
is not Rescher's project, 33
list of major figures assigned to, 37
often conflated with metaphysical project, 31, 185
often thought to be the only truth project, 36
as search for expression intensionally equivalent to 'is true', 9, 14, 30, 314
as search for informational content of 'is true', 9, 30
as search for the meaning of 'is true', 9
as subdivision of speech-act project, 9, 21, 28, 314
thought to be wrong-headed by early Strawson, 29
Assertions, 57–58
Assertive liar, 300, 301
Austin, J. L., 127. *See also* Correspondence as correlation; Correspondence theories of truth
assigned to essence project, 37, 128, 132
assigned to metaphysical project, 37, 128
combines a theory of meaning with a theory of truth, 129
confuses truth projects, 128–129
defines truth, 125
disdains ontological disputes, 129
does not use 'corresponds' to state his theory, 135
and the essence of the correspondence theory, 131
as example of schema (C), 132
and falsity, 126
and hidden similarity of his views to Russell's, 129
influenced Barwise and Etchemendy, 300
influenced Strawson, 29
is mainly interested in subsidiary issues, 126
is an ontological realist, 130
is a Realist about truth, 130, 133
objections to the theory of, 126
objects to correspondence as correlation, 124
as the paradigmatic correspondence-as-correlation theorist, 132, 358 (n. 7)
and performative utterances, 29, 128
presuppositions of the theory of, 126–127